THE
HOUSE OF
GREY

About the Author

Melita Thomas is a co-founder and editor of *Tudor Times*, a website devoted to Tudor and Stuart history. Her articles have appeared in *BBC History Extra* and *Britain Magazine*. She lives in Hitchin.

THE
HOUSE OF
GREY

FRIENDS & FOES
OF KINGS

MELITA THOMAS

AMBERLEY

For my aunt, Melita.

This edition published 2022

Amberley Publishing
The Hill, Stroud
Gloucestershire, GL5 4EP

www.amberley-books.com

British Library Cataloguing in Publication Data.
A catalogue record for this book is available from the British Library.

ISBN 978 1 3981 1242 1 (paperback)
ISBN 978 1 4456 8498 7 (ebook)

Typesetting by Aura Technology and Software Services, India.
Printed in India.

Contents

List of Genealogical Tables

Notes

Land law

Following the Norman Conquest, the Crown granted land to its 'tenants-in-chief' in return for service – usually 'knight's service', which was provision of military support to the king. This was the system of feudalism. The tenants-in-chief then granted land to their feudal inferiors for various types of service. The grant was usually to a man and his heirs, meaning the land could not be sold or willed away without the consent of the feudal superior. The identity of the heir would depend on the original grant, and was often limited to 'heirs male'. When the heir took possession, a 'fine' for entry was payable to the feudal superior. When the heir was a minor (majority was twenty-one for boys and fourteen for girls), he or she was the ward of the feudal superior, who either took the profits of the land or sold the wardship. To avoid this, and some of the other disbenefits of the system, landowners would convey land during their lifetime to feoffees – literally 'those trusted' – on condition they held it 'to the use (benefit) of' named individuals, usually the widow and minor children. Problems arose when the feoffees could not be trusted. Consent of the feudal superior was required for marriage and, again, often required payment of a fine. Land held for monetary rent could be disposed of by will or sale.

Duchy *v*. Dukedom

A duchy is a specific geographic region over which a duke has extensive quasi-sovereign powers. A dukedom is a title which may or may not have lands attached to it, whose duke is merely a peer of the realm. The duchy of Lancaster, granted initially to Henry III's second son, Edmund, was a semi-autonomous province, while the dukedom of York was a title, with various lands pertaining to it, but was not geographically related to York and had no especial legal standing.

Good Lordship

The late mediaeval and Tudor political and social world was one of networking and reciprocal obligation. To gain office, to receive grants, to deal with your land, to make a good marriage for your heir, and sometimes even to succeed in a legal case, you needed to build connections, in a system referred to by historians as 'good lordship'. You would send a present – food, hunting dogs, gloves, even marmalade – to someone more influential than yourself (preferably someone with whom you had connection by blood or marriage, no matter how remote), explain what you needed and ask the recipient to be 'good lord' or 'good lady' to you. In due course, when your 'good lord' wanted something in return – support in battle, putting in a favourable word with the king, a job for a connection, a land exchange – you were expected to return the favour. The nobility and gentry were not numerous, numbering in the thousands among a population of 3 to 4 million, and the upper ranks were even narrower. Repeated marriages (in a time when most people had at least two spouses during their lifetimes) created a complex web of relationships, and it often transpired that individual members of the same family found themselves on different sides of a dispute because of more important or valuable obligations to others. The Wars of the Roses exemplify this – sisters often found their husbands were in conflict, and brothers would sometimes be on opposing sides. In an age of unstable government and volatile monarchs, keeping on good terms with your friends, relatives and connections was not just important for material success – it might save your life.

Money
12 pennies, abbreviated to '*d*', made a shilling, '*s*', and 20*s* made a pound. There were about five crowns to the pound, and a mark was two-thirds of a pound.

Acknowledgements
Many thanks to Dr Lisa Liddy for her transcriptions – her speed and accuracy are amazing. Thanks also to the *Lady Jane Grey Reference Guide* for reviewing my draft. Any errors remaining are entirely my responsibility.

Preface

The early Tudor court remains a source of fascination. The astonishing array of outsize personalities, the tragic tale of Henry VIII and his six wives, the see-saw of religious reform, and the increasingly bloody nature of politics make it a rich source of interest. The only other era which vies with it for allure is that which immediately preceded it – the brutal, violent and bloody period simplified into the tale of a murderous royal family as the 'Wars of the Roses'. This book looks at the period through an unusual lens, focusing not on the monarchs or their spouses, but instead on the fortunes of one branch of the Grey family – who were they, how did they use their connections and what was their place in the polity of late mediaeval and early Tudor England? And, of course, how and why did the family come to a tragic end with the beheading of a girl of sixteen?

The Greys were a baronial family, descended from Anchetil de Grey,[1] who accompanied William of Normandy to England in 1066. By the early fifteenth century, there were several branches, holding different baronies, of which one was the family of Grey of Ruthyn[2] (see Appendix 1 for more). The Greys were typical of the baronial class – they held their share of public offices, quarrelled among themselves and with their fellow barons, sought to marry well and expand their landholdings, and from time to time produced a bishop or a king's councillor. This relative obscurity changed in 1464, when the widow of Sir John Grey, Elizabeth Woodville, married Edward IV, propelling her sons, Thomas and Richard Grey, to the centre of the court. Some of King Edward's courtiers resented the match, but there was little they could do. Edward liked his stepsons, and, while they did not receive the spectacular grants and rewards that his Neville cousins did, they were closely integrated with the royal family. After a dangerous fall from grace in 1483 during Richard III's reign, the Greys returned to the royal family fold as maternal relatives of Queen Elizabeth of York, and in the first half of Henry VIII's reign the Greys were to be found everywhere in the king's network, providing soldiers, courtiers, administrators, and attendants to his first queen, Katharine of Aragon, his daughter Princess Mary, and his illegitimate son the Duke of

Richmond. They even counted among their number a Deputy Lieutenant of Ireland. The position of the family as relatives of the monarch, without the complications of royal blood, saw them involved in everything from jousts to diplomatic missions, military expeditions to christenings, weddings to funerals. But they flew too close to the sun – a marriage into the line of succession, coupled with the divisions brought by the Reformation, caused the family to crash spectacularly from the pinnacle of power to the block.

Prologue

God and posterity will show me more favour.

Lady Jane Grey

At nine o'clock on the morning of 23 February 1554, warders in the Tower of London unlocked the door of an apartment that had served as a prison cell for two weeks. Inside was a thirty-seven-year-old nobleman, Henry Grey, Duke of Suffolk, fully dressed in shirt, doublet and gown. He rose from the bench where he had been seated, and laid aside his book: *Decades* by Heinrich Bullinger, one of the leading proponents of the Reformed faith, who had dedicated the work, in part, to the duke.[1] Suffolk followed the warders out through the stone-lined passage, down the stairs, across the courtyards and out of the Tower. He was not being freed, but, rather, walking to Tower Hill, where a block sat upon a scaffold awaiting his execution. Less than a fortnight before, Suffolk's son-in-law Lord Guildford Dudley had climbed that same scaffold, and died bravely, steadfast in his faith. Guildford's death, and that of Suffolk's daughter, Jane, had been, in large part, Suffolk's fault. He cannot have avoided thinking of them – but, although he might have been sorry that their lives had been cut short, he was confident that within minutes he would be reunited with them in paradise. Jane and Guildford, too, had believed sincerely that they would soon meet again, sending Suffolk loving messages written in a prayer book: 'Your loving and obedient son wisheth unto your grace long life in this world, with as much joy and comfort as I wish to myself, and in the world to come, life everlasting. Your humble son to his death. G Dudley', Guildford had written. Jane's message was similar:

> The Lord comfort your grace and that in His word wherein all creatures only are to be comforted. And though it hath pleased God to take away two of your children, yet think not, I most humbly beseech your grace that you have lost them, but trust that we, by leaving this mortal life,

have won an immortal life. And I for my part as I have honoured your grace in this life, will pray for you in another life. Your grace's humble daughter, Jane Dudley.[2]

As he prepared himself for death, Suffolk was continually exhorted by a priest, fellow Leicestershire man Hugh Weston, to accept the miracle of transubstantiation, as taught by the Catholic Church, believing Suffolk's rejection of it would lead to his eternal damnation. The priest had been sent by Suffolk's distant cousin, Queen Mary I, who was desperate to save the soul, if not the body, of a man whom she had known since childhood, and whose wife, Frances, had been one of her closest friends. Suffolk, firm in his convictions, tried to ignore Weston, but the priest followed him up the steps of the scaffold. Angry at being harangued by a Catholic priest in his last moments, Suffolk shoved him, and the two fell down the steps in an undignified heap. Weston refused to leave – he was there at the queen's command – so Suffolk let him remain, lest the queen vent any anger on Frances or his remaining daughters.

Turning to the crowd, Suffolk told them that he was there to die, having offended the queen and her laws, but that he hoped for her forgiveness. Weston assured him that he had it. Suffolk proclaimed his own Protestant faith, repeating a psalm, before giving his cap and scarf to the executioner, saying, 'God forgive thee as I do, and when thou dost thine office, I pray thee do it well, and bring me out of this world, quickly, and God have mercy to thee.' Even at this last, desperate moment, Suffolk's perennial money problems rose up, as a man pushed through the crowd and asked how Suffolk's debt to him should be paid. The duke could only send the man to his officers: 'Alas good fellow, do not trouble me now!' He removed gown and doublet, bandaged his eyes, and repeated the Lord's Prayer. Laying his head on the block, he stretched out his arms and cried, 'Christ have mercy upon me.' The axe fell.

Part 1

1432–1483
'... sad stories of the death of kings ...'

Descent of the Greys of Ruthyn (simplified)

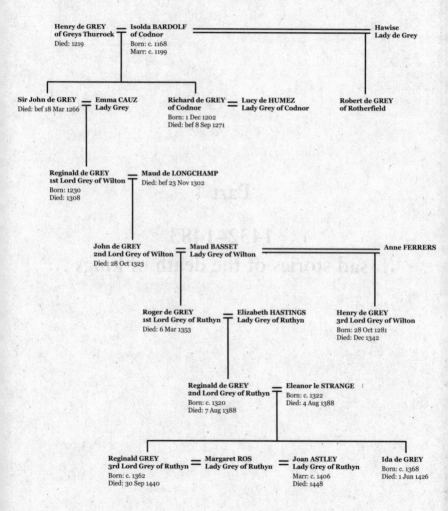

Descendants of Reginald, 3rd Lord Grey of Ruthin

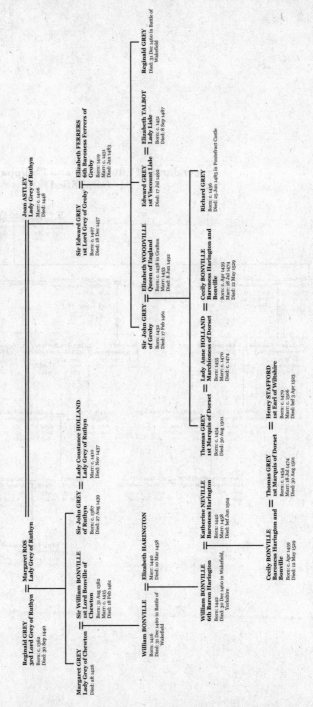

Descendants of Edward III and Philippa of Hainault (simplified)

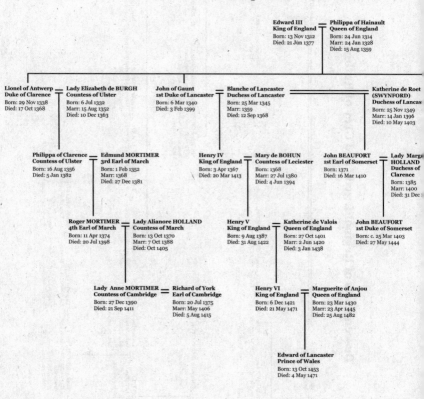

Edward III
King of England
Born: 13 Nov 1312
Died: 21 Jun 1377

Philippa of Hainault
Queen of England
Born: 24 Jun 1314
Marr: 24 Jan 1328
Died: 15 Aug 1359

Lionel of Antwerp
Duke of Clarence
Born: 29 Nov 1338
Died: 17 Oct 1368

Lady Elizabeth de BURGH
Countess of Ulster
Born: 6 Jul 1332
Marr: 15 Aug 1352
Died: 10 Dec 1363

John of Gaunt
1st Duke of Lancaster
Born: 6 Mar 1340
Died: 3 Feb 1399

Blanche of Lancaster
Duchess of Lancaster
Born: 25 Mar 1345
Marr: 1359
Died: 12 Sep 1368

Katherine de Roet (SWYNFORD)
Duchess of Lancas
Born: 25 Nov 1349
Marr: 14 Jan 1396
Died: 10 May 1403

Philippa of Clarence
Countess of Ulster
Born: 16 Aug 1356
Died: 5 Jan 1382

Edmund MORTIMER
3rd Earl of March
Born: 1 Feb 1352
Marr: 1368
Died: 27 Dec 1381

Henry IV
King of England
Born: 3 Apr 1367
Died: 20 Mar 1413

Mary de BOHUN
Countess of Leciester
Born: 1368
Marr: 27 Jul 1380
Died: 4 Jun 1394

John BEAUFORT
1st Earl of Somerset
Born: 1371
Died: 16 Mar 1410

**Lady Marga
HOLLAND**
Duchess of
Clarence
Born: 1385
Marr: 1400
Died: 31 Dec

Roger MORTIMER
4th Earl of March
Born: 11 Apr 1374
Died: 20 Jul 1398

Lady Alianore HOLLAND
Countess of March
Born: 13 Oct 1370
Marr: 7 Oct 1388
Died: Oct 1405

Henry V
King of England
Born: 9 Aug 1387
Died: 31 Aug 1422

Katherine de Valois
Queen of England
Born: 27 Oct 1401
Marr: 2 Jun 1420
Died: 3 Jan 1438

John BEAUFORT
1st Duke of Somerset
Born: c. 25 Mar 1403
Died: 27 May 1444

Lady Anne MORTIMER
Countess of Cambridge
Born: 27 Dec 1390
Died: 21 Sep 1411

Richard of York
Earl of Cambridge
Born: 20 Jul 1375
Marr: May 1406
Died: 5 Aug 1415

Henry VI
King of England
Born: 6 Dec 1421
Died: 21 May 1471

Marguerite of Anjou
Queen of England
Born: 23 Mar 1430
Marr: 23 Apr 1445
Died: 25 Aug 1482

Edward of Lancaster
Prince of Wales
Born: 13 Oct 1453
Died: 4 May 1471

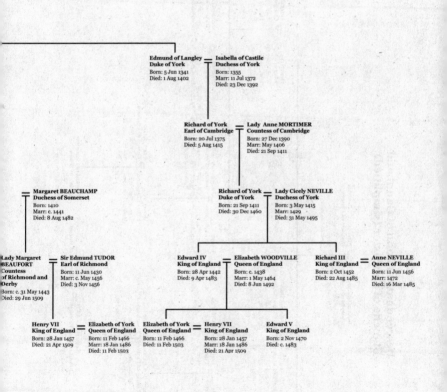

Edmund of Langley
Duke of York
Born: 5 Jun 1341
Died: 1 Aug 1402

Isabella of Castile
Duchess of York
Born: 1355
Marr: 11 Jul 1372
Died: 23 Dec 1392

Richard of York
Earl of Cambridge
Born: 20 Jul 1375
Died: 5 Aug 1415

Lady Anne MORTIMER
Countess of Cambridge
Born: 27 Dec 1390
Marr: May 1406
Died: 21 Sep 1411

Margaret BEAUCHAMP
Duchess of Somerset
Born: 1410
Marr: c. 1441
Died: 8 Aug 1482

Richard of York
Duke of York
Born: 21 Sep 1411
Died: 30 Dec 1460

Lady Cicely NEVILLE
Duchess of York
Born: 3 May 1415
Marr: 1429
Died: 31 May 1495

Lady Margaret
BEAUFORT
Countess
of Richmond and
Derby
Born: c. 31 May 1443
Died: 29 Jun 1509

Sir Edmund TUDOR
Earl of Richmond
Born: 11 Jun 1430
Marr: c. May 1456
Died: 3 Nov 1456

Edward IV
King of England
Born: 28 Apr 1442
Died: 9 Apr 1483

Elizabeth WOODVILLE
Queen of England
Born: c. 1438
Marr: 1 May 1464
Died: 8 Jun 1492

Richard III
King of England
Born: 2 Oct 1452
Died: 22 Aug 1485

Anne NEVILLE
Queen of England
Born: 11 Jun 1456
Marr: 1472
Died: 16 Mar 1485

Henry VII
King of England
Born: 28 Jan 1457
Died: 21 Apr 1509

Elizabeth of York
Queen of England
Born: 11 Feb 1466
Marr: 18 Jan 1486
Died: 11 Feb 1503

Elizabeth of York
Queen of England
Born: 11 Feb 1466
Died: 11 Feb 1503

Henry VII
King of England
Born: 28 Jan 1457
Marr: 18 Jan 1486
Died: 21 Apr 1509

Edward V
King of England
Born: 2 Nov 1470
Died: c. 1483

Descendants of John of Gaunt and Blanche of Lancaster (simplified)

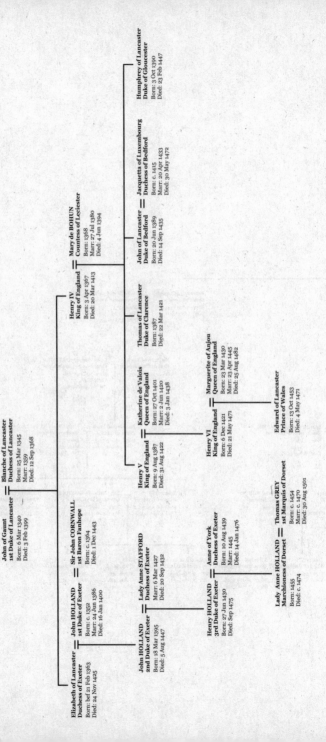

Descendants of John of Gaunt and Katherine de Roet (simplified)

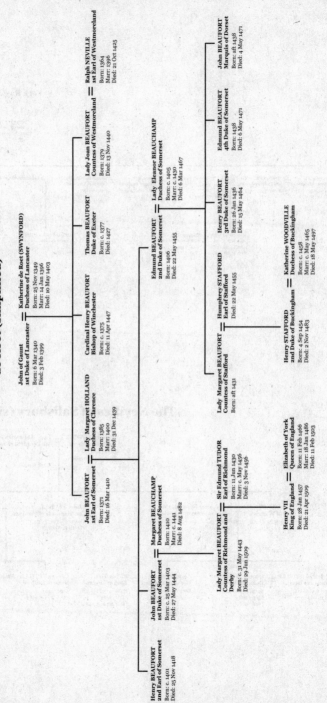

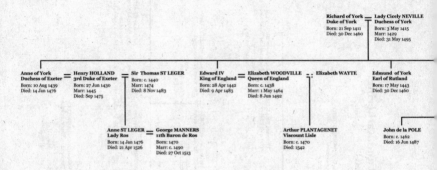

York Royal Family (simplified

Richard of York
Duke of York
Born: 21 Sep 1411
Died: 30 Dec 1460

Lady Cicely NEVILLE
Duchess of York
Born: 3 May 1415
Marr: 1429
Died: 31 May 1495

Anne of York
Duchess of Exeter
Born: 10 Aug 1439
Died: 14 Jan 1476

Henry HOLLAND
3rd Duke of Exeter
Born: 27 Jun 1430
Marr: 1445
Died: Sep 1475

Sir Thomas ST LEGER
Born: c. 1440
Marr: 1474
Died: 8 Nov 1483

Edward IV
King of England
Born: 28 Apr 1442
Died: 9 Apr 1483

Elizabeth WOODVILLE
Queen of England
Born: c. 1438
Marr: 1 May 1464
Died: 8 Jun 1492

Elizabeth WAYTE

Edmund of York
Earl of Rutland
Born: 17 May 1443
Died: 30 Dec 1460

Anne ST LEGER
Lady Ros
Born: 14 Jan 1476
Died: 21 Apr 1526

George MANNERS
11th Baron de Ros
Born: 1470
Marr: c. 1490
Died: 27 Oct 1513

Arthur PLANTAGENET
Viscount Lisle
Born: c. 1470
Died: 1542

John de la POLE
Born: c. 1462
Died: 16 Jun 1487

The Nevilles of Salisbury (simplified)

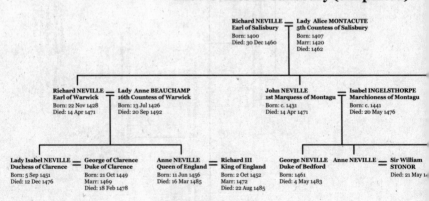

Richard NEVILLE
Earl of Salisbury
Born: 1400
Died: 30 Dec 1460

Lady Alice MONTACUTE
5th Countess of Salisbury
Born: 1407
Marr: 1420
Died: 1462

Richard NEVILLE
Earl of Warwick
Born: 22 Nov 1428
Died: 14 Apr 1471

Lady Anne BEAUCHAMP
16th Countess of Warwick
Born: 13 Jul 1426
Died: 20 Sep 1492

John NEVILLE
1st Marquess of Montagu
Born: c. 1431
Died: 14 Apr 1471

Isabel INGELSTHORPE
Marchioness of Montagu
Born: c. 1441
Died: 20 May 1476

Lady Isabel NEVILLE
Duchess of Clarence
Born: 5 Sep 1451
Died: 12 Dec 1476

George of Clarence
Duke of Clarence
Born: 21 Oct 1449
Marr: 1469
Died: 18 Feb 1478

Anne NEVILLE
Queen of England
Born: 11 Jun 1456
Died: 16 Mar 1485

Richard III
King of England
Born: 2 Oct 1452
Marr: 1472
Died: 22 Aug 1485

George NEVILLE
Duke of Bedford
Born: 1461
Died: 4 May 1483

Anne NEVILLE

Sir William
STONOR
Died: 21 May 14

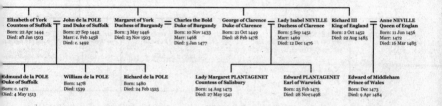

Elizabeth of York
Countess of Suffolk
Born: 22 Apr 1444
Died: aft Jan 1503

John de la POLE
2nd Duke of Suffolk
Born: 27 Sep 1442
Marr: c. Feb 1458
Died: c. 1492

Margaret of York
Duchess of Burgundy
Born: 3 May 1446
Died: 23 Nov 1503

Charles the Bold
Duke of Burgundy
Born: 10 Nov 1433
Marr: 1468
Died: 5 Jan 1477

George of Clarence
Duke of Clarence
Born: 21 Oct 1449
Marr: 1469
Died: 18 Feb 1478

Lady Isabel NEVILLE
Duchess of Clarence
Born: 5 Sep 1451
Marr: 1469
Died: 12 Dec 1476

Richard III
King of England
Born: 2 Oct 1452
Died: 22 Aug 1485

Anne NEVILLE
Queen of Englan
Born: 11 Jun 1456
Marr: 1472
Died: 16 Mar 1485

Edmund de la POLE
Duke of Suffolk
Born: c. 1472
Died: 4 May 1513

William de la POLE
Born: 1478
Died: 1539

Richard de la POLE
Born: 1480
Died: 24 Feb 1525

Lady Margaret PLANTAGENET
Countess of Salisbury
Born: 14 Aug 1473
Died: 27 May 1541

Edward PLANTAGENET
Earl of Warwick
Born: 25 Feb 1475
Died: 28 Nov 1498

Edward of Middleham
Prince of Wales
Born: Dec 1473
Died: 9 Apr 1484

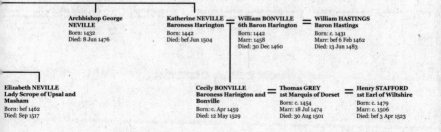

Archbishop George
NEVILLE
Born: 1432
Died: 8 Jun 1476

Katherine NEVILLE
Baroness Harington
Born: 1442
Died: bef Jun 1504

William BONVILLE
6th Baron Harington
Born: 1442
Marr: 1458
Died: 30 Dec 1460

William HASTINGS
Baron Hastings
Born: c. 1431
Marr: bef 6 Feb 1462
Died: 13 Jun 1483

Elizabeth NEVILLE
Lady Scrope of Upsal and
Masham
Born: bef 1462
Died: Sep 1517

Cecily BONVILLE
Baroness Harington and
Bonville
Born: c. Apr 1459
Died: 12 May 1529

Thomas GREY
1st Marquis of Dorset
Born: c. 1454
Marr: 18 Jul 1474
Died: 30 Aug 1501

Henry STAFFORD
1st Earl of Wiltshire
Born: c. 1479
Marr: c. 1506
Died: bef 3 Apr 1523

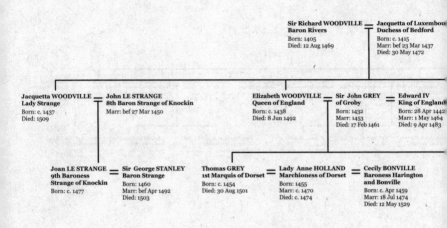

Sir Richard WOODVILLE **Baron Rivers**
Born: 1405
Died: 12 Aug 1469
— **Jacquetta of Luxembourg** **Duchess of Bedford**
Born: c. 1415
Marr: bef 23 Mar 1437
Died: 30 May 1472

Jacquetta WOODVILLE **Lady Strange**
Born: c. 1437
Died: 1509
— **John LE STRANGE** **8th Baron Strange of Knockin**
Marr: bef 27 Mar 1450

Elizabeth WOODVILLE **Queen of England**
Born: c. 1438
Died: 8 Jun 1492
— **Sir John GREY** **of Groby**
Born: 1432
Marr: 1453
Died: 17 Feb 1461
— **Edward IV** **King of England**
Born: 28 Apr 1442
Marr: 1 May 1464
Died: 9 Apr 1483

Joan LE STRANGE **9th Baroness Strange of Knockin**
Born: c. 1477
— **Sir George STANLEY** **Baron Strange**
Born: 1460
Marr: bef Apr 1492
Died: 1503

Thomas GREY **1st Marquis of Dorset**
Born: c. 1454
Died: 30 Aug 1501
— **Lady Anne HOLLAND** **Marchioness of Dorset**
Born: 1455
Marr: c. 1470
Died: c. 1474
— **Cecily BONVILLE** **Baroness Harington and Bonville**
Born: c. Apr 1459
Marr: 18 Jul 1474
Died: 12 May 1529

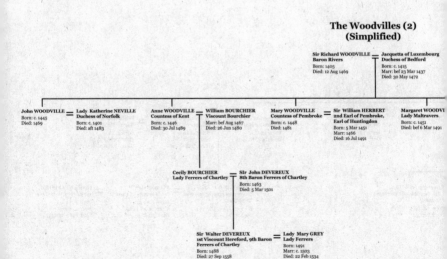

Sir Richard WOODVILLE **Baron Rivers**
Born: 1405
Died: 12 Aug 1469
— **Jacquetta of Luxembourg** **Duchess of Bedford**
Born: c. 1415
Marr: bef 23 Mar 1437
Died: 30 May 1472

John WOODVILLE
Born: c. 1445
Died: 1469
— **Lady Katherine NEVILLE** **Duchess of Norfolk**
Born: c. 1401
Died: aft 1483

Anne WOODVILLE **Countess of Kent**
Born: c. 1446
Died: 30 Jul 1489
— **William BOURCHIER** **Viscount Bourchier**
Marr: bef Aug 1467
Died: 26 Jun 1480

Mary WOODVILLE **Countess of Pembroke**
Born: c. 1448
Died: 1481
— **Sir William HERBERT** **2nd Earl of Pembroke, Earl of Huntingdon**
Born: 5 Mar 1451
Marr: 1466
Died: 16 Jul 1491

Margaret WOODVI[LLE] **Lady Maltravers**
Born: c. 1451
Died: bef 6 Mar 1491

Cecily BOURCHIER **Lady Ferrers of Chartley**
— **Sir John DEVEREUX** **8th Baron Ferrers of Chartley**
Born: 1463
Died: 5 Mar 1501

Sir Walter DEVEREUX **1st Viscount Hereford, 9th Baron Ferrers of Chartley**
Born: 1488
Died: 27 Sep 1558
— **Lady Mary GREY** **Lady Ferrers**
Born: 1491
Marr: c. 1503
Died: 22 Feb 1534

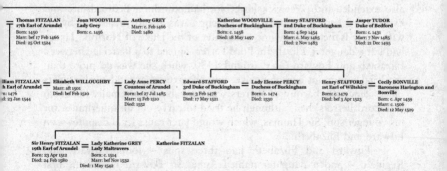

Sir Anthony WOODVILLE
2nd Earl Rivers, Baron Scales
Born: c. 1439
Died: 25 Jun 1483

Elizabeth SCALES
8th Baroness Scales
Born: c. 1436
Marr: bef Apr 1461
Died: 2 Sep 1473

Bishop Lionel WOODVILLE
Born: c. 1453
Died: 1484

Sir Edward WOODVILLE
Born: c. 1454
Died: 1488

Richard GREY
Born: c. 1456
Died: 25 Jun 1483

Thomas FITZALAN
17th Earl of Arundel
Born: 1450
Marr: bef 17 Feb 1466
Died: 25 Oct 1524

Joan WOODVILLE
Lady Grey
Born: c. 1456

Anthony GREY
Marr: c. Feb 1466
Died: 1480

Katherine WOODVILLE
Duchess of Buckingham
Born: c. 1458
Died: 18 May 1497

Henry STAFFORD
2nd Duke of Buckingham
Born: 4 Sep 1454
Marr: c. May 1465
Died: 2 Nov 1483

Jasper TUDOR
Duke of Bedford
Born: c. 1431
Marr: 7 Nov 1485
Died: 21 Dec 1495

illiam FITZALAN
h Earl of Arundel
n: 1476
d: 23 Jan 1544

Elizabeth WILLOUGHBY
Marr: aft 1501
Died: bef Feb 1510

Lady Anne PERCY
Countess of Arundel
Born: bef 27 Jul 1485
Marr: 15 Feb 1510
Died: 1552

Edward STAFFORD
3rd Duke of Buckingham
Born: 3 Feb 1478
Died: 17 May 1521

Lady Eleanor PERCY
Duchess of Buckingham
Born: c. 1474
Died: 1530

Henry STAFFORD
1st Earl of Wiltshire
Born: c. 1479
Died: bef 3 Apr 1523

Cecily BONVILLE
Baroness Harington and
Bonville
Born: c. Apr 1459
Marr: c. 1506
Died: 12 May 1529

Sir Henry FITZALAN
19th Earl of Arundel
Born: 23 Apr 1512
Died: 24 Feb 1580

Lady Katherine GREY
Lady Maltravers
Born: c. 1514
Marr: bef Nov 1532
Died: 1 May 1542

Katherine FITZALAN

1

A Failed State

Cry 'Havoc', and let slip the dogs of war!
Shakespeare, *Julius Caesar*, III ii

About 125 years before the execution of Henry, Duke of Suffolk, Reginald, 3rd Lord Grey of Ruthyn, sought a bride for his son Edward. Edward's older half-brother, Edmund, would inherit the family patrimony, while Edward would be comfortably placed with the inheritance of his mother's barony of Astley. The Astley lands were mainly located in north Warwickshire, not far from the county border with Leicestershire. There was a comfortable fortified manor house, built on a site first occupied in Saxon times and enhanced with crenellation and a moat in 1266. In 1338, Sir Thomas de Astley had constructed a chantry chapel in the nearby church, which, five years later, was upgraded to a college of dean and canons, whose job was to pray for the souls of the family. Edward, therefore, despite being a younger son, had wealth and position to offer any prospective wife. Reginald entered into negotiations with Sir William Ferrers, Lord Ferrers of Groby, whose lands were centred about 25 miles north-east of Astley, at Groby in Leicestershire, although his holdings also extended into Warwickshire, Northamptonshire, Bedfordshire and Essex. Lord Ferrers' eldest son, Sir Henry, was already dead, but by his wife, Lady Isabel de Mowbray, daughter of the Duke of Norfolk, Henry had left a daughter, Elizabeth. Lord Ferrers agreed to a marriage between Elizabeth and Edward Grey around 1430, when she was no more than the legal minimum age of twelve, and the groom around twelve years older.[1] Since the barony of Ferrers was heritable by a female, Elizabeth was Lord Ferrers' heir, although he tried to carve out an inheritance for his younger son, Sir Thomas, which would later cause legal disputes with Edward and Elizabeth.

Sir Edward and Elizabeth had three sons – John, Edward and Reginald – and a daughter named Anne. Sir Edward makes his first appearance in the historical archive in 1441, in an unexciting record of a land transaction alongside the Lord Chancellor, Viscount Beaumont (a personal friend of the king, Henry VI). He and Elizabeth probably divided their time between Astley, the manor house at Groby, and perhaps Woodham Ferrers after the death of Elizabeth's grandfather in 1445. From that time, Edward was styled Lord Ferrers of Groby, holding the barony in his wife's right.

The Greys are likely to have bemoaned the miserable state of England in the 1430s and 1440s. The long minority of Henry VI had seen the loss of most of England's holdings in France, despite the best efforts of the king's uncle John, Duke of Bedford to maintain his brother Henry V's legacy. In 1437, Henry VI, aged sixteen, had taken up the reins of government. Unfortunately for his subjects, Henry was the worst man possible for the job. He lacked the intellectual capacity and force of personality to be a successful king in an era when royal power, although not absolute, was key to good government. He was a man of gentle character, God-fearing and kindly, but he had no stomach for the ruthless acquisitiveness and warlike ambitions of the age. He was generous and suggestible, tending to agree with the person to whom he had most recently spoken. As time progressed, Henry's talents for ruling did not improve. His chief minister, William de la Pole, Earl of Suffolk, by dint of hard work and the maintenance of a good relationship with both the king's uncle Humphrey, Duke of Gloucester and his great-uncle Cardinal Beaufort (who were at daggers drawn), became the power behind the throne.

Suffolk eventually came to be associated with the failure of the war and the heavy taxation needed to prosecute it, and his relationship with Gloucester deteriorated. During this period, taxes were raised only for war or exceptional circumstances. Kings were expected to 'live of their own'. This should have been easy for Henry – he was a man of modest tastes and he personally held the great duchy of Lancaster, the earldom of Leicester, and the moiety of the three de Bohun earldoms that had pertained to his grandmother Mary. Two of his childless uncles and both dowager queens had died by the 1430s, with all their lands reverting to the Crown. He should, therefore, have been more than able to maintain ordinary government, and even contribute to the costs of war. But Henry was in debt – he had given away far too much of his land and income to his friends. The problems this easy generosity caused were compounded by him being haphazard and absent-minded. Henry's incompetence became glaring when he managed to grant the stewardship of the duchy of Cornwall to two different men at the same time. The resulting dispute undermined his authority permanently. One claimant of the office was William, 1st Lord of Bonville and Chewton, who was married to Margaret Grey, Lord Ferrers' half-sister, and commanded extensive estates in the West Country. Bonville's rival was Thomas Courtenay, 13th Earl of Devon. The enmity between the two families was unbridled but the king did little or nothing to impose order, and violence by both sides went unchecked.

As the nobility struggled to respect their king, so too did the wider population. The costs of war were heavy. Little could be wrung from the French populace, and Parliament grew reluctant to vote more funds without any prospect of ultimate victory. By 1439, it was obvious that if a decisive victory could not be won, then a truce would have to be made. Henry himself wanted peace – he saw the long-running war as a source of 'sorrow and misery' to his subjects on both sides of the Channel. Suffolk, Cardinal Beaufort and Archbishop Kempe of York supported him. The Duke of Gloucester, on the other hand, wanted to throw everything into a new offensive. Henry's view prevailed. Beaufort and Suffolk received instructions to negotiate a peace. Unfortunately for the English negotiators, the French were aware of their own growing strength and England's weakness, and proposed terms that Henry's council would not let him accept. Determined to make an overture for peace anyway, Henry released the Duke of Orléans, taken captive after the Battle of Agincourt back in 1415. Gloucester was outraged at this, and he also opposed an extension of the interim appointment of John Beaufort, 1st Duke of Somerset, great-nephew of the cardinal, as English Lieutenant in France.[2] A compromise candidate was found in Richard, Duke of York, whose wife, Cicely Neville, was the cardinal's niece. York had been brought up by the cardinal's sister, Joan, Countess of Westmorland, and might therefore be considered a Beaufort ally, while he was also on good terms with Gloucester, who thought him to be in favour of prosecuting the war.

In 1442, in a strange reversal of his former policy, Cardinal Beaufort promoted a new offensive in France, to be led by Somerset. Somerset was to direct his efforts outside the main theatre of war, Normandy, to relieve Gascony in the south-west and pursue an aggressive war policy, rather than the more defensive one being conducted by York. Whether this splitting of resources was a sensible plan at the time has been debated, but it failed miserably. Somerset was obliged to withdraw, and died soon after – it was rumoured he had taken his own life. By his wife, Margaret Beauchamp of Bletsoe, he left one legitimate child – Lady Margaret Beaufort, who inherited much of his property. The title of Duke of Somerset went to his brother, Edmund.

Somerset's failure made the need for peace even more urgent, and Henry appointed Suffolk to pursue a treaty. Whether the English liked it or not, the French had the whip hand, and Charles VII of France drove a hard bargain. He proposed a two-year truce to allow for further negotiation, and the marriage of Marguerite of Anjou, his wife's fourteen-year-old niece, to Henry. Suffolk espoused Marguerite as Henry's proxy, and on 9 April 1445 she arrived at Southampton. Initially hailed as the bringer of peace between England and France, she was to become a focus of resentment after it became apparent that England was the loser in this exchange. Marguerite, despite an impressive bloodline, brought no dowry, and, it transpired, no hope of an honourable peace. After much discussion, Henry, to the horror of most of his council, ceded the county of Maine in return for a long-term truce. The physical location of Maine – south of Normandy and north of Gascony – gave the French a wedge between the two English duchies. Whether or not Suffolk agreed with these final terms, he worked with Henry to implement them – attracting, unsurprisingly, the hostility of Gloucester. Gloucester was not the only one to think this was a bad bargain – second only to Gloucester in disgust at the apparent pusillanimity of the English government was Richard, Duke of York.

In addition to lacking the warlike spirit of his father and uncles, Henry also failed to provide those other foundations of good mediaeval rule – disinterested justice and the preservation of law and order. Without the war in France to occupy them, the nobility of England turned to their second-favourite pastime – the acquisition of lands, ideally at the expense of their rivals. Private feuding was a regular occurrence, and Henry was unwilling or unable to prevent it, losing respect and authority. Perversely, the nobles who packed juries, maintained private armies and forcibly married heiresses were the very men who complained about lawlessness.[3] The commons, of course, were used to the depredations of their so-called betters, but that did not prevent criticism of the king. The Bonville–Courtenay dispute has already been mentioned, but there were others, including that between Edmund Beaufort, Duke of Somerset, and Richard Neville, Earl of Warwick, whose dispute over the inheritance of their wives, half-sisters Eleanor and Anne Beauchamp, resulted in a bitter hatred between the men. Since Warwick's father, Richard Neville, Earl of Salisbury, was the brother of York's duchess, Cicely, and York's closest friend, York was inclined to support Warwick.

A third great land rivalry was that between Lord Cromwell and Henry Holland, 3rd Duke of Exeter, over land at Ampthill, Bedfordshire. Cromwell was an exceedingly wealthy baron, while Exeter was a very poor duke; however, Exeter was the king's cousin, and he anticipated royal support for his very weak case. The aggrieved Cromwell, who had been steadily losing influence at court after falling out with Suffolk, turned to the York faction for support – which he got, despite Exeter being York's son-in-law. Not content with manufacturing an illegal title to the Ampthill estate, Exeter concocted a charge of treason against Cromwell, Sir John Fastolf and Edmund, Lord Grey of Ruthyn, the latter being Exeter's own cousin.

Exeter probably included his cousin in these accusations because Grey was a third contender for the Ampthill estate, which lay next to the Grey family lands at Wrest, in Bedfordshire. Grey would have resisted Exeter's attempts to accrue local influence – with a duke in the neighbourhood, he himself would necessarily have taken a back seat in county affairs. Although accusations of undue partisanship have been levelled at the Lancastrian court, Lord Cromwell was able to refute the allegations of treason and was exonerated of all charges. Gradually (although it is important not to look too far forward) loyalties were coalescing around those who would remain loyal to Henry VI and those who had little to lose from a change of king.

Edward Grey, Lord Ferrers, was summoned to the parliament of February 1447, to be held at the Benedictine abbey at Bury St Edmunds, in territory held by Suffolk, during a cold so fierce that many poor people died of exposure. Like the other barons, Ferrers received orders to come arrayed for war, Suffolk having persuaded Henry that Gloucester intended to raise rebellion in Wales. Gloucester was nervous, perhaps already aware that Suffolk intended his destruction. The writer of *An English Chronicle of the Reigns of Richard II...* clearly had no doubt that Suffolk, his follower Lord Saye and 'others of their assent' had been planning for some time to make a permanent end of Gloucester, who was difficult and disputatious, and whose wife had been convicted of sorcery and 'compassing' the king's death.[4] The roads in and out of the town were guarded, and orders were sent to Gloucester to come to Bury but not to approach the king until summoned. The following day, some of his knights and squires were arrested; the day after that, the dukes of Buckingham and Somerset, with Lord Beaumont, arrested him. Three days later, the king's uncle was dead 'of sorrow', as the chronicler says – a euphemism suggesting murder.

It is debatable whether Gloucester was, in fact, murdered. He was fifty-seven years old – a natural death of stroke or heart attack brought on by stress is certainly not impossible, and is given colour by one report that he lay for three days in a coma. Additionally, the Chief Justices of England had been summoned to Bury, probably with a view to an open trial and condemnation, which would have been a more savoury outcome, although if the trial had resulted in an acquittal then Suffolk could have expected the tables to be turned. In a way, it does not much matter whether Gloucester was hurried out of the world or not: his demise, either by legal or illegal means, was Suffolk's intention – or so York and the other supporters of the late duke believed. Having been a troublesome, arrogant and overmighty subject in life, Gloucester was now imprinted on the public mind as 'the good duke', whose desire to continue the French wars was entirely laudable, and whose mantle as leader of the war party was now taken up by York.

Gloucester's death also opened the question of the succession. By 1447, Henry VI had been married for two years without his wife showing any signs of pregnancy. Although there is no question that Henry and Marguerite consummated their marriage – there is a charming story of them sitting up in bed together to receive New Year gifts, and spending all morning there – Henry had minimal interest in sex, so while he did his duty from time to time under the velvet bedcovers, he was by no means an enthusiastic lover. Consequently, it was not surprising that pregnancy had so far eluded the royal couple, and speculation was mounting as to who might be the twenty-six-year-old king's heir. None of Henry's dead uncles, the dukes of Bedford, Clarence and now Gloucester, had had legitimate children, and his aunts, Philippa, Queen of Denmark, and

Blanche, Electress Palatine, were also childless. The rules of inheritance to the English crown were fluid, so there were three main candidates: Henry, 3rd Duke of Exeter, Richard, Duke of York, and, as an outside chance, Edmund, 2nd Duke of Somerset.[5] It was therefore urgent that Henry sire children of his own. In the meantime, it appears to have been assumed that York was next in line, although that assumption rests a great deal on hindsight – Exeter's claim was good, if there were no appetite to upset the Lancastrian succession. A joining of the Exeter and York lines probably lay behind the marriage, in 1445, of Exeter's only son, Henry Holland, to York's daughter Anne.

With Gloucester out of the way, Suffolk, still in royal favour, was triumphant. However, the government's French policy could not command support. Nervous of York's growing popularity, the king – for whom we can generally read Suffolk and Marguerite – appointed him as Lord Lieutenant of Ireland in July 1447. York believed, not without reason, that this was punishment for his opposition to the surrender of Maine. He was even more insulted when he discovered that he was being replaced in Normandy by the Duke of Somerset, who showed little enthusiasm for the post, dilly-dallying at home and only arriving in Normandy in 1448.

Meanwhile, in early 1449, Lord Ferrers was in bad odour with Queen Marguerite. He and Beaumont had been 'retaining' men in their livery, contrary to statute, and these retainers were accused of attacking and beating William Newby of Leicester, among others. Worse still, Lord Ferrers' servants and others of his 'wellwilling' had wreaked considerable damage in the royal deer parks and chases.[6] A commission was empanelled in Leicestershire, and Newby's complaints upheld. Marguerite, whose jointure lands in the lordship of Leicester were affected, wrote a stinging letter, ordering Ferrers to pay the substantial compensation awarded to Newby. Ferrers was also forbidden to give livery to anyone in the lordship of Leicester, and was bound to keep the peace with Thomas Farnham and return to Sir Lewis FitzLewis a bond for £20 that he had entered into to 'eschewe the bodely hurte' that might have occurred against William Pecock, another tenant of Marguerite's at Stebbing.

Suffolk, perhaps to prove that he was just as eager to win France as anyone, secretly prompted a raid on a Breton town, in defiance of the truce. Initially successful, the raid turned out to have appalling consequences. The Duke of Brittany, Francis I, called on Charles VII for help. Charles had been waiting for just such an opportunity. Announcing that the English had broken the truce, he declared war on 31 July 1448, whisked through Normandy, and undid the work of nearly forty years of unceasing military effort, capturing Rouen on 29 October 1449. Somerset disgraced himself by buying a safe-conduct from Charles for the staggering sum of 50,000 crowns.

As always in the face of political or military defeat, there began the search for someone, anyone, to blame. The parliament that met in November 1449 was in an ugly mood – huge taxes had been raised to take France, but all that could be shown for it was the dismal stream of refugees who trailed across the English Channel from Normandy. The enormous fortunes that had been amassed from ransoms in the early years of the war were spent, and there was no hope of more. Stone-throwing on both sides began, and the lords gave little thought to the fact that they were all inhabitants of a glass house. The first man to be attacked was Adam Moleyns, Bishop of Chichester, holder of the privy seal and a councillor. Moleyns was close to Suffolk, but more pertinently he was hostile to York, whom he had accused of corruption and incompetence as Lord Lieutenant of Normandy. Whether or not his claims were true, the same accusations were now levelled at him. The king, to protect a man who had been his loyal servant, gave Moleyns permission to resign his offices and go on pilgrimage. The bishop got no further than Portsmouth, where he was murdered by an army captain.

Suffolk was next. In the hopes of evading impeachment, he pleaded his case before the king, pointing out, fairly enough, that he and his family had served the king faithfully. But many of Henry's nobles had lost faith in king and government. While they were not yet thinking of a replacement for the king, they were not going to defend Suffolk. The House of Commons demanded impeachment. Every imaginable accusation was levelled at Suffolk – conspiring with the French, molesting nuns, embezzling funds and giving away towns to France. On 9 March, the duke publicly knelt in front of the assembled Parliament and denied every charge. Henry was in a quandary – Suffolk, although he may have been arrogant, and had slightly sticky fingers, was certainly not the arrant traitor described in the articles against him. The king ruled him innocent of treason but guilty of lesser misdemeanours, deserving a sentence of banishment for five years, to begin on 1 May 1450. The sentence did not please the Commons. Suffolk was smuggled out of London, but news of his departure got out, and provoked a riot. The scale of the discontent led Henry to prorogue parliament, reopening it in Leicester after Easter – the mood not being improved by news of a French-Breton victory at Fromigny on 14 April 1450. While Henry was listening to demands from the Commons that an act of resumption be passed returning all lands alienated by the Crown since the start of his reign, thus enabling the king to 'live of his own', rather than imposing taxes. Suffolk's ship was being intercepted off Dover as he attempted to escape to the Low Countries. After a 'trial', he was found guilty and executed, his head spiked on Dover beach.

Suffolk's execution was not sufficient to calm the country. The men of Kent (and the Kentish men) rose up in rebellion, under the leadership of one Jack Cade, who liked to call himself Jack Mortimer, hinting at noble connections. This rebellion gave rise to one of the most famous lines in Shakespeare – 'The first thing we do, let's kill all the lawyers' – but Cade had more scapegoats in his sights than just the legal fraternity. He led a considerable force towards London. Henry, unlike his predecessor

Richard II, did not choose to meet the rebels in person. Instead, two bands of militia were raised under the Duke of Buckingham and Lord Beaumont, and negotiators were sent to talk to the rebels – with little success. Henry withdrew to his castle at Kenilworth in Warwickshire, having thrown the rebels a titbit in the shape of the arrest and imprisonment of Lord Saye. Emboldened by their success, the rebels marched to London and were permitted to enter the city, where they were joined by other discontented commons from Essex.

The rebels had a well-crafted manifesto in which they claimed that, first, the king was living off the commons, having granted his own lands to other men; second, the lords 'of his royal blood' had been dismissed from his presence and replaced with 'mean persons' – a perennial complaint; third, 'purveyance' – the forcible purchase of goods by the royal household – was bankrupting people; fourth, justice in the royal courts was being undermined by the king's 'menial servants'; fifth, that the loss of the French lands needed to be investigated. There was a long tail of other grievances, but these key ones were echoed across the land in an outbreak of lawlessness. Bishop Ayscough was murdered by a Wiltshire mob in late June, while Henry, cowering at Kenilworth, sent word that Cade was to be permitted to set up a royal court of justice at the Guildhall to try suspected traitors. Cade, mindful that his rebellion had emerged from genuine grievances, attempted to keep control of his men, but discipline inevitably broke down and Londoners were subjected to mob violence.

The City authorities soon became tired of the influx of rebels – if the king would do nothing to manage the situation, they would. They commissioned the experienced soldiers Lord Scales and Matthew Gough, and the rebels were driven out of the city in a bloody skirmish. Marguerite, who had remained in Greenwich, recommended that the rebels be offered pardons, and many dispersed. Cade chose not to escape while he had the chance. On 10 July, he was branded a traitor, and a price was put on his head. A few days later, he was cornered and died from injuries sustained trying to escape. Henry returned to London, where a service of thanksgiving was held at St Paul's. While the Londoners might have been glad that the rebellion had been quashed, Henry had lost even more respect. In an attempt to shore up the leaking ship of state, commissions were sent out to investigate the abuses of which Cade had complained, but there was little improvement.

The nobility of England may have hoped that, with Cade's rebellion more or less defeated, some sort of normality would return, but the political stage was set for nothing less than civil war. York, having been as successful in the lieutenancy of Ireland as anyone could be in that graveyard of political careers, was returning to England, via Beaumaris in North Wales. While this seems innocuous, the king's deputies were only supposed to leave their posts with the king's express permission.

Orders were sent not to permit York to land nor to give the duke or his contingent any succour. This was a hostile act towards one of the king's own senior officers, and the man many thought his rightful heir. Perhaps Henry, or his ministers, chief of whom was now Somerset, were right to be suspicious – some of the unrest of 1450, particularly incidents in East Anglia, can be traced to York's retainers, although government actions certainly exacerbated the situation.

York landed further along the coast and went straight to his own castle at Denbigh. He wrote sorrowfully to the king that he had only returned from Ireland to vindicate himself as a loyal subject. 'I have been informed that diverse language, hath been said of me to your most excellent estate which should sound to my dishonour and reproach and charge of my person,' he complained, requesting permission to answer the charges in the presence of the king.[7] Henry responded with the assurance that he took York for 'our faithful subject and as our well-beloved cousin'.[8]

By the time York arrived in London, he had over 3,000 men with him. It is unclear how many of these he had actively retained as an escort, compared with those who joined him to show support, but from the king's perspective it was hard to see the arrival of such a body of men as anything other than threatening. Nevertheless, Henry received the duke graciously. Seeing his own popularity, and mindful of the grievous state of government – particularly the part that his hated rival, Somerset, was playing in it – York wrote again to the king. This 'bill' was widely circulated and was nothing less than a catalogue of complaints against the government, followed by the suggestion that the king should give York a free hand to resolve the issues of which Cade and the other rebels had complained. Henry may have been an ineffectual king, but that did not mean he would meekly hand over his power to his cousin. He declined with thanks, assuring York that he intended to rule with the help of a 'sad (serious) and substantial council', of which York was to be a member.

York left London to chew this rebuff over, and to commune with his friend, the Duke of Norfolk. The two dukes returned to London, with a forbidding array of men. In a direct affront to the king, York was preceded by an updrawn sword as he rode to Parliament. Parliament demanded that Somerset pay the ultimate price for the loss of France – indictment as a traitor – but the king refused. Within days, the capital erupted in riots. A lynch mob tried to break into the Blackfriars, where Somerset was lodged, but he was escorted to the safety of the Tower by the Earl of Devon, possibly on instructions from York, who wanted Somerset to be condemned by due process rather than murdered. York soon realised he had unleashed more than he intended – the city was only calmed by a show of unity among the lords, who, led by the king and all (except, probably, Henry) dressed in armour, rode through the streets.

Tempers cooled over the Christmas recess, and Somerset tried to clean up the government's act with another act of resumption and efforts to implement a defence of Gascony, to be led by Lord Rivers. But the fragile peace between York and the government collapsed when, in January 1451, further rioting broke out in Kent. Since the leader had been a retainer of York's, the government, rightly or wrongly, saw the duke's hand behind the trouble and the 'sad and serious council' Henry had promised was abandoned. York's position was further damaged when another of his supporters, Sir Thomas Young, put forward a bill in Parliament for York to be recognised as Henry's successor. The king's answer to that was to dissolve the house. Over the next few years, accusation and counter-accusation of mismanagement, financial peculation and general incompetence flew between York and Somerset, and the country slipped inexorably towards civil war.

*

Sometime in the early 1450s, Lord and Lady Ferrers arranged a marriage for John, the eldest of their three sons, who was aged about twenty. We know nothing of John Grey's upbringing, although we can assume that, as the heir to the Ferrers barony of Groby, he would have received the usual military training of his class, and would have been eager for the wars in France to resume, allowing him to win honour and glory. John's bride, about four years his junior, was named Elizabeth Woodville and came from neighbouring Northamptonshire, where her family, originally from Kent, held extensive lands in and around Grafton and Potterspury.[9] Elizabeth's grandfather Richard Woodville had been a squire of the body to Henry V, and later Seneschal of Normandy under John, Duke of Bedford. His son, Richard junior, was knighted at Leicester on Whitsunday 1426, alongside Richard of York, and he too joined Bedford's household, serving in France with the duke until the latter's death in 1435.

Bedford's second wife, Jacquetta of St Pol, was only a young woman when she was widowed, and within months, or possibly even weeks, she married Richard Woodville junior. For the transgression of marrying without the king's permission, which she required as the widow of one of his tenants-in-chief, Jacquetta's dower was forfeit. In 1436, she brought a petition before Henry VI, requesting forgiveness. The petition described how 'Jacquetta, late wife to John, Duke of Bedford, ... took but late ago to husband your true liegeman born of your realm of England Richard Wydeville, knight, not having thereto your royal licence and assent' which had caused the couple to suffer 'right great straitness, as well in their persons as in their goods', leaving Jacquetta with 'neither land nor good her to sustain'. Henry was requested to show his 'righteousness and abundant grace' and forgive them. The king was pleased to accede to this request in return for a fine of £1,000. After payment of this high but not punitive sum, borrowed from Cardinal Beaufort, Jacquetta's dower was restored. As was customary, she retained the title of Duchess of Bedford, and in 1438 she became the highest-ranking woman in England, on the death of the king's mother, Katherine of Valois; she retained this rank until Henry VI's marriage to Marguerite of Anjou

Richard and Jacquetta were among the throng who escorted the new queen to England, and Jacquetta and Marguerite were soon on good terms. It was probably pleasant for them both to converse in their native French. In about 1449, Richard was ennobled as Baron Rivers, with various grants and emoluments, and, as mentioned above, took part in efforts to reclaim Gascony.

Richard and Jacquetta had numerous children, including Elizabeth, the girl now betrothed to John Grey.[10] Elizabeth's dowry was 500 marks, and Lord and Lady Ferrers agreed to enfeoff several manors to the young couple's use, with John able to request the feoffees to vest the property in him. He did this in October 1455, suggesting that the marriage had recently taken place, or perhaps that Elizabeth was pregnant or had given birth. This would give a birth date for their eldest son, Thomas, of 1454–55, rather than the 1453 usually given. The earliest possible date for his birth, inferred from later documents, is April 1452. The second son, Richard, was probably born around 1458. During their married life, John and Elizabeth may have lived in one of the Grey family homes at Groby Hall or Astley, but it is more likely they lived in a manor on their jointure lands.[11]

About the time John and Elizabeth were married, there was rejoicing throughout the land. After seven years of marriage, Queen Marguerite had fallen pregnant. The thought of an assured succession was welcome to almost everyone – although York may have felt some private disappointment. Hopes that this might presage a renewal of prosperity in England were dashed only a few months later, when the last great confrontation of the Hundred Years War took place on 17 July 1453, at Castillon, resulting in a bloody defeat for the English. The devastating news had a dreadful impact on the king, who, on hearing the news, fell into a catatonic stupor, from which nothing could rouse him. Henry's councillors were stunned and frantic. While the king was in his right mind, they could more or less run the country, with Henry consulted and deferred to. With the king lacking capacity, they had no authority at all. The country was, in effect, leaderless.

Such a thing had never happened before in England – but it soon became apparent that some semblance of a regency council would need to be convoked, similar to that which had ruled during Henry's minority. With all the king's uncles and great-uncles dead, and Somerset and York at loggerheads, the royal council was in a quandary as to the right action to take, so it delayed, hoping that Henry's return to the world might be as sudden as his closing off from it. However, there was no change over the summer.

On St Edward's Day, 13 October 1453, Marguerite was brought to bed of a son, whom she named for the saint. Prince Edward of Lancaster was a hale and hearty child, and Marguerite could rejoice in having done her duty. While the birth of Edward was one piece of good news, it floated on a sea of troubles. With no strong central force, an already disorderly country was plunging into chaos. The Percys and the Nevilles in the north, the Bonvilles and Courtenays in the west, and Henry VI's half-brothers Edmund and Jasper Tudor, and the Duke of York in Wales were all conducting private feuds, little less than civil wars.

Summonses went out to all the lords temporal and spiritual to form a Great Council. York received the additional admonition to attend accompanied 'peaceably and measurably' (that is, without so many men as last time), and in a frame of mind to work with, rather than against, Somerset. York's inclusion indicates that the other lords wanted to resolve the running sore of the dukes' dispute. In that, they were optimistic. York was anything but peaceable. He persuaded his ally the Duke of Norfolk to accuse Somerset, in the face of the council, of treason in losing France. Taken by surprise, the council, being led by the Lord Chancellor, Cardinal Kempe, agreed that Somerset should be sent to the Tower while the allegations were investigated. York then put himself forward to lead the council. While the lords were thinking this over, a bid for power came from a surprising quarter – the queen.

As a childless queen, Marguerite had had little power; as the mother of the king's heir, she was now a far more important woman – and she knew it. For women to act as regents for husbands, sons or brothers was by no means a rarity, although there were not many instances in English history.[12] For Marguerite, it would have seemed completely natural. Her mother and grandmother had acted as regents, and her grandmother, Yolande of Aragon, had been a regular councillor to Charles VII. Marguerite composed a bill of five articles, laying out the areas of responsibility she wished to take on, in the name of her husband and son – according to information received by the Pastons of Norfolk, she sought the 'whole rule' of the land. She also sought funds to maintain the king, the prince and herself.

The council debated the rival options of appointing York or Marguerite as regent, but before a decision could be made, Cardinal Kempe died suddenly, compounding the vacuum at the top. Only the king had the power to appoint a new chancellor, and the gravity of the situation became obvious when a delegation of lords was obliged to report 'with sorrowful hearts' that Henry was unable to respond to requests for him to do so. Someone had to take charge, and on 27 March 1454, York was appointed as Lord Protector and Chief Councillor on the same terms as had pertained during Henry's minority – that is, that the protector was to be ruled by the council as a body, and had no power of veto. Marguerite was mollified by the confirmation of Prince Edward as Prince of Wales and Earl of Chester and the assurance that the protectorate would last only as long as the king was incapacitated, or until Prince Edward was of age to be regent.

While the factional fighting that York had indulged in over the previous few years had given some lords misgivings about the advisability of appointing him, the new Lord Protector did not entirely live down to expectations. Although he appointed his brother-in-law Salisbury as Lord Chancellor, in an act that perhaps gave too much succour to the Nevilles in their anti-Percy campaign, and nominated his cousin Thomas Bourchier for the archbishopric of Canterbury, York did not appoint a swathe of cronies. Marguerite's greatest supporter, the Duke of Buckingham (another of York's numerous brothers-in-law), and the king's half-brothers Edmund, Earl of Richmond and Jasper, Earl of Pembroke also received grants. The only losers, it appeared, were Somerset, who languished in the Tower counting his woes, and the Duke of Exeter. Exeter was still snarled up in his quarrel with Lord Cromwell, who now brought a petition to Parliament for the matter of Ampthill to be resolved.

On 20 March, the Lords granted Cromwell's petition and York had it sent to the Commons. Despite the number of servants Exeter had in the lower chamber, he could not prevent Cromwell's petition being accepted. Exeter's already poor relationship with his father-in-law could not survive this, and he and York were now irreconcilable – especially as Exeter was not convinced of York's claim to be the superior peer of the realm. He brought out a couple of hundred men in Lancastrian livery to assert his right to act on the king's behalf, but he had overplayed his hand – York swiftly marched north and dragged his fellow duke out of sanctuary and sent him off to Pontefract Castle. Meanwhile, the other lords were underwhelmed by both York and Exeter, and found pressing business at home, requiring them to absent themselves from York's government. In Calais, too, there was trouble. Calais, and the 'Pale' surrounding it, were all that was left of the English Crown holdings in France – and it was the only place with a permanent body of paid soldiers. The Captain of Calais was the imprisoned Duke of Somerset, who had appointed as joint deputies Lord Rivers and Lionel, Lord Welles – whose wife, Margaret Beauchamp of Bletsoe, had previously been married to Somerset's brother, John, 1st Duke of Somerset. York appointed himself the new Captain of Calais, but it took considerable effort for him to gain any support there, especially as there were internal divisions in Calais, between the wool interest and the garrison, mutinous for lack of pay.

Just as York was getting used to the pleasures and problems of power, in a coincidence that no doubt felt significant to the religious sensibilities of the age, Henry VI emerged from his stupor on Christmas Day, apparently not much the worse for wear, and sufficiently master of himself to order votive offerings for the cathedral at Canterbury. Five days later, Marguerite brought Prince Edward to receive his father's blessing. This proved less than successful. Henry, although he had been aware of Marguerite's pregnancy before he fell ill, looked rather blankly on the baby, not remembering having been told of the boy's birth. Nevertheless, he showed appropriate gratitude and 'thanked God thereof'.

The other man who was thanking God was Somerset. He was released from the Tower towards the end of January 1454, with the approbation of Henry's council, and in early March all the treason charges were dropped. It was obvious that Henry was not going to see Somerset blamed for the loss of France. Had matters ended there, it is possible that the events of the next thirty years might have been different, but York did not just lose the office of protector, which he resigned of his own volition, but was also removed from the captaincy of Calais, which was returned to Somerset, in a vindication of the latter's management of the war. Salisbury was replaced as chancellor by Thomas Bourchier – although that was uncontentious as York had nominated him for the archbishopric – and Salisbury's son Warwick was commanded to release Exeter from gaol. Aware that York was not going to be pleased by Somerset's rehabilitation, Henry's council bound him in the sum of £20,000 to keep the peace. This added insult to injury, and the duke was now faced with two unpalatable truths: the king had a son who had displaced him from his position as heir to the throne, and, with Somerset in the position of confidant to king and queen, York would never recover his power.

York, Salisbury and Warwick decided that their only option was to remove Somerset and the king's 'evil counsellors' (code in the Middle Ages and Tudor period for any minister the rebel did not approve of) by force. They set about raising men. York, the greatest landowner in England and Wales after the king, was able to raise a small army, and Salisbury and Warwick between them could do the same. The royal response, rather than raising a royal army to put down the incipient rebellion, was to call another Great Council to meet at Leicester. In a genuine attempt to defuse the situation, Somerset was replaced as Constable of England by the Duke of Buckingham, with whom neither York nor his Neville relatives had any particular quarrel.

The king did not intend to travel unarmed – orders went out for men to join him en route at St Albans. York, Salisbury and Warwick were summoned to attend with no more than 200 men for the duke and 160 each for the earls – enough to make a suitable entourage but hardly a realistic fighting force. The three men promised that their intentions were good. Unfortunately, the outcome was bad. A vicious skirmish which became known as the first Battle of St Albans was fought in the streets of the town, resulting in the deaths of Somerset, the Earl of Northumberland and Lord Clifford. The king was slightly injured by a stray arrow, and had little option but to accept York's escort to the abbey, where the duke reiterated his loyalty, with oaths that Henry was obliged to accept. Henry was now a puppet in the hands of York. Given York's previously good efforts at managing affairs during the king's illness, this was not necessarily an entirely bad thing; certainly the

Milanese ambassador reported home that many people thought York's control was to be welcomed. He was installed again as Lord Protector on 15 November 1455, when the Commons were told that the king was too ill to open the parliamentary session himself. This second appointment gave York more power than the first and made it possible to dismiss him only by an act of the king in Parliament.

Having grabbed power with the help of a partisan group, it was impossible, even had he wished it, for York to be the impartial representative of the king. Salisbury and Warwick had taken a risk in supporting him and expected their reward. Warwick benefited most obviously, receiving the captaincy of Calais. The incumbent, Lord Rivers, refused to hand over control until his men had been paid their arrears; while this endeared him to the troops, it aroused Warwick's ire, marking the beginning of a feud between the two men that would have dire consequences. The other peers felt marginalised by York and were unenthusiastic about backing his policies, including yet another act of resumption, which the Commons had introduced to try to limit the king's poor financial control. More importantly, there was at least one person implacably opposed to York holding sway – the queen. Marguerite was now twenty-six, and, with her son to protect, was a formidable opponent – everything that Henry lacked in courage, force, determination and will was present in his wife. She was quick to take advantage of York's lack of widespread support, working with the other councillors to appoint men she trusted. Her influence was known throughout the country, commented upon by John Paston, the Norfolk gentleman to whose correspondence we owe much of what we know about the period. York's supporters thought that Marguerite was 'gathering riches innumerable'. If so, it was to support her husband and son.

Henry was persuaded that York had gone too far with the draft bill of resumption – the Commons had suggested that any exceptions that Henry wanted to make would have to be approved by York. This aroused even the mild Henry to protect his authority, and, supported by all the nobles not directly attached to York, he came to Parliament to dismiss the protector. Nevertheless, Henry and his government did not want to leave York and his allies entirely out in the cold. The duke was reappointed as Lord Lieutenant of Ireland – which was a prestigious, if difficult, job; Warwick remained as Captain of Calais; and Salisbury had posts on the Scottish border. In an effort to reconcile York with what was left of Suffolk's family, York's daughter Elizabeth married the new earl – John de la Pole.

A couple of months before this marriage, on 18 December 1457, Lord Ferrers died. Since the barony was Lady Ferrers' own, John Grey would not become Lord Ferrers until her death. Having settled her youngest son, Reginald, in the Duke of York's entourage some years before, Lady Ferrers wanted to make provision for her second son, Edward Grey. While it was the norm for the eldest son to inherit everything, it was by no means rare for parents to try to circumvent the rules of primogeniture by arranging a life-interest in specified lands for younger children. Lady Ferrers elected to do this on 4 October 1459, by enfeoffing land to Edward's use. The settlement itself – four messuages in Higham, a tenement in Leicester, six virgates of land and a close in Carleton Curlegh – was not huge, and worth just 11 marks per annum, but it was enfeoffed to the use of Edward Grey and his heirs. By this means, only if and when Edward's line failed, would the land revert to John's descendants.

Although the government was trying to mend fences, it was proving almost impossible to placate the sons of the men who had died at St Albans. Somerset's son Henry inherited the dukedom as third duke, Northumberland was succeeded by his son – yet another Henry Percy – as third earl, and Lord Clifford's son, John, became 9th Baron Clifford. In what sounds like an initiative typical of the king, it was decided to hold a public reconciliation of the warring factions, a 'loveday'. Lovedays were a recognised part of legal practice in mediaeval England – arbitration and amicable agreement of cases was often sought, rather than recourse to law, which, it will not be a great surprise to readers to learn, was slow, expensive and arcane. Henry favoured conciliation and compromise, which suited his notions of Christian conduct, and, had his peers been as eager to avoid conflict as he was, such efforts might have had some success.[13]

The Great Council was summoned to London, and the city was soon awash with the huge retinues of Somerset, backed by Exeter, Clifford and Northumberland and his brothers, with York, Salisbury and Warwick (newly arrived from Calais) facing them. The council brokered a deal – compensation was to be paid for the deaths of the fathers of Somerset, Northumberland and Clifford, and the Nevilles and Percys (who had been feuding for nearly fifty years, despite intermarriages) were bound over to keep the peace. With the agreement made, the court processed to St Paul's for a special Mass of reconciliation. In front were the young Duke of Somerset and the Earl of Salisbury hand in hand, followed by Exeter and Warwick, then the king in his royal robes, with Marguerite and York bringing up the rear. It is likely that Henry was the only one convinced by the day's spectacle.

Warwick had used his captaincy of Calais as a cover for what was little more than piracy, regularly preying on foreign shipping. While French craft might have been considered fair game, an attack on Hanseatic shipping was unacceptable, as was an even more bloody attack on Spanish shipping in June 1458.[14] Not only was Warwick creating havoc in Calais, he was also, in the opinion of the government at least, causing trouble at home. A commission was established to investigate his activities, headed by Lord Rivers, father-in-law of Sir John Grey. Warwick already saw Rivers as the enemy, and this increased the earl's resentment – he was disgusted at being questioned by a man beneath him in rank. The commission's findings are not known, but we can presume them to have had little positive to say about Warwick's conduct as captain. In November 1458, when Warwick had returned to London to attend Parliament, his servants got into a brawl with members of the king's household. Hearing a rumour that this incident was to be used as a reason to imprison him, Warwick swiftly returned to Calais. Unable to stomach such defiance, the government dismissed Warwick from the captaincy, appointing the new Duke of Somerset in his place. Removing Warwick from office proved easier in theory than in practice, however, and Somerset was unable to take the town. Warwick and his uncle William Neville, Lord Fauconberg, remained there, plotting their next move.

Meanwhile, the government had called another Great Council to the Midlands, which York and his supporters refused to attend. Instead, in a plunge into outright treason, they formed a plan to surround and capture the king. York, together with his two eldest sons, seventeen-year-old Edward, Earl of March and sixteen-year-old Edmund, Earl of Rutland, set out from their estates around Ludlow, while Salisbury brought troops south from Middleham in Yorkshire, and Warwick emerged from Calais to lead a force across the south of England seemingly unopposed. Marguerite and Prince Edward took refuge at Eccleshall, while Henry, at last roused to something like martial fervour, led an army north, preventing Salisbury crossing the Trent. The earl turned west, and despite the numbers not being in his favour, soundly beat a government force under Lord Audley at Blore Heath, leaving some 2,000 dead. Salisbury headed south to join with York and Warwick, and all three swore to be true to each other. Henry, still hoping for reconciliation, offered pardons to anyone not present at Blore Heath, but York and Warwick would not betray Salisbury. They prepared for battle. Henry, with a significantly larger force, faced York across Ludford Bridge.

To bear arms as a way of protesting against weak government was one thing; to fight an anointed king was quite another. Unable to contemplate making war on the king in person, John Grey's brother Reginald, who had been one of York's retainers for at least seven years, defected to the king's side; more significantly, so did one of the Yorkist captains, Anthony Trollope, along with the force he commanded. With their numbers dramatically reduced, the Yorkist leaders abandoned their men and slunk away in the night – York, Salisbury and Rutland to Ireland; Warwick, Fauconberg and March to Calais. Ludlow was sacked, but Duchess Cicely and her children were 'granted grace' by the king.[15]

In anticipation of York and his men returning, the government levied troops in December 1459, with Sir John Grey being commissioned to raise men in his native Leicestershire. The royal party had been right to fear further trouble. Warwick, March and Fauconberg dug in at Calais. From there, they raided the English coast and by early 1460 had established a bridgehead at Sandwich to facilitate a full-scale invasion. On 15 January, a group of Warwick's men came to Sandwich and forcibly 'took away with them in their ship to Calais, Richard Woodville, knight, Lord Rivers, sent by the king for the defence of the kingdom ... and Anthony Woodville, knight, Richard's son, being there in peace as prisoners against their will'.[16] Duchess Jacquetta, was captured too, but not abducted. Once in Calais, the men were roundly abused by Warwick and March. Warwick, as pleased with himself and his drop of royal blood as ever, and no doubt still angry over Rivers' earlier commission, harangued Anthony with the words that 'his father was naught but a squire and brought up with King Henry the Fifth and sithen made himself by marriage, and also made lord, and that it was not his part to have language of the lords being of the king's blood'.[17]

The next pitched battle occurred at Northampton on 10 July 1460. The Yorkists were led by Salisbury, Warwick and Edward of March, as York was still in Ireland. It is unknown whether John Grey fought for the king at Northampton, but if he did, he survived unscathed in person and in reputation, unlike his cousin Edmund Grey of Ruthyn, who turned his coat and let Edward of March know that, in exchange for support in the long-running dispute over the Fanhope estate, he would allow the Yorkist troops to pass him unharmed, despite the trust that had been reposed in him by the king, with his appointment as leader of the left flank. Edmund Grey ordered his men to help the Yorkists enter the barricade protecting the royal flank, a deed described by H. T. Evans thus: 'In the sordid annals of even these sterile wars there is no deed of shame so foul.'[18] With this treachery in the royal ranks, the king's forces were unable to resist the Yorkists. Henry was captured, and, after three days of confinement at Dalapré Abbey, was escorted to London, still treated as king but under the control of Warwick, March and Fauconberg, with Grey of Ruthyn now firmly in the York camp as part of the escort. Marguerite, 'robbed and despoiled of all her goods', fled north with her son.

Parliament was called and a redistribution of offices began: Warwick's brother, George Neville, Bishop of Exeter, became Chancellor;[19] Henry Bourchier (York's nephew) became Treasurer; and Salisbury took the position of Chamberlain of the King's Household, giving him control of access to the king. Not everyone was happy with Henry as a prisoner of the York faction, and the garrison of the Tower kept up a bombardment of London until they were starved into surrender.

York was riding high. On 10 October 1460, escorted by several hundred men, with his naked sword carried before him, he rode into

Westminster, to the cheering of the crowds. He entered the Parliament Chamber and, contrary to all precedent, instead of bowing to the empty throne, climbed the steps to the dais and put his hand on the royal chair, indicating that he claimed it as his own. He turned, expecting a full-throated roar of support. Silence fell. The Archbishop of Canterbury politely enquired whether York were hoping to see the king. Indeed not, was York's response – Henry ought rather to come to see him, as he himself was undoubtedly the true king of England. This claim was met with a baffled silence. Even York's own son Edward of March did not support the move. Eventually, a compromise was reached in the Act of Accord. Henry (who was younger than York) would reign for the rest of his natural life, but be succeeded by York (or York's son). York in the meantime, was to have the revenues and titles of Prince of Wales and Duke of Cornwall. The only sop that poor Henry, separated from his wife and his closest supporters, and bullied mentally if not physically, could manage to wrangle from his oppressors was the reservation of the great duchy of Lancaster for his own son.

Unsurprisingly, although Henry himself had accepted the Act of Accord, Marguerite would have none of it. Henry commanded widespread support as an anointed king and a good man, even if a poor leader, and there were many willing to fight for him. The war dragged on. York, his younger son Rutland, and Salisbury were killed at the Battle of Wakefield in December 1460.[20] Marguerite, in an understandable, if tasteless, act of revenge, had their heads impaled on stakes over the gates of York, the duke's bearing a paper crown. Another casualty of Wakefield was Reginald Grey. While uncertain, it is likely he was fighting for Henry.

The leadership of the Yorkist cause fell to the next generation: Edward, previously Earl of March and now Duke of York, and Warwick. They fought on, with Edward scoring a notable victory at Mortimer's Cross, after which Owain Tudor, the king's stepfather, was executed in the marketplace at Hereford – presumably in revenge for the death of Rutland. Two weeks later, Marguerite's forces triumphed over Warwick at the second Battle of St Albans. Henry was rescued from his ignominious captivity, and the royal army prepared to enter London. Sir John Grey was not so lucky – he fell in the Lancastrian ranks.

Unfortunately for Marguerite, the largely Yorkist capital shut its gates against her, allegedly terrified that the city would be sacked by her victorious northern troops. Jacquetta of Bedford and Lady Scales were sent by the city to request Marguerite to desist. She agreed and withdrew north. This was one of the few occasions on which Marguerite failed to take the bolder course, and it proved her undoing. Edward of York entered the city, and on 3 March 1461 was proclaimed king at Baynard's Castle by Thomas Bourchier, Archbishop of Canterbury; the bishops of Salisbury and Exeter; John, Duke of Norfolk; Richard, Earl of Warwick;

Lord FitzWalter; and Walter Devereux, Lord Ferrers of Chartley. The authority for this action was dubious – neither FitzWalter nor Ferrers had ever been summoned to Parliament, and the others hardly constituted a majority of lords. Nevertheless, the following day, Edward rode to Westminster, where he took the crown and sceptre and was proclaimed as King Edward IV. Now, all he needed to do was to follow this up with a victory in the field, which he did on Palm Sunday 1464 at Towton in Yorkshire – one of the bloodiest battles ever fought on English soil. Queen Marguerite and Prince Edward escaped to Scotland, while King Henry went into hiding somewhere in the north of England.

2

The Triumph of York

Now is the winter of our discontent, made glorious summer
by this sun of York...
Shakespeare, *Richard III*, I i

Following Towton, and Edward's rapid enthronement, the English nobility largely accepted the change of regime – they had not sought it, with few beyond York's immediate circle wanting it, but Henry was not really a king worth fighting for, and his son was only a child. Pragmatism and self-preservation dictated that coming to terms with Edward IV would be a wise move – especially as Edward himself was a man of great promise. Some Lancastrians were attainted at the November parliament, including Thomas, Lord Richemount de Grey, brother of Grey of Ruthyn. The brothers had been on opposite sides for years, so it is unlikely that Ruthyn shed any tears.

Among those who showed themselves willing to accept Edward as king were the late Sir John Grey's parents-in-law, Lord Rivers and Duchess Jacquetta. Rivers had played a major role in the Lancastrian ranks at Towton, but he knew when he was beaten. According to Count Ludovico Dallugo, in a letter to his master, the Duke of Milan, Rivers and his son Anthony, whom Dallugo described as 'very brave men', thought that the Lancastrian cause was irretrievably lost. Edward was eager for reconciliation. The king, 'affectionately considering the state of Jacquetta, Duchess of Bedford and Lord Rivers, of his especial grace', gave them a grant of 333 marks 4s as well as restoring her dower. Having given their loyalty, the Woodvilles did not deviate from it and Lord Rivers, clearly an able man, was a councillor by 1463.

Following the death of Sir John Grey at St Albans, his widow, Elizabeth, was entitled to her jointure lands, and expected the Ferrers inheritance to devolve to her son, Thomas, on the death of Lady Ferrers. However, a dispute broke out between Elizabeth and her mother-in-law about Elizabeth's jointure. Lady Ferrers had married again. Her second husband was Sir John Bourchier, cousin of Edward IV and nephew of the Archbishop of Canterbury – there is no information as to whether this marriage occurred before or after Edward IV took the throne. If the latter, it might have been part of Edward's method of rewarding his supporters by finding them wealthy matches, and also encouraging intermarriage between his supporters and Lancastrians. The quarrel was bitter enough for Elizabeth to leave the Grey family home and return to her own family, which was an unusual step for a widow with children, particularly sons, to take. Unwilling to take the loss of her jointure lying down, Elizabeth went to law. A number of the relevant documents from Chancery still exist, from which it is possible to piece together at least some of the case, although a lack of dates does not make it easy.

According to Elizabeth and her father, the agreed dowry of 500 marks had been paid and the jointure lands enfeoffed to John's use in October 1455 and now that Elizabeth was widowed, the lands should be enfeoffed to her use. Lady Ferrers disagreed. She brought two suits – one, an action for debt against Lord Rivers, claiming that 125 marks of Elizabeth's dowry remained unpaid, and the other against the feoffees, on the grounds that the lands had not been intended for transfer to John and Elizabeth, but to be returned to her at her request. Two of the feoffees, Robert Iseham and William Bovden, confirmed Elizabeth's position and requested the court for damages against Lady Ferrers for 'wrongful vexation'. Lord Rivers made a deposition to the court that he had paid the dowry, although he could not produce any receipt for it, and demanded that Lady Ferrers and Bourchier be brought before the court of Chancery to discharge him of the debt. A third trustee, William Fylding, deposed that the lands had been enfeoffed, and that both Elizabeth and Lady Ferrers were demanding that he make a transfer of the estate, but that he did not know the original purpose of the enfeoffment, so could the court please make a direction as to what he was to do?

The deterioration in the rule of law in the mid-fifteenth century meant that, in order to have any hope of legal redress, a litigant needed friends in high places. Elizabeth's link to the Lancastrian royal family was no longer as powerful as her mother-in-law's new position as a connection of the York royal family, so Elizabeth sought, and found, a 'good lord' in William, Lord Hastings, an intimate friend of the new king, and brother-in-law of Warwick. Her choice may also have been influenced by Hastings' sister Anne being married to Sir Thomas Ferrers of Tamworth, Lady Ferrers' uncle, with whom she and Edward Grey had done battle over the years. Nothing was free in Elizabeth's world. In return for Hastings' help, she had to enter into a complex deal. Her son Thomas, once he reached his majority, was to marry any daughter of Hastings born within the following few years. The groom, should he die, could be substituted by his brother Richard and the bride, if Hastings had no daughters, by one of his nieces. If anything could be wrested from Lady Ferrers, Elizabeth and Hastings would share the income until Thomas (or Richard) was twelve. Hastings was to pay Elizabeth 500 marks for the marriage, but if no marriage eventuated, Elizabeth was to pay Hastings 250 marks.

Elizabeth and her sons remained at her childhood home at Grafton during this period. No remarriage was arranged. This might have been because her finances were in disorder, or perhaps it was because she already had a suitor – the new king himself. The date of Elizabeth's first meeting with Edward IV is unknown. Scofield dates it to June 1461, when Edward visited the Rivers family. Edward was nineteen at that time, and Elizabeth around twenty-three. It would hardly be surprising if two such remarkably physically attractive people, as they are reported to have been, found each other attractive. Edward was described by Philip de Commynes, chief minister first to Charles of Burgundy and later to Louis XI of France, as 'so handsome, he must have been made for the pleasures of the flesh'.[1] But Elizabeth was newly widowed, and Edward was certainly not looking for a wife. While he was notorious as a womaniser even during his own lifetime, to seduce his host's widowed daughter would not have been a sensible action when he had only just laid his hands on the throne.

Three years later, matters were different. Edward was twenty-two, and far more secure on his throne. The story of Elizabeth and Edward's courtship has become a romantic legend. It is said that, on her mother's advice, Elizabeth sought to gain the king's sympathy for her land dispute by waylaying him, flanked by her sons, between Daventry and Grafton while he was enjoying a hunting trip. He became so enamoured of her that he sought to add her to his already impressive list of conquests, but Elizabeth rejected any dishonourable advances, possibly even threatening to kill herself if he forced himself upon her. She knew she was not worthy to be his wife, but she was far too good to be any man's mistress. Genuinely smitten, Edward chose marriage with Elizabeth over the benefits that might have accrued through a foreign match. A private ceremony, witnessed by Duchess Jacquetta, was arranged. A date of 1 May 1464 is often cited, but Elizabeth was still negotiating with Lord Hastings, their final agreement being dated 13 April, indicating that May is too early. She would hardly have needed to be haggling with Hastings if Edward were planning to marry her in a fortnight. In August, Hastings was granted the wardship of Thomas, which is another indication that she had not yet married the king – as queen, she would have liked to have had her son's wardship in her own hand. A later date than May therefore seems more likely.[2]

While Edward was secretly frolicking with Elizabeth that summer, his council, and particularly the Earl of Warwick, was negotiating a match with a foreign princess. Warwick favoured an alliance with France, presumably in the hopes of persuading Louis XI to drop his support of Marguerite and her son. His preferred candidate was Bona of Savoy,

Louis' sister-in-law. Laynesmith suggests that, despite these negotiations, Edward's choice of an English-born wife may have been deliberate. He had painted the marriage of Henry VI to the French Marguerite as part of the problem, writing to the alderman Thomas Cook in 1462 of the French as the enemy, who would 'with all the ways and means to them possible (try) to destroy utterly the people, the name, the tongue and all the blood English of this our said realm'.[3] A parallel for an English marriage could be drawn with that of Edward the Black Prince, son and heir of Edward III, and his cousin Joan of Kent. Joan was not only twice widowed with two children, but had been mired in scandal. Dame Elizabeth Grey would have seemed tame in comparison.[4] Neither the Woodvilles nor the Greys were of a status lower than others of Edward's friends, such as Lord Hastings or Sir William Herbert – and no lower than the Nevilles had been before Warwick's grandfather, Ralph Neville, had clawed his way up in the service of the house of Lancaster and married Henry IV's half-sister Joan Beaufort. Elizabeth's mother, Jacquetta, came from the highest ranks of Burgundian nobility.

Whether his motives were entirely personal or had an element of the political, Edward could not keep his marriage secret forever. He broke the news to his council in September 1464, at Reading. It has generally been the view of historians that Edward's councillors, particularly Warwick, strongly objected to the match, yet it is difficult to disentangle immediate reactions from the views ascribed to them by chroniclers writing a few years later, or modern historians' interpretations. The Chronicle of Jean de Waurin recorded that when Edward informed his council that he was thinking of marrying the daughter of Lord Rivers, he received the answer that

> ... she was not his match, however good and however fair she might be, and he must know well that she was no wife for a prince such as himself; for she was not the daughter of a duke or an earl, but her mother the Duchess of Bedford had married a simple knight, so that though she was the child of a duchess and the niece of the count of St Pol, still she was no wife for him.[5]

Waurin, however, was a strong partisan of the Earl of Warwick, so might be depended upon to express the view of his patron, rather than that of the whole council – he was also writing around five years after the event. The second continuator of the Crowland Chronicle reported that Warwick's anger was merely a rumour. Historians are divided as to whether the marriage caused a rupture with Warwick, or whether it was Warwick's general loss of influence that strained his loyalty to his royal cousin. It is, of course, possible that the marriage itself might have been overlooked by Warwick if Edward had continued to be guided by him, but that Edward cutting the apron strings so publicly, humiliating Warwick in full view of the French, was so painful for Warwick's pride that he would have hated anyone associated with it. He might have been able to cope better with a marriage to the daughter of an ally, but his rage was exacerbated by his long-standing hatred of Lord Rivers, which he now extended to Elizabeth and all Rivers' family. Twenty years later, Dominic Mancini was to write that the king's mother, Cicely, Duchess of York, was so horrified by her son's choice that she denounced him as the bastard of a French archer, rather than York's son.[6] The notion that Cicely committed adultery, admitted to it publicly and yet provoked no mention of it at the time makes the whole thing laughable. Any hint of such a confession would have been trumpeted up and down the land – not least by Queen Marguerite.

Many modern historians write with a tone of disdain for Elizabeth. According to Ross, 'her rather cold beauty was not offset by any warmth or generosity of temperament. She was to prove a woman of designing character, grasping and ambitious for her family's interests, quick to take offence and reluctant to forgive.'[7] If this is a fair representation of Elizabeth's character, then apply the words to any of Edward's male associates, and it suddenly becomes apparent that Elizabeth was no different from Warwick, Pembroke, Hastings, Sir John Howard, George, Duke of Clarence or Richard, Duke of Gloucester. To refer to her beauty as 'cold', hardly a provable allegation, smacks rather of misogyny than historic impartiality. There is an undercurrent of disbelief in Elizabeth's virtue, too, in modern works. We should remember that as a widow, a Christian and the daughter of a duchess, for her to sleep with a man unmarried would have been a sin, and a disgrace.

At the time of the announcement, Warwick put a polite face on the matter, and he and the king's brother, Clarence, led Elizabeth by the hand into Reading Abbey, where she made her first appearance as queen on Michaelmas Day, 1464.[8] She was crowned on Ascension Day 1465, when, as was customary, a whole batch of knights was created. Among them was Thomas Grey, son of Edmund Grey of Ruthyn, rewarded for his early defection to York with the earldom of Kent. Neither of Elizabeth's sons are mentioned as playing any part in the coronation, suggesting that even Thomas was too young to be involved. Elizabeth did, however, have the support of her maternal family – Duchess Jacquetta's brother Jacques of Luxembourg, Count of Richebourg, came to represent the court of Burgundy.

The Great Chronicle of London relates that Elizabeth's family was 'hugely exalted and set in great honour',[9] and the queen has been criticised for promoting them, but, reviewing the facts, the claim is hard to substantiate. Lord Rivers was promoted to an earldom, although without any corresponding large land grant, and was appointed Lord Treasurer in 1466. There is no reason to believe that Rivers did not merit his office. He had many years of experience, and Edward was far too astute to appoint men of little ability. Additionally, there was a deliberately policy in the 1450s and 1460s to appoint rich men to the post to help Crown cash flow. Rivers lent the Crown some £12,259 in the years 1465–69, suggesting that Edward, even if he did not gain in prestige, did not entirely lose from the marriage.[10] From 1467, Rivers was also Constable of England. Elizabeth's brother Anthony Woodville, known as Lord Scales following his marriage to Elizabeth, Baroness Scales in 1462, was widely admired – a notable jouster, courtier and patron of learning, he yet wore a hair shirt under his rich clothes, which insalubrious garment was later venerated by the Carmelite friars of Doncaster.[11] Before 1470, Scales received only four grants. Of these, one was a reversion of an office of his father's, one was a wardship, the third was a minor office, and only the fourth, the governorship of Carisbrooke Castle, was important. John Woodville was appointed as the queen's Master of the Horse, her sister Anne and her sister-in-law Lady Scales were ladies-in-waiting, and her steward was her cousin James Haute.

None of these promotions is particularly outstanding. The younger Woodvilles received nothing until after Warwick's death, when Lionel became Bishop of Salisbury, but the others, Edward and John, received only knighthoods. Elizabeth herself was dowered less generously than her predecessors – receiving only two-thirds the dower of the Lancastrian queens. We can compare these grants to the queen's family with the rewards handed out to the king's Neville relations after Towton: Lord Fauconberg received fifty-six manors and the earldom of Kent,[12] George Neville was promoted to the archbishopric of York, and Warwick himself not only kept everything he had gained under Henry VI, but in 1461 was granted everything his father had once held, or which he himself had held jointly with his brothers Thomas and John, the latter of whom was granted the confiscated Percy earldom of Northumberland along with vast swathes of the Percy lands.

Where Elizabeth's new rank did help her family was in the matter of marriages, and there were complaints that her numerous siblings cornered the marriage market. The Nevilles, led by Warwick and Northumberland, were particularly vociferous in their complaints about the Woodvilles' marriages, despite the Nevilles themselves having risen from minor satellites of the Percy family to being one of the chief families in the land precisely by following a careful matrimonial policy. In total, there were some seven Woodville marriages in the few years following Elizabeth's own. The first match, which might well have raised eyebrows, was that of Elizabeth's brother John, to Katherine Neville, Dowager Duchess of Norfolk, the king's aunt. Duchess Katherine had been married at fifteen and widowed some seven years later in 1432. She had held her generous dower lands since then, to the annoyance of her grandson John Mowbray, Duke of Norfolk, a close ally of Warwick's. Norfolk feared he would be unable to prise the dower lands from Woodville in the event of Katherine's death, as widowers could, in some cases, hold their wives' lands 'by the courtesy'. Perhaps as a sop to Norfolk, when he was granted livery of his lands by Edward, some two months after the marriage, his patent specifically granted him the right to enter Katherine's dower lands after her death. The marriage of Elizabeth's sisters – Margaret to Warwick's nephew Lord Maltravers; Joan to Anthony Grey, son of Edmund Grey, Earl of Kent; and Anne to Sir William Bourchier, son of the Earl of Essex and brother of the John Bourchier who had married Elizabeth's mother-in-law, Lady Ferrers – passed without comment.

Other than the marriage of John Woodville, described as 'diabolical', none of these marriages was in any way remarkable. Criticism is mainly focused on the marriages of the queen's sisters to male heirs who might have been suitable for Warwick's two daughters – Katherine Woodville to the Duke of Buckingham, and Mary to William Herbert. In the latter case, it was not so much the marriage itself that peeved Warwick as the accompanying promotion of Herbert to be Lord of Dunster and Earl of Pembroke – Dunster was the source of a long-running dispute between various heirs, and Warwick was one of the claimants. The marriage of Buckingham to Katherine Woodville was later described as 'forced', but for the king to arrange a marriage for his underage ward was normal practice. We will return to Buckingham's relationship with his wife later.

The match that really stuck in Warwick's craw was the proposal for Thomas Grey to marry Anne Holland, heiress of the Duke of Exeter and niece to the king. Exeter, as we have seen, hated his father-in-law, Richard of York, and his marriage to Anne of York was unhappy. Even if he had not been her family's enemy, it is unlikely Anne would have been a happy wife – all the evidence suggests that Exeter was a violent and angry man. Exeter was, however, loyal to his cousin King Henry. He had commanded the victorious Lancastrian forces at Wakefield and at the Second Battle of St Albans, as well as the defeated army at Towton, following which he went into exile with Marguerite. His wife did not follow him, but stayed in England to enjoy the pleasures of being the king's sister. Exeter was attainted by Edward IV, and his forfeited lands were granted to his wife, with remainder to their daughter. Anne Holland was thus a great heiress, and Warwick quickly organised her betrothal to his nephew George Neville.

Regardless of Warwick's views, Elizabeth and Anne of York agreed to break off the betrothal so that Thomas could marry Anne. It is quite impossible to believe that Elizabeth would have taken this step without the king's permission, so it may be reasonable to see Warwick's anger and hatred of Elizabeth partly as a displaced criticism of Edward IV. Elizabeth paid 4,000 marks to Anne of York, who in turn enfeoffed eleven manors on the queen's feoffees. The marriage took place in October 1466, at Greenwich, but since the bride was only about five, and the groom perhaps thirteen, the union was not consummated. The marriage contract stipulated that should Thomas and Anne die childless, her lands would pass to Thomas's heir, his younger brother, Richard Grey. This was contrary to the common law rule of a childless woman's lands reverting to her natural heirs on her death – her widower could hold her lands for his lifetime if they had had a child.

After years on the run, in the summer of 1465, Henry VI, along with three faithful servants, was captured in a village that could have been named for the hapless Lancastrian king – Bungerly Hippingstones. Warwick was deputed to meet his armed escort at Islington and Henry, subjected to the humiliation of having his feet bound into his stirrups, was carried off to the Tower. Once there, he was not treated unduly harshly: Edward gave orders for him to be treated with respect, and paid 5 marks per week for his upkeep, sending clothes and wine from time to time. Nevertheless, it was a humiliating situation for a man who had been a crowned king of two countries since infancy.

*

Duke Philip the Good of Burgundy was a great-grandson of John of Gaunt, and during the years 1462–65 he had shown his support for his deposed kinsman Henry VI by implementing restrictions on the export of bullion to England, which severely damaged the English economy. Edward had launched reciprocal measures and a full-scale trade war was in operation, a state of affairs that had to be resolved for the benefit of both countries. Guillaume de Clugny, a Burgundian nobleman, was sent to England around the turn of the year 1466 to open talks. Edward responded eagerly, and gave Warwick and lords Wenlock and Hastings commissions to negotiate. Initially, two marriages were to be discussed. The first was between Burgundy's son Charles of Charolais, recently widowed and later known as 'the Bold', and Edward's sister Margaret of York; the second was between Clarence and Charles's only daughter, Mary of Burgundy. Before long, the latter marriage idea was dropped, which Clarence took very hard. Simultaneously, Edward instructed Warwick to pursue negotiations with France, where King Louis scratched around among his nobility for four possible recipients of Margaret's hand. With both France and Burgundy courting him, Edward was in a strong position.

At the end of 1466, an embassy was sent to Burgundy, headed by Lord Scales. The selection of Scales may have been made to trade on Jacquetta's position as a member of the Burgundian nobility. One of her uncles, Jacques of Luxembourg, Count of Richebourg, was a confidant of Charles of Charolais. This rapprochement between England and Burgundy was enhanced by the holding of a grand tournament at Smithfield in London, in June 1467, at which Duke Philip's illegitimate son, the Grand Bastard of Burgundy, jousted with the exceptionally talented Lord Scales. This tournament was so successful that it became a pattern for many of the later tournaments that will be noted in these pages. During the festivities, news came that Duke Philip had died, making Charles an even more desirable brother-in-law for Edward.

In the meantime, Warwick's parallel embassy to France was also going well. Louis was offering very attractive terms, although he could not do much for Margaret beyond an offer of Philippe of Bresse, a claimant to the duchy of Savoy,[13] with the marriage and dowry to be at his expense. He was also prepared to offer his own younger daughter, Jeanne, as a bride for Edward's brother Richard, Duke of Gloucester. If the latter marriage took place, Louis would help Gloucester wrest the provinces of Holland, Zeeland and Brabant from Burgundy. Louis would also drop his rather lukewarm support of Queen Marguerite and her son. Warwick was delighted with these generous terms, and Louis, convinced that Warwick ruled England in all but name, was confident they would be accepted by Edward. But Edward was not so in thrall to Warwick and the Nevilles as Louis supposed.

In 1467, Edward's warmth towards Warwick and his brothers had cooled significantly. For the first time, having escaped the Act of Resumption of 1465, Warwick was stripped of some of his farms and custodies – those in which he had been given a life interest – and George Neville, Archbishop of York, lost the chancellorship. When Warwick arrived home, he was angry and humiliated to find that in his absence Edward been busy building the Burgundian alliance with the support of the Woodvilles and that, having negotiated very good terms with France, the return French delegation was treated with the bare minimum of courtesy. It was soon obvious to all that Edward intended to ally with Burgundy. Another delegation, led by Rivers, Scales and the Bishop of Salisbury, went to Burgundy to thrash out the details. Charles, now he was duke, was somewhat less accommodating than he had been. He demanded a substantial dowry with Margaret and was much slower to reverse trade embargoes than Edward. Why Edward did not abandon the notion and turn to Louis is unclear – perhaps he was so imbued with the idea of France as being the property of the English Crown that he could not, at this stage, stomach an alliance. Edward, of course, was not the only Englishman to be anti-French, and his policy was supported at home. The marriage treaty with Burgundy was ratified in spring 1468.

While the Anglo-Burgundian negotiations were taking place, Warwick took himself off to his estates in the country for a prolonged sulk, refusing to attend the king while Rivers, Scales and Pembroke were part of the royal entourage. He may have vented his spleen by instigating an attack on Rivers' property at Maidstone. Edward made some efforts at reconciliation, granting Warwick the wardship of Francis, Viscount Lovell, retaining him on the council, having the earl at his side in January 1468 and giving him a prominent role in the procession through London as Margaret of York embarked for her new home. Nevertheless, Warwick's star was definitely eclipsed. It was Lord Scales and his wife and younger brothers, John and Edward, who accompanied Margaret to her husband. The earl was beside himself with disappointed ambition – having been obliged, perhaps against his initial inclinations, to make Edward of York king, he could not stand the notion that he was not going to be able to dominate policy. He sought to regain his dominance by fomenting unrest, particularly in the north, where one Robin of Redesdale, probably one of Warwick's retainers, broke out into rebellion.

The king was shocked to learn that on 12 July 1469, Warwick, together with Edward's own brother Clarence, had issued a manifesto against bad government. They raised the tried-and-tested complaint of 'evil counsellors' corrupting the king, saying Edward took 'more honourable account of new upstart gentlemen than of the ancient houses of nobility'. Particularly objectionable were riff-raff such as the Woodvilles, Pembroke, Sir Humphrey Stafford of Southwick, John Audley and John Fogge.[14] In order to save the king from such noxious company, Warwick and Clarence declared their support for the rebels and marched north. While Warwick was angry at the influence of Rivers and Pembroke, it is not clear that anyone other than the Neville brothers and Clarence found it problematic. Edward, confident of his military strength, set out north to quash the rebellion.

At the distance of five centuries, it is difficult to understand the enduring popularity of Warwick. His charisma was such that whenever he entered the field he could be sure of raising substantial numbers of troops. Consequently, learning that there were more rebels in the field than he had anticipated, the king fell back to Nottingham Castle to await reinforcements under the earls of Devon and Pembroke. The northern rebels advanced, bypassing the king but coming up against Pembroke at Edgecote Moor. Battle was joined and Pembroke was captured; the next day, he and his brother, Richard, who had been loyal Yorkists since the 1440s, were executed – quite unlawfully, as they were not in arms against the king (either king!). Other victims of Warwick's jealous greed for power and lands were Earl Rivers and John Woodville, who were hastily executed at Kenilworth after a kangaroo court passed judgement on them. Lord Scales was captured, but not executed. Warwick could now count on the hatred of Queen Elizabeth, as well as that of Queen Marguerite – a matter which was probably of supreme indifference to him. Warwick moved on to Nottingham, and, still protesting loyalty to Edward, much as York had done to Henry VI, 'persuaded' him to take up residence at the earl's own great stronghold of Warwick Castle.

To have a king in your hand is one thing; to use his power when he is not willing is another. It appears that whether or not the other nobles cared much for the queen and her relatives, they cared even less for the idea of rule by Warwick and Clarence. The government of the country ground to a halt, and Warwick was eventually obliged to release Edward when a rebellion broke out (headed by yet another of the widespread Neville clan) but this time in favour of Henry VI. Unable to raise troops without Edward's authority, Warwick was obliged to let the king go. Edward returned swiftly to London, to be reunited with his wife and family, now consisting of three daughters, although as yet no sons. Edward could be ruthless, but he was also a master of pragmatism, and swiftly forgave Warwick and Clarence their treachery, even though it had been compounded by Clarence's marriage to Warwick's daughter Isabel against Edward's express orders.

As we know, no good deed goes unpunished, and despite this leniency, Warwick and Clarence were not to be mollified. They concluded between them that Clarence would be a far better king than Edward, and Isabel a better queen than Elizabeth. Together with Warwick's countess, Anne (who was, in fact, the actual holder of the earldom of Warwick), Duchess Isabel, and Warwick's younger daughter, another Anne, they slipped away to Calais. Isabel, heavily pregnant, lost the baby she was carrying, and upon arrival in France Clarence was no doubt astonished to discover that Warwick was less interested in promoting him to replace Edward than in reconciling himself with the Lancastrians. Louis XI was delighted with the notion, and put pressure on Marguerite to accept Warwick's overtures. Allegedly, she kept him kneeling for a full half hour before deigning to listen to his silver tongue explain how, having contributed to the overthrow of her husband, he had now seen the error of his ways. Warwick was prepared to show his loyalty by suggesting his daughter Anne as a wife for Prince Edward of Lancaster. From Warwick's perspective, this would be an ideal option: he would have one daughter married to Clarence, Edward IV's current male heir, and one to Edward of Lancaster, Henry VI's male heir. That he had proclaimed that Elizabeth Woodville, despite being the niece of the Count of St Pol, was not a good enough match for the king, did not prevent him thinking his own daughters were good enough to be queens. Marguerite agreed, although she may have required consummation of the marriage to be postponed – the sources are unclear. Such caution would make sense – if Warwick won the crown back for Lancaster, he would have his reward in a queen for a daughter; if he failed, he and Anne would be discarded.

Back in England, with Warwick now declared a rebel, Jacquetta brought a private prosecution against him for the murder of her husband and son. Among those named in the sheriff's warrant to be brought to answer the complaint was Sir Edward Grey 'late of Groby'. This can be none other than Queen Elizabeth's brother-in-law. We might ask why Sir Edward would get involved in Warwick's plotting, but the likely answer is his resentment that Thomas Grey would inherit the Ferrers title – even though he himself was his mother's oldest surviving son – and anger over the court case of the early 1460s. No further details of Jacquetta's case have been found – it may have lapsed because of subsequent events.[15]

With French support, Warwick invaded from the south and gathered a huge force. Edward, unable to match him, left London, along with his brother Gloucester, his friend Lord Hastings, his brother-in-law Anthony, now Earl Rivers, and a modest force. They made for Lynn, on the north Norfolk coast, arriving on the evening of Sunday 30 September. They took ship on the following Tuesday, crossing the Channel to the court of Margaret of York in Burgundy,

Edward paying their passage with his cloak, which was lined with marten fur. Queen Elizabeth, heavily pregnant, went into sanctuary at Westminster, accompanied by her three little girls and her younger Grey son, Richard. There is no record of Thomas's whereabouts – he was anywhere between fourteen and seventeen years old, so it is just possible he went with Edward, but it seems more likely he stayed with his mother.

Despite his marriage to Margaret of York, Charles the Bold of Burgundy was in no great rush to involve himself in English affairs. He had always had Lancastrian sympathies, and it was only when Margaret of York was due to arrive that he required the Lancastrian Duke of Somerset, who had been in exile at his court since 1461, to leave. Fearing he had backed the wrong horse by marrying Margaret, it was some time before Charles would even agree to see Edward.

Warwick reached London, which, despite its Yorkist sympathies, did not resist his entrance. Poor Henry was brought out of the Tower, given a quick wash, and led through the city (not in the finery that he should have had) and reinstalled as king. During this second reign of Henry VI (commonly termed the readeption), Warwick was master of all, seconded by that loyal Lancastrian Jasper, Earl of Pembroke, Marguerite's brother-in-law. Jasper quickly sent for his nephew Henry Tudor, son of his dead brother Edmund, Earl of Richmond, and Lady Margaret Beaufort, daughter of the 1st Duke of Somerset, now the wife of Sir Henry Stafford. The Stafford family, headed by the dukes of Buckingham, had been Lancastrian, but Sir Henry and Margaret had accepted Edward IV as king. Richmond had been placed by Edward IV in the wardship of William Herbert, the Yorkist Earl of Pembroke, and after the battle of Edgecote the twelve-year-old had gone into hiding with the family of Pembroke's wife, Anne Devereux. Lady Margaret and her son now saw each other for the first time in several years. According to one legend, she took the boy to meet his uncle Henry VI, who in a moment of prophesy declared that one day the boy would rule all – a charming thought, but unlikely to be more than a *post hoc* justification by later Tudor historians.

Marguerite, nervous about Warwick's loyalty, and fearing to risk her seventeen-year-old son on the battlefield, waited too long, but eventually she and her troops landed on the south coast of England. Meanwhile, Edward of York, with some rather unenthusiastic support from Charles the Bold, sailed from Zeeland on 10 March, landing on the Yorkshire coast after three hideous days tossed on the Channel. He was refused entry by the port of Hull, and that could have been the end of the story. Edward's saviour was Henry Percy, 4th Earl of Northumberland. Northumberland's father and grandfather had died for Lancaster, and he had been sent as a ward to the Yorkist Earl of Pembroke at Raglan Castle. There, he had been brought up alongside the young Richmond, until, having reached the age of sixteen in 1465, he was sent to a reasonably comfortable imprisonment in the Fleet to mull over Edward's offer of restoring his earldom if he swore allegiance to him. After some consideration, Percy agreed, and the grant of the earldom of Northumberland to John Neville was rescinded. Although Neville was compensated by the marquisate of Montagu, which was, theoretically, of higher status, this loss of the prize that the Nevilles had been fighting for against the Percys for fifty years was deeply wounding to John and his brother Warwick. For Edward, however, it proved the best bargain he ever made – Northumberland persuaded the city of York to open its gates for Edward when the latter, copying Henry of Bolingbroke's trick of 1399, claimed that he wished only to reclaim his inheritance of the dukedom of York. Northumberland declined to join Edward himself, representing that his tenants were wholly Lancastrian in allegiance.

As Edward travelled south, crossing the Trent on 25 March, he was welcomed more enthusiastically. Even in Leicestershire, heart of the old Lancastrian fiefs, he was cheered, this being attributed by Eric Acheson to Lord Hastings' domination of the county.[16] There was a skirmish in Leicester which the Yorkists won. Edward himself laid siege to Warwick, holed up at Coventry, and challenged him to try the issue in personal combat. Warwick refused, so Edward, not wanting to waste days on a siege, abandoned it, and headed for London. Clarence had by now had a change of heart – if the man can be said to have had a heart. He submitted to Edward, who was either incredibly forgiving or incredibly far-sighted. By breaking the link between Warwick and Clarence, he was creating a great rent in the Lancastrian–Neville alliance.

Whilst Edward had been away, his queen, still in sanctuary at Westminster, had given birth to a son, yet another Edward. King Henry, gentle and kindly, paid for the provisions for Elizabeth and her family – half a beef and a couple of mutton each week. Henry's newly restored council also paid for Lady Scrope to attend Elizabeth's childbed.[17] Henry's consideration for his rival's wife reflected his conciliatory character – admirable, perhaps, but unsuited to his position, and rendering him quite unfit to lead an army, which remained the most important attribute a king could demonstrate. Henry was no match for Edward of York, the 'sun-in-splendour' who dominated every field he took. Edward whirled into London, undefended while Warwick skulked in Coventry, took control of Henry and the Tower, checked on his wife and children, and within two days had left again to confront Warwick at Barnet, where the Lancastrians were heavily defeated, and Warwick and Montagu were killed. Barnet saw heavy losses, with Edward rescinding his usual policy of killing the lords but sparing the commons. Another casualty was Lady Margaret Beaufort's husband, Sir Henry Stafford, who had chosen to honour his oath to Edward rather than reverting to the Lancastrian cause, despite his wife and stepson's closeness to Henry VI.

Hearing of the rout, which had occurred on the very day of her arrival at Weymouth, Marguerite and her army turned west; if they could cross

the Severn into Wales, and meet up with Jasper, they would be likely
to have a winning army, for although York won more battles than
Lancaster, that was achieved by superior generalship rather than greater
support.[18] Edward of York was the greatest of those generals. He forced
his troops on a punishing march. The city of Gloucester, the first crossing
point of the Severn, was held by Sir Richard Beauchamp. Edward sent
an urgent message, ordering Beauchamp to deny Marguerite entry.
Presumably weighing the odds of a Lancastrian or a Yorkist victory, or
mindful of his personal oath to Edward, Beauchamp followed orders.
Marguerite and her army were obliged to keep north for Tewkesbury,
but before the Lancastrians could cross the river, they were forced
into battle. Edward of York, flanked by his brothers, Gloucester and
Clarence, had the victory.

What happened to the seventeen-year-old Prince Edward of Lancaster
is uncertain – there are two accounts. According to de Commynes, he was
killed in battle. The roughly contemporaneous but pro-Yorkist *Historie of
the Arrivall of Edward IV...* phrases the matter slightly ambiguously, but
implies a battlefield death: ' ... where was slain Edward, called Prince of
Wales, John, brother to the Duke of Somerset, called Marquis of Dorset,
the Earl of Devonshire, the Lord Wenlock, with many notable knights and
squires'. The *Arrivall* continues: 'And then were taken Edmund, called
Duke of Somerset, and the prior of St John's which upon the sixth day of
May were (be)headed at the same town of Tewkesbury and divers others
with them.' Warkworth's Chronicle also has the prince slain on the field,
after crying for help to his brother-in-law Clarence, who had been his ally
when they were last together.

A generation later, Fabyan's Chronicle recounted a different story –
that Prince Edward was brought before Edward of York and questioned.
When the prince answered 'contrary to the king's pleasure', the king struck
him in the face with his gauntlet, and then the youth was 'incontinently
slain' by the king's lieutenants. This account was enhanced by Edward
Hall, who had Prince Edward replying that he sought to recover his
father's kingdom and heritage, at which point Edward of York either
pushed or struck him with a gauntlet and 'they that stood about, which
were George, Duke of Clarence, Richard, Duke of Gloucester, Thomas,
Marquis Dorset and William, Lord Hastings suddenly murdered [him]'.
Where Hall's tale appears wrong is in the naming of Thomas, Marquis
of Dorset as among Edward's men. In 1471, the only man with a claim
to the title of Marquis of Dorset was John Beaufort, brother of the Duke
of Somerset. The title was given to Thomas Grey four years later, so it
is possible that Hall, looking back, gave Thomas the title he would later
have, but it seems more likely to have been a confusion with the marquis,
whom the *Arrivall* reports as killed on the field. It is unlikely that Thomas
was at Tewkesbury. He might have been old enough, if the birth date of
1453 is accepted, but if my calculation of a birth date of 1455 is correct,
then he probably was not. Although it is not evidence, I would also

in 1471 and commanded the Lancastrian left flank at Barnet, where he was badly wounded. He survived, but his marriage did not, and he and Anne of York were granted an annulment in 1472, an unusual but not unknown proceeding. Their daughter was considered legitimate, as the marriage had taken place 'in good faith', so the marriage agreed in 1466 was still advantageous for Thomas.

On 14 August 1472, Thomas was ennobled as Earl of Huntingdon, one of the subsidiary titles of the dukedom of Exeter. Of course, at that time, he was probably expecting that the whole dukedom might come his way, in right of his wife – a hope dashed when Anne died in 1474. Although there is no direct evidence that the marriage between Thomas and Anne had been solemnised, given that she was around eighteen years old at the time of her death, so beyond the usual age of infant mortality, it is possible she died in childbed. Since her mother, Anne of York, was still alive – and, as noted above, the actual grantee of Exeter's forfeited land – Thomas lost all his prospects with his wife's death. Any inheritance was rendered even less likely when Anne of York remarried in 1474, to Sir Thomas St Leger, a faithful adherent of Edward IV. In 1476, Anne of York died in childbed, bearing a daughter, Anne St Leger, who was later declared the heiress of the entire Exeter estate, except for a chunk carved out for Richard Grey. Whilst Edward IV was, technically, within his rights to grant the Exeter lands wherever he liked, the duke having been attainted, it would certainly have been considered more conciliatory to ex-Lancastrians to let Exeter's heirs have some share of the booty.

Thomas, deprived of the Exeter inheritance, needed another source of land and income, and a second rich bride was the answer. Fortunately, his mother's agreement with Lord Hastings from 1464 put just such an heiress in his path – Cecily Bonville, Baroness Harington and Baroness Bonville, one of the wealthiest girls in England. Cecily was a niece of the late Earl of Warwick, daughter of his sister Lady Katherine Neville. Cecily's paternal grandfather and her father, who had inherited the barony of Harington from his maternal grandfather, had supported Richard, Duke of York, largely to gain ascendancy over the Courtenay family, their rivals for influence in the south-west where both baronies had most of their lands. They had been present at the Battle of Wakefield in December 1460, when York was killed and swathes of Yorkists executed. Bonville father and son were no exception, leaving the baby Cecily as heiress to both the Bonville and Harington baronies. Edward IV rapidly arranged Katherine's remarriage to Lord Hastings, and granted Katherine Cecily's wardship and marriage, as well as confirming her jointure from the Bonville and Harington estates of 600 marks per annum.[1]

Hastings had numerous court positions, including Lord Chamberlain of the Household, and he and Cecily's mother lived in high style. His estates were in Leicestershire, at Kirby Muxloe castle and Ashby-de-la-Zouche, where he hugely extended his fortified manor house. Cecily probably spent most of her childhood in these places, with perhaps occasional visits to her own properties in Devon, Dorset and Somerset. These visits would have included spending time with her great-grandfather's widow, Elizabeth Courtenay, Lady Bonville, until Lady Bonville's death in 1471.[2] Cecily was later to pay for a splendid tomb for Lady Bonville at Porlock. Hastings was not just a military man; there is evidence of an interest in scholarship, and patronage. The superb Hastings Hours, an illuminated manuscript of staggering beauty, has been tentatively suggested as the 'primer' that Katherine referred to in her will as the gift of Elizabeth Woodville.[3] The marriage of Hastings and Katherine had taken place before Hastings and the widowed Elizabeth Woodville came to their arrangement in 1464, and since that agreement implied that Thomas would marry a girl of similar age, it is possible that both parties had Cecily in mind, although, given Cecily's wealth compared with the value of the Ferrers and Astley baronies, it is more likely that Hastings hoped to sell Cecily's wardship for a high sum, and keep Thomas for a daughter of his own. If that had been the original intention, Elizabeth's marriage to the king enabled her to ignore it and bag Anne Holland for her son.

Cecily was betrothed to her cousin George Neville, son of the Marquis of Montagu, whose previous betrothal to Anne Holland had been cancelled. With Anne's death, the old agreement was resurrected. Their joint descent from Reginald Grey, 3rd Lord Grey of Ruthyn, required Thomas and Cecily to have a dispensation for their marriage; this was duly obtained in the summer of 1474, and they were married shortly thereafter. Once again the marriage settlement, as approved by Parliament in 1474, flew in the face of accepted modes of inheritance. It stipulated that on Thomas's death, if the couple were childless, Cecily's lands would pass to his brother, Richard, rather than to Cecily's heirs. It was also enacted that the queen would receive all the income from Cecily's estates until she reached the age of sixteen. Elizabeth agreed to pay Hastings 2,500 marks for the marriage, which was satisfied by Edward cancelling the equivalent amount that Hastings owed for the marriage of George, Earl of Shrewsbury, purchased for his own daughter, Anne. We can reasonably infer that Thomas and Cecily were well matched, being educated, sophisticated and wealthy members of the highest ranks of English society. The age gap between them was no more than eight years, and there is no reason to think they would have entered matrimony with anything other than the intention to love and honour each other, as the Church commanded.

The spring of 1475 was a busy time for the couple. They were granted livery of her lands on 12 April, and eleven days later received licence to enter. Since her wardship was not ended until she was sixteen, that gives her a birth date of 1459. The inheritance was bolstered on 18 April with a knighthood when Thomas, Richard and their uncle Edward Woodville were dubbed as knights of the Bath during the investiture of Prince Edward as Prince of Wales.[4] Immediately after, Thomas surrendered the earldom of Huntingdon to receive the marquisate of Dorset, 'upon which day he sat in his habit at the upper end of the table amongst the knights in St Edward's Chamber'.[5] The title of marquis of Dorset was an important one, first created for the oldest Beaufort son, John, in 1397. The resurrection of this title was perhaps intended to indicate that, like the Beauforts, the Greys were members of the extended royal family. The grant of a marquisate allowed Thomas to take precedence over all earls, and rank only below dukes, of whom there were seven – the king's brothers, Clarence and Gloucester; his brothers-in-law Suffolk and Exeter (still clinging on to the king's toleration, if not favour); and, at a further remove, Buckingham and Norfolk. To support Thomas's new title, there was a grant from the king worth £35 – hardly riches, but a pleasant addition to Cecily's inheritance. From now on, Thomas is referred to as Dorset. Two weeks later, Dorset was admitted to the Order of the Garter, but Richard Grey received nothing beyond his knighthood.

*

During this period, Dorset and Richard were spending at least a part of their time at Ludlow, Shropshire, alongside the Prince of Wales. In 1473, the prince had been appointed as head of a new council created by Edward to reinvigorate government in Wales and the notoriously lawless Marches, the breeding ground of many of the quarrels that coalesced into the Wars of the Roses. The president of the council was the prince's tutor, John Alcock. Alcock had risen rapidly in Edward's service, appointed first to the position of Master of the Rolls and then to the bishopric of Rochester. The prince's chamberlain was Sir Thomas Vaughan, who was well into his sixties and had served Henry VI but converted to the Yorkist cause early on. The prince's governor, who had overall responsibility for him, was his uncle Earl Rivers. The queen herself was closely involved, and named as the head of Prince Edward's councillors with authority to appoint other councillors and to hear trials in Hereford alongside the prince in the king's absence. The council was to act with her advice and express consent. She, Rivers and Alcock had the only keys to the coffers containing the council's funds and, initially, she went with the prince to Ludlow. Edward had complete trust in his wife, brother-in-law and stepsons. A letter was issued in the prince's name on 8 June 1475, to the bailiffs of Shrewsbury:

> Whereas there have been perpetrated great and heinous complaints of robberies, murders, manslaughters, ravishing of women, burning of houses by the inhabitants of the Marches and now of late by arrant thieves and rebels of Oswestry hundred and Chirkland, for redress of same I am commanded to assemble the people to punish the misdoers, and I entrust Thomas, marquis of Dorset and Richard Grey, knight, to do the same.[6]

With Wales and the Marches now more firmly under royal control, Edward, secure on his throne, with a growing family, and his brothers apparently onside, decided that he would make England great again, and eclipse the house of Lancaster, by conquering France. He began negotiations for offensive alliances with Charles of Burgundy and Francis of Brittany. The negotiations between Charles and Edward were spearheaded by Louis of Luxembourg, Count of St Pol and Constable of France, who was Dorset's great-uncle. The king and duke entered a treaty in July 1474.

Edward's stated purpose was 'the recovery of his duchies of Normandy and Aquitaine and his realm of France'. Louis of Luxembourg, having once been a close friend of Louis XI, had quarrelled violently with him, and now promised that he would deliver up the town of St Quentin to the Anglo-Burgundian alliance. The matter was complicated by Charles of Burgundy's activities on his eastern borders, where he was besieging Neuss, intending after its capture to combine with England, and turn their joint armies on France. Simultaneously, Edward was busy with the complex task of raising an army – calling Parliament, being granted a subsidy, and collecting it – which took the best part of a year. Edward's other preparation was the drawing up of his will. His trust in his queen was so great that she was named as first among his executors. He did not, though, give written instructions as to how the government of the kingdom was to be conducted should he die while Prince Edward was still a minor. He may, of course, have given verbal instructions – or perhaps assumed that a regency council would be formed, as had been done for Henry VI.

Once the English were ready, Edward sent Rivers to urge Charles to abandon Neuss and join him in the attack on France, but Charles stubbornly declined to give up the siege. In the meantime, Louis XI was working with the Swiss, the Duke of Austria and the Duke of Lorraine to attack Charles on other fronts. The French assaulted a couple of minor Burgundian towns, then ransacked Arras, where they captured Jacques of Luxembourg, Dorset's great-uncle, and a cousin, Antoine of Luxembourg, Count of Roussy. Flushed with success, Louis approached the emperor, Frederick III, hoping for an agreement by which they would confiscate all of the territories held of them by the duke.

Edward sent a formal declaration of war to Louis via his herald, which Commynes thought was 'written in such fine language and style that [he] believe[d] no Englishman could have had a hand in it'.[7] Louis perused it thoughtfully, then responded that an alternative to war might be available, as he knew that Edward had been encouraged into war by the Constable of France and Charles of Burgundy, but that the former would certainly betray him, and the latter was in no state to fight. Surely it was better that he and Edward should come to terms? The lucky herald received 300 French crowns, and 30 ells of crimson velvet, with the promise of another fat purse should an agreement be reached. Edward might have been interested in peace at this point, but he certainly would not remove the threat, so he and his army set forth from Dover. Urgent messages were sent to Charles to abandon Neuss and join with England immediately. Reluctantly, Charles capitulated. The siege was raised on 27 June 1475, just as Edward's impressive army was arriving in Calais. The English force was huge: it consisted of some 13,000 men – archers, infantry and cavalry – and nearly all the English nobility. Dorset, listed after the dukes but before the five earls, received 10s per day in pay, compared with the 13s 4d allotted to the dukes and the 6s 8d the earls received. It took three weeks for the entire force to cross from Dover, with Edward and his immediate entourage arriving on 4 July.[8]

The siege of Neuss had cost Charles dear – his army had been reduced by attrition, internal wrangling and the general tendency of mediaeval armies to dissipate over time. His forces were in no fit state to join with the English, and, contrary to the treaty, he did not appear with a mighty force but rolled up on 20 July with the ragtag army that remained. Similarly disappointing was Louis of Luxembourg's failure to deliver St Quentin, despite repeated assurances. This left Edward with two options: agree a truce, or attack with a smaller army than anticipated. He weighed the odds, and, finding that they were not in his favour, indicated that he would accept Louis XI's overtures. A three-man team was appointed to discuss terms, comprising John, Lord Howard, Thomas St Leger and Dr John Morton, in a commission witnessed by Dorset on 13 August 1475.[9] The result was the Treaty of Picquigny, confirmed in a meeting between Edward and Louis. The terms included a marriage between the king's eldest daughter, Elizabeth of York, and Louis' only living son, the Dauphin Charles. In addition, Louis was happy to cover much of the cost of the fruitless expedition. 75,000 crowns were delivered immediately, and an annual pension of 50,000 crowns promised – this pension was to be a bone of contention for the next eighty years. Another provision of the treaty was the return of Marguerite of Anjou to France. Edward's nobles were mixed in their reception of the treaty – many considered it a good deal, and were happy to accept pensions; others, including Gloucester, felt it was dishonourable, and that it would be better to earn their money by slaughtering the French and ransoming captives, as Henry V and his army had done. Dorset may have received a pension – de Commynes records that he did, but there are no extant English records confirming it.

In 1476, Dorset was elected as the 212th knight of the Garter, filling the stall vacated by the death of John de Mowbray, 4th Duke of Norfolk. The Garter might have been a sign of royal favour and a symbol of chivalry, but it was also deeply rooted in faith – the knights were members of a religious order. That St George's Day, which fell on a Sunday, the king and the knights, including Dorset, processed to Matins, then breakfasted with the dean, Bishop Beauchamp, before attending High Mass. The queen, the Duchess of Suffolk, Cecily Dorset and Dame Anne Hastings were all present. The following day, the king and the knights went in procession to the Chapter House, then into the choir, where each stood in front of his stall. Edward made an offering of a superb new set of vestments, after which Dorset and Suffolk offered up the sword of the late Duke of Norfolk, and the lords Howard and Maltravers presented his helmet.

It was around this time that Dorset began his jousting career. The joust in which he is first mentioned lists the challengers as Thomas Dorset, Richard Grey, Edward Woodville, James Tyrrell, Walter Ferrers and John Cheyne. *Excerpta Historica* dates this joust to 28 May 1474, to mark the elevation of the king's second son, Richard of Shrewsbury, born August 1473, to the dukedom of York, but since Thomas did not yet have the title of Dorset, 1474 must be too early. More likely, this tournament was to celebrate the investiture of Prince Edward as Prince of Wales, or Prince Richard as Earl of Nottingham in 1476.

The other great court ceremony that year was the re-interment of Richard, Duke of York and Edmund, Earl of Rutland at Fotheringhay in July 1476. This was a declaration of the strength and unity of the house of York, and was described in great detail, by Chester Herald:

... the bodies were exhumed, that of the duke garbed in ermine-furred mantle and Cap of Maintenance, covered with cloth of gold, lay in state on a hearse blazing with candles, guarded by an angel of silver, bearing a crown of gold as a reminder that by right, the duke had been king. On the journey, Richard, Duke of Gloucester, with other lords and officers at arms, all dressed in mourning, following the funeral chariot, drawn by six horses, with trappings of black, charged with the arms of France and England and preceded by a knight bearing the banner of the ducal arms ... Fotheringhay church was reached on 29th July where members of the College and other ecclesiastics, went forth to meet the cortège. At the entrance to the churchyard, King Edward IV waited, together with the Duke of Clarence, the Marquis of Dorset, Earl Rivers, Lord Hastings and other noblemen. Upon the arrival, the king made obeisance to the body right humbly and put his hand on the body and kissed it, crying all the time. The procession moved into the church where two hearses were waiting, one in the choir for the body of the duke and the other in the Lady Chapel for that of the earl and after the king had retired to his closet, the princes and officers of arms had stationed themselves around the hearse, masses were sung, and the king's Chamberlain offered him seven pieces of cloth of gold which were laid in a cross on the body. The next day three masses were sung, the Bishop of Lincoln preached a very noble sermon and offerings were made by the Duke of Gloucester and the other lords. There were presented the Duke of York's coat of arms, his shield, his sword, his helmet and his courser on which rode Lord Ferrers in full armour, holding in his hand an axe reversed.

The continuity of the house of York was further emphasised by Edward in another grand ceremony, the swearing of allegiance to Prince Edward on 9 November 1477, in which Dorset participated – as did all the nobles, including Gloucester. By then, Dorset had become a father for the first time. Thomas was born in June 1477, and Dorset and Cecily went on to produce at least thirteen more children.

Richard Grey's career was also burgeoning. On 4 July 1475, he was appointed to the Commission of the Peace in Herefordshire, which perhaps indicates an earlier birth date than discussed above – it seems unlikely he would have been appointed to that type of position before he was of age, although appointment at eighteen might be possible, giving a latest date of 1457 for his birth. He was reappointed regularly over the following years to commissions of peace and oyer and terminer hearings in numerous southern counties. On 10 February 1479, he was given the office of Constable of Chester Castle, and on 24 April 1482, he was granted Kidwelly in tail mail. Six months later, he was appointed constable and steward of Wallingford. In the parliament of early 1483, he was granted further lands in tail male worth 500 marks per annum, for which Queen Elizabeth paid her husband 2,000 marks.[10] All of this suggests that Richard Grey had enough education, intelligence and ability to carry out the regular functions of the baronial class from which he came.

Although Dorset was not yet a member of the king's inner circle of councillors, he was certainly an important contributor to ceremonial. In 1478, when his half-brother Richard of Shrewsbury, Duke of York, was married at the ripe old age of five to the even younger Anne Mowbray, Countess (not duchess) of Norfolk, he played a part in the accompanying tournament.[11] He appeared 'on horseback in great triumph for the jousts royal. The Duke of Buckingham bore his helm, accompanied with great estate and degrees, knights and esquires clothed in his colours, that is to say, white and murrey embroidered.'[12]

Once again, Edward IV bent the rules of inheritance, persuading Parliament to agree that Anne Mowbray's lands would not only be held by her husband during her life, but would remain his permanently, even if they had no children, rather than passing to her heirs general. This was exactly the arrangement he had made for Dorset on his marriage to Anne Holland, but in that case there had been some excuse, as the Duke of Exeter was considered a rebel. This particular subversion of the rules of inheritance, however, was deeply troubling for the nobles. Given the rates of child mortality, the possibility that Anne of Norfolk would not live to have children was quite high. The heirs general who were thus potentially disinherited were the descendants of the 1st Duke of Norfolk – John, Lord Howard, and the children of Lady Isabel de Mowbray, who included Dorset's grandmother, Lady Ferrers of Groby, and Lady Ferrers' half-siblings, a litter of Berkeleys.

It seems unlikely that Dorset would have been particularly concerned about the potential loss of the small part of the Mowbray lands that may have been due to his grandmother – his wife was wealthy, he had a grand title, and he might hope for more favour in future. He was perhaps more concerned about cutting a fine figure at the jousting that formed part of the celebrations. He and Rivers had been in charge of the arrangements – the challenges were drawn up weeks before, and proclaimed at Westminster Hall, at Cheapside, at Leadenhall, at Gracechurch, and at London Bridge.[13] The whole enterprise was couched in the language of the Arthurian romances so beloved of the English court. Dorset, Richard, Edward Woodville, Sir James Tyrrell, Lord Ferrers and John Cheyney challenged all comers, two for each of the three competitions: first, the joust-royal, with 'helm and shield'; second, running in full armour 'along a tilt', armed as they wished; finally, sword work in tourneying armour. Each competition was represented by a shield, painted in blue and tawny, with a letter 'A' and a diamond in the first quarter for the first competition, an 'E' and a ruby for the second competition, and an 'M' and an emerald for the third.

Dorset was first to enter the lists, banners of white and murrey fluttering, and his helmet carried by Buckingham. Behind him came five coursers, with trappings 'enramplished' with embroidered 'A's for Anne and a sixth horse to carry the armour. Then came Richard Grey, dressed in blue and tawny, with his three coursers trapped in crimson cloth of gold and tissue. Lord Rivers made his own display, entering 'disguised' in white as a hermit with a black velvet hermitage. All the men acquitted themselves well, although the prizes, distributed by Dorset's half-sister Princess Elizabeth, went elsewhere.

*

Among this display of family solidarity, one figure was missing: George, Duke of Clarence. Clarence, having taken part in the bloody Battle of Tewkesbury alongside his brother, and dispatched the Lancastrian leaders he had previously allied with, had done as much as he could to prevent the marriage of his sister-in-law, Anne Neville, to his brother Gloucester, hoping to prevent any sharing of the Warwick and Salisbury lands. An accommodation had been reached, but there was a canker at the heart of the royal family.[14] So far as can be ascertained, neither Dorset nor his mother had a dog in this particular fight, and they are more likely to have favoured Gloucester, given Clarence's involvement in the unlawful executions of Elizabeth's father and brother.

This was not the only source of disagreement in the royal family. Two years earlier, following the death of his duchess, Isabel, Clarence had sought a new bride. In 1478, he set his sights on Mary, the new Duchess of Burgundy, Charles the Bold having been killed at the Battle of Nancy in 1477. The match was very much favoured by Mary's stepmother, Margaret of York. King Edward, however, was not in agreement with his siblings: if Clarence were duke of Burgundy in right of his wife, who knew what trouble he might cause for the brother of whom he was so bitterly jealous? Duchess Mary, too, was unenthusiastic, favouring the candidacy of Maximilian of Hapsburg, King of the Romans, who would, in due course, be elected to his father's position of Holy Roman Emperor. Edward thought he had a better solution for Mary than either Clarence or Maximilian, in the shape of his loyal and talented brother-in-law

Earl Rivers, widowed in 1473. Rivers was not of the rank that might be considered suitable for a sovereign duchess, but he did come with the promise of military support against Louis XI, who was eager to snatch back those elements of Mary's territories that were held in appanage from the French Crown, on the reasoning that they were not heritable by a woman. Mary was still not impressed – she preferred to be an empress, and continued with her plans to marry Maximilian. Meanwhile, Edward had seriously annoyed Clarence, without having the marriage of Rivers to show for it.

Edward's suspicions about his brother's trustworthiness were not just based on a past history of treachery. The duke was openly flouting the law. He had unceremoniously had three people tried and hanged for the alleged poisoning of Duchess Isabel and her infant son. Not only that, but a member of his household, Thomas Burdett, and two others were found guilty in a Church court of attempting to predict the death of the king and his son. Clarence claimed that the charges were false, that Burdett and his colleague's executions were unwarranted, and, shockingly, that it was Edward himself who had resorted to the black arts. Thoroughly fed up with his troublesome brother, Edward had him taken to the Tower, where he languished for some months, before being brought to trial in early 1478, in the high court of Parliament.

The scene that unfolded was unparalleled in English history. Edward read the indictment himself, and it spared no detail of Clarence's treachery, including an alleged conspiracy against 'him [the king], the queen, their son and heir, and a great part of the nobility of the realm'. Even worse, Clarence was alleged to have accused Edward of being illegitimate, and supposedly sought to send his own heir abroad while bringing a false child to Warwick Castle in the little boy's place. Individuals accused of treason did not have the right to representation by legal counsel – instead, they were obliged to defend themselves. They could question any witnesses; according to the Crowland Chronicle there were some, but, as the chronicler sorrowfully relates, it was not clear whether they were witnesses or further accusers. Clarence offered to settle the matter by personal combat with his brother – it is difficult to believe that he thought the suggestion would be seriously entertained by Edward.

Parliament, hardly able to disbelieve the king's own word, and well aware of Clarence's history, found the duke guilty and passed the death sentence. Edward did not immediately put it into effect – presumably some scruples as to the execution of his brother stayed his hand, although it's unlikely Clarence would have had similar doubts. Two weeks after the verdict, Parliament petitioned the king for the sentence to be carried out, and Clarence was executed privately in the Tower of London. The means of death is uncertain, but the general belief was that the duke was drowned in a butt of malmsey wine.

Dominic Mancini, whose account of the happenings of 1483 was discovered in the early twentieth century, but who was not present in London at the time of Clarence's execution, wrote that Queen Elizabeth had urged her husband to dispatch Clarence because she feared that he would claim she and Edward were not legally married, and would, in the event of Edward's death, keep her children from the throne. Clarence had shown no hesitation in joining the Lancastrians against his own brother, so he was unlikely to care much about his brother's children. We will come back to the matter of the marriage later, but, regardless of that, it is feasible that Elizabeth feared Clarence would try to usurp the throne if Edward died while their sons were still underage, and we can suppose that she certainly was not sorry about Clarence being finally brought to book for his treachery. We can conclude, too, that there were no crocodile tears from the Grey brothers. It was fairly unusual during this period for people to know their grandparents well, but the presence of the older Lord Rivers and Jacquetta at Edward's court during the late 1460s when the Grey brothers were growing up, meant that they did know theirs. Since all sources suggest that Elizabeth was very family-minded (indeed, it is the great criticism of her by historians), it is probably fair to assume that the Grey brothers were close to their family.

Mancini added that Gloucester was so upset at the death of Clarence that he withdrew to his northern estates and blamed his sister-in-law. Gloucester's duties required him to be in the north, but he did make forays south. If he did blame Elizabeth, it was irrational to do so – Edward was perfectly capable of making up his own mind, and Clarence had been asking for it for years. In fact, Gloucester was petitioning for Clarence's estates before his death, hardly the actions of a man eager to prevent the execution. Certainly, if Edward felt any grief or remorse over his brother's death, he did not show it.[15] If Gloucester resented the queen's family, he would have had to contain himself when Dorset was appointed alongside him to the commission of oyer and terminer in York in September 1478. Other appointees were Lord Stanley and the Earl of Northumberland. By spring, Dorset was back in the south, taking part in the sombre ceremonies surrounding the funeral at Windsor of Edward and Elizabeth's youngest son, George.

Practically, Dorset did well out of Clarence's death. In 1478 he received a number of the stewardships and other offices Clarence had held, and on 16 September 1480 he was granted the wardship and marriage of the duke's son, the five-year-old Earl of Warwick, for which he paid £2,000. This would allow him to take the profits of the earl's lands until the latter reached his majority, and Edward generously allowed him to pay only after he had received the sum in income from the estate. It is likely that he anticipated marrying Warwick to his own eldest daughter. Dorset's purchase also entitled him, in the event of the earl's early demise, to the wardship and marriage of Warwick's sister, Lady Margaret of Clarence.

It is not impossible that Gloucester had anticipated receiving Warwick's wardship and thus having the whole Warwick inheritance available to him for at least ten years. If he did, losing it to Dorset would have been a considerable annoyance. As it was, Gloucester appropriated two manors in Rutland that the 1474 settlement had allocated to Clarence, which, despite repeated demands from the Exchequer, he refused to relinquish. Disputes about landholdings were bread-and-butter to fifteenth-century nobles, so we need not assume that any argument between Dorset and Gloucester over the Warwick lands would necessarily lead to bad blood between them, although it would be unlikely to enhance their relationship. Gloucester may have seen the grant to Dorset as an affront, and turned his dissatisfaction with the king upon the queen and her son. Warwick, aged five, probably joined the Dorset family's growing nursery.

Dorset was now so well thought of by his stepfather that he was worth courting for his 'good lordship'. In January 1480, he was thanked by the Merchant Adventurers, alongside Hastings, Rivers and, most of all, the queen for they 'ha[d] been right friendly and laboured for us in our matter of subsidy. And we] have prayed them of their good lordships.'

In 1480, Edward turned his mind to the marriage of his eldest daughter, now fourteen, and promised by the Treaty of Picquigny to the dauphin. Edward urged Louis to arrange the marriage, to extend the lifetime truce between them and to pay the arrears of his pension, all matters on which the French king was proving cagey. Louis supplied his ambassadors with various arguments for placating Edward while delivering nothing. He also wished to decline Edward's offer of arbitration between himself and Maximilian over Duchess Mary's territories. Louis thought that Edward's involvement in Burgundian affairs related more to English trade interests, and the position of Dowager Duchess Margaret, than any actual concern about the limits of Mary's territory. He therefore was willing to assure the English king that if he conquered any of the territories where Margaret's dower lands lay, she could continue to enjoy them, and English merchants, who had not been involved in any fight against him, could go about their business unmolested. But Edward was tired of Louis' hollow promises, and kept his ambassadors waiting for some time.

Edward was also revolving in his mind the news he had received from Scotland – Louis was encouraging James III to break off the Anglo-Scottish truce, which included a pledge for Prince James of Scotland to marry Edward's daughter, Cicely. They had been solemnly betrothed on 25 October 1474 and Edward had kept up the regular payments of his daughter's dowry, at 2,000 marks per annum. Edward now demanded that the prince be sent to England as surety that the marriage would take place and that the town of Berwick be handed over. Berwick, strategically placed at the mouth of the River Tweed, had been a bone of contention for centuries, and had last changed hands when Marguerite of Anjou had given it up in return for Scottish aid against the Yorkists. If James would not accept Edward's demands and make reparations for the alleged damages in the borders, then Edward would declare war.

James returned a very cool answer, so Edward prepared for war, commissioning Gloucester as Lieutenant of the North and authorising the gathering of forces. Lord Hastings was sent to Calais to ward off any surprise Franco-Scottish attacks there. Edward still hoped to defuse matters by keeping Louis onside, and again offered to mediate between him and Maximilian, but Louis refused on the grounds that if Edward did the right thing and confirmed Louis' rights, the English people would be angry with their king, and Louis generously abhorred this idea. On the other hand, if Edward wanted to please his people and support Maximilian, he would have to run counter to his conscience – which, thought the considerate French king, would be equally difficult for Edward.[16] Margaret of York had no such qualms about persuading her brother to be partisan – in particular, she hoped to hurry on an agreement for Mary and Maximilian's only son, Philip of Burgundy, to marry Edward's daughter Anne of York – and proposed a visit to agree terms. Edward was delighted. Edward Woodville was deputed to fetch the duchess on the ship *The Falcon*, the men sporting new purple and blue velvet jackets. Coldharbour, formerly the London home of Clarence, but now in the king's hands, was fitted up for Margaret's use. Both Dorset and Rivers received robes from the king of three yards of white tissue cloth of gold, enough for a 'short gown', and a further grant of spectacular purple cloth-of-gold on satin.

The visit was one of great pomp, with Dorset again one of the chief participants in the ceremonies. While children were not generally involved in adult activities, we might note that this was the only occasion on which Margaret met her nephews and nieces. Richard, Duke of York was seven. But it was not all junketing – Margaret had a complex set of negotiating points to make, relating to pensions, truces, marriages and their financial ramifications, and potential alliances against France. Maximilian's chief desire was for Edward to provide him with 2,000 men for his campaign against Louis. Louis, hearing of the discussions, immediately sent over arrears of Edward's pension and made noises about beginning wedding preparations for Princess Elizabeth and the dauphin. He would also enter a hundred-year truce – provided Burgundy and Brittany were excluded.

Edward did not answer these blandishments immediately, but continued to discuss options with Margaret – on one point, though, he was adamant. He would not ally with Maximilian against Louis, unless Maximilian swore to replace the pension that would be lost. Since Maximilian never made a promise he wouldn't break, he agreed. There were promises and counter-promises, but the only immediate result was preparation for the dispatch of 1,500 archers and thirty men-at-arms to swell Maximilian's army. Before they could embark, however, the stunning news arrived at the English court that Maximilian and Louis had agreed a truce. Poor Margaret was obliged to excuse her stepson-in-law's dubious activities in such a way as to preserve everything she had gained. She was even more mortified upon the discovery of letters from Maximilian to Scotland, in which he indicated he would continue to allow trade even if Edward declared war on the Scots – the very thing Margaret had agreed would not happen. Despite this, Edward pretended to accept Maximilian's excuse that his negotiators had agreed terms with Louis without his knowledge, and sent Margaret home, laden with presents.

Louis was not only angry with Edward for offering archers to Maximilian, but was also aware that the English king was negotiating a marriage for the Prince of Wales with Anne, daughter – and likely heir – of Francis of Brittany. Louis was 'wonderfully displeased', and blamed Margaret, saying she hated him for refusing to help Clarence to the throne of England. There was a good deal of huffing and puffing on all sides, but no open warfare between England and France at this juncture – Edward had his hands full with the Scottish campaign and was far too sensible to contemplate war on two fronts.

Soon after Margaret's departure, Edward and Elizabeth had their last child – Bridget, born November 1480. Dorset played a prominent part in the christening. We can infer from his frequent public appearances that he was a man of personal grace and distinction – perhaps he took after his beautiful mother. Edward's court was magnificent and designed to show English wealth and power – no matter how fond he might have been of his wife and stepson, Dorset would not have played a public role had he not been able to carry it off elegantly. On this particular occasion, he helped the lady carrying the young princess to the font – none other than Lady Margaret Beaufort, Dowager Countess of Richmond, widow of Sir Henry Stafford, now the wife of Thomas, Lord Stanley. Lady Stanley was in favour at the Yorkist court and was courted by the king as the most important landowner in north-west England. Lady Stanley's previous incarnation as the sister-in-law of Henry VI was no doubt glossed over. The entire court had once been loyal servants of the Lancastrian kings, so she was not unusual.

*

An initial raid on Scotland led by Gloucester was successful, so Edward contemplated leading a larger army north. He collected a fleet under the command of Lord Howard, and approval from his council – but the old problem of cash flow hampered him. Unwilling to ask Parliament for a grant, he sought 'loans' from his subjects, who proved remarkably keen on the old saying 'neither a borrower nor a lender be'. Simultaneously, Maximilian pressed him to invade France – or at least send more men and money to Burgundy to shore up Maximilian's own campaign. War was intensifying in the Channel, with the capture of a couple of French ships. The fleet, under Lord Howard, also dealt some vicious blows to Scottish shipping, and the towns in the Firth of Forth. Meanwhile, James III's brother Alexander, Duke of Albany, who was quite as troublesome to his king as

Clarence had been to Edward, was proving an irresistible temptation to Edward. Albany had fled to France in 1479, and Louis had given him a wealthy wife, and had used his own attempts to reconcile the brothers as a cover for his encouragement to James to break the truce with England. Edward now suggested to Albany that the English would help him usurp his brother's throne, provided that, once king, he would cede Berwick and various other towns, and do homage to Edward as his overlord.

Albany accepted the offer with alacrity and sailed for England, where Edward's Master of Horse, Sir John Cheyne, met him at Southampton and escorted him in some state to Coldharbour. Mustering orders were issued to Dorset, Stanley, Rivers, Edward Woodville (who raised his troops in the name of the Prince of Wales) and the others whom Edward had engaged for service in Scotland. Dorset brought 600 men from Warwickshire, paid 6*d* per day, while Rivers had 1,000 men and Stanley 3,000 – these relative strengths show how important the Stanleys were. Before the king and these reinforcements could travel to Scotland, the royal family was enveloped in grief when fourteen-year-old Princess Mary died on 23 May 1482. She was buried in St George's Chapel, Windsor, with her brother, the Prince of Wales, as chief mourner.[17] Edward at least had something to distract him from his grief – the very day of the burial, he and his men were heading north. The army made a stop at Fotheringhay, in Northamptonshire, and it was there, on 11 June, that Edward entered into a formal treaty with Albany, who signed himself Alexander R. in an advanced case of counting his chickens.

Despite this, Edward, surprisingly, never moved further north than Nottingham, returning to London while Dorset and the others joined Gloucester. The king was still in communication with Louis, who continued his flattery: assuring Edward that a recent visit to Normandy had no sinister connotations, sending reassuring messages to Lord Hastings in Calais, and even paying another instalment of the pension. By October, Edward had agreed to renew the lifetime truce with France, probably in return for Louis agreeing to cease meddling in Scotland. Gloucester continued his campaign with some success. The town of Berwick (although not the castle) was taken and Gloucester marched, more or less unopposed, into Scotland, laying waste as he went. The English army entered Edinburgh before the end of July 1482, and Garter king-of-arms proclaimed that the Scots must pay reparations, restore Albany to his rights, and repay the dowry already sent for the marriage of the Lady Cicely. But, like Clarence before him, Albany would turn his coat at the prospect of a better offer. As soon as it became apparent that the Scots lords, disgruntled though they were with their king, didn't fancy Albany as a replacement, the duke was persuaded into reconciliation with James. Considering the hapless plight of the Scots, Gloucester agreed generous terms and withdrew – probably mindful that his brother could not afford to keep an army in the field indefinitely, which is what would have been required to hold the northern kingdom in subjugation. On his way home, he forced Berwick castle into submission, and the town returned to English control. Gloucester knighted Edward Woodville during the campaign, but there is no information as to his personal relationships with Woodville or Dorset. Stanley, he considered a friend.

Across the Channel, Maximilian was being hard pressed by Louis – the French king was closing in on Burgundian territory. Duchess Mary had died in March 1482 in a fall from her horse, and Maximilian, claiming the regency during the minority of their son, Philip, was not uniformly popular in Burgundy. With Edward refusing to send substantial support, Maximilian felt he had no option but to come to terms with Louis in the Treaty of Arras, signed on 23 December 1482. Under its terms, the dauphin, instead of marrying Elizabeth of York, was to marry Marguerite of Austria, the three-year-old daughter of Mary and Maximilian. The little girl was to be sent to France for her upbringing, and, although everyone was too polite to say so, as a hostage. This unceremonious jilting of his daughter so enraged Edward IV that he was rendered speechless. But there was nothing he could do. Burgundy and France were at peace, and he had snubbed the Scots by rejecting the marriage alliance. All his efforts in foreign policy had been no match for the wily Louis XI.

*

Against the backdrop of war and diplomacy in these years, Dorset and Cecily had familial and financial responsibilities of their own. In spring 1482, Cecily was resident at Taunton. Taunton was a royal castle, and her presence there probably related to Dorset's appointment in 1477 as Lord Warden of the Stannaries. The Stannaries were a form of local government concerned with the management of the tin mining industry, central to Cornwall's economy. He also received the office of Steward of the Crown Lands in Devon and Cornwall in 1482, with a fee of £40 per annum. Among Cecily's guests was her cousin Lady Anne Neville, daughter of John, Marquis of Montagu. Lady Anne was the wife of Sir William Stonor, a member of Edward IV's household who held lands from Cecily and Dorset in Clyst, Devon. In surviving correspondence relating to Stonor's various landholdings, there are at least two instances of his bailiff urging him to seek resolution of a local issue by 'get[ting] ... a letter from my Lord Marquis'. The two men were on good terms: '... ye be the greatest man with my Lord and in his conceit [affection] because of your horse given and your attendance unto him at London,' wrote one of Stonor's servants.[18]

Lady Anne stayed with Cecily for some time – she wrote to her husband that had she known she would be so long parted from him she would have been more loath to leave, and come to this 'far country'. However, she was 'much beholden to my lady ... (who) makes right much of me'.[19] She anticipated that Stonor would join them for the Easter assizes, and sent a list of the gowns she would like him to bring. Cecily and Lady Anne moved on to Cecily's manor at Dartington, and Stonor was informed of his wife's whereabouts by John Payne, one of his own servants, who was on an errand to Dorset. Cecily's household would have been bustling and full – she had a growing family, and she and Dorset were already taking part in the usual hard-headed business decisions of marriages and lands. Her lands were extensive and her ownership of them not without argument; there had even been a disagreement with Lord Rivers, with whom Dorset was normally on the best of terms, about land at Knighteston, in the parish of Ottery St Mary, once owned by the Bittelsgate family. The last male Bittelsgate, Thomas, had given the land in remainder, should he have no grandchildren, to Cecily's grandfather William, Lord Bonville. Thomas Bittelsgate's sister, Joan, was the paternal grandmother of Lord Rivers, who claimed the land as heir general of the estate. There are no details as to how the matter was settled, but by 1494, Cecily and Dorset were in possession.

It is impossible to be certain of either the order of births of their children, or even the year, other than the oldest. The analysis of all the records available suggests an order of: Thomas, Richard, John, Eleanor, Anthony, George, Cecily, Dorothy, Leonard, Mary, Elizabeth, Margaret and Edward. There may have been another daughter, Bridget, who died young, and it is possible the second son was another Edward who also died in infancy. There were also Dorset's wards, Edward, Earl of Warwick, and Joan Durnford, who later married Sir Piers Edgcombe, another great West Country landowner.

Life in a great mediaeval household followed a regular pattern. There are no records of Dorset and Cecily's arrangements, but, inferring from the information about other households in the late fifteenth century, the pattern of the day may have been similar to the following. Just after dawn, the gates of the castle or manor would open and the servants would begin work. The master and mistress would rise and dress at about 7 a.m. and hear an early service of Matins, after which they ate a light breakfast of bread and small beer. The business of the day followed, working with an army of clerks checking finances, dealing with correspondence, ordering supplies and giving instructions to the household. The main meal of the day was eaten any time after 11 a.m. and, depending on whether it was a fast day (Wednesday, Friday, Saturday and specific holy days), would consist of several courses of meat or fish. After dinner, the lord or lady might meet tenants and hear petitions, or take exercise. For women, there was the endless task of needlework. All of a household's linen had to be made – only the most elaborate clothes being produced by tailors. Evensong was celebrated towards the end of the afternoon, then supper was served around nightfall. Evening recreation might consist of chess, backgammon, cards and other gambling games, music and dancing, or reading aloud from the ever-popular chivalric tales, such as *The Romance of the Rose*, *Le Morte d'Arthur*, *The Book of the City of Ladies*, *The Canterbury Tales*, or, for more devout households, religious texts.

Bedtime depended on the time of year as the light changed. The gates were closed and locked before 10 p.m.

The size of the Dorset household is unknown, but, comparing them with nobles of similar status, it probably consisted of 50 to 100 people, including Cecily's lady attendants, the children's nurses, the chaplain, the officers (such as the steward and clerks), the cooks, pages and stablemen. Other than Cecily's ladies and the nurses, the staff would have been all male, divided into different departments – pantry (bread and napery), buttery (wine and ale), kitchen, stable, wardrobe or chamber (finance) and marshalsea (responsible for keeping order). The whole was ruled by the steward. Members of the household might be paid wages or just board, and often included dependent relatives. It was the practice for those who had more than one property to move between them, to allow proper cleaning and also to make it easier to find food for such large numbers. To facilitate this, most furniture was plain and demountable. Luxury was achieved with soft furnishings – tapestry if it could be afforded, 'counterfeit arras' or painted cloth if not, as well as cushions of all shapes and sizes, and elaborate bedclothes. As Cecily moved from Taunton to Dartington in the spring of 1482, her household equipment would have been loaded onto carts, bundled under trussing cloths and trundled off, while she and those children who were old enough would have ridden to their destination.

*

In early 1483, Dorset's grandmother Elizabeth Ferrers died. As she had not had any children by her second husband, her lands now descended to Dorset, who was given licence to enter.[20] This addition to his income may well have helped in the purchase Dorset now made of the marriage of Anne St Leger, heiress to the Exeter inheritance. Having been cheated of it by the death of his first wife, he was keen to secure it, intending Anne for his eldest son. Once again, it was agreed that his brother Richard Grey would have some part of the estate, and 500 marks' worth of manors were allocated to him. Dorset and St Leger worked together regularly as St Leger was Edward IV's feodary for the county of Devon.[21] Dorset's own offices were expanding – he took over the deputy constableship of the Tower of London in the spring of the following year, 1483, replacing Lord Rivers, whose primary role as mentor to Edward, Prince of Wales, was growing in scope and importance. The prince was now twelve, rapidly heading for manhood (his uncle Gloucester had fought his first battle at the age of sixteen). Revised orders were issued for the prince's council and the conduct of his household.

From February 1483, Sir Richard Grey was to take over from Queen Elizabeth as the third holder of the keys to the princely coffers. The prince himself was not permitted to write, do or say anything without taking advice from Sir Richard, Rivers and Bishop Alcock. As some compensation for these restrictions, his bedtime was extended from

8 p.m. to 9 p.m. In a letter concerning various administrative matters, Rivers asked one of his officers, Andrew Dymmock, to send him a copy of the patent he already held, for gathering troops in the Prince of Wales' name. Since Edward Woodville had already raised troops for Scotland in the name of the prince, there is nothing sinister in this request. It certainly is not evidence, as has been suggested, that Rivers planned to poison the king and seize power! Rather, it was an indication that he would need to raise troops for the king's new Scottish campaign, plans for which were brought to Parliament in January 1483.

There was no reason at this time for Dorset to doubt that the coming years would bring him an increase in both wealth and influence at his stepfather's court. But the established world of the Yorkist court was about to be turned upside down.

Part 2

1483–1509
'... uneasy lies the head that wears the crown ...'

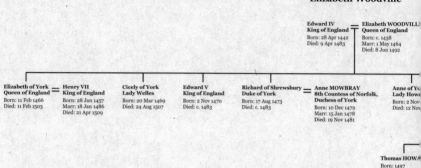

Family of Edward IV and Elizabeth Woodville

Edward IV
King of England
Born: 28 Apr 1442
Died: 9 Apr 1483
—
Elizabeth WOODVILL
Queen of England
Born: c. 1438
Marr: 1 May 1464
Died: 8 Jun 1492

Elizabeth of York
Queen of England
Born: 11 Feb 1466
Died: 11 Feb 1503
—
Henry VII
King of England
Born: 28 Jan 1457
Marr: 18 Jan 1486
Died: 21 Apr 1509

Cicely of York
Lady Welles
Born: 20 Mar 1469
Died: 24 Aug 1507

Edward V
King of England
Born: 2 Nov 1470
Died: c. 1483

Richard of Shrewsbury
Duke of York
Born: 17 Aug 1473
Died: c. 1483
—
Anne MOWBRAY
8th Countess of Norfolk,
Duchess of York
Born: 10 Dec 1472
Marr: 15 Jan 1478
Died: 19 Nov 1481

Anne of Yo
Lady How
Born: 2 Nov
Died: 12 Nov

Thomas HOWA
Born: 1497
Died: 3 Aug 1508

Family of Thomas, 1st Marquis of Dorset and Cecily Baroness Harington and Bonville (1)

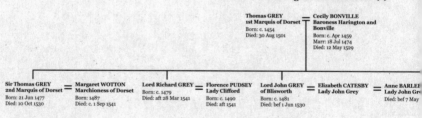

Thomas GREY
1st Marquis of Dorset
Born: c. 1454
Died: 30 Aug 1501
—
Cecily BONVILLE
Baroness Harington and
Bonville
Born: c. Apr 1459
Marr: 18 Jul 1474
Died: 12 May 1529

Sir Thomas GREY
2nd Marquis of Dorset
Born: 21 Jun 1477
Died: 10 Oct 1530
—
Margaret WOTTON
Marchioness of Dorset
Born: 1487
Died: c. 1 Sep 1541

Lord Richard GREY
Born: c. 1479
Died: aft 28 Mar 1541
—
Florence PUDSEY
Lady Clifford
Born: c. 1490
Died: aft 1541

Lord John GREY
of Blisworth
Born: c. 1481
Died: bef 1 Jun 1530
—
Elizabeth CATESBY
Lady John Grey
—
Anne BARLE
Lady John Gre
Died: bef 7 May

John ARUNDELL
of Lanherne
Born: c. 1500
Died: 7 Nov 1557
—
Katherine EDGCOMBE
—
Elizabeth DANETT

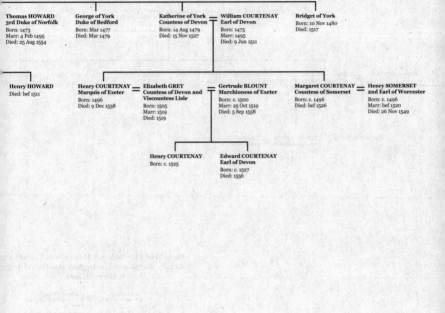

Thomas HOWARD
3rd Duke of Norfolk
Born: 1473
Marr: 4 Feb 1495
Died: 25 Aug 1554

George of York
Duke of Bedford
Born: Mar 1477
Died: Mar 1479

Katherine of York
Countess of Devon
Born: 14 Aug 1479
Died: 15 Nov 1527

William COURTENAY
Earl of Devon
Born: 1475
Marr: 1495
Died: 9 Jun 1511

Bridget of York
Born: 10 Nov 1480
Died: 1517

Henry HOWARD
Died: bef 1511

Henry COURTENAY
Marquis of Exeter
Born: 1496
Died: 9 Dec 1538

Elizabeth GREY
Countess of Devon and
Viscountess Lisle
Born: 1505
Marr: 1519
Died: 1519

Gertrude BLOUNT
Marchioness of Exeter
Born: c. 1500
Marr: 25 Oct 1519
Died: 5 Sep 1558

Margaret COURTENAY
Countess of Somerset
Born: c. 1496
Died: bef 1526

Henry SOMERSET
2nd Earl of Worcester
Born: c. 1496
Marr: bef 1520
Died: 26 Nov 1549

Henry COURTENAY
Born: c. 1525

Edward COURTENAY
Earl of Devon
Born: c. 1527
Died: 1556

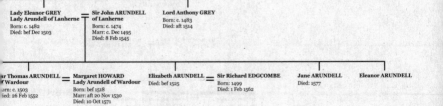

Lady Eleanor GREY
Lady Arundell of Lanherne
Born: c. 1482
Died: bef Dec 1503

Sir John ARUNDELL
of Lanherne
Born: c. 1474
Marr: c. Dec 1495
Died: 8 Feb 1545

Lord Anthony GREY
Born: 1483
Died: aft 1514

Sir Thomas ARUNDELL
of Wardour
Born: c. 1503
Died: 26 Feb 1552

Margaret HOWARD
Lady Arundell of Wardour
Born: bef 1518
Marr: aft 20 Nov 1530
Died: 10 Oct 1571

Elizabeth ARUNDELL
Died: bef 1525

Sir Richard EDGCOMBE
Born: 1499
Died: 1 Feb 1562

Jane ARUNDELL
Died: 1577

Eleanor ARUNDELL

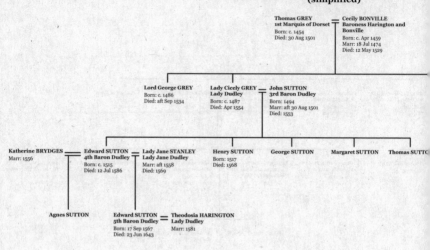

Family of Thomas, 1st Marquis of Dorset and Cecily, Baroness Harington and Bonville (2) (simplified)

Thomas GREY
1st Marquis of Dorset
Born: c. 1454
Died: 30 Aug 1501

Cecily BONVILLE
Baroness Harington and Bonville
Born: c. Apr 1459
Marr: 18 Jul 1474
Died: 12 May 1529

Lord George GREY
Born: c. 1486
Died: aft Sep 1534

Lady Cicely GREY
Lady Dudley
Born: c. 1487
Died: Apr 1554

John SUTTON
3rd Baron Dudley
Born: 1494
Marr: aft 30 Aug 1501
Died: 1553

Katherine BRYDGES
Marr: 1556

Edward SUTTON
4th Baron Dudley
Born: c. 1515
Died: 12 Jul 1586

Lady Jane STANLEY
Lady Jane Dudley
Marr: aft 1558
Died: 1569

Henry SUTTON
Born: 1517
Died: 1568

George SUTTON

Margaret SUTTON

Thomas SUTTO

Agnes SUTTON

Edward SUTTON
5th Baron Dudley
Born: 17 Sep 1567
Died: 23 Jun 1643

Theodosia HARINGTON
Lady Dudley
Marr: 1581

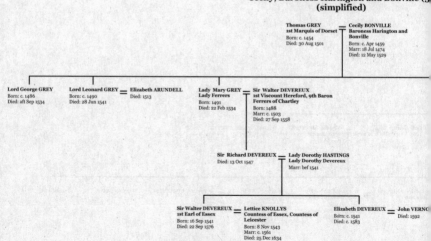

Family of Thomas, 1st Marquis of Dorset and Cecily, Baroness Harington and Bonville (3) (simplified)

Thomas GREY
1st Marquis of Dorset
Born: c. 1454
Died: 30 Aug 1501

Cecily BONVILLE
Baroness Harington and Bonville
Born: c. Apr 1459
Marr: 18 Jul 1474
Died: 12 May 1529

Lord George GREY
Born: c. 1486
Died: aft Sep 1534

Lord Leonard GREY
Born: c. 1490
Died: 28 Jun 1541

Elizabeth ARUNDELL
Died: 1513

Lady Mary GREY
Lady Ferrers
Born: 1491
Died: 22 Feb 1534

Sir Walter DEVEREUX
1st Viscount Hereford, 9th Baron Ferrers of Chartley
Born: 1488
Marr: c. 1503
Died: 27 Sep 1558

Sir Richard DEVEREUX
Died: 13 Oct 1547

Lady Dorothy HASTINGS
Lady Dorothy Devereux
Marr: bef 1541

Sir Walter DEVEREUX
1st Earl of Essex
Born: 16 Sep 1541
Died: 22 Sep 1576

Lettice KNOLLYS
Countess of Essex, Countess of Leicester
Born: 8 Nov 1543
Marr: c. 1561
Died: 25 Dec 1634

Elizabeth DEVEREUX
Born: c. 1541
Died: c. 1583

John VERNO
Died: 1592

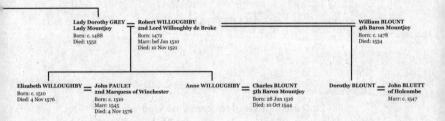

Lady Dorothy GREY
Lady Mountjoy
Born: c. 1488
Died: 1552

Robert WILLOUGHBY
2nd Lord Willoughby de Broke
Born: 1472
Marr: bef Jan 1510
Died: 10 Nov 1521

William BLOUNT
4th Baron Mountjoy
Born: c. 1478
Died: 1534

Elizabeth WILLOUGHBY
Born: c. 1510
Died: 4 Nov 1576

John PAULET
2nd Marquess of Winchester
Born: c. 1510
Marr: 1545
Died: 4 Nov 1576

Anne WILLOUGHBY

Charles BLOUNT
5th Baron Mountjoy
Born: 28 Jun 1516
Died: 10 Oct 1544

Dorothy BLOUNT

John BLUETT
of Holcombe
Marr: c. 1547

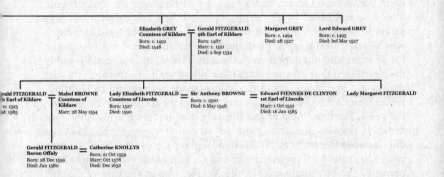

Elizabeth GREY
Countess of Kildare
Born: c. 1492
Died: 1548

Gerald FITZGERALD
9th Earl of Kildare
Born: 1487
Marr: c. 1521
Died: 2 Sep 1534

Margaret GREY
Born: c. 1494
Died: aft 1527

Lord Edward GREY
Born: c. 1495
Died: bef Mar 1527

rald FITZGERALD
h Earl of Kildare
n: 1525
d: 1585

Mabel BROWNE
Countess of Kildare
Marr: 28 May 1554

Lady Elizabeth FITZGERALD
Countess of Lincoln
Born: 1527
Died: 1590

Sir Anthony BROWNE
Born: c. 1500
Died: 6 May 1548

Edward FIENNES DE CLINTON
1st Earl of Lincoln
Marr: 1 Oct 1552
Died: 16 Jan 1585

Lady Margaret FITZGERALD

Gerald FITZGERALD
Baron Offaly
Born: 28 Dec 1559
Died: Jun 1580

Catherine KNOLLYS
Born: 21 Oct 1559
Marr: Oct 1578
Died: Dec 1632

4

Turmoil

... desire of a kingdom knows no kindred.

Sir Nicholas Throckmorton

In April 1483, King Edward IV lay dying, the queen, Dorset and Hastings at his side. He was not yet forty-one, but he had lived hard – a youth spent on the battlefield, followed by a life that was conspicuous for its fleshly indulgence. His son and heir, Edward, Prince of Wales, was twelve years old. Edward was aware of the dangers and difficulties the boy would face as an underage monarch, and in his last days did what he could to smooth the boy's path, including engineering a reconciliation between Dorset and Hastings, who apparently loathed each other.

The reasons for Dorset and Hastings' mutual antipathy are difficult to discern. Professor Michael Hicks in his *Richard III* suggests that Elizabeth and Hastings' agreement of 1464 began the enmity: '[she] had to pay with her eldest son's inheritance and marriage for access to the king that, surprisingly, made her queen'.[1] This seems to me to be a misreading of the situation. First, a marriage between Thomas, whose inheritance was good but not spectacular, and a daughter of Hastings, the king's friend, would be welcomed by Elizabeth; second, if this arrangement did give access to the king, it was a perfectly normal example of good lordship – why would Elizabeth ask Hastings for help, and then both resent him for giving it and not expect to reciprocate? Third, no one could possibly have predicted that Edward would fall in love with Elizabeth, so the fact that he did marry her would surely have made her grateful to Hastings, rather than the reverse. While enmity between the families developed over the years, Hastings' help at this juncture does not seem a plausible root cause. Hicks also maintains (without proffering a source) that Hastings did not want Dorset to marry his stepdaughter, Cecily. It is hard to know whom he could have preferred – he had no sons of his own. He may have preferred the betrothal with George Neville, who at the time of Cecily's marriage to Dorset was Duke of Bedford, but George had already lost any prospect of inheritance with the attainder of his father, Montagu, so would have been a bad bargain. George's property went to Gloucester for as long as George or his heirs lived.

Writing in 1483, Mancini ascribed the animosity between Dorset and Hastings to jealousy 'as a result of the mistresses they had abducted or attempted to entice from each other' but does not name these petticoated bones of contention. Sir Thomas More, writing some thirty years later, names Elizabeth Shore, the favourite mistress of Edward IV, as the lady for whom the men were rivals.[2] Mrs Shore had been the king's mistress for some time, and according to More 'many he had, but her he loved'. After the king's death, More continued, Hastings and Dorset became rivals for her affections and Hastings was jealous that she chose Dorset. No one other than More, however, records that Hastings had an interest in Mrs Shore. If he were jealous over Shore, that does not seem a sufficient foundation for a quarrel before Edward's death, although it may have exacerbated previous rivalry, or it may be that Hastings resented Dorset conducting an affair with Shore not because he wanted her himself, but on behalf of Cecily.

Mancini also claimed that the queen resented Hastings for encouraging Edward in his debaucheries – indeed, Mancini's description of Edward was hardly flattering:

> He was licentious in the extreme; moreover it was said that he had been most insolent to numerous women after he had seduced them, for, as soon as he grew weary of the dalliances, he gave up the ladies, much against their will, to other courtiers. He pursued with no discrimination the married and the unmarried, the noble and lowly. However, he took none by force. He overcame all by money and promises and having conquered them he dismissed them. Although he had many companions and promoters of his vices, the more important and special were ... relatives of the queen. Her two sons and one of her brothers.[3]

Mancini was not especially enamoured of Dorset either, noting that other, wiser, men had been passed over for the marquis's sake. While it is not impossible that Dorset roistered with his stepfather, it seems unlikely that his younger brother did – Richard was considerably younger than the king, and spending much of his time in the Marches.

The other chronicler of the period, Crowland, whom most scholars believe to have been a member of Edward IV's council, also recorded animosity, but says nothing about licentious behaviour on the part of Hastings, Dorset or Grey. He attributes the quarrel to a very different cause.

> ... for [Hastings] was afraid lest, if the supreme power should fall into the hands of the queen's relations, they would exact a most signal

vengeance for the injuries which had been formerly inflicted on them by that same lord; in consequence of which, there had long existed extreme ill-will between the said lord Hastings and them.[4]

This hints at a more plausible root for a rift between Rivers and Hastings, which expanded to include Dorset, centred on political rivalry, which Manicini also mentions: '... as well for that the king had made him (Hastings) deputy of Calais, which offer the queen's brother, Lord Rivers, claimed of the king's former promise, as for divers other gifts which he received that they looked for'. It is highly likely that Rivers did desire to have the lieutenancy of Calais, as his father once had, and that he resented Hastings being awarded it. Instead of accepting his failure to gain the office, Rivers apparently told the king that Calais was in danger of being betrayed to the French by Hastings. Hastings responded to this incendiary accusation by torturing one John Edwards into making (unknown) allegations against Dorset, Rivers and Robert Ratcliffe, the Gentleman Porter of Calais. The accusations must have been serious, as Edwards was brought before the king, his ministers, three bishops and six other peers on 8 August 1482, to be examined again. Edwards then retracted his allegations, but it may well have been hard for either side to forgive the serious accusations each had made. Whatever the causes, the rivalry between Dorset, Rivers and Hastings was about to explode in a way that destroyed the legacy of the king they all loved.

*

With the king dead, the council, entirely properly, continued to sit. The royal council was not a formally designated body – while certain offices, such as Lord Chancellor, Treasurer and Archbishop of Canterbury, would always give an individual a right to be part of a council advising the king, he could pick and choose other men to give advice. At the time of Edward IV's death, his councillors included Thomas Rotherham, Lord Chancellor and Archbishop of York; Thomas Bourchier, Archbishop of Canterbury; Hastings as Lord Chamberlain; Bishop Russell of Lincoln as Lord Privy Seal; Dorset; Bishop Morton of Ely; Thomas, Lord Stanley; John, Lord Howard; John Elrington as Treasurer of the Household; and Oliver King as Secretary. The queen, although she had no formal role, had influence and joined the council meetings after Edward's death.

Among these councillors, although his actual identity is disputed, was a man referred to as the Crowland Chronicler – the closest we have to an eyewitness, although the composition of the document probably dates to after 1486, so may require some caution. Within forty-eight hours of the king's death, the council sent two lords to the City of London to instruct its corporation to maintain order. Letters were sent across the country for Edward V to be proclaimed, and announcing a coronation date of 4 May. The council also dispatched letters to the prince, which arrived at Ludlow on 14 April, informing him that he was now king, and requesting that he return to London, accompanied by Earl Rivers, Sir Richard Grey and Sir Thomas Vaughan, the three chief men of his household. According to Crowland, Lord Hastings, fearing that the king's maternal relatives would have too much influence, insisted that Rivers provide only a modest escort to bring Edward V to London.

> The queen most beneficently tried to extinguish every spark of murmuring and disturbance, and wrote to her son, requesting him, on his road to London, not to exceed an escort of two thousand men. The same number was also approved by the before-named lord [Hastings]; as it would appear, he felt fully assured that the dukes of Gloucester and Buckingham, in whom he placed the greatest confidence, would not bring a smaller number with them.[5]

This satisfied the whole council, and 'everyone looked forward to the eagerly desired coronation day of the new king'.[6]

Mancini reported that Hastings kept Gloucester informed of the deliberations of the council. This has been taken to mean that it was Hastings who informed Gloucester of his brother's death, but that is not the most obvious construction – it is more likely the council sent the duke an official missive. Crowland does not say when or how Gloucester was informed of the death of the king, but only that the duke sent

> ... most soothing letters in order to console the queen, with promises that he would shortly arrive, and assurances of all duty, fealty, and due obedience to his king and lord, Edward the Fifth, the eldest son of the deceased king, his brother, and of the queen.[7]

While the king and the duke were making their ways toward London, the council deliberated on how the government should be carried on. The prince's youth need not have been a catastrophe – sixteen or so was considered manhood enough to fight, if not to exercise all the powers of a king, so a minority would not be lengthy. The prince had been brought up from childhood as the heir and was already accustomed to the activities of his own council in Wales, and the country was at peace, with no obvious Lancastrian claimant to muddy the waters. It was better than the situation on the death of Edward III, whose grandson and heir, Richard II, was only ten, or at the accession of Henry VI when he was less than two years old. In both cases, a regency council had been set up, presided over by the king's uncles, but with no single individual having the power of a regent. There was no reason why such a step could not be taken for Prince Edward, who would be able to contribute to government, at least in part, from the outset. Aware of these examples, it seems that the king made some updates to his will of 1475, although, as no 1483 will has ever been discovered, the contents of any codicils are matter of hearsay only. Mancini believed, although Crowland does not mention it, that Edward

IV named his brother, Richard, Duke of Gloucester, as Protector of the Realm – that is, quasi-sovereign. If Edward IV had appointed Gloucester as protector, it would make sense for him to have been thinking of a long-term appointment.

If Mancini was right, and Edward did want his brother to take control, then the question arises as to why the council, the queen and Dorset rejected the idea, and decided that Gloucester should be protector only until the coronation. Was the council's decision the result of adherence to precedent, or concern about being led by Gloucester, or the natural desire of the council to promote its own collective importance? Why would Dorset and the queen not want Gloucester to be protector if Edward had mandated it? Dorset had apparently worked happily with Gloucester in the Scottish campaign, and Earl Rivers had recently asked the duke to arbitrate in a dispute. Later reports refer to bad blood between Gloucester and the queen and her Grey sons, but there is no evidence of it before the death of Edward IV. Perhaps the enmity between Dorset's grandfather, the first Earl Rivers, and the late Earl of Warwick still resonated. Although Gloucester had been unfailingly loyal to his brother, he had spent much of his childhood with Warwick, whose charisma was powerful, and he may well have imbibed Warwick's hatred of Rivers – and, by extension, the whole of the queen's family. The idea that Mancini put forward for their enmity – that Gloucester blamed the queen for the death of Clarence – is undermined by the fact that he was petitioning Edward IV for parts of Clarence's estates even before the duke had been tried, as well as between trial and execution. Despite this, it would not be incompatible with human nature to look for a scapegoat for the trauma of Clarence's death at his brother's instigation.

Dorset's guardianship of Warwick might also have caused resentment. However, it is hard to believe that Dorset and Elizabeth between them (assuming she was present at council meetings, although this is not clear) could have been so persuasive that the other councillors would go against Edward IV's dying wishes – especially if, as is often contended, Elizabeth and her family were unpopular and despised as greedy and ambitious. Perhaps the idea of a protectorate was floated not by Edward IV, but by a member of the council who feared that the queen and Dorset would have too much influence once Edward V was crowned. The obvious man to fit that bill is Lord Hastings, perhaps anticipating that, as soon as Edward V had been crowned, the captaincy of Calais would be taken from him and given to Rivers. It was therefore in his interest to promote the rule of his friend Gloucester.

The decision of the council that Gloucester should only be protector until the coronation would, therefore, indicate that Edward did not name Gloucester as protector, although concern was raised, perhaps by Hastings, about making a final decision before Gloucester arrived. Dorset responded to this by saying, 'We are so important that even without the king's uncle, we can make and enforce these decisions.' This has been represented as Dorset suggesting that he, his mother and his uncles were more important than the council, but in the context of the report, he is referring to the importance of the council as a whole. The proposition that Mancini relates that Dorset favoured was that 'the government should be carried on by many persons, of whom the duke, far from being excluded, should be the chief'.[8] This would have been consistent with the roles which the dukes of Bedford and Gloucester had had during the youth of Henry VI – that is, leader of the council, but without the sovereign power of veto.

The discussion over the future was put on hold for the funeral. On 16 April, Edward IV's coffined body was taken from the royal chapel to Westminster Abbey to lie in state, followed by a vast throng of ecclesiastics and nobles. Chief among them were John de la Pole, Earl of Lincoln, the late king's nephew; Dorset; William Herbert, Earl of Huntingdon; Viscount Berkeley; Lord Stanley; and Lord Hastings. Also in the procession were Sir Edward and Sir Richard Woodville, the mayor and aldermen of London, and the judges. The service was conducted by Archbishop Rotherham. Everything was done according to strictest etiquette – the coffin, draped with black cloth of gold and topped with an effigy of the late king, robed, with crown, sceptre and orb, seated in a chair of black velvet, was borne by six horses, trapped with black velvet. It was preceded by Lord Howard, dressed in a mourning hood, bearing the king's banner and other heraldic emblems. The procession left London, resting overnight at Syon Abbey, where the Bishop of Durham presided over another service.

The next day, the cortège travelled to St George's Chapel, Windsor. The body lay in state overnight, surrounded by the gentlemen and esquires of the king's household. In the morning, the Archbishop of York conducted the requiem Mass. Garter king-of-arms gave the Mass penny in turn to the Earl of Lincoln, Dorset, and Huntingdon to offer. Similarly, Clarencieux, Norrey, March and Ireland kings-of-arms gave the shield and the sword to Lord Maltravers, Lord Berkeley, and Sir John and Sir Thomas Bourchier to offer.[9] Edward's squire of the body, Sir William Parr, entered on a horse, fully armed except for his helmet, and carrying an axe which he offered, followed by the lords with their offerings of palls. Dorset and the Earl of Lincoln, as the highest-ranking men present, gave four palls each, while Huntingdon gave three, and Maltravers and Berkeley two. Thus was King Edward IV honoured in death.

Meanwhile, the business of government continued. Commissions were set up for assessing the subsidy recently granted by Parliament. The factions were treated even-handedly. Hastings had seven commissions, while Dorset and Rivers combined had eight. Sir Edward Woodville and Dorset were given orders and money to raise forces in the southern counties to take to sea to combat the depredations of Philippe de Crèvecoeur, one of Louis XI's captains. The inevitable confusion caused by the death of a king was a handy opportunity for foreign powers to create mischief. Cash was allocated by the council to fund a force of 2,000 men to be raised by Woodville, and a further 1,000 by Dorset.

By 23 April, the Duke of Gloucester was heading south, having first proclaimed Edward V's accession in York, and sworn his loyalty. On the same day, Edward V, accompanied by Rivers, Grey and Vaughan, set out from Ludlow, reaching Stony Stratford in Northamptonshire on 29 April. Gloucester was behind the royal entourage, 11 miles further north at Northampton, where he had rendezvoused with Henry Stafford, 2nd Duke of Buckingham. In the usual mix of Lancastrian and Yorkist loyalties, Buckingham was the grandson and son of men who had died fighting for Henry VI, yet his grandmother Anne Neville was Edward IV's aunt, and he himself had sworn loyalty to Edward IV when his estates were restored after the attainder of his father. Buckingham had played little part in Edward IV's reign. He went home early from the 1475 jaunt to France, for unspecified reasons, and spent most of his time on his estates in the Welsh Marches, where he was thoroughly unpopular with his tenants. Despite his already vast land holdings, Buckingham wanted more – specifically, his share of the de Bohun inheritance, which Edward IV had improperly retained. Once again, Edward IV's cavalier treatment of the rules of inheritance gave rise to resentment.[10] Buckingham was also the brother-in-law of Queen Elizabeth and Rivers. According to Mancini, but no other source, he had strongly objected to his marriage to Katherine Woodville on account of her rank. Regardless of their personal feelings, the Buckinghams had produced four children – two boys and two girls.

Having settled their charge in a suitable inn, Rivers and Grey rode north to join the dukes, and all four spent a convivial evening in a local inn – certainly suggesting that, even if they were not the best of friends, they were on good enough terms to spend an evening together. This meeting at Stony Stratford is the best evidence that Dorset and his uncle Rivers had no idea of undermining Gloucester's position as interim protector now that it had been agreed by the council. The only way the two parties could have converged would be by prior arrangement. If Rivers had harboured the slightest desire to avoid the duke, either because he wanted to keep control of the king as part of some dastardly plot or because he had any suspicions of Gloucester, he would have taken the king to London by the more obvious route via Banbury and Oxford.

On the morning of 30 April, Rivers and Grey waited for the dukes before setting out south to join the king. It was the courteous thing to do, and since Gloucester and Buckingham had been all smiles the night before, there was no reason to think that anything might go wrong. But rather than all heading south together to meet the royal retinue, Gloucester ordered his men to take Rivers and Grey prisoner and carry them north immediately, Rivers to Sheriff Hutton and Grey to Middleham. The dukes rode on and met the king, who was waiting for Rivers and Grey before setting out. Gloucester and Buckingham both bowed to Edward, and Gloucester explained that he had been obliged to arrest Rivers and Grey, and was now also constrained to arrest Sir Thomas Vaughan, the seventy-three-year-old knight who had been set at Edward's side by his father. The king protested that he knew no evil of the men, who had been set around him by his father, and that until anything were proved against them, he wanted them restored. Gloucester smoothly informed him that that was not possible, and that he himself was now in charge. Edward was twelve years old – he was well educated, and had been prepared for kingship since babyhood, but with the three leaders of his council removed, no one dared overrule Gloucester and his troops. Edward had no choice but to bow to the inevitable, and Vaughan was soon heading for Pontefract Castle.

The news reached London later that day. The queen, unsurprisingly, was horrified – her brother and son had been arrested on unspecified charges, and her royal son was now stripped of the men whom his father had appointed, while he was in the power of an uncle whom he hardly knew. Elizabeth took the step she had taken in 1469 when the Lancastrians returned – she fled into sanctuary at Westminster Abbey, along with her daughters and younger son, Richard, Duke of York. It is unclear whether Dorset went with her. Given his age, it seems unlikely, and certainly Gloucester believed him to be at large. He had probably already left London on his council-appointed mission to raise a force to join Edward Woodville at sea. Despite it often being cited as a fact, based on Mancini's account, there is no evidence for the story that Edward IV's treasury went with Elizabeth, and that it was divided between her, Dorset and the young king. The matter has been comprehensively investigated by Rosemary Horrox, who has identified that there was no treasure to be stolen. At Edward IV's death, he left £490 in his exchequer, and £710 in his chamber – not enough to pay his funeral costs. That is not to say there was not a rumour at the time, perhaps based on Gloucester's letter to Cardinal Bourchier of 2 May, requesting that he see to the 'safekeeping of the Tower and the treasure therein', a term used to mean valuables, but not necessarily large quantities. Alternatively, it may have been provoked by the disbursement by the council of funds for Woodville's naval squadron.

Gloucester justified his arrest of Rivers, Grey and Vaughan by announcing that he believed the Woodvilles were plotting against him. This cannot be substantiated by any real evidence. If such had been Elizabeth's intention, why did she accept the council's curb on the number of troops sent to fetch Edward, and why did Rivers and Grey wait for Gloucester and Buckingham at Northampton? Why would they not have set out from Ludlow immediately on hearing of Edward's death, allowing them to reach the safety of London before the dukes could get there? And of course, why would Elizabeth plot against Gloucester anyway? Her son was king, and it seems highly unlikely she would have suspected Gloucester of any ill intent. There is no evidence from before the spring of 1483 to indicate that there was bad blood between Gloucester and the queen and her family.

If both sides were harbouring deep-seated resentments, these can only be inferred from the events of 1483; there is no evidence. Of course, absence of evidence is not evidence of absence, and far more may have been going on than we are now aware of. Clearly, something sparked Gloucester's actions – perhaps he genuinely believed that the queen's family wished him ill, predicating this conviction on a mere hunch, on what Hastings told him or on evidence that was either not produced at the time or has since been lost. Alternatively, naked ambition may have been the catalyst. Perhaps if the young king had shown himself more amenable to rule by Gloucester at Stony Stratford, events might have unfolded differently, but Gloucester's precipitate action in arresting the men whom the king loved immediately set them on a collision course. With Edward aged twelve, the council would pay some attention to his views, and with his majority not that far off, Gloucester might have feared that retribution would follow his cavalier action.

Whether Gloucester had thought through his actions is questionable – he seems to have made decisions on the hoof that then put him in a position where he could not back down. He now had to show some reasonable grounds for having arrested Rivers and the others. So, as Edward V was accompanied through London on 4 May (which should have been his coronation day), he was followed by cartloads of arms, which Gloucester claimed had been confiscated from stashes made by the queen's brothers and sons with the intention of ambushing him. According to Mancini, this claim was widely believed to be nonsense, as it was well known that the arms had been collected for further war against the Scots. Gloucester complained to the council anyway, and demanded that Rivers, Grey and Vaughan be pronounced guilty of treason and executed. The council was not convinced. It pointed out that there was no evidence of ambushes being planned, and, in any event, Gloucester was not the king, nor even sworn in as protector, so no one could commit treason against him. If the council were all in thrall to the Woodvilles, that would rather negate the idea that the family was widely hated. Indeed, Crowland mentions that the council was concerned that the queen was not being treated with sufficient respect. If she had been considered unsuitable at the time of her marriage, nearly nineteen years as Edward IV's beloved consort, during which time she had done her duty handsomely, had worn away any resentment.

Mancini was impressed by Gloucester's men. 'There is hardly any without a helmet, and none without bows and arrows ... they seem to have hands and arms of iron ... there hangs by the side of each one a sword...' This description indicates that the retinue that accompanied Gloucester from the North was not a mere retinue of servants, but a band of trained soldiers, presumably fresh from the Scottish wars. Their presence may have influenced the reactions of the council.

On 7 May, Thomas Rotherham, Archbishop of York, was relieved of his seals of office as Lord Chancellor, to be replaced by John Russell, Bishop of Lincoln. According to More, but no one else, Rotherham had disgraced himself by handing the Great Seal to Elizabeth, which, if true, was a most improper proceeding. He had taken the seal back, but this obvious sympathy with Elizabeth was not welcome to Gloucester. By the next day, at the latest, the council had sworn Gloucester in as protector – an office which Crowland reports the duke 'exercised with the consent and goodwill of all the lords'. The office was to last until the young king's coronation, now set for 22 June. Plans for the ceremony went ahead and the young king was moved from the Bishop of London's palace at St Paul's, to the Tower of London, consistent with the tradition of monarchs lodging there prior to their coronations. Nevertheless, there were murmurings about the plight of the queen, and the continued holding of Rivers and the others. Dorset had disappeared from view – he had probably heard by now of the arrest of his brother, and Gloucester's installation as protector. It would make sense for him to remain out of reach in the south-west until he could get the lay of the land – although Desmond Seward in his *Wars of the Roses* postulates that Dorset was being hidden in London by Elizabeth Shore.

As Lord Protector, Gloucester replaced Rivers and Edward Woodville in their constableships of Carisbrooke and Portchester castles, and on 14 May, orders were issued for Sir Edward to be arrested while any of his companions who 'surrendered' peacefully could be allowed to leave – with the exception of Dorset and Robert Radcliffe. Woodville had put to sea no later than 30 April, so can have had no idea of events in London. A ship bearing the protector's orders arrived among the fleet, and some of the vessels returned to England. Woodville himself, refusing to accept arrest from Gloucester, sailed with two ships to Brittany. There he joined the entourage of Henry Tudor, the exiled Earl of Richmond, who had slipped out of Wales with his uncle, Jasper, Earl of Pembroke, in the wake of the Battle of Tewkesbury twelve years before. Efforts had been made during Edward IV's reign by the earl's mother to bring him back to England, and perhaps marry him to one of Edward's daughters – although one can't help feeling that Edward would have wriggled out of any such arrangement once he got his hands on Richmond.

The continued presence of the king's mother in sanctuary was embarrassing. On 23 May, the Common Council of London had two oaths read to them. The first offered the allegiance of the dukes of Gloucester and Buckingham to Edward V, while the second was a draft of an oath the dukes were prepared to swear should Elizabeth emerge. However, Elizabeth was not sufficiently reassured to emerge. Unable to gain her acquiescence to his actions, Gloucester undertook a wholesale confiscation of the lands of her family. Sir Richard Grey wouldn't be needing his property, immured as he was at Middleham – his manor of Thorpe Waterville slipped into the grasp of Gloucester's friend Francis,

Viscount Lovell. Richard Woodville, who had played no part in Edward IV's court or government, had his manor of Wymington in Bedfordshire taken by Gloucester, and the queen's cousin Richard Haute was obliged to hand over Igtham Mote. Dorset, of course, was not immune to this confiscation. Simon Stallworth wrote on 9 June 1483 to his master, Sir William Stonor, that 'where so ever can be found any goods of my Lord Marquis it is taken. The Prior of Westminster was and yet is in a great trouble for goods delivered to him by my Lord Marquis.'[11] This latter sentence indicates that Dorset had initially gone into sanctuary, or at least taken his goods there to be secured by the prior. Dorset also lost the wardship of Anne St Leger, who, rather than being returned to her father, was granted to Buckingham.

*

Preparations for the coronation continued apace, as reported by Simon Stallworth. The council, including Gloucester and Buckingham, was meeting daily between 10 a.m. and 2 p.m., but the queen was not being consulted, something Stallworth clearly thought surprising. Meanwhile, Gloucester was preparing another assault on her. On 10 June 1483, he wrote to the Mayor of York, a city where he was popular, and to Hull, requesting troops be sent to protect him 'to aid and assist us against the queen, her blood (not bloody) adherents and affinity which have intended and daily doth intend to murder us and our cousin the Duke of Buckingham and the old royal blood of this realm'. The letter was taken by one of Gloucester's closest friends, Sir Richard Radcliffe.[12] There was another letter, for Ralph Neville, Earl of Westmorland, to similar effect. The troops were to muster at Pontefract on 18 June. A third missive was sent to Northumberland at Pontefract.

Lord Hastings, Crowland assures us, was very happy with the turn of events. He was 'bursting with joy' and 'asserting that nothing had been done except to transfer government from two blood relatives of the queen, to two nobles of the blood-royal (Gloucester and Buckingham)'. He presumably had no worries on 13 June when Thomas Howard, son of Gloucester's close friend John, Lord Howard, came to fetch him to attend a council meeting at the Tower. En route, Hastings stopped to speak to a priest but was chivvied along with a laugh and the words, 'My Lord, you have no need of a priest, yet.' Gloucester requested that someone send for strawberries from Bishop Morton's garden. He then leapt up, shouting, 'Treason!' Armed men rushed in, and arrested at least four of the councillors – Hastings, Archbishop Rotherham, Morton of Ely and Oliver King. Hastings was bundled into the yard, forced to lay his head upon a log, and executed, without even being granted the solace of a priest, let alone a trial.

Exactly what Gloucester thought Hastings was doing is unclear – there may have a been an accusation that he was engaged in treasonable conspiracy with the queen. It seems to defy all logic that at one moment Hastings hated Elizabeth, Dorset and Rivers to such an extent that he thought that the strongest means possible should be used to prevent them having influence in government, and then, at the next, that he was conspiring with them to undermine Gloucester in his role of protector. A more credible explanation is that Gloucester now had designs on the crown and needed to remove Hastings before he could lead any opposition. Crowland and Mancini say nothing except that Hastings was innocent of any crime. Sir Thomas More, writing some thirty years later, and only a child at the time, wrote that Gloucester had displayed a withered arm, and accused Elizabeth Shore of conspiring with the queen to use sorcery against him.[13] Vergil, perhaps a more reliable source than More, reported that Gloucester accused Hastings himself of attempting to destroy him. One man who benefited from Hastings' death was the queen's brother-in-law Edward Grey of Groby. Grey was already Baron Lisle in right of his wife, Elizabeth Talbot, and was now promoted to a viscountcy, as well as Hastings' office of Lord Chamberlain, and the Garter.

Unable to mete out the same rough justice to clerics as had been given to Hastings, Gloucester had Rotherham and Morton imprisoned, Morton at Buckingham's castle at Brecon in South Wales. John Morton had graduated as a doctor in both canon and civil law from Oxford in 1452. His merit was quickly recognised, and he was appointed as chancellor in the household of Prince Edward of Lancaster. Although, as a cleric, he was not a fighting man, he was sufficiently important to the Lancastrian party for the victorious Edward IV to exclude him from the general pardon of 1461. He escaped to France, and served in Marguerite's court-in-exile, returning with Warwick in 1470. With the death of Henry VI and Edward of Lancaster, Morton accepted the inevitable, and swore allegiance to Edward IV. More's *History* quotes Morton: 'Had the world gone as I wished, King Henry's son had had the crown and not King Edward. But after that God had ordered him to lose it, and King Edward to reign, I was never so mad that I would with a dead man strive against the quick.'

By 1472, Morton was a councillor and Master of the Rolls, and was frequently used for diplomatic missions; indeed, Louis XI considered him influential enough to deserve a pension. In 1478, he was provided to the see of Ely, and appeared to be a stalwart of the Yorkist regime, officiating at Edward's funeral and ostensibly accepting Gloucester as protector. Perhaps Gloucester believed that Morton would be an obstacle to any plans he was developing to take the crown. It appears that Gloucester's allegations against Hastings were accepted as true by the council – although it is hard to believe that no one questioned, even if only silently, the execution of a councillor without a formal charge or trial for an offence that was not a treasonable act against the king. While such outrages might have been overlooked during the wars, when men were executed after battles, it was not acceptable in peacetime, and was nothing less than murder. Gloucester was acting as accuser, judge, jury and, by the proxy of a servant, executioner. From that time, according to Crowland, Gloucester and Buckingham had free rein. It can never be proven whether, as Mancini maintains, Gloucester had intended from the start to usurp his nephew's crown, or whether temptation simply crept up on him, but it is apparent from this point that Gloucester was intending to displace his nephews, although it seems unlikely that the council anticipated such an astonishing intention.

The two dukes made their way to Westminster with 'a great crowd with swords and clubs'.[14] Archbishop Bourchier led a delegation to the queen, requesting that she release the ten-year-old Richard, Duke of York into his custody, to be taken to the Tower as company for his brother – although he hardly knew him, Edward having spent most of his time at Ludlow.[15] Elizabeth refused for some time, but eventually, perhaps fearing violence, or perhaps trusting in the archbishop, she let Richard go, on the understanding that he would be returned to her after the coronation. Thus Queen Elizabeth lost the fourth of her five sons. The coronation was postponed again, to coincide with the king's thirteenth birthday on 9 November. But London was growing restive. As Stallworth reported to Stonor, 'with us is much trouble, and every man doubts other'. Stallworth could find no explanation for the presence in the capital of thousands of Gloucester's and Buckingham's men-at-arms, other than to suggest they were there to keep the peace. This sentence can be read entirely at face value or as sarcasm, and historians have done both.

On 22 June 1483, the Londoners who assembled for the sermon at St Paul's were astonished to hear that their late king, Edward IV, had been illegitimate – the offspring of Duchess Cicely and a Norman archer. He had not, therefore, been the legitimate king, and his sons could not inherit. While this must be a tissue of lies – surely any rumour of adultery by Duchess Cicely would have been seized upon by the Lancastrians years before – people have taken the matter seriously. The Londoners, at any rate, were unconvinced. An alternative means of declaring Edward's line unlawful was therefore needed, and so it was suggested that Edward and Elizabeth's marriage had been invalid, because Edward had already been precontracted to Lady Eleanor Talbot, daughter of the Earl of Shrewsbury, and widow of Sir Thomas Butler. There is no record of any evidence being adduced at the time to substantiate this claim, nor was any brought forward in an ecclesiastical court, the proper place for such a contention. No word of it had been heard during the lifetimes of either party, and the claim has been argued over endlessly since.

Nebulous claims are one thing, large numbers of men-at-arms another. Buckingham, on or around 24 June, suggested to the council the benefit of passing over King Edward V and accepting the Duke of Gloucester as the legitimate king. Perhaps convinced by the illegitimacy claim, or cowed by the death of Hastings, the council acquiesced, and a petition was brought to Gloucester at Crosby Place, requesting him to accept the crown. Blushing becomingly, he allowed himself to be convinced, and was proclaimed as Richard III.

In the meantime, Henry Percy, Earl of Northumberland, had arrived at Pontefract as instructed. This was the same earl who had persuaded the city of York to open its gates to Edward on his return from Burgundy in 1471. Northumberland and Gloucester's relationship in the North had been uneasy, as Gloucester's increasing pre-eminence there overshadowed Northumberland's own in a land which had once 'known no king but Percy'. They had come to an accommodation, but Gloucester may have underestimated Northumberland's resentment when the royal duke retained Percy men. At this point, however, Northumberland obeyed Gloucester's instructions to execute Rivers, Grey, Vaughan and Haute, who had been brought there from the various locations of their incarceration. Richard Grey had been held at Middleham – costs of 20s 6d had been allowed for his servants and horse there, while a further 20s 3d was paid to transport him to Pontefract and another 6s 8d for his servants at that grim place.[16]

According to Crowland, there were no trials, although Rivers at least was entitled to trial by his peers. Rous (the chronicler of the earls of Warwick) wrote that they were 'cruelly killed ... lamented by almost all and innocent of the deed charged against them, and the Earl of Northumberland their chief judge ... so these lords were condemned to death as if they had ... plotted the death of Richard, Duke of Gloucester ... a thing they never contemplated'.[17] If there were a trial, no evidence of it or from it remains, but the execution of the men, supervised by Sir Richard Ratcliffe, is not in doubt. Grey was executed first and hastily interred.[18] A few days later, Rivers died, requesting he be buried next to his nephew. Hicks infers from Northumberland's willingness to execute the king's uncle and half-brother, of whom Edward was clearly fond, that the duke knew that Gloucester was planning to take the throne, and, further, that the idea that the usurpation came at the end of a series of decisions, rather than being a deliberate plan, is misplaced. In Hicks' view, Northumberland would not have taken such a step without being certain he would never be held accountable for it – a logical inference. If Northumberland knew that Gloucester intended to take the throne, he must have been supportive of the plan, or why not act in concert with others to prevent it? If he did know of such a scheme, what did he think would be the fate of Edward V and his brother? Deposed kings do not live long. Either Northumberland was naive beyond belief or his co-operation gives him some responsibility for the eventual outcome.

On 1 July, the men from the North whom Richard had called for arrived in London, and three days later he invited the mayor to admire their strength in a review at Moorfields. This excursion no doubt helped the mayor to appreciate the necessity of Richard being crowned, and the ceremony duly took place two days later at Westminster Abbey. Holding Queen Anne's train was Margaret Beaufort, Lady Stanley, whose son, Richmond, was still in Brittany, but whose husband was high in the new king's favour. The ceremony was carried out with punctilious attention to detail. As previously mentioned, Lady Stanley had been in discussions with Edward IV about allowing Richmond to return, settling some of her own estates on him, and perhaps allowing him to marry one of Edward's daughters. She now began negotiating a similar deal with Richard III, using Buckingham as her intermediary. She knew Buckingham well – he was the nephew of her second husband, Sir Henry Stafford, and had often been entertained by her in his childhood. But this minor matter was not at the forefront of King Richard's mind: his priority was to travel around his new kingdom, along with his queen, reassuring everyone that his occupation of the throne was legitimate and for the good of the realm.

Westminster now became a fortress, rather than a sanctuary, as Queen Elizabeth and her daughters were trapped inside, surrounded by armed guards. Edward V's attendants were relieved of their offices on 18 July, and over the summer the boys were seen less frequently, until they vanished from sight altogether. According to Mancini, Edward's physician, Dr Argentine, informed him that the boy feared he would soon die. With Richard away from London, a plan was laid to rescue the boys from the Tower. Richard, hearing of the plot, did not think it sufficiently serious to warrant a return to the capital, but instructed the chancellor, Bishop Russell, to sort the matter out. Three men were executed on Tower Hill for their part in the 'enterprise' – none of them were of high rank, but two of them – John Smith, formerly Edward IV's groom of the stirrup, and Stephen Ireland, a wardrober from the Tower – had personal loyalty to Edward IV and his sons. The French chronicler, Thomas Basin, recounted that the conspiracy comprised some fifty men, who had also contacted the exiled earls of Pembroke and Richmond. This is the first hint that Lady Stanley might have been taking an interest in events – probably envisaging her son returning home to be a loyal servant, and perhaps brother-in-law, of a restored Edward V, rather than to be king in his own right.

There is no information about how Cecily Dorset reacted to the sudden execution of her stepfather, Lord Hastings; at the very least, she must have been concerned for the welfare of her mother and half-siblings. Katherine Hastings wrote to the king, begging for mercy for herself and her children. Fortunately, Richard was fond enough of his 'well-beloved cousin' to promise to be a 'good and gracious sovereign lord' to the family. He forbore bringing any act of attainder against Hastings, leaving Katherine and her children in possession of their inheritance, even allowing her to retain the wardship and custody of Cecily's eldest half-brother, Edward, now Lord Hastings.[19]

As the summer of 1483 wore on, a more widespread resistance to Richard's usurpation took shape. By early August, the king was aware that trouble was brewing. On the thirteenth of that month, Lady Stanley's half-brother John, Lord Welles, had his lands confiscated. Richard turned to the man he believed to be his right hand, Buckingham, giving him a commission to enquire into treasonable activity in eight counties surrounding London. Buckingham had received huge rewards for his support of Richard after being consistently overlooked by Edward IV for all the offices that, as a royal duke, he thought he deserved. He was appointed Constable of England, Chief Justice and Chamberlain of both North and South Wales, steward of all the royal castles in Wales, had the constableship of fifty-three other castles, and, on 27 August 1483, even received the king's signature on a warrant granting him the Lancastrian moiety of the de Bohun inheritance he had so long coveted. But by this date, Buckingham was plotting against the king he himself had made.

The Crowland Chronicler believed that Buckingham 'had repented of what he had done' – that is, conniving in Richard's usurpation. Even if we discount later suggestions that Buckingham either advised Richard to murder his nephews, or even did it himself, sudden repentance seems hard to believe – although perhaps, like many men of the time, his strong stomach for political violence did not extend to the murder of children. This view of Buckingham's actions is, of course, predicated on the boys being dead, or him believing they were. This motivation is unconvincing – as before, with regard to Northumberland, it would be an extraordinarily naive man who believed that a king could be deposed and not end up dead. The generally accepted theory is that, suborned by his prisoner, Bishop Morton, Buckingham rose up in support of the little-known off-shoot of Lancaster, the exiled Richmond.

This seems equally unlikely. Richard had been more than generous to Buckingham after he helped him to the crown. Why would an unknown Richmond be more grateful? If Buckingham's heart were Lancastrian, then his own claim could be argued to be the equal of Richmond's – they were both descended in the female line from John of Gaunt, and while Buckingham's claim derived from a younger branch, he was also descended from Edward III's fourth son, giving him a double dose of royal blood. Professor Hicks has identified that the idea that Buckingham was trying to make Richmond king dates only from later, Tudor, sources, and so it is fair to conclude that Buckingham sought the throne for himself, and conspired with Richmond's supporters as a way to gather forces, either promising Richmond rehabilitation should he succeed, or planning to double-cross the exile should he harbour his own ambitions for the throne.

Closely involved in the rebellion were Dorset and his uncles Lionel Woodville, Bishop of Salisbury, and Richard Woodville, brothers to the Duchess of Buckingham, probably with Morton as the go-between. In August 1483, Dorset could have believed any of three things. First was that Edward V and the Duke of York were alive, and that Buckingham had repented and intended to restore them to the throne. Second, that the boys were dead and that, once Richard III caught up with him, he would follow his uncle Rivers and brother Richard to execution; and that he would be better off with Buckingham, married to his aunt, as king (which would not tie in particularly well with the idea that Buckingham hated his Woodville wife, although, as mentioned before, there is no real evidence of that). Finally, Dorset could have believed the boys to be dead, and that Richmond as king, married to his half-sister Elizabeth, would be the most desirable outcome.

Dorset therefore had much to gain from rebellion, regardless of whether Buckingham or Richmond were the intended beneficiary, and little to lose. He did, of course, need to think of his wife and children, and what might happen to them if the rebellion failed and he were executed and attainted. Here, the ownership of the property by Cecily was beneficial. If a man were attainted, he would lose lands that he owned in tail, but his wife would not lose her lands unless she, too, were involved in the treason and attainted. Thus, for the Dorsets, provided Cecily did nothing to attract punishment, there would be little to lose – in theory, anyway.[20] Dorset might also have been inspired by a more noble motivation – he had been sincerely attached to his stepfather, and had sworn allegiance to both him and Edward V – he would not have been the first man during the Wars of the Roses to risk his life in loyalty to his king.

The rebellion received widespread support from the friends and officers of Edward IV, somewhat negating the idea that the queen's family were as disliked as Richard's supporters claimed. Many of Edward IV's household men were involved – and all had a lot to lose. Their commitment to deposing Richard, either for Buckingham or for the practically unknown Richmond, is eloquent testimony to their views of Richard and their horror at the deposition and assumed deaths of the boys. The actual fate of Edward V and Richard, Duke of York has of course, been hotly debated for centuries. All that can be said for certain is that they went into the Tower in 1483 and were never definitively seen again. Whether or not Richard had them killed, or they were killed without his knowledge, or they died of natural causes, or even that they escaped, is ultimately irrelevant. What matters is that people at the time believed that Richard was responsible; they were in his power, he was their uncle, and he had sworn allegiance to Edward. He was accountable for their fate.

Lionel, Bishop of Salisbury, visited his sister and brother-in-law at Thornbury Castle on 22 September, just before the king issued an order confiscating the bishop's secular properties. A day later, Buckingham wrote to Richmond, inviting him to England. The letter is no longer extant, so far as is known, so its original existence is based on the parliamentary attainder against Buckingham the following year, which only records that Buckingham invited Richmond to take part, not that he was suggesting Richmond as a replacement king. From Thornbury, Buckingham took his duchess and their sons to Weobley Castle in Herefordshire, leaving their daughters behind at Brecon castle – another hint that his marriage was no more unhappy than most arranged aristocratic marriages, for if he did not like his wife, why not leave her with his daughters, about whose safety he was so careless that they were abducted in his absence? Weobley was the home of Sir Walter Devereux, Lord Ferrers of Chartley, where

Richmond had been taken to safety after the summary execution of his guardian William Herbert, the Yorkist Earl of Pembroke, following the Battle of Edgecote.

Richard was deeply hurt and angered by Buckingham's perfidy, calling him 'the most untrue creature living'. Rewards for the capture of Buckingham, Lionel, Dorset, Morton and Bishop Courtenay of Exeter were issued. To preserve rank, the rewards were tiered from £1,000 for whoever captured the duke to a lesser 1,000 marks for Dorset and a mere 500 marks for the others. At this time, Richard was seemingly unaware that Richmond might be in any way involved. Among the rebels was Sir Thomas St Leger, widower of Anne of York, and father of the girl betrothed to Dorset's son. The St Legers had been York supporters for many years – this defection of Richard's brother-in-law underlines the lack of support for him from the traditional Yorkists. Other rebels included Sir William Stonor, even though he had received a letter from his 'loving cousin' Francis Lovell on 18 October, requesting him to join Lovell and muster for the king. Dorset raised the standard of rebellion in Exeter, while Lionel Woodville did the same in his bishopric.

The proclamation against the rebels did not just offer a reward for capturing them, or proclaim the importance of loyalty to the king, it also launched a damning indictment of the individuals concerned, particularly Dorset, concentrating heavily on sexual slander. According to the proclamation, Dorset, 'not fearing God, nor the peril of his soul hath many maids, widows and wives damnably and without shame, devoured, deflowered and defouled, holding the unshameful and mischievous woman called Shore's wife, in adultery'. Richard's emphasis on the alleged sexual peccadilloes of the rebels was intended to discredit them, and to suggest that the rank-and-file supporters were being 'abused and blinded' by 'adulterers and bawds'. Notions of sexual morality were very much stricter in the fifteenth century than they are today, and accusations of adultery should not be underestimated as an indicator of evil. Having called on the moral majority for support, the king headed for Salisbury, to scotch the rebellion in its heartland,

Buckingham was disappointed of the mass of followers he had evidently anticipated. He slunk out of Weobley, first sending his eldest son, Edward, disguised as a girl, to retainer Sir Richard Delabere for safekeeping. Unpopular with his tenants, the duke had also fallen foul of the gods: the autumn was one of winds and lashing rain. Few rebels had the heart to turn out, and Buckingham was constrained to hide among his tenants. One, Sir Ralph Bannister, decided either that his loyalty to the crowned king was a higher priority than any loyalty to Buckingham or that he fancied the considerable reward – or even that it was a great opportunity to rid himself of a grasping landlord. He revealed Buckingham's location, and the duke was arrested and taken by Sir James Tyrrell to Salisbury, where he arrived on 31 October. He requested permission to enter the king's presence, his son later alleging that he intended to murder Richard with a knife. If that were his plan, then it was thwarted by Richard's refusal to see his former ally. On 2 November, Buckingham was executed in the marketplace at Salisbury.

Either unaware of Buckingham's death, or unperturbed since the focus of the rebellion was the institution of Richmond, on 3 November, rebels at Bodmin proclaimed King Henry (Henry was the Christian name of both men). Richmond himself had put to sea and come in close to the English coast. A small body awaited him on shore, and informed the scout sent ahead that they were there to proclaim him king. Richmond, always cautious, smelt a rat and declined to land, returning to Brittany, where Dorset soon joined him and received a generous grant of 400 livres per annum from Duke Francis – four times as much as Sir Edward Woodville received. Bishop Lionel took sanctuary in Beaulieu Abbey. Richard Woodville was eventually pardoned, but St Leger was executed, along with two others from the south-west, and six from Kent. Morton did not leave England with Dorset. Instead, he travelled to the centre of his bishopric in Ely to gather funds before crossing to the Low Countries, where he kept a low profile.

Richard took steps to confiscate Dorset's property. The lands of Ferrers of Groby that were Dorset's patrimony were given to his grandmother's widower Sir John Bourchier for life, with reversion to the Crown. His lordships of Tremwell in Cornwall and Kentsbeare, Blackborough and Charlton in Devon were granted for life to Sir Robert Manners, augmenting that gentleman's annual income by some £125. Sir William Catesby, a close friend of Richard's, received numerous manors in Northamptonshire, and Broughton Astley in Leicestershire. The Duchess of Buckingham and her younger children were summoned to London, but where they were housed is unknown; nor is there any information about Cecily Dorset and her children. Richard's hardest dilemma was the punishment of Lady Stanley. Her husband had remained loyal, so Richard could not afford to anger him – Stanley was the greatest landowner in the north-west of England. On the other hand, it appeared that Lady Stanley had been involved in the plot, possibly even suborning Buckingham. The king compromised by forfeiting all of Margaret's considerable inheritance, but permitting Stanley to keep the income. Thus, Stanley was no worse off, but on the death of Margaret, rather than being inherited by Richmond, the lands would revert to the Crown. Stanley was ordered to keep her close, watch her servants, and prevent her from communicating with her son.

make him one of the most admirable of the men involved in the Wars of the Roses; he was one of the few who never changed sides, never betrayed his friends, and was consistent in all his dealings. To give common cause to the mixture of Lancastrians and Yorkists, following the Christmas Day Mass at Rennes Cathedral in 1483, Richmond swore that as soon as he recovered the kingdom that he now claimed was his by right, he would marry Elizabeth of York or, if she were unavailable, one of her sisters.

For the time being, such a marriage seemed no more than a pipe-dream as the parliament that opened in January 1484 passed acts of attainder against the rebels of the previous summer. The bishops, Morton, Woodville and Courtenay, were stripped of the temporalities of their bishoprics but spared their lives, while the Earl of Oxford, Jasper, Richmond and Lady Stanley lost their titles and lands. Richmond will therefore be referred to now as Henry. The other business of the parliament was the passing of the bill Titulus Regius, which enacted Richard's claim that the marriage of Edward IV and 'Dame Elizabeth Grey', had been invalid, and that their children were ineligible to inherit the crown. For good measure, the brother whom Richard had claimed to love and be loyal to was memorialised as of 'ungodly disposicion' and ruled in 'self-will and pleasure, feare and drede, all manner of equity and lawes layd apart'.[1]

Elizabeth and her daughters were persuaded to leave sanctuary as a result, according to Crowland, of frequent intercessions and dire threats. While some have suggested that Elizabeth's surrender is proof of her belief in Richard III's innocence in the matter of the disappearance of her younger sons, she certainly knew he had executed her brother Rivers and her son Richard Grey without due process or legal authority, so she is unlikely to have believed him to entertain warm feelings towards her or the rest of her family. However, she and her five daughters, ranging in age from three to eighteen, had been in sanctuary for eight months, living on the charity of the monastery. The place was surrounded by Richard's soldiers, and she knew that the recent rebellion had failed. There was no way out, other than to submit. Nevertheless, Elizabeth drove a hard bargain. Richard was obliged to swear publicly that the girls would be 'in surety of their lives', that they would not be imprisoned, either in the Tower of London or anywhere else, that they would not be 'disparaged' by forced marriages to unworthy men, and that they would have dowries of 200 marks per annum. Elizabeth herself was to have an income of 700 marks. The household of the former royal ladies was to be supervised by John Nesfield, Constable of Hertford Castle, where they may have resided. Perhaps Queen Elizabeth was lucky – Edward IV's other love, Elizabeth Shore, was whipped at the cart's tail as a common harlot.

During 1483, Richard's extensive progress had culminated in a grand ceremony at York, where his son, Edward of Middleham, was created Prince of Wales. The boy was delicate, so did not travel to London with his parents on their return, but remained at Middleham until his untimely demise in April 1484. His death on the anniversary of that of Edward IV would have seemed ominous to mediaeval minds, used to seeing coincidences as signs of divine favour or wrath. Both personally and politically, Richard was devastated. So far as is known, Edward of Middleham had been Anne's only pregnancy. She was twenty-seven to Richard's thirty-two, so the couple might live many more years with no heir.

Throughout the summer of 1484, rumour and counter-rumour spread. One William Collingbourne was arrested for nailing a verse to the door of St Paul's Cathedral: 'The Cat, the Rat, and Lovell the Dog, rule all England, under an hog.' This referred respectively to Sir William Catesby, Sir Richard Ratcliffe and Viscount Lovell. The hog indicated the king, whose personal badge was the white boar. Of more concern than scurrilous verses was the charge that Collingbourne had invited Henry to invade. He was found guilty of treason, and hanged, drawn and quartered. Despite the quashing of the risings of the summer of 1483, further insurgencies took place. On 2 September 1484, more men were indicted in England for conspiring with Henry, among them John Risley of Colchester, a former squire of the body to Edward IV, and his servant, William Coke of Lavenham; Sir William Brandon and his two sons, William and Thomas; and Sir William Stonor. As we have seen before, the Stonors had close links to Dorset and Cecily, and Sir William Brandon and his wife were friends of Morton's.

Over in Brittany, things were not going as smoothly as Dorset and the others might have hoped. Francis had plenty of troubles of his own. His chief minister, Pierre Landais, was cordially hated by many of his nobles, who scorned the man's humble background. Landais' enemies had support from Anne of Beaujeu, who was hoping to force Francis to agree that, if he had no male heir, Brittany would fall to the French Crown. It was perhaps to raise money or troops to counter French influence while Francis was on his sickbed in September 1484 that Landais came to an accommodation with Richard III, agreeing to hand Henry over. In return, Richard would cease his campaign of seizing Breton shipping and goods, grant Brittany the income from the lands of the exiles, and support the duchy against France with 1,000 archers.

Morton had retained links with home, and when he discovered Landais' plot he sent Christopher Urswyk to Henry to warn him. Henry and Jasper sent a request to Anne of Beaujeu to admit them to France. The men separated, with Jasper taking a group of followers to visit Francis on his sickbed, conveniently close to the French border; but rather than visiting the duke, Jasper crossed the border and headed for the city of Anjou. A couple of days later, Henry, with a retinue of only five men, set out, ostensibly to visit a friend. Having ridden 5 miles, the party disappeared into a forest where Henry changed clothes with one of his servants and, with just one other man, rode as fast as he could for the border, crossing it just an hour before Landais' men arrived. Francis, when he recovered from his illness, was ashamed of Landais' actions, and paid for the passage of the other exiles to the court of France, Dorset among them.

While English writers sneer at Henry's descent from Owain Tudor, a Welsh gentleman of the blood of the native princes of Wales, he was also a great-grandson of a king of France. Charles VIII and Anne of Beaujeu welcomed their kinsmen with open arms. From the French perspective, nothing could be better than Henry's presence. Richard III was maintaining the York relationship with Burgundy, where Dowager Duchess Margaret was still influential, and Maximilian, despite the Treaty of Arras that had so enraged Edward IV, was still bitterly opposed to France. By harbouring Henry, the French government could annoy Richard, without having to do much in the way of practical support for the exiles beyond cash for their maintenance. Henry was given 3,000 livres per annum (slightly less than £3,000). With this, he had to support his not inconsiderable retinue of 400, housed at Senlis.

The exiles were soon to be joined by a man even more experienced in war than Jasper – John de Vere, 13th Earl of Oxford. The de Veres had been loyal Lancastrians, and the twelfth earl and his son Aubrey, father of the current earl, had been executed for plotting against Edward IV. Edward IV, hoping for reconciliation with leading Lancastrians, had allowed the current earl to inherit, and he had been made a knight of the Bath for the coronation of Elizabeth Woodville. But his Lancastrian loyalty was too strong to allow Oxford to be reconciled with the Yorkist regime. He had taken part in the Battle of Edgecote, escaping afterwards to France, where he joined Marguerite and Prince Edward. Returning with Warwick (his brother-in-law) in 1470, he had commanded the left flank at Barnet, but the mischance of the battle (which took place in fog) and the similarity of his streaming star badge to Edward IV's sun-in-splendour led the Lancastrians to fear treachery, and turn on their own men. Oxford escaped again and spent the next three years harassing the English Crown, even capturing St Michael's Mount.

Finally obliged to surrender, Oxford was imprisoned at Hammes Castle in Calais. By October 1484, Richard III was taking no chances, and decided to bring Oxford back to England – presumably for execution. Oxford persuaded the Governor of Hammes, Sir James Blount, to join him in a final throw of the Lancastrian dice – the men rode into France, and joined Henry, who was 'ravished with joy incredible'.[2] Oxford returned to Hammes and, clearly silver-tongued, brought the garrison onside. Henry could now begin to feel that he truly was the representative of the Lancastrians. CSL Davies argues that the Calais captain's willingness to join Henry stemmed from Blount being one of Hastings' affinity, and therefore anticipating a fairly short tenure under Richard III. It is a more convincing argument than a sudden conversion to the cause of an unknown sprig of Lancaster. The other man who joined Blount and Oxford was John Fortescue, Gentleman Porter of Calais, whose uncle, Sir John Fortescue, had been tutor to Edward of Lancaster in exile.

The two sides began a propaganda war. Whether or not Richard had dispatched Edward V and Richard of York is, as mentioned above, unknowable, but it certainly did not stop his enemies accusing him of the heinous crime – and Richard neither publicly denied the charge nor produced the boys alive. In the autumn of 1484, Henry sent open letters to England calling on true men to unseat 'that homicide and unnatural tyrant', repeating his own claim to the throne and promising an invasion. Richard retaliated with a proclamation in December, in which Henry was accused of being willing to sell the rights of the English Crown to France, and attacked Henry's supporters, opening with the men who had rebelled with Buckingham:

> Forasmuch as the king our sovereign lord hath certain knowledge that Piers, Bishop of Exeter, Thomas Grey, late Marquis of Dorset, Jasper, late Earl of Pembroke, John, late Earl of Oxford and Sir Edward Woodville, with others divers his rebels and traitors attainted by the High Court of Parliament, of whom many be known for open murderers, adulterers and extortioners ... departed ... into France ... under the obeisance of the king's ancient enemy Charles calling himself king of France and to abuse and blind the commons of this said realm ... have chosen to be their captain one Henry late calling himself earl of Richmond which of his ambition and insatiable covetousness stirred and excited by the confederacy of the king's said rebels and traitors encroaches upon him the name and title of royal estate of this realm of England, whereof he hath no manner interest right or colour as every man well-knoweth.

It seems unlikely that Richard would have taken the threat of Henry terribly seriously at first. He himself had been a successful commander in the field – he knew how difficult it was to conquer England via invasion, and he had little respect for the men surrounding the exiled earl. Nevertheless, he was not a fool, and implemented plans to stave off any invasion.

In the meantime, there were the Christmas festivities to be enjoyed at his court – although the loss of his son and the deteriorating health of his queen were no doubt preying on his emotions. During Christmas 1484, the daughters of Edward IV were also at court. The eldest, Elizabeth, was just short of her nineteenth birthday. Her physical similarity to the queen was mentioned, and also that she and Queen Anne wore the same gown. This might mean that Anne gave Elizabeth her gown – it was not uncommon for kings and queens to give favoured courtiers their clothes, or, alternatively, that there were two copies of the same gown – later, Elizabeth and her mother-in-law wore identical gowns. Whether it was the same gown or one of the same style, it was taken as an indication that Richard was displaying an inappropriate level of interest in his niece, and that Elizabeth was encouraging it.

Crowland thought that Richard was considering marrying Elizabeth. Anne was in poor health and unlikely to bear more children, so political necessity might demand that Richard remarry. It would not have been particularly difficult for the king to obtain an annulment – he and Anne were in the forbidden degrees of consanguinity (her father was his cousin) and they had married before receiving any papal dispensation. These rumours were fuelled to hysteria when Anne fell ill after Christmas and Richard avoided her – probably on the orders of his physicians. If he were to remarry, then contemplating Elizabeth of York made sense – for those who assumed her brothers were dead, she was the next heir. It would also prevent her marriage to Henry. Against this was the fact that Elizabeth was his own niece. According to Crowland, it took the best efforts of the Cat and the Rat to put Richard off the notion – they brought in legions of priests to inform him that no pope would grant a dispensation for such a marriage. Leaving aside the morality, Catesby and Ratcliffe were concerned that Elizabeth might wish to avenge the deaths of her uncle and her three brothers (Edward V, the Duke of York, and Sir Richard Grey) and look for scapegoats. Additionally, the followers of Warwick, who were still loyal to his memory, did not wish to see his daughter disparaged. The latter argument would have had less weight after the queen died in early 1485, but the former two were strong.

Whatever Richard's private thoughts, and the story may just have been an ugly rumour, it had enough credibility for him to be forced to deny it in a public announcement in the Great Hall at St John's, Clerkenwell, to the mayor and alderman. He informed them that he was grieving the loss of his queen and had never dreamed of marrying 'in such a manner wise'. What Elizabeth thought has also been subject to speculation, with many believing that a fragment of a letter, quoted by Sir George Buck (but now lost), indicated that she was keen to marry her uncle. Against this is the context of the letter, which can just as easily be interpreted as a desire for fulfilment of marriages that Richard was negotiating for both of them to members of the Portuguese royal house.

Beyond their close blood relation, there is also the sheer unlikelihood of any woman wanting to marry the man who deposed her brother, was responsible for the disappearance of her younger brothers (whether or not he had them killed), had executed her half-brother and her uncle, driven her other half-brother and uncle into exile, slandered her parents as evil-living adulterers and disparaged her as a bastard. That Elizabeth had been fond of her uncle Rivers seems to be indicated by a payment from her, twenty years later, to a man in whose house Rivers had stayed, waiting for execution at Pontefract. No matter how attractive Richard might have been, it seems an unlikely crush. To reduce the scandal, and prove the rumours unfounded, Richard sent Elizabeth to Sheriff Hutton Castle, in Yorkshire, to reside with her cousins Edward, Earl of Warwick, and Margaret, but not before the gossip had reached Henry. It was bad news – he was 'pinched ... by the very stomach' at the idea of the loss of his potential bride.[3]

In January 1485, Dorset sent an envoy to Bruges to meet Jacques of Savoy, Count of Romont, the leader of the Flemish forces resisting the rule of Maximilian. Jacques' wife, Marie of Luxembourg, was Dorset's second cousin. The purpose of the journey is not known – he may have been sounding out support for Henry, or perhaps looking for other opportunities for himself in case Henry's mission came to nothing. The messenger he chose was Roger Machado, formerly Leicester Herald, who had previously been involved in Anglo-Burgundian diplomacy and had taken part in Edward IV's funeral. How he came to be in Dorset's employ is not clear – perhaps he was another man who resented the passing over of Edward IV's sons, and saw an accommodation with the Lancastrian rump as the answer. According to Machado's journal of expenses,[4] Dorset paid him £2 3s 4d for the journey to Ghent to see Romond, and he sold six pieces of Dorset's plate, totalling 9 lbs in weight, for which he received £11 8s. Machado left Romont and travelled on to see Jacques of Luxembourg, Dorset's great-uncle, arriving on 2 February 1485. A journey to Jean II of Lannoy was next. Once a friend of Louis XI, Lannoy was now an ally of Maximilian's, and had been involved in negotiating the Treaty of Arras. Dorset was not just concerned with politics – another entry in Machado's account is for £2 paid to the marquis's painter.

Machado was later well-rewarded by Henry – this has been attributed by Davies to Machado perhaps betraying Dorset's intention to leave Henry and return to England.[5] The marquis had received a letter from his mother, urging him to forsake Henry and return home, where he would be well received by Richard and 'be called of the king unto high promotion'.[6] Perhaps Elizabeth had become resigned to the status quo and been slightly comforted by the knowledge that Richard intended to pardon her brother, Richard Woodville, which he did on 30 March. Dorset decided to heed his mother – maybe he was tired of exile, maybe he thought that Henry had no real chance of winning the crown. He may have missed his wife and young children, as well as his mother and half-sisters. Dorset had lost his uncle and brother, his stepfather, and his two half-brothers all within the space of eighteen months. If he craved the comforts of home and the family that was left to him, should we be surprised? At any rate, whether his motives were political, personal or a combination of both, he decided to return, slipping away into the night.

When Dorset's disappearance was discovered, there was consternation among the exiles – he had been privy to all the plans for invasion. Humphrey Cheyne was sent after him to secure his return – by force if necessary. Dorset cannot have been travelling fast, or very secretly, as Cheyne caught up with him at Compiègne, a mere 50 miles from Paris. The ease with which Dorset was found and persuaded to return suggests another possibility – that he signalled a willingness to go home and be reconciled with Richard so that the king, if he believed Dorset to be in France under duress, might relax the pressure on his family. This may have worked, as he was not included in Richard's proclamation against Henry in June 1485, yet, having been prevented from leaving, he was not held in captivity, so could probably have made a dash for England had he really wanted.

It was obvious to Henry that he needed to hasten his invasion – every day Richard remained in power would consolidate his hold on the throne and make it more likely that his own supporters would drift home. Henry also needed to make the most of Oxford and the Calais garrison, whose defection had encouraged the French to take him seriously. Not that Charles VIII was entirely committed to supporting his cousin. His government was weighing the likelihood of Richard invading France, the problems posed by the continuing conflict with Maximilian, now gaining support in Burgundy, and the possible future of the duchy of Brittany.

On 4 May 1485 the French parliament agreed to lend 40,000 livres tournois for an invasion fleet, although only the first instalment of 10,000 livres was actually disbursed.[7] This was enough for Henry's preparations to begin, allowing Charles and Anne to evaluate the situation in Brittany and determine whether Richard was likely to invade, before handing over any more cash. If Richard were not going to prove a problem, they would not wish to waste their money. Henry and Jasper set up their headquarters in Rouen and wrote copious letters to England requesting support, including to Sir William Herbert, whom Henry knew from the period he had spent as the ward of Pembroke's father, alongside William, his sisters Katherine and Maud, and Henry Percy, Earl of Northumberland. Pembroke had intended Henry to marry Maud, but, with Henry in exile from 1471, she had married Northumberland, and by the summer of 1485 was dead. Henry agreed that, should he be unable to keep his vow to marry Elizabeth of York, or one of her sisters, Katherine Herbert would share his throne.

As the summer progressed, Richard began to prepare in earnest. He sent out commissions of array from his central base at Nottingham Castle calling for all his subjects to be ready 'in their most defencible array … for the resistance of the king's rebels, traitors and enemies'. They were to levy a fixed number of men, who were to be provided with weapons and protective clothing, suitable to their rank. One man who did heed the call to arms, although his intentions can only be inferred, was Northumberland, who made his will on 27 July. On 23 June, Richard published another broadside against the exiles. Henry was impugned as coming of two illegitimate lines. His Beaufort great-grandfather had been born before the marriage of his parents and Richard also alleged that Richmond's grandfather, Owain Tudor, was illegitimate, although no doubts were cast on the marriage of Owain to Katherine of Valois. In this proclamation, Dorset was not mentioned – perhaps Richard was still hoping that a reconciliation was possible.

With no further funds forthcoming from Charles, Henry was obliged to borrow to make up the shortfall. He entered a contract on 13 July 1485 with Philippe Luillier, Sieur de Saint-Jean-le-Blanc and Captain of the Bastille, notarised by Pierre Pichon of Rue Saint-Antoine, Paris. Luillier would lend 30,000 livres, but on tough conditions. Henry was obliged to pledge all his personal belongings, and give two sureties – Sir John

Bourchier, and the Marquis of Dorset. He also promised to pay for the upkeep of the two men at the Bastille during their time as pledges. Dorset and Bourchier provided their own letters of obligation – as knights of the Garter, and men of honour, they would be obliged to stand by their word. This puts a rather different complexion on Henry's relationship with Dorset. It has usually been presumed that Dorset was left behind because Henry did not trust him, but Lullier would have been highly unlikely to accept hostages whom Henry did not value. The banker must have thought that Henry would be keen to redeem them. Equally, it shows that Dorset and Bourchier had considerable faith in Henry's ability to win the throne – if he did not, there would be no possibility of the loan being repaid.

With cash in hand, Henry could raise an army. He collected around 4,000 men, while his uncle Jasper was in communication with his former friends and tenants in Wales. According to Vergil, among the messages of support was one from Rhys ap Thomas, one of the most powerful influences in south-west and west Wales. Without his support, it would be difficult for Henry to make a landing on the Welsh coast.

Finally, Henry set sail. He landed near Milford Haven on 7 August sporting the Welsh Dragon banner of the ancient British king Cadwaladr, as well as the red cross of St George. The Tudor forces quickly moved through south Wales, keeping to the west coast and heading for Aberystwyth. The Herberts did nothing to prevent their advance, but neither did Rhys ap Thomas immediately fulfil any promises he might have made. In fact, the next news was that Rhys ap Thomas and Sir Walter Herbert were marching in parallel up the valley of the Teifi. The Tudors cannot have known whether these men were intending to join their ranks or cut them off at the knees. Fortunately, it was the former. With these increased numbers, Henry's march continued through Wales and he crossed into England at Shrewsbury, meeting Richard III at the Battle of Bosworth on 22 August 1485, where his troops were commanded by Oxford.

Bosworth was notable for the lack of enthusiastic support from Richard's nobles. Lord Stanley, and his brother Sir William, equivocated. Northumberland brought his men, but did not fight; even Richard's beloved city of York sent few men, and those came late. His most valiant adherent was John Howard, Duke of Norfolk, who fought to the bitter end. Another of the men who fought with Richard was Sir John Bourchier, widower of Dorset's grandmother.[8] The battle was short, but bloody, culminating in a last, desperate, courageous charge by Richard III and his bodyguard to rush Henry's banners. Sir William Stanley's men joined the fray, careering down the hill to trap Richard, who was cut down and killed. With his demise, the battle was over. Lord Stanley bowed to his stepson and proclaimed him King Henry VII. Richard's stripped and broken body was unceremoniously bundled off to Leicester, where it was quietly buried in the church of the Greyfriars. Henry later paid for a modest memorial.

Henry processed slowly to London, where he was proclaimed king, no one dwelling too closely on his claim. Dorset's half-sister Elizabeth of York was brought to London, where she was placed in the care of the new king's mother, Lady Stanley, in her house at Coldharbour. The Earl of Warwick and Margaret of Clarence probably accompanied her.

Henry was crowned on 30 October and opened his first parliament the following week. Again, his title to the throne was lightly skated over. The new king was a man of measured temper and shunned bloody antics – of Richard's men, only Sir William Catesby and two men of humbler background were executed. Henry also remembered his friends. Stanley received the earldom of Derby, and Lady Stanley's attainder was reversed, meaning she was now referred to as Countess of Richmond and Derby, or more usually as my Lady, the King's Mother; Sir Edward Woodville regained his former post of keeper of Portchester Castle, and gained that of Carisbrooke Castle and the captaincy of the Isle of Wight; Richard Woodville was recognised as Earl Rivers; Queen Elizabeth's marriage to Edward IV was confirmed as valid, and she was restored to her state and dignity, while the odious Titulus Regius Act was ordered to be destroyed unread. Henry's other early action was the redemption of Dorset and Bourchier, who returned to England before Christmas. Dorset's reward was fair, but not over-generous: the attainder against him was reversed, and the lands and titles he had inherited or married were restored, followed by confirmation of his title of Marquis of Dorset and his grant of £35 per annum. He also had a place on Henry's council, although the offices granted by Edward IV were not regranted, nor the wardship of Warwick.

Henry's strategy was one of reconciliation. He had spent his youth in Wales, away from the English court, and the only nobles he knew, other than the Herberts and Northumberland, were those who had joined him in Brittany. He therefore did not have the personal likes and dislikes that had so influenced the Wars of the Roses. While he was eager to reward his supporters appropriately, he did not wish to indulge in wholesale revenge against Yorkists, nor to create new overmighty subjects such as York and Warwick had been. General pardons were issued and a policy of forgive and forget was the order of the day. By far the most generously rewarded was Jasper, who was reconfirmed as Earl of Pembroke and granted the dukedom of Bedford, raising him to higher rank than Dorset. The ceremony was part of a general show of reconciliation, with prominent Yorkists taking part. Jasper was led to the foot of the throne by the Duke of Suffolk, brother-in-law to Edward IV and Richard III, and his son, John de la Pole, Earl of Lincoln. Jasper was also found a wealthy wife – Dorset's aunt Katherine, Dowager Duchess of Buckingham. Jasper was some twenty-five years older than her, and had led a hard life, but she could feel safe in the knowledge that he was the new king's closest friend and ally.

The most important plank of Henry's strategy was his marriage to Elizabeth of York, which took place on 18 January 1486, immediately after a dispensation had been granted. On 2 March 1486, the dispensation was confirmed personally by Pope Innocent, at the request of the king and queen. He followed this up with a bull on 27 March, excommunicating anyone who challenged either the marriage or Henry's personal right to the throne. The couple swiftly fulfilled their dynastic duty. Elizabeth bore a son at Winchester on 21 September 1486. The whole court was *en fete* – Arthur's birth seemed to show that the new dynasty, linking Lancaster and York, had the blessing of the Almighty. The christening was as sumptuous as the king could make it, and, once again, balanced the factions. The godfathers were the Earl of Derby and Lord Maltravers, married to Dorset's aunt Margaret Woodville; the Earl of Oxford, second only to Jasper in the king's esteem, was godfather for the confirmation; the godmother was the dowager queen, Elizabeth. The baby himself was carried by his aunt, the seventeen-year-old Cicely of York. The christening robe was so long that it required its own little retinue to support it: Sir John Cheyne, Dorset and Cecily, and Lincoln. At the feast which followed, Dorset, Lincoln and Lord Strange (Derby's son, who was married to Dorset's cousin) served the queen.

Everything in the royal garden seemed rosy – Henry had won a kingdom and a wife, and now had an heir.

*

The sunny opening to the new reign was soon darkened by the spectre of rebellion. An early threat of insurrection under Lincoln and Francis, Viscount Lovell faded when Bedford travelled north, armed not only with men but with pardons for any rebels who would submit to the king, and, handily, a bull of excommunication from the pope for any who persisted in rebellion. The tactics were effective, so Lovell and Lincoln took refuge in Burgundy with Margaret of York. Bedford was then called to Wales, where, together with Sir Rhys ap Thomas, he suppressed a rebellion by Thomas Vaughan.

Soon, a more serious rebellion threatened, centred on a boy known to posterity as Lambert Simnel, who was crowned on 27 May 1487 in Christ Church, Dublin as Edward, King of England, under the aegis of Gerald FitzGerald, 8th Earl of Kildare, Deputy Lieutenant of Ireland.[9] Aware that Lincoln and Lovell were involved, Henry anticipated that Margaret of York would supply them with troops. To counter this threat, he decided to fortify the whole east coast, travelling to Bury St Edmunds in Suffolk himself to see it done. While there, he heard that Dorset was also en route to the shrine of St Edmund 'in order to purge himself' – hopefully spiritually, rather than corporeally. Dorset's approach made Henry nervous – why would he be heading towards the east coast? The king decided that it was better to be safe than sorry, and sent Oxford to intercept Dorset and escort him back to London for a brief sojourn in the Tower. Vergil explains that if Dorset were an enemy this would neutralise him, and if he were a friend, which Vergil assures us he was, then he would not mind his dignity being ruffled for the greater good.

This nervousness over Dorset, coupled with Henry's alleged treatment of Dorset's mother, the dowager queen, Elizabeth, has been taken as an indication that perhaps Simnel really was who he said he was. But who did he say he was? According to Vergil, Simnel was presented in Ireland as Edward, Earl of Warwick, son of Clarence. There has been speculation by Matthew Lewis in his recent book *The Survival of the Princes in the Tower* that perhaps the boy claimed to be the missing Richard, Duke of York, and was crowned as Richard IV, but I believe the overwhelming evidence supports the coronation of the boy as Edward VI, and therefore that Warwick's was the identity claimed.[10] Impersonating Warwick was only feasible if it could be suggested that the real Warwick had escaped from captivity. Perhaps it was assumed that, having been sent to the Tower and not released, the boy had been murdered and that Henry would not be able to produce him. Even if secret murder had been Henry's inclination, the example of the loss of support that Richard III had suffered because of suspicion about the fate of his nephews would have put him off. Henry executed comparatively few of his enemies, and always publicly, under at least a fig-leaf of judicial process. Warwick was produced from the Tower, marched up and down, taken to St Paul's and obliged to talk to people who knew him.

That the boy known as Simnel was a real member of the House of York is an inference sometimes drawn from Elizabeth Woodville's retirement to a convent and the reassignment of her jointure to her daughter. This, it is asserted, indicates that Henry believed Elizabeth Woodville to be complicit in the rebellion. Even if the boy were genuinely Warwick, it is preposterous to think that Elizabeth would have preferred the son of Clarence, whom she hated, to be king, rather than her own daughter as queen consort, with her grandson to inherit the crown. Or, if the plan were to substitute the Earl of Lincoln, as seems probable, how could that improve Elizabeth's position? She could only have had any interest in the matter if the claimant were being named as a son of her own, and, as we have seen, that is not the case. Suggestions that Elizabeth 'intrigued' or 'meddled' for the sheer sake of it have more than a whiff of misogyny about them. Her decision to retire to the abbey at Bermondsey is perfectly consistent with mediaeval ideas of piety, and with the actions of previous dowager queens, such as Eleanor of Provence and Katherine of Valois. Elizabeth had lost more than almost anyone in the Wars of the Roses (a husband, a father, two brothers and three sons), so she may well have desired a quieter life. It is possible she struggled with the dominance of Margaret Beaufort at court, but Elizabeth still outranked her as dowager, and the two had been friends for years – Margaret's second husband had died supporting Edward IV at Barnet. That she was an unwelcome reminder of the heyday of the Yorkist court seems unlikely – Henry's whole political plan had been to promulgate the union of himself and Elizabeth of York as a new future for both houses.

In any case, Elizabeth's seclusion was by no means total. On 28 November 1487, Henry agreed a marriage for her with James III of Scotland. If he feared his mother-in-law's support for pretenders, such a match would have been the last thing the king would want. As Queen of Scots, she would have had far more opportunity to plot with disaffected Yorkists – the other York widow, Margaret, Dowager Duchess of Burgundy, was causing the king enough headaches. If Henry did put pressure on Elizabeth to retire from court, he is far more likely to have had financial motives – he wanted her jointure lands, restored on his accession, for his wife. It would not be the first time a dowager queen's lands had been taken to support the new queen – Isabella of France had had to surrender her property to Philippa of Hainault, and Johanna of Navarre was conveniently accused of witchcraft and deprived of her property to the benefit of Katherine of Valois. Henry, always slippery in the matter of money, would not have hesitated to follow such examples. Even so, Elizabeth was not penniless – Henry gave her an income initially of 400 marks, later increased to £400 per annum (twice what Richard III had promised to her daughters as dowries, although less than that king had given Elizabeth herself.) She also retained a property in Westminster, and visited the court from time to time, even standing in for her daughter to greet ambassadors when the queen was in childbed.

Dorset's position in regard to the Lambert Simnel affair may have been different. As discussed above, he had been granted the wardship of Warwick, and probably intended him to marry one of his own daughters. He had lost the wardship after Richard III took the throne, but if he had already built up a relationship with the young earl, and believed that Simnel might be Warwick, then it is possible to argue that the idea of his daughter as queen consort, rather than his half-sister, might have encouraged him to support the rebellion. This argument would have to be predicated on Dorset believing that Warwick, whom he had not seen since early 1483, had escaped from the Tower, and there is no information as to what he actually thought, nor whether he was one of the people who talked to the Warwick produced from the Tower. It is likely that it was Henry's cautious nature, rather than any evidence, that impelled him to imprison Dorset.

The scheme had been prepared in advance, enabling Lincoln and Lovell to arrive in Dublin just before the coronation, with up to 2,000 troops supplied by Margaret, under a captain named Martin Schwartz. Ten days later, they landed at Furness in Lancashire, crossed the Pennines and marched south. Meanwhile, Henry had propitiated heaven by a quick trip to the shrine of the Virgin at Walsingham in Norfolk, before heading to Kenilworth Castle – a convenient central location for him to wait to be informed of the rebels' path. His mother, wife and son joined him there. While some former Yorkists, including Sir Thomas Broughton, joined Lincoln, and his force eventually numbered around 6,000, Henry probably had about double that number – many supplied by Derby. He also had the support of the Earl of Shrewsbury; George, 5th Lord Grey of Ruthyn (married to Anne Woodville); Cecily's half-brother Edward, Lord Hastings; and Sir Edward Woodville, who led an advance cavalry troop. Oxford and Rhys ap Thomas led the vanguard, with Bedford commanding the centre, and Henry himself the rearward. Only Oxford's contingent took part in the battle near East Stoke, in Nottinghamshire on 16 June. It was a fierce confrontation in which the royal troops were victorious. Lincoln was killed, Lovell disappeared, and the Irish troops, who had no armour, suffered badly, dying in their thousands. Simnel was captured – he was later paraded in London at St Paul's, alongside the real Warwick, before being given a job in the king's kitchens, whence he was eventually promoted to be the king's falconer.

Henry having won his victory, Dorset was released from the Tower and returned to his position on the king's council. He was described by Vergil as 'a good, prudent man', but never had the level of closeness to Henry that Oxford or Bedford enjoyed.

Following the Battle of Stoke, Henry felt a little more secure on his throne, but the granting of a subsidy in January 1489 led to rioting in the north, in the worst of which Northumberland was killed. The rebels, perhaps terrified that they had put themselves outside the royal mercy, encouraged a more widespread rising. They were not dynastically motivated – there was no call for Henry to be replaced by any Yorkist claimant – but it was still a threat that Henry took seriously. He led substantial numbers of troops north,[10] being joined by a swathe of peers. Although his uncle, 3rd Earl Rivers, is named among Henry's men, there is no record of Dorset being involved. The rebels dispersed, and Henry progressed to York, where he was seated in majesty, and heard several days of trials at the Guildhall. A few men were hanged, and around 1,500 pardoned. Henry departed, leaving the Earl of Surrey as his lieutenant in the North. Surrey, once a close adherent of Richard III, and the man who had led Lord Hastings to the meeting that ended in his death, had sworn allegiance to Henry, and been released from the Tower. There followed eighteen months or so of calm for the royal family, during which time Elizabeth of York bore a daughter, Margaret.

6

Royal Service

There's no trust, no faith, no honesty in men; all perjured,
All forsworn, all naught, all dissemblers.

Shakespeare, *Romeo and Juliet*, III ii

Thinking that domestic matters were running smoothly, Henry had more leisure to consider European affairs. His old friend Francis, Duke of Brittany had died in 1488, leaving eleven-year-old Anne as his heir. Within the duchy were opposing camps – those who wanted an accommodation with France, and those, led by Anne herself, who were determined to escape Charles's clutches. In February 1490, Henry entered the Treaty of Redon with Brittany, giving him control of the port of Morlaix to ship troops in to aid the duchess. Throughout that year, the English fleet, led by Lord Willoughby, harassed French shipping in and around the Breton coast. A substantial force of 8,000 men was raised, under the Earl of Shrewsbury, to defend the duchy, and on 11 September Henry entered a treaty with Maximilian for a joint attack on France. As an indication of their alliance, Maximilian received the Order of the Garter, and shortly afterward married Anne of Brittany by proxy. As usual, Maximilian was strapped for cash, disorganised, and unreliable: when French troops took Rennes on 4 April 1491, he was nowhere to be found. Henry's efforts to help were not exhaustive, and his troops were repulsed from the Normandy coast, leaving him to consider the risks of all-out war with France to protect Brittany at a time when Maximilian was concentrating on conflict in Hungary.

A more immediate threat for Henry than French expansionism was the news that another young man had been garnering support in Ireland, claiming to be Richard, Duke of York, the younger of Edward IV's sons, last seen entering the Tower in June 1483, aged nine. Later, the man said that his name was Peter or 'Perkin' Warbeck, and that he was a native of Flanders. He is called that here for ease and because, although I acknowledge the possibility that he was Richard, I think it unlikely.

In 1483–85, the belief that Richard had ordered his nephews murdered was sufficiently common among supporters of the House of York that Henry was able to win the throne. However, no one knew for certain, nor knows now, whether either or both boys were dead. It was the most likely scenario, but the actions of Henry VII and many former Yorkists over the years suggest that they feared – in Henry's case – or hoped – in others – that the younger boy had survived. By 1492, Richard would have been sixteen – a period of life when a child changes, not necessarily beyond all recognition, but enough to make any positive visual identification uncertain. The claimant seemed to be about the right age. He had arrived in Cork on a ship from Portugal in the company of a silk merchant, so, perhaps not surprisingly, was well dressed. There, he was allegedly spontaneously acclaimed as the Earl of Warwick, but he denied this. Actually, he said, he was Richard of York.

S. B. Chrimes, Henry VII's chief biographer, believes the whole impersonation was a plot hatched by Charles VIII of France, who, having been surprised at how successful he had been in destabilising England by supporting Henry against Richard, now wanted to repeat his action to prevent Henry interfering in Brittany. According to Warbeck's own confession, he had been a member of the household of Sir Edward Bampton. Bampton had arrived in England in the 1470s as a destitute Portuguese Jewish immigrant. He converted to Christianity and had a spectacular career under Edward IV and Richard III (being one of the men sent to pursue Sir Edward Woodville in 1483). Bampton left England after Bosworth and continued his mercantile interests between Burgundy and Portugal. A familiar face at the Yorkist court, he could easily have coached Warbeck, or even worked with Margaret of York on a scheme. Whoever came up with the idea, there were enough Yorkists in Ireland to bring the plot to fruition. Warbeck was taken to the court of Charles VIII, where he was recognised as Duke of York, although with little fanfare – Charles would have weighed up the risk of provoking Henry into war by vigorous support of the pretender, compared with biding his time. Giving countenance to Warbeck was probably a miscalculation on Charles's part – Henry took it as sufficient provocation to pursue the invasion of France he had agreed with Maximilian.

Henry did not have the grandiose ambitions of his Plantagenet predecessors. Despite officially claiming the French crown, he was not aiming at the reconquest of France, but at containing French power, which, after Brittany's capital, Nantes, fell to the French and Anne was forced to marry Charles VIII, looked dangerously resurgent.[1] In the spring and summer of 1492, Henry began thorough preparations to pursue a full-scale campaign in France. Henry is not generally thought of as a military king but he was victorious in all the military engagements he was involved in and planned diligently. Bedford and Oxford were again to be Henry's chief commanders, along with Sir Edward Poynings as naval commander. Among others called to fight was Dorset, but it appears that

Henry was not entirely convinced of his loyalty, and the marquis was obliged to enter into a complex set of bonds with the king.

The whole issue of bonds and recognisances is one for which Henry VII is much criticised. A recognisance was a written recognition that an individual owed money to the Crown, which the king might request to be paid at any time. A bond was a promise to do something, with a financial penalty for failure, secured on the individual's land. It had been common practice for an individual to give a bond when he received an office. No money changed hands immediately, and if the office were conducted effectively, the bond was returned. If not, it became a debt, and the usual legal remedies could be pursued. Henry extended this use of bonds to bind his nobles to good behaviour, and often required them to bring fellow sureties – 'mainprisors' – who would be required to pay heavy fines if the individual defaulted. This threat of financial loss encouraged peers to keep a watchful eye on each other. This strategy felt oppressive because it was corrosive of trust between friends and families, and the threat of the financial axe was always hovering – although it seems preferable to the physical axe, which fell much more frequently in the reign of Henry VIII.

On 4 June 1492, Dorset received a general pardon for unspecified offences. General pardons were common – they did not indicate that the recipient had deliberately been guilty of anything specific but protected them from past misdemeanours being dragged up. In return for the assurance of royal favour, Dorset was obliged to enter into a very onerous bond. First, he had to give up all grants made by Edward IV, other than those directly connected with the marquisate of Dorset; in particular, he had to repudiate any property agreements concerning the lands of the dukedom of Exeter and the wardship, custody and marriage of Edward, Earl of Warwick. Second, he had to convey to twelve feoffees 'all castles, honours, manors, lands, rents and services, whereof he, or Cecily his wife [was] seised, or any other person to his use or by recovery', with the exception of two manors in Essex (Stobbyng and Fairested), which could be left in the hands of their current farmers to the use of Dorset and Cecily, and for the performance of Dorset's will. An additional clause allowed manors to be sold to pay a ransom if he were captured abroad. Third, he must not 'do misprision (concealment of treason) to the king's person, but disclose such treason to his highness in writing'. Fourth, he was to 'labour' to have his or his wife's remaining lands in Lancashire included. All of the properties thus enfeoffed would be forfeit if he offended the king. If Dorset kept his nose clean, the agreement would cease on his death, and his son would be permitted to inherit, without hindrance.

There was more – Dorset had to grant Henry the marriage of his son and heir, who was to be 'found (maintained) in the king's service at the cost of the marquis'. If the boy were returned unmarried before he was nineteen, Dorset was to pay £1,000. Finally, he had to pay a recognisance of £1,000 immediately and it may have been to raise this sum that

Dorset sold three manors to the Archbishop of Canterbury for £120 in September 1492. He had to find mainprisors for £10,000 and replace any of them at three weeks' notice. If he were found guilty of any default, he would have to pay another £1,000.

This agreement was extraordinarily harsh, but there is no evidence that Dorset suffered any immediate financial difficulty beyond the initial £1,000 and the loss of his son's marriage. Although the lands were now enfeoffed, he and Cecily would continue to enjoy their use, so long as he did nothing to forfeit them. He certainly had no problem finding mainprisors: fifty-five men were willing to support him – including, surprisingly, his uncle Edward Grey, now Viscount Lisle, perhaps finally reconciled to Dorset having the Ferrers inheritance, and Grey's wife, Joan. Lisle, together with more distant Grey cousins – the Earl of Kent, Lord Grey of Codnor and Lord Grey of Wilton – contributed to mainprises totalling £9,225. There was also support from the bishops of Ely, Lincoln and Worcester, three of Henry's most favoured councillors. The negotiations must have taken some time, as the mainprisors were enrolled on 19 and 22 May 1492, two weeks before the indenture itself.

Dorset was not the only man who had to make this sort of arrangement with the king, but this was particularly onerous, perhaps indicating that Henry feared Dorset might believe Warbeck to be his half-brother and involve himself in the conspiracy. The king was a cautious man – even with little to go on, it was better to tie up Dorset and his mainprisors so tightly that the king would be informed immediately of any approach from Warbeck's backers. The core of the agreement was enacted in the parliament of 1495, but over time it was modified to make it less harsh. At around the time of the original bond, Henry paid Dorset £100 for a ring of gold – perhaps another contribution to the £1,000 immediately required.[2]

Just before being obliged to enter this cumbersome bond, in March 1492, Dorset inherited the property of his uncle Richard, 3rd Earl Rivers. Rivers had no children – although he did have a wife, Joan, who predeceased him[3] – and so he bequeathed everything to his nephew. It was not a huge estate: four manors in Kent, worth around £60 per annum, a couple of other parcels of land, the manor and advowson of Theydon in Essex and some property in Calais.

Three months later, on 8 June 1492, Dorset suffered a much greater personal loss – the death of his mother, Elizabeth, the dowager queen. So far as can be inferred, the bonds of family affection had been strong and Dorset is likely to have grieved her sincerely. Elizabeth's will, made three months prior to her death, requested her 'dearest daughter, the Queen's Grace and [her] son, Thomas, Marquis of Dorset, to put their good wills and help for the performance of this [her] testament'. She had no lands to bequeath to any of her children – not because, as has been speculated, Henry VII ill-treated her, but because she had never possessed any lands of her own. All her interests in, and income from, land, both as Lady Grey and as queen, were for life only, and died with her, as did her pension from Henry. Elizabeth expressed a wish to be buried beside Edward IV with minimal pomp; having once been a woman who thrived on the magnificence of the world, she had come to realise that it was but dust and ashes. Such a stipulation was not unusual in the wills of noble ladies.[4] The few possessions Elizabeth did have were to be used to pay her debts and 'for the health of her soul' – that is, payments for the performance of Masses for the dead – although, if her children wanted any of her goods, they should have the preference.

In accordance with her wishes, the funeral was not extravagant. Her body was accompanied to Windsor by an attendant named Grace, apparently an illegitimate daughter of her late husband's, a Mr Haute (presumably one of her Haute cousins), and her chaplain, Dr Brent. Her coffin was immediately put into the tomb with that of Edward IV, overseen by one of the priests of the college. The following day, the Bishop of Rochester came to offer the funeral Mass. A hearse was set over the tomb, draped in black cloth of gold and surrounded with candlesticks of wood and silver-gilt. The next day, three of her daughters, Anne, Katherine and Bridget (who was a nun at Dartford), came to pay their respects, accompanied by Cecily Dorset and one of Cecily's daughters. Two of the late queen's nieces were also in attendance: a daughter of Katherine, Duchess of Buckingham and Bedford, probably the elder, Lady Elizabeth Stafford; and Lady (Elizabeth) Herbert, daughter of Mary Woodville. Queen Elizabeth did not attend – she was awaiting the birth of another child and it is likely that her sister, Cicely of York, was with her.[5]

The menfolk came as well: Dorset; Henry, Earl of Essex, the late queen's nephew; and Viscount Welles, husband of Cicely. According to the disgusted chronicler, who thought the whole show paltry, the dirge was not sung by twelve poor men in black, as was customary, but by twelve old men 'dressed in the many-coloured garments of poverty'. On the Wednesday, a college canon, Mr Vaughan, sang Our Lady Mass, while Dorset knelt at the head of the hearse. The marquis offered a piece of gold, while Anne of York offered the Mass penny, preceded to the altar by her officer of arms, with her train carried by Dame Katherine Grey. This offering entitled Lady Anne to the carpet and the cushion from under the head end of the hearse. Lord Welles offered on behalf of his wife, then all the other gentlemen, the knights of Windsor, the dean and canons, yeomen and officers of arms. Dorset paid the funeral costs.[6]

Over the summer, naval warfare continued, but Henry was not yet ready to embark his army. Part of the delay was down to Maximilian's failure to provide the promised support. Considering Maximilian's record in this regard, it is unlikely that Henry ever anticipated substantial help. Nevertheless, there were risks in attacking alone, which had to be weighed against the likelihood that, if he failed to do anything, the English populace would be angry at having been taxed for a campaign that did not materialise. Henry decided to go ahead, and in early October crossed to Calais. Hostilities opened with the English army besieging Boulogne. Charles VIII, keen to pursue his far more exciting claims in Italy than to get involved in a muddy campaign in northern France, copied Louis XI's trick of buying off the English king – something that Henry was probably well aware was a likely outcome. With both kings eager to negotiate, it did not take long for a treaty to be agreed – that of Etaples. Dorset's was the first of the twenty-two signatures on the document recommending the terms to the king, just as it had been on the 1475 treaty.[7] Henry, well satisfied with his show of strength, departed with a pension of 50,000 crowns and the promise that Perkin Warbeck would no longer receive succour from the French.

Despite his failure to keep his end of their agreement, Maximilian affected to be outraged at Henry's treaty with the French and welcomed Warbeck to Burgundy with open arms. Margaret of York was thrilled and claimed to recognise the boy immediately as her nephew. She had, presumably, seen him in 1480 on her state visit to England, when he was seven. Given the formality of court life, and the little part that children played in it, it is unlikely she spent any prolonged time with him, so immediate recognition twelve years later sounds like the triumph of hope. Margaret certainly did hope, and perhaps believe, the boy was her nephew, and was willing to ensure that he was as like a prince of the House of York as he could be made by training.

*

Just as he had emulated Edward IV in his negotiations with France, in 1493, Henry again emulated him by sending his eldest son, Dorset's nephew Arthur, Prince of Wales, to Ludlow as nominal head of the Council for Wales and the Marches. Arthur was accompanied by a full show of royal and noble strength – Bedford, Dorset, the Earl of Arundel, Lord Bergavenny and Sir William Stanley, the Lord Chamberlain, all trooped to Hereford Castle to hear a commission of the peace in late April. A bevy of lesser men from the Marches sat with them. This was old ground for Dorset, and he remained with Arthur until the end of the summer, returning to London by October.

Henry's action was intended to make a dynastic point, necessary in the face of the growing threat from Warbeck. The young man had been invited to attend the funeral of Maximilian's father, the Emperor Frederick III, presented as the rightful king of England. In retaliation, Henry banned trade with Burgundy – a punishing blow both to the Burgundians and to the English merchants. Security was stepped up at home, and, to take people's minds off Warbeck and confuse the issue, Henry created a new Duke of York – his second son, another Henry, born in June 1491, whose christening Dorset, Cecily, and their eldest son, Thomas, Lord Harington, had attended.[8]

The creation of Prince Henry as Duke of York was one of the magnificent set-piece pageants of Henry VII's reign, and Dorset and his family took a prominent part. A great joust to 'honour the said creation and feast; and for the pleasure of our sovereign lord, the queen's grace and the ladies'[9] was proclaimed. The festivities lasted several days, beginning on 27 October 1494 with the king, the queen and 'my lady the king's mother' sailing downriver from Sheen to Westminster, while three-year-old Prince Henry was transported upriver from Eltham, accompanied by a festive flotilla, bearing the mayor and aldermen of London. Prior to Prince Henry's ennoblement, he, Lord Harington and twenty-one others were dubbed knights of the Bath. The complex ceremony began with the budding knights waiting on the king at supper: Prince Henry served the king with his towel, Harington offered 'sey' (perhaps salt), while Lord Clifford offered the basin, Lord FitzWarren, the water, and Lord Dacre of the South, the king's potage.

Once night fell, baths and beds were prepared for each knight. The first, in the king's own closet, was for Prince Henry, who was bathed, then royally dressed. The Earl of Oxford read the patent of knighthood, after which the king crossed the prince's shoulder with holy water and kissed it. All then processed to the queen's closet, where Harington and Clifford received the same treatment. The remaining twenty knights were bathed and knighted in the Parliament Chamber. The king having done his part, the knights dressed in the outfits of hermits and went to the chapel, where they were fed spices and sweetmeats; each tipped the Sergeant of Confectionery a rose noble (a coin worth 10s). After that, they retired to the beds arranged in each of the chambers. Early the following morning, each knight was shriven, and heard Mass. After Mass, they gave their russet gowns to the minstrels before returning to bed for another sleep.

On waking again, each paid a sum consistent with his rank to the Sergeant of Arms and the officers. Harington paid the highest fee, £10; the barons paid £9 and the lower ranks 20s. They clubbed together to create a 'common purse' for the usher, the porter and the esquires of honour. The earls of Oxford, Northumberland and Essex, and Lord Daubeney helped the new knights to robe, starting with the prince, followed by Harington. Dressed, the knights trooped through St Stephen's Chapel to the foot of the stairs leading to the Star Chamber, where they mounted their horses. It is not clear if they rode somewhere, or just waited, mounted. Lord William Courtenay (soon to marry Katherine of York) brought Prince Henry a sword and spurs. He then carried the little boy into his father's presence. The king gave the right spur to the Duke of Buckingham and the left to Dorset, to fit on the prince's heels. The king affixed the sword to his son's hip, and dubbed him knight. The rest of the knights had the same treatment. Sir William Sandys led the procession, carrying the prince to the chapel, where all the new knights offered their swords at the altar. On leaving the chapel, the new-made knights' spurs, along with another rose noble, were given in tips. The knights dined in the Parliament Chamber, served by their squires, taking advantage of the special licence they had from the king to eat meat on a fast day. The day was still not finished. After eating, they took off their mantles, girdles, surcoats and coifs, giving them to the officers of arms. Finally, they clad themselves in blue cloaks with hoods, then sent Sir Robert Litton to the king to give their thanks.

The following day, the king came in state to the Parliament Chamber and stood under his cloth of estate, flanked by Morton, now Cardinal Archbishop of Canterbury, and his chief nobles. Awaiting him were the other peers in their parliament robes, the mayor and aldermen of London, and the judges. Garter king-of-arms entered the chamber and presented a patent of nobility to the king. The Earl of Suffolk followed, carrying a sword; Northumberland, coming after, bore a rod; then Derby, carrying a rich robe of estate, furred with ermine, and a coronet. Shrewsbury came in with the prince in his arms, and Dorset and Arundel led him up to the king. Oliver King, Bishop of Exeter and the king's secretary (as once he had been secretary to Edward IV), took the patent of nobility from Garter and read it aloud. The prince was named as Duke of York, with a grant of £1,000 a year.

The ceremony complete, the king, wearing his crown, went to the chapel, followed by the nobles – there was some arguing over who should take precedence, but Henry gave the final word, favouring the Earl of Suffolk over the Earl of Kent, and the Lord Grey above the Lord Clifford. The archbishop, dressed in his pontifical robes, offered the Mass, assisted by most of the other bishops and abbots. Following the Mass there was a grand procession, with the various earls carrying symbolic accoutrements – Arundel led, carrying the royal sword, then Derby, bearing his staff as Constable of England. Shrewsbury came next, carrying the little duke, with coronet, robe and golden rod. More nobles and ecclesiastics followed, then came the king, in his crown, followed by the dukes of Bedford and Buckingham, the Earl of Northumberland and the other lords, including Dorset. The judges were next, and finally the ladies, led by the queen in her crown, followed by the king's mother with a coronet, and the various duchesses, countesses and ladies in order of rank, with Cecily following the duchesses. Dorset was honoured by Henry creating a new officer-of-arms, Dorset Herald. That done, Henry dined, with only the Archbishop of Canterbury sharing his table. Largesse was cried for the prince, naming him as Duke of York, Lieutenant of Ireland, Earl Marshal, Marshal of England and Warden of the Cinque Ports.

Over the following days, the jousts and tourneys were held. Two prizes were offered, with one for jousting and the other for tourneying – rings of gold set with a ruby for the first, and a diamond for the second. The winners were the earls of Suffolk and Essex, with various others also doing well. The winning earls were in their early twenties. Dorset did not take part: past forty, his jousting days were behind him, while Harington was too young. They were both present at the grand feast that closed the proceedings, as was Cecily. No Lady Harington is listed, but the lists are incomplete, so we cannot be sure that Harington was still unmarried. Given that Henry had taken his wardship, it seems reasonable to expect him to have had a marriage in mind.

Despite this show of unity, Henry was not above employing spies and informers in the houses of his nobles. Since listeners seldom hear good of themselves, Henry should not have been surprised to learn that even in the royal household there were those who believed, or wanted to believe, that Warbeck was the missing Richard of York. Sir William Stanley, Lord Chamberlain, whose support at Bosworth had swung the battle in Henry's favour, was one of them. He had been told by Sir Robert Clifford, who had seen the boy in Flanders, that Clifford was certain Warbeck was the duke. Stanley had been a faithful supporter of Edward IV, and apparently declared to Clifford that, if he knew the boy was indeed York, he would never bear arms against him. He did not say positively that he would fight for him, but the ambiguity in a man so close to Henry was shocking and hurtful.

Stanley was arrested and tried. He admitted his fault, which seems slight, but if he hoped that his past service and his honesty would save him, he was wrong. He was executed on 18 February 1495. The later discovery of £10,000 and a Yorkist livery collar at his castle of Holt certainly did not do anything to suggest that Henry had taken the wrong action. That he took it as much in sorrow as anger is indicated by him sending Stanley £10 on the day of his execution to tip the headsman – the customary incentive to do the job swiftly. The king also paid for the funeral and burial at Syon Abbey, at a cost of £15 9s. How Derby felt about the death of a brother to whom he had been close can only be surmised. Certainly, there was no overt cooling of his relationship with his son-in-law, and Henry undertook an extended visit to Derby and Margaret at Knowsley Castle in the summer of 1495.[10]

Henry sent agents abroad, who reported that Warbeck was the son of a man 'of low degree' from Tournai. This pleasing information was quickly disseminated by the king, who requested that the court of Burgundy cease supporting the pretender, dispatching Sir Edward Poynings and William Warham (later Chancellor and Archbishop of Canterbury) to give his request gravitas. According to Vergil, the two men were instructed to point out to the Burgundians that Richard of York and his brother had been murdered by their uncle – for what would be the point of killing one brother, but not the other? Philip and his advisors decided that they did not wish to offend Henry further, and agreed to desist from supporting Warbeck. As for Margaret, they lamented, she was not under their control – if she wished to spend her considerable dower on supporting Warbeck, they could not prevent it.

If Dorset's recognisance of 1492 was related in any way to Warbeck, it seems to have satisfied Henry, especially as he paid the required £100 regularly each Whitsuntide and Hallowtide.[11] In 1495, he was still in possession of his £35 annuity from 1475, and the offices he held were exempted from an act of resumption of later that year, covering Wales and the lands of the Prince of Wales. He and Henry were on good terms, even shooting at the butts together. On 26 February 1495, Lord de la Warr gave a mainprise of 500 marks for Dorset's loyalty during life, but too much should not be made of this; a few days later, the Archbishop of Canterbury himself, Henry's chief minister, along with the Bishop of Salisbury and several others, gave bonds of 500 marks each.

On 18 April 1495, Dorset was summoned to the parliament Henry had called to make further preparations for fending off the Warbeck conspirators – the affair was becoming more than a minor irritation for the king. On 3 July, with a small fleet of eleven vessels, provided by Margaret of York, Warbeck landed at Deal in Kent. His followers received short shrift from the residents, so Warbeck did not disembark. Ten days later, Dorset was named in the commission of the peace for Kent, to deal with fallout from the attempted landing. The disheartened Warbeck sailed to Munster, in Ireland, where he had first found followers. Here, he was somewhat luckier, in that the Earl of Desmond gave him support, but once again, he failed to achieve anything when his siege of Waterford was raised by a royalist force under Sir Edward Poynings.

Warbeck moved on to Scotland, where the king, James IV, was delighted to have a stick with which to beat his southern neighbour. Whether or not James really believed Warbeck was York, he affected to do so, publicly acknowledging him as Richard of York, rightful king of England, and giving him a noble bride, Lady Katherine Gordon, daughter of the Earl of Huntly. The marriage took place in Edinburgh around 13 January 1496, accompanied by a tournament, with the groom dressed in an outfit given him by James. Probably, James did not care one way or the other about Warbeck's origins. If he could invade England and help Warbeck to the throne, he would have a grateful ally, with a Scots queen. If Warbeck failed, James was not much worse off – low-level warfare with England was a continuing state of affairs anyway. Having the pretender in his hand would give him a negotiating tool in discussions for a long-term peace. Henry had offered a noble bride as part of a peace treaty, but James wanted a royal one – the king's own daughter – so James would make what use he could of the pretender.

James's response to Warbeck was also germane to his concurrent negotiations with the sovereigns of Spain, Ferdinand of Aragon and Isabella of Castile. They had promised their youngest daughter, Katharine, to Prince Arthur, and were concerned about the threat posed by Warbeck. James assured them he would drop Warbeck and agree a treaty with England if he could thereby secure the hand of a Spanish princess for himself. Given that the Spanish had run out of daughters, they could not accept James's offer. Consequently, James used Warbeck to stage an invasion of England. They crossed the border on 20 September, and the Scots began the usual raiding and pillaging that characterised border warfare. Warbeck was horrified – fearing that such treatment of his 'subjects' would not endear them to him. James pointed out that no one seemed that pleased to see him anyway – there had been no uprising in his favour. Warbeck withdrew into Scotland, leaving James to carry on as usual. It was a successful raid – James destroyed a number of English border fortresses before retreating across the Tweed, hearing that an army under the Earl of Surrey was en route.

While the outraged Henry was contemplating his best course of action against James and Warbeck, Dorset and Cecily were continuing with their plans for their children. Dorset had purchased the wardship and marriage of Walter Devereux, son and heir of Lord Ferrers of Chartley, from the king for £200, payable in instalments.[12] Walter, born around 1488, was the son of Dorset's cousin Cecily Bourchier, daughter of Anne Woodville and Sir William Bourchier. The Devereux family were favoured by Henry VII – Walter's great-aunt Anne, Countess of Pembroke had been the wife of Henry's guardian in the 1460s, and her family had protected him after Pembroke's execution by Warwick in 1468. Walter was to marry Dorset's daughter Lady Mary. Dorset also came to an agreement on 20 May 1496 about the marriage of his daughter Lady Eleanor to Sir John Arundell of Lanherne, a leading man in Cornwall, and later the duchy's receiver-general. One might have expected Dorset to have wanted a title for his eldest daughter – this suggests either that Eleanor was not the eldest, or that the marriage was, perhaps, at the instigation of the king.

Arundell's father had been a supporter of Henry's before Bosworth, and an alliance with the daughter of a marquis would be a convenient way of rewarding the family at no cost to the king. However, there is no information on the point, so it may be that Dorset wanted to consolidate his influence in the south-west. The document refers to an earlier contract, so probably indicates the actual marriage date, giving Eleanor a latest birth date of May 1484, and a more likely birth date of 1481–82.[13] Eleanor was to have a dowry of 1,000 marks, and in return she was to have an estate of her own, to the value of £20 per annum, as well as jointure lands with her husband, of which a third would be seised to the use of Eleanor as her dower, should her husband predecease her. Dorset had paid 200 marks down the previous Christmas and was to pay the remaining 800 marks before 6 May 1497. As surety, various of Dorset and Cecily's lands were enfeoffed to the use of the Arundell couple, until the 800 marks was paid. Since these lands were among those enfeoffed in the bond of 1492, the king's permission must have been obtained. Both Dorset and Arundell gave a bond of 1,000 marks for performance and there were several other sureties.

Dorset's financial dealings in 1496 do not seem to have been inhibited by the requirement from Henry for yet another bond for good behaviour. In September 1496, nine men put up mainprises for Dorset totalling £2,776 13s 4d.[14] The mainprisors, who were called to swear at Okehampton on 26 August, were all West Country men, headed by the Earl of Devon, husband of Dorset's niece Katherine of York, and including Sir James Audley of Audley.

As though the new bond were not financial pressure enough for Dorset, he and everyone else in the country faced a large tax bill in 1497. Henry was preparing for war against Scotland in earnest, and he was voted a large subsidy by Parliament. While Parliament, as a central body, could see, or at least be persuaded of, the necessity to protect the northern border, the men of Cornwall had little or no interest in a part of the country so far away. They contended that the subsidy contravened the Stannary Charter of 1305, which exempted Cornwall from certain types of tax. Dorset had lost his office of Lord Warden of the Stannaries under Richard III, and Henry had not regranted it. The office was in the hands of Sir John Halliwell, who had already had to manage disputes with the king. Eager to protect their rights, the Cornish rose up in rebellion under Thomas Flamank (whose father had been one of the commissioners charged with raising the levy) and Michael An Gof, and marched on London, protesting, as was the custom, against the king's 'evil counsellors', specifically, Sir Reginald Bray and Cardinal Morton. While the county of Devon remained largely unbothered, support was gained in Somerset, and James Tuchet, Lord Audley, joined the rebels. This was probably the same man as had stood as a mainprisor for Dorset the previous autumn.[15] The reasons for Audley's disaffection are unknown – perhaps he was genuinely sympathetic to the plight of the Cornish.

By 13 June, a rumoured 13,000 rebels were at Guildford. Henry had only 8,000 troops; they had been mustered for Scotland under Lord Daubeney, but were quickly redeployed, while the queen and the royal children were sent to safety in the Tower. There was a brief skirmish in Surrey, before the rebels encamped on Blackheath, capturing the river crossing at nearby Deptford. Henry himself gathered another force in the Thames valley, and joined Daubeney by 16 June. Dissension broke out in the rebels' ranks – submit to the king now, for a pardon, or press on? About a third decided that discretion was the better part of valour and began the long trek home. Henry, detail conscious as ever, sent a wing of his army to the rear of the rebels. There was a short bout of fighting at Deptford Bridge, but Henry's forces were triumphant and the rebels surrendered – estimates as to the number killed vary from a couple hundred to a couple thousand. The king rode into the city to give thanks at St Paul's.

Henry was not bloodthirsty, but he was ruthless. The three leaders were executed – Flamank and Michael An Gof by hanging (they were spared drawing and quartering) and Audley by beheading. All the other rebels were allowed to live. Henry's preferred punishments were financial – exorbitant fines were handed out to anyone involved. To quote Henry's early biographer Sir Francis Bacon, 'The less blood he drew, the more he took of treasure.' Some biographies of Henry VII mention that Dorset had command of one of the sections of men at Deptford, but I cannot find any original source that places him there. The earls of Oxford and Suffolk commanded the van and the centre guard. Perhaps the rearguard, which did not go into action, was led by Dorset.

Smarting under the fines, the people of Cornwall remained disgruntled, making it a suitable destination for Warbeck, banished from Scotland by James IV after the Scottish king had secured a marriage to Princess Margaret. Warbeck landed in the west of the county in September and was proclaimed as Richard IV at Bodmin. Leaving his 'queen' at St Michael's Mount, he marched towards Exeter, gathering significant support en route, but failed to take the city. He continued to Taunton, but either he did not receive as much support as he had anticipated, or the whole enterprise overwhelmed him: hearing of Daubeney's approach, he abandoned his army to seek sanctuary in Beaulieu Abbey.

Winkled out by the king's forces, Warbeck made a confession – true or not – that he was the son of a Tournai man and not the Duke of York. Henry followed Daubeney to the south-west. On 3 November, he was at Ottery St Mary, around 10 miles east of Exeter, and shortly after he was at Newenham Abbey at Axminster. Cecily was a patroness of both these churches, which were close to her chief manor at Shute, and Henry may well have stayed there, in the comfortable surroundings created by Cecily's extensive refurbishment of the old manor. In the aftermath of the rebellion, Henry treated Warbeck and his wife leniently. They had rooms at Sheen Palace, and Lady Katherine was admitted among the queen's attendants. But life in a gilded cage did not suit Warbeck, who tried to escape. Caught, he was imprisoned in the Tower of London and executed in 1499, along with the real (and blameless) Earl of Warwick, under the fig-leaf that they had conspired to escape together. The execution of Warbeck and Warwick was the price Henry had to pay for Prince Arthur's marriage to the Spanish princess Katharine of Aragon. Warwick's death was a stain on Henry's character that apparently haunted him ever after. What Dorset and Cecily thought of the judicial murder of their former ward can only be guessed.

*

During the 1490s, Dorset began renovations at his old family seat of Groby Hall in Leicestershire, which was set in a park with a circumference of 6 miles and contained a lake. The village was described as 'poor' and the old castle had fallen into disrepair, so the ditch was filled in for a garden, and work began on a gatehouse, probably in the fashionable style of the late 1490s – red brick with two towers, or perhaps like the stone gatehouse Cecily was building at Shute. Dorset undertook various land exchanges to consolidate the area around Groby, including disposing of land around Grafton, inherited from Earl Rivers. Before long, Dorset had begun a far more impressive house, a few miles away at Bradgate, and it was to this property, at Christmas 1499, that he invited a young priest named Thomas Wolsey, who was a Fellow of Magdalen College, Oxford, and had been his sons' tutor. Magdalen was a new style of foundation, in that it was designed to educate not just men studying for degrees but younger scholars, known as Commoners, usually the sons of rich men.

It is not surprising that Dorset chose Magdalen – it was patronised by Edward IV and Elizabeth Woodville, and his uncle Lionel, Bishop of Salisbury, had been its chancellor. The boys tutored by Wolsey must have been one or more of Dorset's younger sons – Richard, John, Anthony, Leonard, George or Edward – as Lord Harington would have been too old. Wolsey remained with the Dorsets until mid-January 1500, and according to George Cavendish, later Wolsey's Gentleman Usher and his biographer, impressed Dorset so much that he received a benefice – the Bonville parish of Limington in Somerset. The chantry chapel there is dedicated to St Leonard, and this may perhaps lie behind the choice of Leonard as a Christian name for one of the Grey sons.[16] Despite these activities in Leicestershire, Dorset and Cecily were still spending time at court. In 1499, Henry paid for Dorset's livery gown for the annual Garter celebration: 5 yards of blue cloth for a gown and hood, at 8s the yard; 110 garters of silk, costing 45s 10d; and 5 timbers (a measure of fur) of miniver pure, at 16d per timber.[17]

In June 1500, King Henry and Queen Elizabeth travelled to Calais to meet Archduke Philip of Burgundy, to conclude another treaty with Burgundy and Austria. Dorset was not in Henry's retinue, but Lord Harington was. Dorset's absence may have been owing to declining health. On 30 August 1501, while in London, rather than at home in Leicestershire, he made his will. Three weeks later, Dorset breathed his last. His will was long and complex, suggesting that although he may have been stricken in body, he was perfectly sound in mind. After the usual bequeathing of his soul to the Lord, and requests for intercession from the Blessed Virgin and saints, his first instruction was for his burial. His chosen resting place was in front of the Holy Trinity in the collegiate church of Astley. He requested 100 Masses for his soul from each of the four orders of friars in London, and the sum of 100 marks was to be distributed among the poor at the funeral. The hospital of Lutterworth that he had patronised was appropriated to Astley, to pay the dean and canons to pray for the souls of his stepfather, his mother, his father, his wife, and all Christian souls, as well as his own. Further arrangements for the dean and canons were minute and expensive. There were also alms for the Friars Observant of Greenwich and exhibitions for scholars at both Oxford and Cambridge universities.

Having dealt with his soul and other charitable matters, Dorset passed on to his children. Each of his unmarried daughters was to receive £1,000 towards her dowry – a third more than Eleanor had received in 1496. The marriage between Mary and Lord Ferrers had been performed, but not yet consummated, so if the groom repudiated the match on attaining the legal age for consummation of fourteen, then Mary was to have £1,000 for another marriage. The marriage between his daughter Cicely and Lord Sutton's son John Dudley had been agreed, but not performed – hardly surprising, as the groom was probably only around seven years old. If the marriage didn't go ahead, Sutton was to return the element of the dowry already paid so that Cicely might marry elsewhere. Had Dorset known that Cicely's husband would turn out to be feckless and lose his patrimony, he might have made other arrangements. He also requested any debts that could be proved against him to be paid – in particular, money he owed to Dr Sutton of Walbrook for 'such stuff as [he] had of Queen Elizabeth [his] mother'. Cecily was appointed as executor, alongside neighbouring Leicestershire gentleman Sir William Skeffington, among others. The executors were to hold several properties, including the manor of Astley, for the performance of his legacies, while his other manors, including Groby and Bradgate, as well as his lands in Calais, were to pass immediately to his eldest son, Lord Harington, along with his plate and tapestries. Dorset could not have foreseen that his bequests would still be contributing to family quarrels nearly forty years later.

7

Marriages and Money

A son can bear with equanimity the loss of his father, but the loss of
his inheritance drives him to despair.

Niccolò Machiavelli

With the death of his father, Thomas, Lord Harington fell heir to the
marquisate of Dorset and the baronies of Groby and Astley. There are
no details of his childhood. His early childhood would have been spent
at his mother's properties in the south-west, where he probably remained
until Henry VII's accession. Subsequently, he may have been a Commoner
at Magdalen, like his brothers. He seems always to have associated
himself with Leicestershire and Warwickshire, rather than any of the
south-western counties where his mother's lands were, so after 1485 he
was probably largely at Groby or Astley. A suggestion that Harington was
with his father during Buckingham's rebellion of 1483, and subsequently
went into exile in Brittany, seems highly unlikely – why would Thomas
I have risked the life of his six-year-old son in such a fashion? The boy
was too young to take an active part in the rebellion and could only have
hampered any escape.

Harington's marital status in 1501 is uncertain. The *Dictionary of
National Biography* refers to a marriage to Eleanor St John, daughter of
Sir Oliver St John of Lydiard Tregoze, but I can find no contemporary
record. Such an alliance would have been entirely logical. Sir Oliver
St John was Lady Margaret Beaufort's half-brother, and a marriage that
would have given her niece the position of Lady Marquis of Dorset would
have been typical of Henry's pattern of promoting his mother's half-blood
relatives and integrating the various Yorkist and Lancastrian families. But
there are no references to a Lady Harington, nor is there any evidence
of children. It may be that there was a betrothal or marriage, but that
Eleanor died young.

As soon as his father's funeral was over, Harington began the necessary
administration to 'sue out his livery', that is pay the feudal 'fine' to his

superior lord – in his case the king – and receive formal confirmation of inheritance. He was permitted to pay the 500 mark fine in instalments and was granted livery of his lands on 18 November 1502. He will now be referred to as Dorset. Soon after his father's death, Dorset took part in the celebrations to mark the arrival in London of Katharine of Aragon, Prince Arthur's bride. This marriage was the most important political achievement of Henry VII's reign, and he arranged the whole magnificent spectacle to signal the parity of the English monarchy with those of France or Spain. Dorset, along with the Archbishop of York, the Bishop of Winton, the Earl of Essex, lords Strange, Bergavenny and Willoughby and Lord William Courtenay of Devon, attended Henry, Duke of York as he met his new sister-in-law at St George's Fields.

The wedding took place on 14 November at St Paul's, and was followed, in best mediaeval tradition, by a public bedding ceremony. Dorset and the other gentlemen led Arthur, in his night clothes, to the princess's chamber, and left him there to perform his new conjugal duties – a matter over which the gentlemen were later to be interrogated. Four days later, on 18 November, a great tournament was held at Westminster Palace to celebrate the wedding, presided over by the prince and princess. Arthur, even if he had not been the guest of honour, was too young at fifteen to take part. Jousters seem to have been at their peak in their early twenties. Dorset was one such – at twenty-four, he was in the prime of his physical strength. The man in charge of the tournament was the Comptroller of the Household, Sir Richard Guildford, yet another of Dorset's connections.[1] The 'challenger' was the Duke of Buckingham, a notable jouster, while Dorset was the first of the 'answerers'. After the festivities, Arthur returned to Ludlow, accompanied by Katharine.

Not long after the marriage of Arthur and Katharine, there was another great celebration at the English court – the proxy wedding of James IV of Scotland and Princess Margaret at the new palace of Richmond. The occasion was once again marked with jousting – this time, Dorset was the leader of the challengers, flanked by Essex, Lord William Courtenay, Sir John Peche, Sir John Neville and Guillaume de la Ryver. The answerers were Sir Roland Veyville, Sir John Carr, Charles Brandon and Reginald de Sechells.[2] Buckingham confined himself to entering the lists with his horse richly trapped and showing the audience his skill at performing 'gambades' – a type of dressage in which the horse leaps off the ground, a feat requiring enormous skill from both horse and rider. The ladies, including Cecily, ranking fifth after Queen Elizabeth, the new Queen of Scots, the Princess Mary and the Dowager Duchess of Norfolk, watched in admiration as the courses were run. The Queen of Scots presented the prizes to Brandon, Sechells and Carr, with Lord William Courtenay considered the best performer overall.

With these weddings, Henry VII's reign reached its apogee – from which it hurtled downward into a bleak and oppressive anti-climax.

Disaster struck in April 1502 when the court was stunned and horrified to receive the news that Prince Arthur was dead.[3] Within the year, Dorset's aunt Queen Elizabeth and her newborn daughter had followed Arthur to the grave. The king was distraught, and withdrew from sight for weeks, comforted only by the honour he paid Elizabeth in the pomp of her funeral. On the day after her death alone, 636 Masses were sung for her across London. The body was taken in procession to the chapel, from her apartments in the Tower, with Buckingham's sister Lady Elizabeth Stafford following, just as she had done for the queen's mother some ten years before. The Requiem Mass was performed by the king's chaplain, with Katherine of York as chief mourner. The body lay in state for ten days, with ladies, gentlemen and officers of arms taking turns to keep vigil.

On the twelfth day, the body was removed, on a chair draped in black velvet. Atop the coffin was an effigy of the queen, dressed in her royal robes, with a crown and sceptre. The procession walked slowly to Westminster, with the Earl of Derby and various other peers behind the coffin. At Westminster, Dorset and Arundel were waiting, dressed in their robes, as the coffin was carried into the abbey, and placed under the hearse. After the Mass, the peers retired to the Queen's Great Chamber in the palace for a supper of fish, while a watch of ladies and officers of arms was kept overnight. During the funeral oration, delivered the next day by Richard FitzJames, Bishop of Rochester, the queen's ladies covered the hearse with thirty-seven palls, one for each year of her age. Another Mass was offered, then Elizabeth's effigy was placed in the shrine of St Edward the Confessor before the laity left the church. A tomb was opened in the floor and the coffin placed in it, with further prayers and rituals. Later, Elizabeth and Henry VII would have a magnificent effigy in bronze, cast by Pietro Torregiani, erected over their common grave.

The king was further saddened by the necessity of sending Margaret, Queen of Scots, to her new home. Henry was reluctant to let his daughter go – she was not yet fourteen, and he did not want to part with another child, having lost four children to premature death. But duty was duty, and Margaret had to leave her family and travel north. The whole court, including Dorset, accompanied her to Collyweston, Lady Margaret Beaufort's grand home in Northamptonshire. By 8 July, Henry could delay no longer. That morning, Margaret set out, flanked by the familiar figures of her cousins Dorset and Essex, and her grandmother's husband, Derby. After a mile, the gentlemen bowed, kissed her hand, and drew their horses back to let the rest of the procession pass, headed by the Earl of Surrey and his wife, who were to guard Margaret until she was handed over to her husband.

With the deaths of Arthur and Queen Elizabeth, it seemed that God's favour was no longer with the king and his new royal house. Although the king's second son, Henry, had quickly been proclaimed Prince of Wales, his was not the first name mentioned as the right person to take the throne in the event of the king's death. Buckingham's name was being whispered, as was the most obvious candidate other than Prince Henry: Edmund de la Pole,

Earl of Suffolk, younger brother of the Earl of Lincoln killed at Stoke in 1487. Despite his brother's rebellion, Suffolk had been permitted to inherit part, although not all, of his father's lands, and the lesser of his father's titles, becoming earl, rather than duke, on payment of a large entry fine. There was no reason to suppose he could not forge a successful path as one of Henry's senior peers, but in 1498, Suffolk and some of his friends were brought before the King's Bench for brawling in Aldgate. The altercation had resulted in the deaths of three men, and the earl was indicted for murder. This might seem to be exactly what the law required, but noblemen were usually spared capital charges of this nature. Suffolk certainly took it as a deliberate slight – especially as the man presenting the indictment was Sir Reginald Bray, one of Henry's closest councillors.

Suffolk refused to grovel to the king for the pardon that was hinted at, and left the country without permission, for the court of his aunt Margaret in Burgundy. Since yet another plot involving yet another impostor pretending to be a lost Yorkist price had recently been uncovered, in the king's suspicious mind that plot and Suffolk absconding were linked. Henry immediately threatened Philip of Burgundy with a re-imposition of the sanctions that had bitten cruelly a few years earlier if he encouraged Suffolk in his disobedience. At the same time, he sent Sir Richard Guildford to persuade Suffolk to return. If he did so, Henry would believe in his loyalty, and, over time, allow him to regain favour. Suffolk decided to return, presumably because he was innocent of plotting, even if guilty of brawling. Henry, a man of his word, accepted Suffolk back into the fold, and in 1500 he was one of the witnesses to the marriage treaty between Arthur and Katharine. He had also attended Henry and Elizabeth on their visit to Calais that June, when Henry agreed a long-term treaty with Philip of Burgundy to be cemented by a marriage between the Duke of York and Philip's daughter Archduchess Eleonora of Austria. But Suffolk had neither the patience, nor the skills, to win back Henry's trust over the long term. He felt himself to be hedged in on all sides by rivals. In East Anglia, where he should have reigned supreme, Henry's support of Thomas, Earl of Surrey was especially galling – Surrey had fought valiantly for Richard III at Bosworth, yet was now one of Henry's most trusted men, even being given Anne of York as wife.

Suffolk became more and more disgruntled – whether he initially wanted the throne or just the dukedom and pre-eminence over the other nobles (a position now taken by Buckingham) is not certain, but he became increasingly disaffected, and two months after the Calais summit, in August 1501, he and his younger brother Richard de la Pole sailed down the Thames and took ship for Burgundy. From Burgundy, he crossed into the territories of Maximilian, now Holy Roman Emperor, who, to Henry's horror, had extended a personal invitation to this sprig of the House of York. Suffolk travelled to St Johann, in the Austrian alps, where Maximilian welcomed him with glee. Given the treaty between Maximilian's son, Philip, and Henry, open military backing of Suffolk was not a wise course of action (not that Maximilian ever planned very judiciously). But permission for Suffolk to stay in Imperial territories, and support for him as a prince-in-exile, was Maximilian's plan for the meantime – with a promise of more substantial help in future.

Suffolk began to draw support from erstwhile Yorkists – Richard III's former retainers, who had appeared reconciled to the Tudor regime, and had posts in Henry's household. The most high-profile man to indicate support for Suffolk was Sir James Tyrrell. Tyrrell had served Edward IV, and then Richard III, as Lieutenant of Guisnes Castle, one of the outposts of English military command in Calais. After a brief sojourn in the Tower following Bosworth, he had been accepted into Henry's service and reappointed to his post. During Suffolk's first foray abroad, the earl had visited Tyrrell on his way home – perhaps the two men talked, remembering 'the good old days' when York was in the ascendant and Suffolk's brother tipped as heir to the throne. By 1501, Tyrrell had declared his support for Suffolk, as had the neighbouring fortress of Hammes – whose defection to Henry in 1485 had significantly improved his chances of gaining the throne. On this occasion, Hammes had no opportunity to support a new challenger. Henry sent Sir Thomas Lovell to arrest Tyrrell, who was tried at the Guildhall, in front of a large panel of peers, including Dorset. He was found guilty and executed. Sir Thomas More later claimed that Tyrrell admitted to the murder of the Edward V and Richard, Duke of York, but if he did, no one mentioned it at the time, so it seems a spurious claim.

Suffolk and Richard de la Pole were declared outlaws in December 1502, and in the following January the earl was stripped of all his honours, including his knighthood of the Garter. The fourth de la Pole brother, William, was sent to the Tower, where he languished, uncharged and untried, for the rest of his life. Henry, knowing that Maximilian was perennially broke, offered him a staggering £10,000 to banish Suffolk. Maximilian dallied, changed his mind, took the money, and promised Suffolk would be banned from the territories he ruled personally, but claimed to be unable to control the Imperial Free Cities. Conveniently, one of them, Aachen, was prepared to take Suffolk as a long-term guest.

Henry does not appear to have entertained any suspicions about Dorset's loyalty. The marquis was elected to Suffolk's Garter stall and the king paid for the Garter livery, just as had been done for Thomas I.[4] In 1504, Dorset sat alongside Prince Henry, Buckingham, the two archbishops and numerous other peers in Parliament, and later that year, he gave his recognisance to support Sir William Blount, Lord Mountjoy, who had been appointed as Governor of Hammes Castle, in place of the disgraced Tyrrell.

*

The first few years of the new century were difficult for Cecily. As well as the loss of her husband, her daughter Lady Eleanor Arundell died around 1503, leaving five children: John, Thomas, Eleanor, Elizabeth and Jane. The following year saw the death of Cecily's mother, Katherine,

Lady Hastings. Lady Hastings had not remarried after the sudden execution of her second husband in 1483. Instead, she had brought up their family of five children alone. The oldest, Edward, was about seventeen at the time of his father's execution. Later, he was to write affectionately of his mother that she had endured 'great trouble, pains, heaviness and labour ... in his bringing up ... and especially since the decease of his good lord and father ... [and had shown him] manifold motherly kindnesses'.[5] Like many other widows, Katherine Hastings had experienced financial problems fulfilling her husband's will and arranging her daughters' marriage portions. She had been constrained to borrow from Cecily from time to time, but still died in debt. To Cecily, as recompense for the money she owed, she bequeathed the bed of arras, complete with tester and counterpane, that Cecily had recently borrowed from her. Cecily had also taken a 'tabulet' of gold as a pledge for a loan, which she was now to keep. Additionally, Cecily was bequeathed three curtains of blue sarcenet, a traverse of the same material, three cushions of 'counterfeit arras' with imagery of women, a long cushion and two short ones, all of blue velvet, and two carpets. Cecily was also the first named of the executors. For her mother's sake, Cecily charged one of her own manors for five years to repay Katherine's debts.

In November 1505, the Grey family was drawn to the king's attention in a less positive way than performance at tournaments. Dorset and his mother Cecily had fallen out so spectacularly that Henry and his council felt obliged to take a hand to resolve their quarrel. Intending to 'see and sette the seid parties atte unyte and peas of and for almaner of variance, controversies, matters and causes dependyng betwene them', Dorset and Cecily were summoned to appear before a panel that, along with the king, included the Earl of Surrey, Lord Treasurer; Richard Fox, Bishop of Winchester; Sir Giles Daubeney, the Lord Chamberlain; Sir John Fyneux, Chief Justice of the King's bench; Sir Thomas Fowick, Chief Justice of the Common Pleas.[6]

The cause of the dispute was, of course, money, and the fulfilment of Thomas I's will. As mentioned above, various manors, including Astley, had been allocated to Cecily and the other executors, for the performance of this will – that is the executors were to retain the income until all the legacies had been paid. Once those had all been paid, Astley would remain with Cecily as her dower, while the other manors would pass to his son. Since her daughter Mary's betrothed, Lord Ferrers of Chartley, was still underage at Thomas I's death, Cecily had had to buy his wardship and marriage from the king again for £1,000, in a transaction brokered by Sir Reginald Bray, paying £200 down, then a further £200 yearly at Hallowtide for four years. She had provided six sureties and had given a further bond of 1,000 marks, to replace any of the sureties within three months if necessary.[7] Money for the rest of Thomas I's bequests would have to be collected over time. It was not unusual for a widow to receive a life-interest in one of the chief manors, so Thomas granting

Astley to Cecily, now that Bradgate was the chief family home, was not unreasonable. Dorset, in truth, had little to complain of, although he might have wished his father had left fewer bequests, as the Grey lands were not extensive – the chief wealth was in Cecily's lands. Then Cecily dropped a bombshell: she intended to marry again.

Cecily's new husband would be entitled to hold her estates during her life, and, should he have a child by her, would retain a life interest in her lands after her death, possibly even including an interest in her dower from Thomas I. From Dorset's perspective, this was a nightmare. He did not want his mother to remarry at all, and he particularly abhorred her choice of husband – Lord Henry Stafford, the younger brother of the Duke of Buckingham. Stafford, although already widowed with a son, was around eighteen years Cecily's junior – in fact, probably two years younger than Dorset. The likelihood was that Dorset would never collect his mother's lands, and possibly not even his father's manor of Astley either. Cecily's motivation for remarriage can only be speculated on – she was approaching forty-five, and had survived thirteen or possibly fourteen childbirths. Either she was certain that she would have no more children, or perhaps felt that, if she did fall pregnant again, she would continue to be lucky. She did not need to marry for money – she was rich from her own estates, and as a widow could control them completely. She did not need a title, as she would retain the rank of lady marquis, unless she married an even higher-ranking man – and that meant only the royal family, or the married Buckingham. One can only suppose it was love.

The other possibility is that the king suggested the marriage, to give an estate to the younger brother of Buckingham, whom he may have wished to favour. He certainly seemed to think well of Stafford, appointing him to the Garter in April 1505, but there is no evidence of Henry organising the marriage, and it seems unlikely – why enrich a young man, when the estates were probably least likely to be used for nefarious purposes in the hands of a widow? Stafford's motivation is of course, easier to see – a wealthy widow was a good deal even with a significant age gap. He may, of course, have been in love with her person as well as her money.

As Cecily was a tenant-in-chief of the Crown, she needed royal permission to marry. Henry gave the requisite licence, on payment of a fine of £2,000 – less, the king implied, than the 'right great and chargeable sums' to which he was entitled. Once again, the king was willing to stagger payments. Stafford was to grant an obligation to the king of £1,000, which would be discharged on condition that he 'demeane[d] and behave[d] himself truly to our said sovereign lord and to his heirs and [was] not … retained or towards any other person; otherwise than shall stand with the king's pleasure'. The other £1,000 was to be payable in instalments at Christmas and St John's Day over five years, since the king was 'not willing the said lady and Henry to be grieved with the hasty or sudden payment of the same nor that their honourable port and countenance thereby should [di]minish or decay'. A list of Cecily's manors, to the value of 400 marks per annum, was made, from which goods could be distrained if the couple failed to pay.[8]

Having dealt with the marriage so far as Henry's own rights were concerned, king and council turned to managing the row between Cecily and Dorset, and the latter's fear that he would lose his inheritance to Stafford. The king and his council agreed a compromise between mother and son on 10 June 1504. Cecily was to retain Astley, accounting for it to the Archbishop of Canterbury, to make sure she did not drag her feet over the satisfaction of Thomas I's bequests. The rest of Thomas I's lands were to pass to Dorset, who was to make a reasonable dower settlement within three months. All the lands of Cecily's own inheritance remained with her, but her rights to manage them were curtailed. The inheritance was divided into two parts. She had free rein to manage the first part as she wished, including disposing of them for a term of lives, after which they were to pass to Dorset, and, failing him, her next heirs. These lands were then subject to an indenture between Cecily and her fiancé, under which they were enfeoffed to forty-two feoffees, beginning with Stafford himself. The feoffees were to hold these manors to the use of Stafford after her death; if he predeceased her, a subset of the manors was to be held for the performance of Stafford's will, with the remainder to Dorset or Cecily's right heirs. The residue of Cecily's inheritance, including the manor that she had charged to pay her mother's debts, was to be enfeoffed to a long list of Henry's councillors. She could not make any grants greater than the value of 100 marks, so all of that element of her property would pass, unencumbered, to Dorset on her death.

This was a personal agreement between Cecily and her son. If he predeceased her with no heir, the agreement would be void. If he died before her, with an heir, then the lands would be held to the use of Henry Stafford for his lifetime, and then pass to her 'right heirs' – either daughters of Dorset or Cecily's younger sons. The result of this compromise was that Dorset could claim half his mother's inheritance at her death, rather than having to wait for the death of her widower to claim the whole. If Dorset predeceased her, her next heir would have to wait until both she and Stafford had died to inherit. The real losers from the agreement were Cecily's daughters. With only Astley available to pay their dowries, and all of Thomas I's other bequests to pay out of it, it might be a long time before they received their fair share. No doubt Dorset thought that Cecily should pay his sisters' dowries out of her own money, but that was neither the custom, nor what his father had willed. As might have been expected, no one was happy with the arrangement, and the resentment between mother and son was never assuaged.

*

In January 1506, King Henry was surprised and delighted to have an unexpected opportunity to play host to Philip of Burgundy and his wife, Juana of Castile – more delighted, certainly, than they were.

The archduke and his wife (sister of the widowed Katharine, Princess of Wales) had been en route to claim Juana's kingdom of Castile, after the death of Queen Isabella. Ferocious storms in the English Channel had obliged them to put into port at Melcombe Regis in Devon. Philip requested that he and his party might be swiftly refitted with new vessels and allowed to proceed, but news of his arrival was sent post-haste to London, and Henry immediately ordered that the archduke and queen be treated as honoured guests but not found any shipping. Nothing could have served Henry better – he was still angry with Philip and his father, Maximilian, for harbouring the Earl of Suffolk, who was now referred to, aggravatingly, as the 'White Rose'. Philip was deluged with ceremonial, taken first to Winchester and then Windsor, where he was met by Henry, flanked by Dorset, 'riding upon a bald sorrel horse, with a deep trapper full of long tassels of gold of Venus, and upon the copper of his horse a white feather, with a coat upon his back, the body goldsmith's work, the sleeves of crimson velvet, with letters of gold'. Also present were the Prince of Wales and as many nobles as could be found at short notice.[10] Dorset's new stepfather, Lord Henry Stafford, was among them, sporting a hat of 'goldsmith's work', decorated with diamonds and rubies which probably caused Dorset to grind his teeth, seeing his mother's money decking out her lusty young husband.[9]

Helpless to escape Henry's toils, Philip was obliged to sign several treaties to England's advantage – the key ones being an agreement for a marriage between his son the Archduke Charles and Henry's youngest daughter, Princess Mary, and a trading agreement that was so advantageous to England that it was known in Burgundy as the 'Intercursus Malus'. Henry also showed an interest in marrying Philip's only sister, the Archduchess Marguerite. In return, Henry would recognise Philip as King of Castile in right of his wife. The other concession required by Henry before he would let his guests leave was the handing over of Suffolk. Philip had no alternative but to accept Henry's demand, his conscience being slightly eased by a promise from Henry that the White Rose would be spared his life. Orders were sent for the White Rose to be apprehended, but, unwilling to trust Philip's word, Henry detained the restive archduke until he had received word that Suffolk had been handed over to his own men. As always, Henry kept his promise, to the letter if not the spirit: he spared Suffolk's life, but confined him to the Tower. Before Philip and Juana could depart, there was a final grand joust at Richmond, that of Lady Winter and Dame February, where Philip and his dazzling entourage impressed Prince Henry with their chivalric glory. Charles Brandon was one of the English team, but it is not clear whether Dorset was – it seems likely, given his expertise. Dorset, obviously an athletic man, also played tennis with the archduke.

With the White Rose safely immured, it might be thought that life at the Tudor court would settle down, but Henry, probably severely depressed after the traumas in his personal life, and in declining health, became more difficult and suspicious with every passing day. Despite Dorset having been granted the White Rose's confiscated manor of Wyveston in Suffolk in December 1506, at some time in the following year he was arrested, along with Lord William Courtenay, and sent to the Tower, on suspicion of involvement in Suffolk's schemes. The basis of Henry's concerns seem to have been the discovery that five or six days before Suffolk's secret departure in August 1501, Dorset and Courtenay had dined with him, along with Lord Essex, and Sir Thomas Green, and that Courtenay had treated Suffolk with such 'great reverence' that it implied he saw Suffolk as a potential king. Taxed with this, Suffolk responded that it was often the case that the men were together, but that they had not known of his plans, even though he had given Dorset and Lord William horses, with a request to send them to his stable. As for the idea that Courtenay had treated him unduly politely, Suffolk could only reply that people could judge what they liked from appearances.

None of this seems a solid foundation for Henry's suspicions, but as time passed, Henry needed less foundation for suspicion to take root. The idea Dorset would have preferred Suffolk as king – a man with whom he had no connection of kinship, even if they were friends – rather than Henry's son, who was his cousin, seems unlikely. Nevertheless, Henry was convinced that Dorset and Courtenay were up to no good, and they remained in the Tower until, in October of 1508, they were taken across the sea to Calais, to be imprisoned in the castle there, under the guard of Sir Richard Carew. This seems an even stranger undertaking – why put prisoners in a place far more vulnerable to attack or susceptible to changing sides than the Tower? The whole scenario seems bizarre. While Dorset was in prison, Henry at least had the grace to pay his debts; nor were the men ill-treated in Calais – the governor was later to write that he could not have made ends meet without the substantial allowance he was paid for Dorset's keep.

It was probably while her brother was languishing in prison that Lady Dorothy Grey sued the executors of her father's will for failing to produce her £1,000 dowry. Her father's will required her, if she wanted her dowry, to marry by the 'advice of her mother and [his] executors', and now, according to her submission to the Lord Chancellor, her mother and her stepfather had found a suitable husband for her – a man with a good living of over £1,000 per annum. Frustratingly, neither of the other two executors, Robert Alday and William Skeffington, would either answer her request for their opinion on the match, nor hand over the dowry, despite them having received 'great sums of money' from her father's lands. If the Lord Chancellor did not command them to act, then she would be 'like to lose her preferment and not only that but also to lack exhibition and her finding necessary for ever hereafter to her utter undoing'.[10] The marriage went ahead, although not all of the dowry was paid. Dorothy's new husband was Sir Robert Willoughby de Broke – a widower with two children, around fifteen years her senior.

8

A New Dawn

Heaven smiles, earth rejoices; all is milk and honey and nectar.
William Blount, Lord Mountjoy

The Chronicle of Calais opines that, had Henry VII lived longer, Dorset would have been executed. As it was, Henry VII died on 21 April 1509, to be succeeded by Dorset's cousin as Henry VIII, to the delight of the populace. Initially, this did not bode well for the Grey family. Dorset was specifically excluded from the customary general pardon, issued for all offences, and Lord Henry Stafford, who had been an associate of Henry VII's widely detested councillors Sir Richard Empson and Sir Edmund Dudley, was arrested. Cecily's feelings can only be imagined – one son in gaol in Calais and her husband in the Tower. Other members of the family were welcome at the new court – three of the Grey brothers, lords Richard, John and Anthony, received the cloth allowance for barons to take part in Henry VII's funeral procession, and Lord Richard took part in the great joust of 'Lady Pallas', held to celebrate the coronation of the new king and queen – Henry VIII having married his late brother's widow, Katharine of Aragon, within weeks of succeeding.

Events like the Pallas joust delighted Henry for many years, and the structure was always similar – one spectacularly disguised group pitted against another, fighting for praise and honour based on a tale from myth or legend. The fighting was not mock: real blows were given, and men could be seriously wounded or even killed. This particular joust opened with Lady Pallas being carried into the lists in a mock tower fashioned of cloth of gold, embroidered with roses for the king and pomegranates for the queen, bearing a shield of crystal. Simultaneously, 'fresh young gallants' with horses draped in exotic fabrics of gold, silver and tinsel pranced around the lists, showing off their horsemanship. Following Lady Pallas were her five knights: Lord Thomas Howard, married to the king's aunt, Anne of York; his brother, the Admiral Sir Edward Howard; Sir Thomas Knyvett, brother-in-law to the Howards; Charles Brandon, a close friend of the king's; and Lord Richard Grey. They were fully armed, with their horses trapped in green velvet, again decorated with roses and pomegranates. Pallas presented them to the king as her 'scholars', who wished to serve him to the 'increase of their honour'. Another hundred or so men entered, dressed in velvet with matching hose and hats. Pallas requested that her scholars be permitted to defend the king against all comers, which he graciously allowed. Yet another sixty men entered, dressed in gold and silver, on horses trapped to match, each man wearing a collar of chain of gold and a great helmet with a plume of feathers. Accompanied by drums and fifes, they performed some species of dressage, 'every man taking up his horse, as well for their ladies as for laud or praise'.

This exhibition of horsemanship complete, the challengers entered the lists: Sir John Peche, Sir Edward Neville, Sir Edward Guildford, Sir John Carew, Sir William Parr, Sir Giles Capell, Sir Griffith Dwnn and Sir Roland Veyville, dressed and trapped in cloth of gold and silver. Their leader, dressed and trapped in blue and gold velvet with a golden spear, approached the queen. His men had heard, he said, that Lady Pallas had brought her scholars, but whether they were to learn wisdom or feats of arms he did not know. His knights were come to do feats of arms for 'love of ladies', and he requested her permission to challenge the Lady Pallas. If Pallas's team won, they would have the golden spear; if his men broke more spears, they would have Pallas's crystal shield. Queen Katharine agreed, and the joust began. The chronicler observed that all men acquitted themselves well, but he did not know the outcome. The following day, Pallas's knights reappeared, still with pomegranates and roses decorating their robes, followed by the other knights, dressed this time in green satin with bramble bushes embroidered in gold. A cage, decorated to look like a park, with green and white palings and replica trees and bushes, was brought in, containing fallow deer that were released into the lists. Greyhounds were loosed to kill the deer, whose carcasses were presented to the queen and her ladies – a spectacle that, presumably, Katharine and her ladies enjoyed, however revolting it seems to modern ideas. The challenger knights reappeared, announcing that they represented Diana, and further combat ensued.[1]

While Lord Richard was enjoying the coronation festivities, his brother Dorset remained confined in Calais. But in July, Henry, remembering how much he admired his cousin's jousting, sent Sir Thomas Lovell to fetch him. Once back at court, Dorset soon recovered his lost favour. On 13 August, he was granted the office of Forester of Sawsey Forest, Northamptonshire, with the same rights as his forebears, the earls Rivers, had enjoyed. He had power to appoint officials, to enclose and convert 20 acres of underwood into coppice each year, and to sell underwood to pay the fees and maintain Sawsey Lodge. The grant was followed up by a general pardon. Over the course of years, Dorset received various lands and offices, and was also involved in land exchanges with the king. Known to be in the king's favour, he received other appointments too, such as the stewardship of the lands of the Priory of St Augustine, Daventry. At the end of December, Henry VIII collected a list of the outstanding debts owed to his father – they were not forgiven but were 'put in respite and suspense till our mind and pleasure be further known'. Among those 'respited' were Dorset and Cecily. No doubt they were suitably grateful.

Dorset was summoned to Henry's first parliament, second among the secular lords after Buckingham, who had the honour of carrying the cap of maintenance in the procession, while Lord Henry Stafford, who had been released from the Tower within a few weeks, carried the sword. A week later, Stafford was granted the earldom of Wiltshire. Wiltshire soon became one of the men who attended Henry regularly, joining in his boisterous games and disguisings. Although references to the queen and her ladies are not frequent, it is likely that Cecily was often in attendance, with both her husband and sons being among the king's intimates.

In the spring of 1510, Dorset played a prominent part in the Garter festivities for the commemoration of St George's Day at Greenwich, Henry's favourite palace. Four of the stalls were vacant, and the incumbent knights were asked for nominations. Dorset put forward King Manuel of Portugal and the King of Aragon (the queen's brother-in-law and father, respectively), and the Duke of Urbino. Closer to home, he suggested Lord Bergavenny, Lord Thomas Howard, Lord de Vere, Sir Henry Marney, Sir Nicholas Vaux and Sir Thomas Knyvett. All these gentlemen were stalwarts of the early Henrician court and well known to Dorset – Howard had been his tennis partner during the visit of Duke Philip in 1506. The following day, after the annual Requiem Mass for the departed knights, the king selected King Manuel, Lord Thomas Howard, Lord de la Warr, and Sir Henry Marney. Howard and Marney were brought into the chapel by Garter king of arms for installation. Henry gave the highest-ranking knights – Buckingham and Dorset – the garters for the new knights. The duke fixed his to the leg of Howard, and Dorset embellished the stocking-clad calf of Marney.

Henry VIII was, in many ways, a very different man from his father. Certainly, at the beginning of his reign, when he was only just eighteen, he was much less interested in the day-to-day business of government, rarely attending council meetings. The late king's councillors were largely retained (excepting the unlucky Empson and Dudley, who were both executed). Chief among them were William Warham, Archbishop of Canterbury and Lord Chancellor; Thomas Howard senior, Earl of Surrey and Lord Treasurer; Bishop Fox of Winchester; Sir Thomas Lovell; George Talbot, Earl of Shrewsbury; Charles Somerset, Lord Herbert, who was descended from the Beaufort family; and Sir Henry Marney. Dorset was soon attending meetings, as was Charles Brandon. As time passed, the old guard began to be overshadowed by Thomas Wolsey, who had risen from the parish at Limington granted by Dorset's father to the post of King's Almoner. Wolsey, an extraordinarily talented and hard-working man, soon took on all of the dull administration that the lords thought beneath them, and, by dint of acting as a conduit between Henry and his councillors, became indispensable to the monarch.

*

On 1 January 1511, bells rang out, bonfires were lit, and free wine was distributed across London. Queen Katharine had given birth to a boy. Henry went on pilgrimage to Walsingham to give thanks. The Tudor dynasty was safe for another generation – or so the ecstatic parents believed. A lengthy series of pageants and jousts was planned, and this time Dorset was able to take part. He was partnered with Sir Thomas Boleyn, the two of them dressed as pilgrims to the shrine of Santiago de Compostela, in honour of the queen. Of course, their robes were not of pilgrim-coarse cloth, but of black velvet, as were their horses' trappings. Wiltshire took part as well, dressed in silver embroidered with his motto and with sheaves of golden arrows (another of Queen Katharine's badges), as did lords John and Leonard Grey. But all the junketing was in vain – the little Duke of Cornwall died on 22 February. Henry took this 'dolorous' news wisely, and underplayed his grief in order to comfort his wife, who, 'like a natural woman', was heartbroken. Henry expressed his grief with a solemn funeral, at which Dorset had the great honour of being the chief mourner. The little boy was laid to rest at the feet of his grandparents in Henry VII's Lady chapel in Westminster Abbey.

Perhaps to distract himself, Henry turned from the mock battles of tournaments to the real thing. In 1498, Charles VIII of France had invaded Italy, a move that would result in sixty years of almost continuous warfare. There were four main protagonists, who combined in different ways, but all were in pursuit of control of the Italian peninsula. The first three were Henry VII's old sparring partner Emperor Maximilian, once again in control of Burgundy as Duke Philip had died not long after his unintended trip to England; Louis XII of France, who claimed the duchy of Milan; and Ferdinand of Aragon, who was also regent for his daughter, Juana, in Castile. Ferdinand and Maximilian had grandchildren in common, the eldest of whom was Charles, born in 1500, who had yet to take control of his patrimony of Burgundy but was expected to inherit the territories of Maximilian and Ferdinand in due course. Charles was still betrothed to Henry's sister, Mary. The fourth player was the pope, Julius II, who was far more interested in achieving papal control of the central belt of Italy than in attending to the corruption that was rife in the Church – with disastrous consequences for Christian unity in Europe.

As well as the kingdom of Naples, Ferdinand had the kingdom of Navarre in his sights. Navarre was an independent realm that straddled the Franco-Spanish border in the Pyrenees. He claimed it, rather unconvincingly, as heir to his half-sister Leonor, who had been its queen regnant, while Louis XII supported the claims of Leonor's granddaughter

Catherine, daughter of a French princess and married to a French nobleman.² There was also Scotland to consider. Henry VII's treaty with James IV, sealed by the marriage of Margaret in 1503, had been intended to inaugurate a 'perpetual peace', but the Scots had an older alliance, with France. If France and England were in conflict, the Scots would have to choose between their old friend and their old enemy.

In late 1511, Ferdinand requested Henry to furnish him with a company of knights and 200 archers to fight against the Infidel – while crusading was not so fashionable as it had once been, everyone believed in it in theory. It was only sixty years since Constantinople had fallen to the Turks, and only twenty since Ferdinand and Isabella had conquered the Moorish kingdom of Granada. Ferdinand's immediate target was North Africa, where many of the dispossessed Moors of Granada had taken refuge. There were numerous volunteers to join Ferdinand, among them Lord Anthony Grey. The company of some 1,500 men, under the leadership of Thomas, Lord Dacre, set sail for Cadiz. Whether Ferdinand had been serious or not in his initial plan, by the time Lord Anthony and the others arrived he had changed his mind about the campaign, and told the Englishmen to go home. Some things never change – the bored young Englishmen in the south of Spain got drunk and behaved abominably, damaging property, accosting a young woman and getting into a brawl in which three men were killed.

Dorset was still partying with the king – on May Day, the court went out to the woods early to fetch in the may, after which there was another tournament. Henry, Sir Edward Howard, Sir Edward Neville and Charles Brandon competed against Dorset, the Earl of Essex, William Courtenay (now Earl of Devon) and Lord Thomas Howard. The party lasted three days, at the end of which Queen Katharine hosted a banquet (not a full meal, but a special feast of sweetmeats). She presented four prizes: first, unsurprisingly, went to the king, and Dorset squeezed in at fourth. Dorset was certainly high in the king's favour. Over the following couple of years, he was appointed as Master of the Hunt in Canford, Constable of Corfe Castle and Master of the Hunt in Purbeck, steward of the lands in Somerset and Dorset that had passed to Henry VIII on the death of his grandmother, Lady Margaret Beaufort, steward of various lands from the Salisbury inheritance confiscated by Edward IV from George of Clarence, and Master of the Hunt in those locations. Soon, he was to be given the opportunity to test his martial prowess on a real battlefield.

In October 1511, a Holy League was formed by Julius, Maximilian and Ferdinand to combat Louis XII and the Venetians. The catalyst was a call from Louis for a General Council of the Church to be held at Pisa. Popes, in general, did not like General Councils, widely considered to be the ultimate authority in the Church. Julius denounced Louis as schismatic and called for aid against him. While Henry's councillors had previously discouraged his ambitions for war against France, with a call from the Holy Father himself, they could no longer resist the king's desire.

Henry was young and idealistic, and although with the benefit of hindsight we may be amazed to remember it, he was a hot defender of the pope, and the Church hierarchy. He accused Louis XII of 'lacerat(ing) the seamless garment of Christ', and 'wantonly destroy(ing) the unity of the Church'. Ferdinand was delighted at the warlike nature of his son-in-law, and the two kings agreed that an Anglo-Spanish army would be raised to conquer Guienne, once part of the English Crown's lands in the south and west of France. That was the plan for English consumption, at least – Ferdinand, whose cynicism knew no bounds, had other ideas.

Preparations began. The English nobleman was psychologically bred for war, but the men who surrounded Henry had little or no real experience of it. Their fathers and grandfathers had learnt from the experience of their fathers in France, and themselves had faced combat during the Wars of the Roses, but the men born after 1470, who made up the bulk of Henry's warriors, had little practical experience. There were exceptions – those who had fought in the Scottish campaigns of the 1490s, such as the Howard brothers; Lord Dacre, who had fought for Richard III at Bosworth and been Henry VII's Warden of the Marches; and the Earl of Shrewsbury, who had also fought at Bosworth. But these men were a minority. Dorset and his brothers had never been within sniff of a battle, nor had Brandon, Neville or, of course, Henry. To them, it was a glorious game. Even those who had experienced the Wars of the Roses knew only pitched battles, which, once fought, had no lasting effect on the surrounding countryside. European wars were quite different – during the French wars of the fifteenth century and the Italian wars of the sixteenth, tens of thousands of common people had their lands and crops ruined, died of hunger and disease, had troops billeted on them and were raped and murdered by the opposition. Warfare of this sort was better understood on the Anglo-Scots border, where campaigns, although seldom longer than a few weeks, were accompanied by livestock theft and destruction of towns.

Despite his lack of practical experience, Dorset was appointed Lieutenant-General of the king's forces. He entered into a bond on 4 March, in the sum of £1,000, which was cancelled on 18 April following the successful completion of his first task, the mustering of forces from all over the country to meet at Southampton. The Venetian ambassador, Badoer, wrote that Lord Talbot was to take around 15,000 men to attack Normandy while Dorset would be leading a similar number of men to attack Guienne. The actual numbers were probably closer to 10,000.

Dorset's formal commission to act as Lieutenant-General of the whole king's army 'going beyond the sea' was granted on 2 May. We can guess that Dorset was extremely proud of the document, and perhaps that Lord Thomas Howard, who had had real experience of war, thought he had been unfairly passed over. Howard had to be content with a commission appointing him to take charge should Dorset be killed. Three of Dorset's brothers were also part of the expedition: Leonard, Anthony and John. His brothers-in-law Lord Ferrers, Lord Willoughby de Broke and John Dudley were also included, along with Dudley's father, Lord Sutton; Lord Ferrers' other brother-in-law, Sir Thomas Cornewall; Lord Willoughby de Eresby; and Lord Thomas Howard's brother, Sir Edmund. The treasurer for the expedition was Sir William Sandys, and among the men was Dr William Knight, once secretary to Henry VII and now closely associated with Thomas Wolsey, whom he kept informed of every detail.[3]

Dorset had orders to embark on 4 May, to rendezvous with Ferdinand and a similarly sized host at Fuenterrabia. The port, now known by its Basque name of Hondarribia, is located on the River Bidasoa, marking the Franco-Spanish border, slightly west of Navarre. The troops went aboard ships under the command of another Howard brother, Admiral Sir Edward. Contrary winds forced them to land on the Isle of Wight, where they were trapped until 3 June. This was an inauspicious start, and the expedition never improved. Some of the ships became separated from Dorset's flagship, and his men suffered so badly with seasickness that they were at the mercy of the sailors, who, according to Knight, stole some of the rations. After four more gruelling days at sea, the little fleet landed at Bermeo in Aragon, a little to the north-east of Bilbao. There, they were glad to receive 'everything needful' and sent their thanks to Ferdinand. Somewhat recovered, the ships slipped up the coast to Pasaia at the mouth of the river now known as Oiartzun Ibaia. The narrow river mouth was already crowded with shipping, including one great ship loaded with artillery and powder, and navigation was hazardous. The troops disembarked and encamped at Errenteria. The victuals were poor, and the rain incessant, which was miserable for the soldiers, who were lying out rather than under tents. Dorset was anticipating that Ferdinand, or his general, the Duke of Alba, a noted warrior who had taken part in the conquest of Granada, would be waiting for him – or at least be en route – but he was greeted only by the Bishop of Siguença, with a letter from Ferdinand.

Knight reported on the situation to Wolsey. There was thought to be a pro-English faction within Guienne, including the Lord of Urtubia, a castle and district near St Jean-de-Luz. The pro-French faction was led by Louis' Governor of Guienne, François, 2nd Duke of Longueville, whom Knight hopefully reported had to contend with a quarrel between his brother, M. Dunois, and the citizens of Bayonne, a major town within Guienne, immediately over the border. This quarrel had led many of the leading burgesses of Bayonne to flee into Navarre, which might have been positive for the English, except that, while Ferdinand had agreed with Henry that Guienne was the target, he was far more interested in getting his hands on Navarre, using the pretext that Queen Catherine and her husband, King Jean, had declared the kingdom neutral, to avoid joining in the Holy League against France. Knight wrote to Wolsey that he had heard that a French ambassador was with the King of Navarre, to negotiate terms to help the Navarrese against Ferdinand. This, Knight thought, was ominous. If King Jean were to come to an agreement with King Louis, and 'slack' the supplies, the English army would need victualling from England.

Dorset moved his men north to Fuenterrabia and waited for the promised troops from Ferdinand. The rain continued to fall, and it is hard to imagine that anyone was especially cheered by the delivery of three banners, direct from Henry. They were symbols of the king's trust in his cousin – the first was of white sarcenet, with a red cross of St George; the second was of green sarcenet with a picture of the saint; the third was of red sarcenet, with the arms of the duchy of Guienne. All three were fringed in silk of the Tudor colours of green and white. Henry was no doubt fondly imagining them fluttering from the towers of the Palace of Justice in Poitiers, where his ancestors Henry II and Eleanor of Aquitaine had once held sway.

Letters were dispatched to Ferdinand to send troops, but the king countered with a request for Dorset to lead the English army into Navarre to support him – it would be best, Ferdinand explained, to overcome Navarre before attacking France. Dorset wrote home for orders on 1 July but had received no response by 8 July. As the men waited, encamped about a mile outside Fuenterrabia, sickness began to stalk the local population. Howard wrote to Wolsey that, although only one of them had died so far, compared with five in a nearby village, if illness did strike it would be hard to keep order. There had already been one night of brawling between the English and the locals, whom they condemned as interested in nothing but money – it is indeed extraordinary that the Spanish were more interested in making a living than supporting English military fantasies! Howard continued that he wished the king had not trusted Ferdinand any more than Howard himself did. They should not have had to rely on Ferdinand for horses and carts but should have had their own to launch their attack. If Ferdinand refused to bring his troops up, Howard did not know what might happen – but he feared the worst. He urged Wolsey to talk to the Lord Privy Seal and the Lord Chancellor and, between them, persuade Henry to allow the men either to attack Guienne without waiting for Ferdinand, or join Ferdinand in Navarre. While they were eking out supplies as well as they could, they would run out before long, and needed to take action.

Howard added that all of Dorset's colleagues – himself, Willoughby de Broke, Lord Ferrers and the others – had urged Dorset to write again for orders, but that Dorset had refused, having already sent his man, Vincent, with a request for instructions, and claiming that Vincent would return before anyone else could arrive in England. Despite his own experience of being caught by contrary winds, Dorset seemed certain that no mishap could have befallen his messenger. In an exercise that might be seen as covering his back, but which may well have been born out of a real feeling that Dorset was not making sensible decisions, Howard asked Wolsey to keep his letter 'as proofs of the truth hereafter'. Perhaps his urging had some effect, as he added in a postscript that Dorset had written again to the king, and that the reason for that letter not being counter-signed by all of the officers, as was customary, was that Sir Henry Wyatt and Sir William Sandys were out of the camp, guarding the ordnance, which had been positioned in Fuenterrabia itself.

On 14 July, Dorset declined another request from Ferdinand to lead his men against Navarre, because he had still received no instructions to do so. He added that if Ferdinand would send troops to him to commence the attack on Guienne, he would be extremely glad. Ferdinand, however, ignored this request. The arguments continued. Dorset pressed Ferdinand for men and horses, while Ferdinand claimed that, since he had heard that the King of Navarre was plotting with France to attack the English from the rear, the best course of action was for the armies to combine to subdue the Navarrese. Dorset refused – it was against his orders, and besides, to withdraw from the border confronting the French might smack of cowardice. Dorset did not have sufficient experience or confidence to act against explicit orders in the face of a changed situation – even if the endless rain had not made the roads impassable.

The Duke of Alba wrote on 1 August to Dorset that as soon as Navarre was pacified, he would agree a date for advancing with the English. He added in his own handwriting that he longed for nothing so much as to be of service to the marquis. The next day, Ferdinand sent another missive via Dorset's courier, Richmond Herald. Ferdinand was full of the joys of spring – the location of Dorset and his men on the border had been extremely helpful, preventing the French crossing into Navarre. As for the complaint that he had not kept Dorset up to date, nothing could be further from the truth – he had written as soon as Navarre's capital, Pamplona, had been captured, and followed that up when he knew that Alba had received the surrender from King Jean. He assured Dorset that just as soon as Navarre was pacified, they would make a joint assault – he himself was quite as anxious as King Henry to see that monarch in rightful possession of his duchy of Guienne.

A few days after this, John Stile wrote a long letter in cypher to Henry. Stile was the permanent English ambassador at Ferdinand's court, having been sent there as early as 1505 to promote the friendship between England and Aragon. He had joined Dorset when the latter first arrived in Spain, and now he decided that the king needed to know exactly what was going on. He opened with assurances that Dorset and the other commanders were in good health, as were the most part of the soldiers, but that morale was terrible. The men were 'not contented in their hearts and minds' that they had been there so long without doing anything 'to the purpose of the enterprise'. Stile confirmed that Dorset and the others were eager to press forward, but that Ferdinand had failed to send the men and materials promised, making Navarre his excuse. He told Henry that Dorset had sent more messengers to Ferdinand and Alba, with requests for information and a plan for moving into Guienne, and that they were all dissatisfied with the evasive answers of the Spanish leaders. The English commanders were worried about the depletion of stores and money with nothing being achieved, and the increasing restiveness of the men. They were fatigued with lying out in the field, and prices were rising. Stile gave a long list of prices of supplies, and the little that could be bought for the money the soldiers had – wages were 6*d* per day, while a loaf cost a penny and a gallon of wine ten pennies. Besides, the local wines were not desirable – they were too 'hot' and the cider made the men ill. They needed beer. The men were demanding an additional two pennies per day – they were hungry, their clothes were worn, and they would not stay any longer without either more money or some action being taken by their leaders.

Stile continued that Dorset and the others wanted Henry to issue orders, based on Ferdinand's and Alba's letters – they themselves had little trust in Ferdinand now. Stile seemed to have a similarly low opinion of Ferdinand, whom he nevertheless referred to throughout his missive as 'your good father'. He told Henry that the English army being in position to attack France had led Louis to withdraw from Italy, leaving Ferdinand in possession of Naples and Sicily, his real aim, and also able to dictate terms in Navarre. Stile was in a quandary as to what ought to be done, since Ferdinand and his council '[had] certified unto your grace that their words and writings be so diligent and so fair [but] their deeds so immeasurably slack'. The ambassador had even angered Ferdinand by challenging him, only to be told that Ferdinand's whole intent was for the protection of Holy Church and the obtaining of Guienne for Henry. If only, Stile observed, Ferdinand had supplied horses, the English would have made great inroads into Guienne, but the men of Bayonne would never 'issue out' to give battle. All Ferdinand. had so far contributed to the enterprise against Guienne was permission for Stile to purchase saltpetre from Cadiz for the making of gunpowder, although not without Stile having written and importuned him repeatedly. The English had been obliged to purchase seventy-five mules and 100 oxen with their harness for pulling the artillery, since Ferdinand had also failed to provide transports.

Stile wanted personal instructions – was he to return home to report to Henry, or to stay with the army, as Dorset and his colleagues wanted? If the latter, Stile would need more money – he was already out of pocket with going back and forth to Ferdinand and ordering supplies. So keen was he for Henry to receive his letters that he chartered a pinnace from San Sebastian, at the cost of 96 ducats of gold. The boat was to go to Plymouth and wait fifteen days for Henry's response.

A spy had been captured, who gave the information that the Duke of Bourbon, one of Louis' commanders, was en route with some 9,000 or 10,000 men. If Bayonne could keep the English contained, Louis had no doubt that they would be forced to return home within the month. If this were Louis' plan, he was soon proved right.

Knight wrote to Wolsey on the same day, informing him that Ferdinand had been busy trying to suborn the bishops of Guienne from their allegiance to France, to support Henry. It was Knight's view that, even if the said bishops did come over to the English side, they should be replaced once the province was conquered. Not, he added, that the bishoprics were worth much, and that of Bayonne was now worth less, because the English troops had destroyed the country 'both contrary to our statutes and to our hindrance'. The soldiers were on the verge of all out mutiny. One group had refused to serve for less than 8*d* per day, and although the mutiny had been contained, and one man hanged, it was ready to burst out again, with many declaring that they would stay no longer than Michaelmas (29 September). It was Knight's opinion that all of this was owing to the army being idle – they were not being kept up to the mark with proper exercises, not even mustering for payday, and had no experience of victory to keep them cohesive.

Knight was also concerned that many of the commanders would 'suffer no counsel'. It is probable that by this he meant Dorset – he was the man in charge, so it was up to him to listen to advice and make decisions. Knight wrote that Wolsey had been roundly condemned – presumably for failing to provide enough stores. Knight was nervous that he was seen as Wolsey's man and asked for an early recall without it being known he had requested it. If that got out, he was afraid he would be killed – which seems a rather exaggerated concern. He also said that his correspondence was being read. It all smacks of too many men, with too little to do, rounding on each other with blame and suspicion. On 26 August, Wolsey sent Knight's letter on to Fox. He summarised its contents, saying that the men's desire to return home would be as great a hindrance to Henry conquering Guienne as Ferdinand's slackness.

Ferdinand decided to send a messenger, Luis Carroz, to Henry, to explain, yet again, why he could not possibly aid Henry in Guienne at that juncture, despite its recovery by England being so dear to his heart. Whatever he had said earlier about Navarre being under his control, it was undermined by a treaty of 7 September between Navarre and Louis, in which King Jean agreed that, the English being in Fuenterrabia, and menacing France, the Navarrese would declare war on them – perhaps Ferdinand had been right all along to claim that the Navarrese needed to be completely subdued before a worthwhile campaign could be mounted against Guienne.

On 4 October, Knight wrote again to Wolsey, informing his master that on 28 August Dorset's council had resolved that Knight and William Kingston should be sent to England for orders and money. Sir William Sandys had objected – in his view the whole debacle was Wolsey's fault, and if the two men went to him, they would persuade Henry to leave Dorset and the others in Spain. Quite why Sandys blamed Wolsey is not clear – at this time, Wolsey was the King's Almoner and a councillor, but not yet the power he was to become. However, the resolution had been to send them, so they went to San Sebastian for a ship. Once again, the weather was against them. The ship had beaten up and down in a storm for six days but been obliged to return to port.

Kingston and Knight had therefore returned to the camp, where Knight was cross to find that his post that had arrived in the meantime had been opened. He revenged himself by saying that little attention was being paid to the king's letters. Instead, the council was preparing to follow Ferdinand's instruction to join his forces at St Jean-Pied-de-Port. They would initially assemble at Errenteria, where Lord Willoughby de Broke remained stationed. Knight had protested that this would be contrary to orders. Howard, impatient, had declared that with a small force he would endure a winter war, and would prefer to die for the honour of the realm, the king and himself than return empty-handed, 'contrary to the king's [honour?] with rebuke and shame'. At this point, someone (Knight does not name him) slipped out of the tent and informed Lord Willoughby's men that, unless they mutinied, they would be obliged to attack Béarn, where King Jean and Queen Catherine had taken refuge. In Knight's words, 'great uproar ensued'.

Knight clearly had a very low opinion of most of the commanders – describing them as 'light', and worrying that the king was 'unlovingly served'. Howard's eagerness to fight, even without orders, caused Knight to except him from his general condemnation, saying that Wolsey could believe what Howard and Richmond Herald told him. All that Knight could offer by way of comfort was that Henry could be pleased that the main point of the expedition – the deliverance of Holy Church – had been accomplished and that England's enemies were 'men of long continuance in war, full of policy, and privy to all our deeds'. Back on the theme of Dorset's incompetence, Knight wrote that discipline among the men was poor and supplies mismanaged, and that Sir Henry Willoughby had told him that of the 800 bows the army had, only 200 were serviceable. Nevertheless, Knight added, it was of no use to blame anyone in particular, as that would just lead to mutual recriminations.

Dorset had sent Sir Guyot de Hedley to Bilbao on 17 September to charter ships to take the men home – another proceeding Knight thought rash, as the French were still haunting the Channel. He hoped that the returning army would meet with Sir Edward Howard's fleet for protection. Despite the local wine being too 'hot', Dorset had been obliged to order more. He himself was now ill, and Ferdinand had sent a physician to attend him. The decision to go home having been made, Dorset and his council were surprised, and probably angry, to receive a missive from Ferdinand, that the moment was now favourable for invading Guienne, and that he would be moving the Spanish forces towards the English. Dorset, perhaps not believing Ferdinand, perhaps with no choice in the face of mutiny and lack of supplies, responded that the English would meet the Spanish, but could only remain for twenty-five days in the field – perhaps an allusion to the men's determination to walk away at Michaelmas – after which, if Ferdinand did not provide shipping, they would march home through France.

This answer from Dorset was relayed to Henry in a letter directly from Ferdinand. Faced with Dorset's intransigence (despite, as Ferdinand said, his own 'unavailing remonstrances'), he had had to call the whole campaign off. Dorset, he said, had been utterly unreasonable, and he even suspected that there were French sympathisers in the English camp – especially as he had been informed by the Bishop of Siguença that Dorset had mentioned he was negotiating to marry one of the daughters of the King and Queen of Navarre. Howard and the other officers had approved of Ferdinand's plan – or so he said. In Ferdinand's opinion, the greatest fault of English soldiers was their inability to work together with others.

Ferdinand continued with the stunning information that, since he knew of the difficulties Henry was experiencing with the French fleet and the Scots, and that Henry was requesting aid from the Spanish fleet, he had taken it upon himself to agree a six-month truce with Louis, in which England was included. The truce covered the territories of England, Scotland, France and Spain, but not Italy, so France and Spain could continue their hostilities in the peninsula. He would be very happy to conquer Guienne on Henry's behalf in the following summer, if Henry paid half the cost. He assured his son-in-law that he would never make peace with France without consulting him – the truce had only been made because of the English failure to attack either Guienne or Calais. The truce would also, lied Ferdinand, make the pope more dependent on England and Spain, to fend off the French in Italy, enabling him to openly deprive Louis of Guienne and Normandy, in favour of Henry. This incendiary missive was dispatched to Henry with Ferdinand's two envoys, Luis Carroz and Martin de Muxica, in late September, after Dorset and his men had sailed, the day after Henry's instructions to join with the Spanish arrived.

Carroz and Muxica presented their letters, copies of the correspondence between Ferdinand and Dorset, and Ferdinand's criticisms of the campaign, first to the king and queen, and then to the council. The council accepted the criticisms, and the following day, Dorset, Lord Herbert, Lord Ferrers and the other captains were brought before king and council. Archbishop Warham asked for an explanation of their failure. The scene was witnessed by Carroz, who reported that they cited the mutiny of the men and the lack of supplies. Apparently, Dorset either took all the blame himself, or the others piled it on him, although he did dispute that he had written one of the letters Ferdinand claimed, saying that it had been composed by the Bishop of Siguença. This public dressing-down completed, the council assured Carroz that Henry would be guided by Ferdinand. Additionally, Katharine informed her father's ambassador that she had supported the notion of Ferdinand conquering Guienne on Henry's behalf, with the costs to be shared.

While the public humiliation following the complete failure of his first military command was doubtless extremely unpleasant for Dorset, it does not seem to have done him lasting damage with Henry. Dorset's brothers, too, were in favour. Lord Leonard and Lord Richard had both been granted positions in the king's new company of 'Spears', intended to form part of the king's personal entourage, with both ceremonial and military duties. Fifty men were appointed; each Spear was to be followed by an archer, a demi-lance and a custrell (the squire who carried the knight's sword) and to have three warhorses. The Earl of Essex was appointed as lieutenant, with Sir John Peche as his second-in-command. But the costs of being part of such a young and fashionable outfit were too much for Peche – according to Hall, the horses were trapped in cloth of gold, silver and goldsmith's work, and the servants were also 'richly apparelled'. One can imagine a band of eager young warriors, keen to outdo each other and obtain favour from the king. While the Spears received wages of around £60 per annum, the level of capital outlay must have been high. Presumably the Grey brothers' outfits were paid for by Cecily.

9

The Golden Years

My son, you are going to dupe the English, and I am going to
dupe the French.

Maximilian to Charles

Perhaps Henry believed that Dorset only needed a strong leader, such as
himself, to do great things on the battlefield. The following June (1513),
the king mounted a full-scale campaign against France, and named Dorset
and Buckingham as his fellow commanders of the rearguard. Henry's
friend Charles Brandon and lords Bergavenny, Berners and Darcy were
all in the same division. The experienced Earl of Shrewsbury was to lead
the vanguard, along with the Earl of Derby and lords Hastings, FitzWalter
and Cobham. Lord Herbert, together with the earls of Northumberland,
Wiltshire and Kent, Lord Dacre of the South, Lord Zouche's oldest son
and Sir Ralph Brereton, led the mid-section. Each commander brought
a contingent of men. Dorset provided 300, while Brandon led 900.
Brandon was appointed as marshal, and he and Dorset were to take the
musters of foreign mercenaries.[1]

As mooted the previous autumn, and agreed in a league sworn in April
1513, Ferdinand was to invade France from the south, subsidised by
Henry. Meanwhile, Maximilian was to enter from somewhere unspecified
on the long border between his territories and France, the pope's troops
were to join from the south-east, and Henry was to push out from the
Calais Pale. Henry meant business. A large grant had been wrested from
Parliament and was expended on armour, artillery, supplies (including the
obviously essential English beer), tents and all the accoutrements of war.
Great ships were under construction, and stockpiles of bows, arrows and
pikes laid in. Hundreds of naval craft of every sort were hired or bought
to ship 40,000 men plus horses, guns and gear across the Channel. But for
Henry it would all be worthwhile – the glittering prospect of the French
crown was within his sights. In his last sermon before the court, John
Colet, the Dean of St Paul's, had exhorted Henry to pursue peace, and

had been brushed aside. Henry could be certain of his destiny – the pope had even agreed that a vanquished Louis would be stripped of any rights to his kingdoms, which would be bestowed on Henry – for so long as the English king remained in 'faith, devotion and obedience to the Roman Church and Apostolic See'.[2] Henry, a devoted son of the Church, could have had no problem with that injunction. For the time being, however, Julius II preferred his grant of Louis' crown and kingdom to Henry to be kept secret.

There were two other pieces of business for Henry to deal with prior to his departure: safety on the home front, and the rule of the country in his absence. For the first, Henry cut off the risk of any Yorkist insurgency by executing Edmund de la Pole, formerly Earl of Suffolk, who had been languishing in the Tower since 1507; he meanwhile charged the Earl of Surrey to guard the Anglo-Scots border. James IV, having desperately tried to patch up a peace between his brother-in-law and his oldest ally, had decided that Scots honour lay with the alliance with France, and was rumoured to be ready to mount an invasion. Surrey was deeply unhappy with this relegation, as he saw it, as was his son, Lord Thomas Howard. The matter of government was solved by the appointment of Queen Katharine as regent, supported by those members of Henry's council not involved in the military effort.

Before Henry set sail, he received bad news: Ferdinand, once again, had slipped his collar and agreed a year's truce with Louis. Henry, although presumably enraged privately, made little of the matter in public, and pressed on with his plans. Another setback, which was also a personal blow, occurred in April when Admiral Sir Edward Howard was killed in an unsuccessful naval engagement off Brest. His admiral's whistle was sent as a trophy to Anne of Brittany, Queen of France.[3]

May and June were worn away with the transport of Henry's troops, often contending with contrary winds. Henry himself arrived in Calais on the last day of June. He did not travel light, bringing his choir, his chapel, his musicians, his numerous changes of clothing and his royal bed to keep him comfortable. His chief councillors, including Wolsey, were also in attendance. Henry VIII's idea of campaigning was very different from that of his heroic predecessor Henry V. For three weeks, he played at war, negotiating with Maximilian as to who would conquer what, and how the costs, and the spoils, would be divided. On 21 July, the English army set out for the town of Thérouanne on the Burgundian-French border, a regular bone of contention which Maximilian was keen to recover. As always, troops in northern France attracted rain. Henry, drenched on the first day of marching, took the opportunity to emulate Henry V by walking around the camp in wet clothes, urging his men to great feats of courage. The English sought the French to give battle, hoping for another Agincourt, but in vain. Louis had given orders to avoid pitched battle, given historic English superiority in set-piece confrontations. So, there was nothing for Henry's men to do but besiege Thérouanne. Maximilian arrived, not with the large force promised, but with a small escort. Flatteringly, he announced that he was under Henry's orders, a mere soldier in the victorious English king's army. He calculated, correctly, that Henry (still only just twenty-two years old) would be so impressed with the notion of the emperor being under his command that he would not push Maximilian on his failure to adhere to the terms of their league.

It was while this siege was in operation that the one battle of the campaign took place – a confrontation that was more spectacular in the retelling than in the event. A body of the French cavalry, including the Duke of Longueville, who had opposed Dorset in Guienne the year before, arrived to lift the siege, but had to make a headlong dash for safety, chased by the English, in what became known as the Battle of the Spurs. The French lost their banners, the Vice-Admiral of France, a marquis, and the aforementioned duke. Henry was not present in person, but he was nonetheless delighted. Thérouanne capitulated within days, and Henry, fond of the grand gesture, handed it over to Maximilian, who promptly had every building except the church destroyed.

With a victory of this magnitude under his belt, Henry accompanied the emperor to the Flemish town of Lille, to be fêted by Archduchess Marguerite, Maximilian's daughter, who was regent for her nephew Charles. Having enjoyed his rest and relaxation, Henry returned to his army, and arranged for Longueville to be sent as a prisoner of war to his admiring wife. It was probably with slightly mixed feelings that he learnt from that same adoring spouse that, in his absence, Surrey had won a crushing victory over the Scots at Flodden, leading an army inspired by Queen Katharine, who had made a speech reminding the men that 'English courage exceeded that of all nations'. James IV and a significant proportion of his nobles lay dead on the field. The speedy fall of the town of Tournai was not really comparable as a victory – although, to be fair to Henry, in military terms this campaign was the most successful that the English had fought in France since 1453. Whether it was a better outcome than Edward IV or Henry VII's campaigns, which had resulted in hard cash being paid by France to England annually, is a moot point.

Tournai was not given to Maximilian but garrisoned by the English. Other winners from the war were lords Richard and Edward Grey, both knighted at Thérouanne. Lord Edward also received a gift of £20. Henry was eager to follow up his victory, and on 17 October, Dorset and Fox were the English negotiators for a new agreement with Maximilian, Ferdinand, Juana, Charles and Henry against Louis XII. The campaign completed for the year, the army was paid off. Lord John sent his servant, William Prestgrave, to the paymaster, Sir John Daunce, and asked for the money to be given to Prestgrave 'to bestow in trifles against Christmas, for I am bare of money at this time'.

After further partying in Lille and a joust at Tournai that cost over £125, Henry returned home, confident that he now had an extended bridgehead in France. He had agreed with Maximilian that a new campaign would be launched the following summer. With hope still triumphing over experience, Henry was eager for Ferdinand to be, once again, the third member of the triumvirate, agog to dismember France. Naturally, Henry would pay for it all – or rather, Henry's subjects would. Before the new campaign began, Archduke Charles, who would turn fourteen on 24 February 1514, would complete his 1508 proxy marriage to Henry's sister Mary.

The year 1514 opened well for the English court. Surrey's contribution to English arms was recognised with the grant of the dukedom of Norfolk, held previously by his father, and before that by his Mowbray relatives. His son Lord Thomas Howard, Dorset's companion from the 1512 campaign, became Earl of Surrey and Charles Brandon was elevated to the dukedom of Suffolk. Dorset is unlikely to have been pleased by these elevations. As a marquis, he ranked only below a duke, and had been used to having none but Henry and Buckingham ahead of him in the pecking order. He had now been pushed down two notches. Still, given his poor showing in Guienne, he was not in a position to be openly offended. The king did not appear to be bearing any grudge, and, as usual, Dorset was present at the annual Garter ceremony at Greenwich. A month later, he was deputed, along with the new Duke of Suffolk, to meet the papal protonotary, Spinelly, who had been sent by Leo X to bestow the cap of maintenance on the king. This was a highly prized gift which popes conferred from time to time on monarchs whom they wished to honour. Spinelly was met at Canterbury and Rochester by Archbishop Warham and Bishop Fisher respectively, who conducted him to Blackheath where Dorset, Suffolk, the Bishop of Lincoln (none other than Thomas Wolsey), the Earl of Essex and Henry's Spears, including Dorset's brothers, were waiting. The protonotary entered London with Dorset at his left hand and received all the honour due to him as the pope's representative.

The preparations for Princess Mary's nuptials continued apace, with messengers racing between London and Marguerite's court. Henry was willing to lavish enormous amounts of money on the wedding in the anticipation that his sister would one day be empress. But the Imperial side began to drag its feet. Charles, aged fourteen, was heard to remark that the eighteen-year-old bride was old enough to be his mother. The politics of Europe had changed with the death of the bellicose Julius II and his replacement with Leo X in spring 1513. Leo was seeking reconciliation with France to limit Spanish power in Italy, and in return Louis had abandoned his scheme of his own General Council and accepted Leo's plans for one to be held in Rome. Leo now sought to pacify Henry, sending a delegation which Henry, uninterested in reconciliation with France, declined to receive. Yet again, Henry was to be frustrated by his allies. Before long, he was astounded to learn that, far from readying his army for an advance, Ferdinand had signed a truce with France, and was busy suborning Maximilian. Even more outrageously, Ferdinand purported to sign for his son-in-law as well. Ferdinand would not even take responsibility for his betrayal, instead ordering his ambassador to say that he, Ferdinand, had heard from Maximilian that Henry was eager for his name to be appended to the truce.

This time, Henry was ready to wash his hands of his father-in-law. He determined to press ahead with the war, negotiating with the Swiss for them to invade France from the east, at Henry's expense. Soon, though, the king changed his mind – probably on the urging of Wolsey and Fox, backed up by papal exhortations. He accepted Louis' indication that he would consider terms, and, angry and humiliated by the failure of Charles to marry Princess Mary, he agreed that she should marry Louis himself, Anne of Brittany having died in March 1514. Fifty-six-year-old Louis was thrilled with the thought of an eighteen-year-old bride, and Mary, persuaded by Henry that she must do her duty as a princess, publicly withdrew her consent to the marriage with Charles. A few days later, on 13 August 1514 at Greenwich, in the presence of king and queen, Buckingham, Norfolk and Suffolk, Dorset, the bishops of Winchester and Durham and the earls of Shrewsbury, Essex, Surrey and Worcester, Mary entered into a proxy marriage. Louis was represented by the Duke of Longueville, handily still at the English court following his capture at the Battle of the Spurs.

*

To demonstrate English delight with the new alliance, Henry threw himself into the celebration of the match with even more gusto than he had shown for the marriage with Charles. The preparations for Mary's trousseau, her escort to France and her long-term household were munificent. Meanwhile, Archduchess Marguerite tried to scupper the French match by claiming that Charles and Mary's proxy marriage had been binding, so that any new marriage with Louis would be invalid. These threats were ignored, and on 14 September, Louis entered a proxy marriage with Mary – the princess represented by the Earl of Worcester. The French king was in a great hurry to have his bride – he wrote to Wolsey that, although he was pleased that arrangements were being made for Mary to have clothes in the French fashion, he was content for the lengthy preparations to be shortened, so that she might embark as soon as possible. The tailors were certainly hard at work – Henry's accounts show that Mary received fifteen gowns in French fashion, six in Milanese style, and seven English ones.

Henry, Katharine, Mary and her large escort departed London for Dover on 19 September. While waiting for the wind to change, Mary apparently persuaded Henry to promise that, when Louis died, which everyone thought could not be far off, considering his general decrepitude, she could marry the man of her choice. Henry, on 23 September, issued formal instructions to the official embassy which was to deliver the princess. Dorset, Norfolk, Suffolk, Worcester and Docwra, Prior of

St John, were the chiefs. They were to obtain from Louis a receipt for the 220,000 crowns of Mary's dowry, and two copies of the grant of dower, with the great seal of France – one to remain with her, and the other to be brought back. Longueville accompanied them, thrilled to have been released from captivity.

The leader of the English embassy was Norfolk, accompanied by his wife, Cecily Dorset's sister-in-law Elizabeth Stafford; his daughter, Anne, Countess of Oxford; and his son, Lord Edmund Howard. Between them, they had 100 horses. Next in rank was Suffolk, followed by Dorset, named with his wife and brother, Lord Edward; the three of them received £80. This is the first mention of Dorset's wife. Since the Spanish had accused him of having his eyes on a marriage with Navarre in 1512, the probability is that he married in the intervening year, although most references to his marriage give a date of 1509. The lady in question was Margaret Wotton, once a maid of honour to Elizabeth of York. Margaret's family was not especially exalted – gentry from Boughton Malherbe, Kent – but her mother, Anne Belknap, was a cousin of Lady Ferrers of Chartley, so they were connected to the Yorkist affinity. Margaret made a first marriage to William Medley, by whom she had at least one son, George. A grant made in September 1514, varying an earlier grant to Dorset of the manor of Wyverston from tail male to tail general, is perhaps an indication that Dorset now had a daughter, but no sons. In all, Dorset and Margaret were to have eight children. His first son was to be born in 1517, followed by two others. The birth order, as always, was uncertain, but I will postulate that the eldest daughter was either Katherine (named for the queen) or Margaret, named for her mother.

Further down the list were lords Richard, John and Leonard Grey, in receipt of £20 each. There is no mention of either Lord Anthony or Lord George on this occasion, although later references confirm they were still alive. Margaret Dorset was named as one of Mary's ladies for the marriage itself while among the long-term appointments were Dorset's sister, Lady Elizabeth Grey, Anne Devereux, sister-in-law of Mary Grey, and Margaret Dorset's sister, Mary Wotton.

After being tossed about by storms, the group landed in France on 3 October, and accompanied Mary to Abbeville, the appointed meeting place with Louis. Louis' subjects were wild with enthusiasm for their new queen, cheering her all the way from Boulogne to Abbeville – perhaps as much in hopes for a more permanent end to hostilities between England and France as for her beautiful face. Before the official meeting, Mary came upon her fiancé 'by accident', as was the custom. A similar chance meeting had occurred between Mary's sister Margaret and James IV, when the king came across his new bride during a hunting party. Louis, therefore, pretended to be hawking when he encountered Mary's train. Fortunately, he was wearing his best clothes (which just happened to match Mary's outfit of cloth of gold and crimson) and was accompanied by his court. Mary, playing up to expectations, blew Louis a kiss, which he returned, before riding up to her, and kissing her without dismounting. Louis greeted Mary's attendant lords, including Dorset, before continuing his hawking expedition.

Mary's official entrance to Abbeville was of unparalleled splendour. The crowds thronged to see her, and reports of her beauty and the brilliance of her clothes, jewels and carriages raced around Europe. She was conducted to the Hôtel de Gruthuse where Louis, François of Angoulême, the king's son-in-law and heir-presumptive, and the rest of the French court awaited her.[4] Norfolk presented Mary, then regaled the company with a long speech, assuring Louis of Henry's friendship. Mary and Louis dined with a few of his closest friends, while Dorset and the other English lords were entertained by François.

The following day was the feast of St Denis, patron saint of France, and thus eminently suitable for the wedding, which took place in the Great Hall of the Gruthuse. Mary, dressed in the French style, was led in by Norfolk and Dorset, whose wife, brothers and sister Elizabeth were all in attendance. Louis was waiting, dressed in cloth of gold, with the nobles of France lining the room. During the service, the canopy of state was held above the couple by François and the Duke of Alençon. In accordance with custom, after the ceremony Mary withdrew to spend the day with the great ladies of France, led by Louis' daughter Claude, while François entertained the gentlemen. There followed the ceremonial public bedding. There was much speculation as to Louis' ability to perform his conjugal duties, but in the morning he loudly proclaimed his prowess. One gentleman thought it was probably true as Louis appeared 'most uncomfortable'. Louis was reported by all observers as besotted with his new bride. He gave Mary copious gifts of jewellery, requiring her to pay in kisses. The Venetian ambassador complained that Louis was spending too much time attending to his wife, rather than concentrating his energies on keeping Maximilian out of Italy.

If Lady Elizabeth Grey had been hoping for a glittering career as lady-in-waiting to the Queen of France, she was to be rudely disappointed. Despite Louis' fawning on his new bride, he had no compunction about dismissing most of her attendants. A distressed Mary wrote to Henry a mere three days after her wedding, upset by the dismissal of her chief companion, 'Mother' Guildford. Without that mature lady's advice, how could she be sure how to conduct herself? The young women left to her were not of the age or experience she would need to rely on if 'any chance [were to] happen other than well'. Norfolk, she thought, had been worse than useless in supporting her. If Wolsey had accompanied her instead, he would have protected her better. As it was, she was obliged to ask Henry to request Lady Guildford's reinstatement. Suffolk agreed with Mary that Norfolk was to blame. In Suffolk's view, Norfolk and his son Surrey had connived in the ladies' dismissal because they had been chosen by Wolsey in a show of power that Norfolk resented. Suffolk advised Wolsey to 'redress' the matter, for if Queen Mary were not 'well-handled',

Norfolk and his cohort would cast the blame on Suffolk and Wolsey. In this early show of rivalry between Wolsey and Norfolk, although there is no evidence of Dorset's views, it seems likely that he would have been at one with Suffolk, who was his friend, and he may well have had some personal feeling for Wolsey, given that it was his own father who had given him a start to his career.

Wolsey did his best for Mary and wrote personally to Louis requesting Lady Guildford's reinstatement: whatever Louis had been told, she was 'wise and discreet', and Henry had brought her out of retirement specifically to serve Mary. Despite his efforts, however, Louis would not have Lady Guildford back. He asserted that his wife and he 'be in good and perfect love as ever two creatures can be, and both of age to rule themself, and not to have servants that should look to rule them'.[5] Lady Guildford would not permit anyone to come near Mary without herself being present and he did not want a woman whom he hardly knew hovering about when he wished to be 'merry' with his wife. A few of Mary's more junior people were permitted to remain, including Lord Edward Grey.

Soon, another diplomatic contretemps arose. In mid-September, in anticipation of the marriage, François had issued a challenge to the knights of Europe to attend a tournament in honour of Mary, to take place forty days from the original proclamation date. A triumphal arch had been set up in the Rue St Antoine, near Tournelles, hung with six coloured shields denoting the various competitions and prizes. The challenge was brought to England by France's Mountjoy Herald, and proclaimed at Canterbury on 28 September, the very day that Mary and her entourage were due to embark. By that time, some 150 knights had signed up. Henry thought the forty days' notice too short, and an amended date, sixty days forward, was agreed by Mountjoy, but François was now reluctant to change the date. While there was no man more 'desirous' to do the new Queen of France honour than he, François claimed, he was not in charge of preparations for her state entry into Paris (French queens could not enter the capital until the day of their coronation), upon which the tournament depended. He would consult Louis on the matter, but would advise against it. In fact, anyone less pleased to see Mary than François could hardly exist – if Mary bore Louis a son, he would lose his chance of inheriting the kingdom.

King Louis, finding married life taxing, was laid low by gout. Mary was solicitous, attending him every day and sitting by his bed. He was sufficiently recovered by the last week of October for the royal party to leave Abbeville and make for Paris with a two-day rest at Beauvais. During that interval, Dorset and Suffolk were invited by François to hunt two wild boar which had been 'entoyled' in a wood. Suffolk killed the first and Dorset the second. The next day, after arriving in Paris, they met François to discuss the forthcoming jousts and undertake some practice. Dorset was surprised to discover that, despite what he had previously heard, once armed, François and his men were not particularly adept – although they handled themselves well with light staves. Dorset himself had nothing prepared at this point – neither horse, nor armour, nor weapons – and needed to gather everything before the tournament began. Before he had left England, Henry had given him £500 and he was sure that if he spent the money as generously as Henry had given it to him, he would be 'as well trimmed' as any man in France.

Despite this, neither he nor Suffolk were sure that they wanted to take part. Some 200 or 300 knights had already signed up, suggesting a lack of exclusivity that they thought would give the victors little honour. The duke may have hinted at his concern, because Louis asked François to appoint Suffolk and Dorset as his 'aids' – that is, supporting François personally. In due course, François summoned the two Englishmen to dine with him and the Duke of Bourbon, and told them that, rather than being his 'aids', they would be his 'brothers'. The talk at table was of Henry's athletic prowess. Nothing, wrote the sycophantic Suffolk, pleased François so much as to talk of Henry. The challenge was still set down for seven days hence, but on Suffolk and Dorset protesting that they could not be ready in time, François requested Louis to grant a week's postponement.

On the morning of 3 November, Dorset, Suffolk and their colleagues were summoned to attend Louis at St Denis, to receive official information about Mary's entry to Paris. The delegation gave Louis thanks for the honourable treatment of Mary and confirmed that they were commissioned to agree details of a meeting between the two kings. Two days later, Mary was crowned in the cathedral at St Denis. Dorset and the rest of the embassy were sent for by the Constable of France to take their seats early, before the multitude of spectators was permitted to enter. They waited for about an hour before Mary was led in by François, and the dukes of Alençon, Longueville, Bourbon and Albany. Albany was, in fact, a Scottish lord, who had been invited by the Scots to replace Henry's sister Margaret as governor of Scotland during the minority of her son James V, and Henry was desperate for Louis to keep him in France.

Later that day, Dorset and his colleagues were requested to attend Louis' council to discuss the meeting between the kings. Both sides claimed to be eager for it to take place, but found it surprisingly difficult to agree the details. The location, in particular, was contentious: the English wanted Calais, while Louis was reluctant to leave French territory, given his age and infirmity. The French suggested Ardres, but the English had no order to offer anywhere but Calais or St Peter's. All that could be agreed was that Henry would go to Dover, and Louis to Boulogne, and they would then settle a meeting location. Louis wanted the summit as early in April as possible, because he intended to send another army into Italy in May, and planned to supervise operations from Grenoble, but would 'in no wise' join his army before he and Henry had met.

When it was Dorset's turn to write the report from the delegation to the king, he was full of praise for Suffolk's handling of the embassy.

His final sentence contained the information that 'awle my money be spende'. However, every penny appears to have been used to good effect for the tournament which took place on 13 November at the Hôtel des Tournelles. Louis, in declining health, was unable to sit on his chair of state to watch it, so lay on a couch, Mary beside him, attended by Claude and the other great ladies. The five-day tournament was not a mere show – some 305 knights took part, of whom, according to Hall's Chronicle, 'diverse were slain and not spoken of'. The nine French champions were led by François, the English champions by Dorset and Suffolk. Patriotic as always, Hall recorded that the English did as well as the best of any other nation. Suffolk was the hero of the first day, running fifteen courses. He did not win them all, but gained extra points for detaching his opponent's plumed hat. François was obliged to retire after ten courses, having an injured hand. With François out of commission, Dorset and Suffolk took the position of Defenders, holding the barrier against all comers. Suffolk nearly killed one man, and Dorset struck a M. Grew, described as an 'Albanoys', so fiercely with his spear that the man's helmet was pierced and his death anticipated – Hall does not record whether the man recovered.

In the tourney round, both Dorset and Suffolk overthrew mounted horsemen, but the French were so jealous of their success that they refused to offer them the praise they deserved. Hall then recounted that François was so aggravated by the brilliance of Suffolk that he had a German man, larger than any man in the whole court of France, disguised as a knight to challenge the duke. The two men fought fiercely, the judges allowing many more 'strokes' to be given than had been laid down in the rules. Once the judges saw the German 'reel and stagger' they dropped the barrier, and ended the round. Meanwhile, Dorset was engaged with a French opponent, whom he managed to disarm of his spear. After this, there was a short break, during which our two English heroes took off their helmets to get some fresh air. Before long, they started again, this time with blunted swords. Once more, Suffolk was attacked by the gigantic German, but again he had the best of it. François whisked his man away before he could be unmasked. Louis remarked drily of François that '*ce grand gaillard gatera tout*' (this great lout will ruin everything). Lord Edward, whom Hall notes as Dorset's youngest brother, giving him the age of nineteen, took a turn, and he too 'was of such strength, power and policy that he so stroke his adversary that he disarmed him'.

Dorset's account of the tournament in his letter to Wolsey on 22 November, was rather less florid. While he mentions one man being killed, he notes that he and Suffolk only took part on the first day of the jousts, because the following days there were no noblemen to fight – instead, they sent their seconds. Once the fighting on foot began, he and Suffolk took part. He excused himself from saying more than that the English had acquitted themselves with honour, because he was 'a party therein'. Suffolk, like François, had injured his hand, but Dorset was unscathed. In his own handwriting, he added that Mary had told him that Louis was so impressed with their performance in the tournament that he thought they had put France to shame, and that the prizes, which were to be distributed by Mary on 26 November, ought to be awarded to them to carry into England. After the prize-giving, Dorset and Suffolk intended to return home.

Before departing, Dorset and the others had a further discussion with Louis' council, having been instructed by new letters from Henry to broach the matter of Navarre. This was probably a rather sensitive point for Dorset, considering the embarrassing failure of his 1512 campaign, but he made no mention of that in his report. Each side endeavoured to 'grope' the mind of the other, without giving anything away. Seeing that nothing was being revealed, Louis invited the men to have supper with him, by the side of his sickbed. The following day, after further verbal fencing, the French 'opened [their] king's pleasure and mind to us that we well-perceived they dealt plainly with us'. Dorset plumed himself that they had handled the matter so well that Louis had, unusually, agreed to commit his intentions to writing, rather than mere words – he had promised that the Duke of Albany would not be allowed to go to Scotland. Dorset was eager to receive the letters so that they could return home. Louis had told them, in the presence of the queen, that no king alive had such a servant as Suffolk (and we may suppose Dorset, although he was too modest to say) for both peace and war.

A few days later, Monsieur de la Guiche made a formal response on how Henry and Louis would combine to attack Ferdinand. As usual, Henry was to provide most of the men and money – 10,000 English soldiers, plus pay for 5,000–6,000 French. La Guiche would bring 300–400 horse and would be delighted to serve the English king. With this, Dorset and Suffolk's French embassy ended. By 28 November, they had reached Clermont, whence they sent a messenger ahead to request ships. They did not intend to arrive home in anything less than the style suitable for the king's envoys: twenty-two hoys were sent to carry them and their train back across the Channel.

Two days before the opening of Parliament in February 1515, Dorset took part in yet another tournament. He and Henry, along with an unnamed aid, were the Challengers. Dorset was issued with 'apparel' of white satin with 'sleeves volant', lined with blue and white sarcenet at 4s a yard and suitable harness for his horse, all of which he was granted at the end of the tournament. The fun and frolics continued – for May day, there was an entertainment, for which Dorset, Suffolk and the Earl of Essex were issued with base coats, harnesses and trappers of green velvet, embroidered with cloth of gold. While Dorset was enjoying court life, his brother Lord Edward had left Queen Mary's household, and was in the garrison at Tournai, being paid at a rate of 4s per day.

While Dorset had probably thoroughly enjoyed his time in France, the fundamental point of the trip was negated when Louis died on

1 January 1515, worn out with 'dancing', as it was politely termed, with his young wife. If, as seems suggested by Dorset's strong commendations of Suffolk, the two were friends, then he must have had his heart in his mouth when he learned that Suffolk, sent to France to collect the widowed Queen Mary, had married her, without Henry's permission. The king was in a fine rage, and it was not until Suffolk and Mary (referred to thereafter in England as the French Queen) had agreed to pay an enormous fine and hand over many of the jewels she had received from the doting Louis, that Henry calmed down.

*

The accession of François had a detrimental effect on Anglo-French relations, exacerbated by Archduke Charles having reached his majority, throwing off his aunt Marguerite's pro-English regency and taking a pro-French stance. Henry and Wolsey kept a close eye on happenings in the Low Countries through the agency of Thomas Spinelly – Spinelly, originally Italian, was not an ambassador in the modern sense, but resided near the Burgundian court as a representative of England. He was at the centre of a nexus of bankers, merchants and diplomats across Europe, enabling him to share up-to-date information with the English government, and he wrote to Wolsey to warn him against the machinations of one Don Diego whom he characterised as a 'subtil' fellow, a pensioner of both the late Queen Anne of France and Margaret, late Dowager Duchess of Burgundy.

Spinelly feared Don Diego might be harbouring sympathy for the last of the de la Pole brothers, Richard, who, having been expelled from France by Louis as part of the marriage treaty, was now in Lorraine, under the protection of an imperial duke. Don Diego was planning to visit England, and, under cover of bringing personal messages from Lord Fiennes and Lady Ravenstein, intended to visit Buckingham, Dorset and Sir Thomas Boleyn.[6] Fortunately for Dorset, this hint of a Yorkist conspiracy does not seem to have given Henry or Wolsey any concern about his loyalty. In July he was appointed to the commission of the peace for Northamptonshire and was granted, for life, the reversion of the manors of Loughborough and Shepshed, in his home county of Leicestershire, on the death of Elizabeth Scrope, Countess of Oxford. The grant was extended in 1520 to a grant in survivorship with Margaret and later into a permanent grant in tail male. At the outset, as Lady Oxford was still in possession, Dorset was to receive £82 per annum until the king could persuade her to exchange the land for the cash.

Henry was intensely envious of the new French king, especially after François won a decisive battle at Marignano in September 1515. This galling incident brought Henry back into harmony with his untrustworthy father-in-law, Ferdinand, and they entered a defensive treaty, in part as counterbalance to François' decision to send Albany to Scotland to replace Queen Margaret as governor. Margaret had lost her position by making a second marriage to Archibald Douglas, Earl of Angus. Unable to come to an accommodation with Albany, the queen escaped by night from Linlithgow, and, crossing the border, took refuge at Harbottle Castle, where she bore a daughter, Lady Margaret Douglas, in October 1515. Margaret remained there over the winter, confined to bed by severe sciatica but regularly importuning Henry to help reinstate her in Scotland.

During 1515, another dispute between Dorset, his mother and his stepfather arose, regarding his sisters' dowries. It was arbitrated by Wolsey, who seems to have forced Cecily and Wiltshire to contribute, rather than the dowries being paid out of the Grey estates. Since none of the sisters married in that period, it was probably brought to a head by either John Dudley or Lord Willoughby claiming Cicely or Dorothy's unpaid portions.

The key event at the English court in the autumn of 1515 was the arrival of a cardinal's hat from Rome. Wolsey, already Archbishop of York, had recently been appointed as Lord Chancellor, and now, after much badgering on the part of himself and Henry, was elected to the college of cardinals. The red hat that he coveted so much was dispatched and treated with extraordinary ceremonial, 'as though it were the greatest prince in Christendom come into the realm.'[7] On 15 November, it was conveyed to London and placed on the high altar at Westminster, to be viewed reverently by the great and good of the realm, including Dorset. The new cardinal rode behind the three dukes – Buckingham, Norfolk and Suffolk – with Dorset and Surrey immediately following. Mass was celebrated by Archbishop Warham, flanked by the bishops of Armagh and Dublin. The sermon was preached by Colet, who observed, no doubt to Wolsey's chagrin, that the cardinal's role, like that of his ultimate master, Christ, was to minister rather than be ministered to.

*

In February 1516, Henry was delighted when Queen Katharine bore a living child, although disappointingly, rather than the longed-for male heir, it was a girl, who was named Mary. Dorset carried the salt at the christening, which took place at Greenwich, while his wife bore the chrism. Meanwhile, Queen Margaret had been sending a barrage of requests to her brother for help. She was at last invited to London, to visit the brother she had last seen twelve years before, when he himself was only twelve. Accordingly, Henry required his chief nobles to attend the court at Whitsuntide. The Earl of Shrewsbury sent his not-entirely-sincere regrets – he was ill and there was contagion in his household. Wolsey was not wholly convinced by the earl's excuses, but there was little he could do, especially as there was a genuine outbreak of contagion in the capital and 'they beg[a]n to die in London in divers places, suddenly, of fearful sickness'. Henry's well-known fear of infection meant any plea of illness was almost certain to be accepted. Buckingham was in London, staying at his house at Coldharbour, whence he travelled regularly to the court by barge, and Dorset and Northumberland were also in attendance.

Margaret arrived in London in early May, entering the city from Tottenham, as was the custom for visiting kings of Scotland, riding a white palfrey, sent by Katharine. A great train of ladies and gentlemen accompanied her to Baynard's Castle, where she took to the river to travel to Greenwich. This addition of the Scottish queen made the tournament in celebration of the birth of Princess Mary even more splendid. Henry, Suffolk, Essex and Sir Nicholas Carew were the Challengers, while Dorset led the Knights Waiters, supported by the Lord Admiral (Surrey), Lord Bergavenny, Lord Hastings, Lord Ferrers and numerous others. Dorset's team were dressed in blue velvet again – perhaps reusing the garments from earlier events. After the jousts, Henry declared that he would not joust again unless it were with 'as good a man as himself', from which we may infer that his team had triumphed, and that perhaps Dorset was showing his age.[8]

While Shrewsbury was lying on his sickbed, his agent, Thomas Alen, kept him abreast of events at court, where Wolsey was implementing root-and-branch reforms in the king's council and his household to save money and improve efficiency. Dorset was listed as entitled to 'livery', that is a fixed amount of food and drink at the king's expense. Alen noted that both the cardinal and Sir William Compton were 'great' with the king, while Suffolk and the French Queen were 'out of the court' and had withdrawn to Suffolk – possibly because Mary had borne her first child, a son, Henry Brandon, in March. Alen reported the others on the losing end of Wolsey's reforms to be Dorset, the Earl of Surrey and Lord Bergavenny, all of whom had been 'put out of the council chamber within this few days, whatsoever that did mean'. Alen also noted that Dorset was to keep the Feast of St George the following day. This is an allusion I cannot explain, since 23 April is St George's Day, unless it were the custom for the Garter knights to take turns to host a feast.

Henry was in a bad mood – having commanded his nobles to court to do his sister honour, he was not happy when he saw that some of them had excessive retinues dressed in their liveries. This was a serious offence, prohibited by the statutes against maintenance – that is, maintaining men beyond the number required for household service, dressed in livery and indentured to serve. The Earl of Northumberland was the first to feel royal wrath, being sent to the Fleet prison, and Alen wrote to Shrewsbury that he had been informed by the king's solicitor that Dorset, Lord Hastings, Sir Richard Sacheverell, Lord Bergavenny and Sir Edward Guildford might soon follow.

Dorset's troubles stemmed not from suspicion of retaining but from a rivalry with his cousin Lord Hastings concerning influence in the East Midlands. By her second marriage to William, Lord Hastings, Dorset's grandmother Katherine Neville bore five children. The eldest son, Edward, became Lord Hastings following the sudden execution of his father and later married Mary Hungerford, who was Baroness Botreaux, Hungerford and Moleyns in her own right. This couple had two children: Anne, who married the Earl of Derby, and George, who, born around 1487, was ten years younger than Dorset. In 1509, three years after Edward Hastings' death, his widow married her late husband's receiver-general, Sir Richard Sacheverell. Mary Hungerford (always referred to by her own title), George Hastings and Sacheverell lived in a permanent state of petty warfare with Dorset. All three men were now brought before the Star Chamber and bound over to keep the peace.

*

The birth of a living child, although only a daughter, had been of considerable relief to Henry and his ministers. The optimistic king was confident that sons would soon follow, and over the next few years indulged in complex diplomacy for Mary's marriage. Much of it involved negotiations with the ever-unreliable Maximilian and rested on giving him financial support in his quest to push the French out of Milan. Henry and Wolsey had tried to interest the pope in the same cause, along with Charles, who, since the death of Ferdinand in January 1516, had been King of Spain as well as Duke of Burgundy. As noted above, at this stage in his life Charles was inclined to a French alliance, and, much to the horror of Maximilian and Henry, in August 1516, he entered into the Treaty of Noyon with François. Henry was determined to contain France within its borders, so, in response to Noyon, he agreed a treaty with the Swiss Confederation against France. Maximilian was delighted by Henry's offer to cancel his debts and even allow him to pocket yet more English gold – this time, 40,000 florins to keep the Venetians out of Verona. As part of the English contribution, Dorset was to receive a command to attack the south coast of France with some sixty ships over the autumn.[9] The treaty was agreed on 15 November 1516, and ratified by Maximilian, resplendent in his Garter robes, on 9 December. He promised to meet Henry for talks in person the following month.

Unfortunately, Henry was about to lose again. The Swiss changed their allegiance to François, and Maximilian quickly followed suit, accepting the Treaty of Noyon on payment of 60,000 francs from François, although he continued to protest to Henry that this was a ruse to lull the French into a false sense of security. This claim appeared somewhat thin when it was revealed that he was planning to take a French bride, and had received 20,000 florins from the Venetians to let them enter Verona. Henry and Wolsey's foreign policy was in ruins. But, undeterred, they continued to work for a defensive league against France, and, on 5 July 1517, yet another agreement was made with Maximilian and Charles. Charles sent an impressive embassy to sign on his behalf, led by Jacques of Luxembourg, supported by three other ambassadors, 100 horses and twenty-four baggage-wagons. Henry sent some 400 assorted barons and prelates to greet them and conduct them to his presence. He was dressed in Hungarian fashion, with a collar of 'inestimable value', flanked by

Katharine, the French Queen, Buckingham, Norfolk, Suffolk and Dorset, all dressed in cloth of gold.[10]

Dorset was a witness to the signing of the treaty, which was celebrated, as usual, with jousting. Henry, Suffolk, Dorset and Surrey took part, along with at least thirty others, watched from the windows by Katharine and the French Queen. After Henry and Suffolk had run eight courses against each other, in which they both 'shivered' their lances each time, a new spectacle was shown. A beam of wood, 20 feet in length and 9 inches in diameter, was balanced on the head of a Master Carol, who ran up and down the length of the tiltyard without dropping it, to thunderous applause. Appetites sharpened by the physical display, the court and honoured guests consumed a celebratory feast. Dorset was seated between Lady Guildford the elder – she who had been sent home from France by Louis XII – and one Lady Willoughby, probably Lady Willoughby de Eresby, who was Katharine's close friend, rather than his sister Dorothy, Lady Willoughby de Broke. Also at his table were his wife, his sister Elizabeth, Norfolk, Suffolk and the Venetian ambassador. Surrey, along with lords Richard and Leonard Grey, had the honour of bearing towels and basins for the king, while Lord John Grey did the same for the queen.

Ten days later, Lady Elizabeth Grey acted as proxy for the infant Princess Mary, who had been invited to be godmother to her new-born cousin Frances, daughter of Suffolk and the French Queen. In August, Dorset was part of the embassy to Brussels for the counterpart ratification. While he was away, Lord Leonard got into some unspecified trouble – Dorset wrote on his behalf to Wolsey, requesting the cardinal to be 'good lord' to his brother, with the words 'myserycordy shulde be used to warde ever man, and specyally to the yowng wytt' (mercy should be used towards every man, and especially the young).[11] With the uncertainty of the brothers' birth order, and the date of their father's death, Leonard could have been any age between seventeen and thirty-seven, but we can perhaps infer that he was closer to the lower end of the scale.

10

Local Politics

A plague on both your houses...
Shakespeare, *Romeo and Juliet*, III i

Although Dorset was, as head of the family, the focus of Henry's friendship and generosity, his brothers were not neglected. Lord Edward was retained in the household of Mary the French Queen and Suffolk, while in December 1516, Leonard was given the position of carver in the king's household and Lord John received an annuity of £20 during the king's pleasure.

Details about the marriages of Dorset's siblings are scarce and have to be pieced together from external evidence. A number of books suggest that Lord Edward married Anne Jerningham, who served with him in the household of Suffolk and the French Queen. However, I cannot find any substantial evidence that they ever did marry – or, if Edward did marry a lady of that name, whether she was the same Anne Jerningham who subsequently married Henry Barlee, Robert Drury and Edward Walsingham. A suggestive link is the name Barlee – Lord John Grey married Henry Barlee's sister Anne as his second wife, so the families may all have been connected.

Lady Dorothy was still married to Lord Willoughby, the mother of several children who died young and two daughters who lived: Elizabeth, later Lady Marquis of Winchester, and Anne, later Baroness Mountjoy. Lady Mary, wife of Lord Ferrers of Chartley, had three sons: Richard, Henry and William. Lady Cicely, married to John Dudley, heir to Lord Dudley of Sutton, produced a quiverful, with five sons and three daughters. Lord Leonard appears to have married Elizabeth Arundell, the widow of Lord Daubeney, his father's old companion-in-arms – the evidence is suggestive, but not compelling. Elizabeth was the aunt of the Sir John Arundell whom Leonard's sister Eleanor had married, and was probably considerably older than her husband. She had wardship of her two sons by Daubeney, which would have made her an attractive proposition for a younger son. In 1513, she, Leonard and Dorset were bound in an obligation to pay the king £300 by ten annual instalments at Easter, a reduction from the £600 Elizabeth had previously owed the king.[1] There does not seem any reason for the Greys to be involved unless Leonard was married to the lady, and there is a later reference to a wife of Lord Leonard's named Elizabeth. Lord John first married a lady named Elizabeth Catesby, but quite where she fits into the Catesby family I cannot tell; then, as his second wife, he wed Anne Barlee, widow of Robert Sheffield.

Rather than marrying, Lord George Grey graduated from Oxford as a bachelor in Civil Law in 1511 and took holy orders. Disappointed of the office in Colchester that Dorset had requested for him from the king, he was appointed as Dean of the College of the Annunciation of St Mary in the Newarke, Leicester, in 1517. St Mary Newarke was founded by Henry of Grosmont, 1st Earl of Lancaster, and was an important religious site for the Lancastrian royal family. It was the burial place of Constanza of Castile, second wife of John of Gaunt, and of Mary de Bohun, first wife of Henry IV. This important Lancastrian shrine had found a protector during the Yorkist years in William, Lord Hastings. He granted it lands, in return for a £20 annuity, and obits for himself and his wife, Katherine Neville. Following George's appointment in 1517, the visitation by the Bishop of Lincoln paints a picture typical of the years leading up the Reformation: there were no very great sins to report, but the dean and canons were lax in their attendance at divine service, frequented taverns and admitted women to the premises without licence. The canons took the opportunity to complain that Lord George was arbitrary in his rule of the college.

In 1517, Elizabeth, Lady Scrope, née Neville, died. She was the daughter of John Neville, Marquis of Montagu, who had died at Barnet in 1471, and she was thus a first cousin of Cecily, and the sister of Lady Anne Stonor, whom we met in the 1480s as Cecily's guest. In her will, Elizabeth Scrope left 'Mary daughter in base unto Thomas Grey Marquis Dorset my bed that my said Lord Marquis was wont to lie in and all the apparel that belongs thereto and all the apparel of the same chamber'. She also appointed Dorset as the overseer of her will, for which he was to receive £25. Harris, in *English Aristocratic Women*, infers from this bequest that Dorset and Elizabeth had been lovers and that Mary was their daughter. This seems unlikely – Elizabeth was first married in 1477, and even if she had been only the legally minimum age of twelve, rather than the more usual fourteen or fifteen, that would still make her considerably older than Dorset. Although the size and value of the bequest certainly suggests a closer relationship than mistress and servant, other explanations seem more likely – the cousinship may have resulted in Dorset, or perhaps Cecily, requesting a job for his illegitimate daughter, a very common proceeding.

*

Dorset's first son, named Henry, had been born in March 1517. As a sign of royal favour, and to encourage another generation of his extended family who could be relied upon to serve him without posing a threat to his throne, the king granted Dorset and young Lord Henry several offices in survivorship: steward to the dean and canons of the college of Warwick, and to the priories of Nuneaton, Merivale, Coventry, Stoneley and Kenilworth. These offices reinforced Dorset's influence in Warwickshire and Leicestershire, where he was concentrating on local affairs and building his affinity. He wrote to Wolsey from Bradgate in February 1518, concerned that three men of Leicester had conspired to steal horses from his own servant, George Hynde. Dorset had sent out twelve men in pursuit, who had captured the thieves at Doncaster. He enclosed their confessions, observing that the case was unusual: 'Such stealing of horses as is in these quarters I have not much heard of before.'

With all his available funds going into the development of Bradgate, Dorset had little left over to maintain the properties that he owned in Calais. As a frontier town, Calais needed to be kept secure, but there was never enough money to do it. The Calais council had recently complained to the king that Dorset and the other landowners had allowed their properties to 'fall into decay'. They should be reprimanded and commanded to 'amend' their holdings, as this state of affairs caused the king to lose money. The security of Calais was vital as Henry and Wolsey were contemplating a volte-face in foreign policy. By 1518, it was apparent that there would never be support from Charles and Maximilian to overrun France, so a more pacific approach was taken. The idea of a mutual defence treaty in Europe, with England as the arbiter, was mooted. This was partly designed to outmanoeuvre Pope Leo, who was trying to develop something similar with a view to a crusade against the Turks, and partly to give England a higher level of prestige as a promoter of peace than could be achieved by military means.

Two treaties were agreed, one between France and England, and the other, which was to be open to all European monarchs, was a pact for mutual protection and non-aggression. The Anglo-French element was cemented by the betrothal of Henry's two-year-old daughter, Mary, to the baby son of François and Claude. The betrothal was celebrated with great ceremony over several days in early October. Dorset was a signatory for both treaties, but departed London immediately after the signing, before the formal ceremony on the 5th. He headed for Bradgate, but no sooner had he arrived than he received a letter from Wolsey, requesting his presence at 'a solemn ceremony' to take place on the 14th – this was Henry's public swearing to the treaty, with failure to observe it to be punished by excommunication and an interdict on his kingdom. Dorset begged to be excused, although he would very much have liked to attend, saying he was suffering 'from his old sickness'. There are no details as to what ailed him; it may be that the sickness he had picked up in

Fuenterrabia was recurrent. Perhaps it was malaria, endemic in Europe in the sixteenth century. Or perhaps he just wanted to go home to enjoy the pleasures of domesticity amid a growing family.

Dorset's greatest rivals for influence continued to be Lord Hastings, Sacheverell, and a third man from Hastings' affinity, Sir John Villers. Family ties were, in this case, no bar to enmity. The hearing in Star Chamber of 1516 had not resolved their differences. Dorset wrote to Wolsey from Bradgate for help, complaining on 28 January 1519 that Leicestershire was in 'great disorder'. Two tame harts, with bells about their necks, belonging to Leonard, had been killed in the night, and their heads set upon stakes, at the suggestion of Sir John Villers. The same Sir John had also impeded an inquest due to take place in Leicester when '[he], who was wont to ride with eight or nine horses at the most, came to town with 26 or 30 well weaponed, and himself a sword and buckler by his side, who never used to ride with one before, and set him down upon the bench, the said sword and buckler by his side, facing and braving the quest with his adherents, so that justice could take no place'.[2]

This mafia-style slaughter of deer and intimidation was probably designed to impede a charge of murder against a priest named Edward Alen, who had been indicted but subsequently released. Alen was part of Hastings' and Sacheverell's affinities. Subsequent to his release, Alen sent two men to London to be questioned about their alleged transmission of a letter from the latest 'White Rose', Richard de la Pole, addressed to TMD, whom Alen identified as Dorset. The men denied all knowledge of such a letter. Henry's secretary, Richard Pace, warned Wolsey that he thought Alen a 'crafty fellow' and suspected he was actually a spy for the White Rose. Nothing in the records shows Wolsey finding anything to question Dorset about, but it does indicate that hinting at involvement with Yorkist conspiracies was considered a useful tool against an adversary.

During March and April 1519, Dorset had recovered sufficiently from his winter illness to attend court. He was present when Charles's ambassador, Signor Bartholomew, arrived and complained bitterly of the behaviour of the King of France in connection with the imperial election. Maximilian had died, and Charles and François were straining every sinew to be elected to the coveted throne. According to Charles, François was attempting to wrest the crown from the electors by 'violence and tyranny', supported by the pope, the Venetians, the Swiss, the Genovese and the Florentines. Dorset expressed his 'extreme regret' to the French ambassador that such things were being said of his master, to which the ambassador responded that, while François was not, of course, contemplating violence, it would be better to obtain the crown 'magnanimously, by force of arms' than by seduction and fraud – a reference to the enormous sums being poured out in bribes by Charles. At one point, Henry himself was suggested as a candidate, but he probably did not think that he stood a realistic chance of election. Instead, he promised support to both François and Charles, while generally favouring the latter. Charles did indeed win the election, but the level of bribes he had had to shell out rendered it a pyrrhic victory – he was indebted for the rest of his reign.

Wolsey took the opportunity of Dorset's presence at court to conduct another arbitration between Dorset, Hastings and Sacheverell, perhaps combining this with investigation into the allegations by Alen. Many of the issues seem to have related to the management of Leicester's royal deer parks. As part of the agreement, Dorset agreed an exchange of lands with the king. Dorset would surrender the park of Birdsnest, Leicestershire, where his brother Lord John and John's wife were living, for lands elsewhere, and Sacheverell would be appointed as the new royal keeper of the park, while he and Lady Hungerford would leave Newarke. Accordingly, Dorset, Lord John, Hastings and Sacheverell were all told to discharge their servants. At the same time, Dorset confirmed that at the royal park of Frith, where he was warden, he had maintained at least 3,000 beasts. Arbitration complete, Dorset departed for Waltham Forest, in Essex, to undertake his duties as a member of the commission for the peace, arranging to meet Leonard at St Albans afterward, to travel together to Bradgate.

Leonard came directly from the court with bad news from the king. Henry was cross that Dorset had not kept his promise regarding the number of deer in Frith. As soon as he reached Bradgate, Dorset hastened to justify himself in writing to Wolsey. He could confirm that there were 1,200 deer in Frith just after Easter, a number which had been confirmed by William Catour, one of Lord Hastings' keepers, to the king's commissioners only the week before the date of writing. The Frith deer, together with those in the parks at Toly and Baron, and some additional beasts he had under the king's warrant, made up the number to at least 3,500.

Dorset now complained that Sacheverell had raced home and, before he had even dismounted from his horse, sent two servants to Birdsnest to tell Lord John and his wife that they must depart. Lord John was not at home, so Lady John asked Sacheverell's men to produce written orders, either from the king or Dorset. On being told that they had come on Sacheverell's bare word, she refused to leave, but 'made them good cheer'. The following day Sacheverell himself arrived, flanked by twenty-four men, armed with bows and arrows, which they shot off around the house in threatening fashion. Alarmed, Lady John refused to admit Sacheverell, instead sending out a servant to ask his business. He sent back the message that he was merely calling to thank her for her hospitality when they had last been at Bradgate together and denied any knowledge of the servants who had come the day before. Lady John still refused either to come out herself, or let him in, so he departed, his servants continuing to shoot randomly, and breaking down the palings to the edge of the park, which, Dorset said, had resulted in the death or injury of many of the king's deer. To add insult to injury, Lady Hungerford was claiming to be too ill to make the reciprocal move from Newark.

Dorset went on to relate that, until the arrival of the king's servants to manage the park, Sacheverell's men had been walking the parks and forests as keepers. 'Under colour thereof', on the day after Trinity Sunday, one of Sir William Ashby's servants, riding through the park, had been shot and killed by Sacheverell's servant Parker in an entirely unprovoked (according to Dorset) attack. The following day, three more of Sacheverell's servants had impounded Parker's goods. The bailiff, Sir William Skeffington, demanded the goods be lodged with him as pertaining to the king, but Sacheverell had refused to release them, on the grounds that they had been seized in satisfaction of a prior debt. It is not easy to disentangle what is going on here, but probably it was a ruse to ensure that Parker's goods were kept safe from confiscation in the event of a conviction for murder.

Dorset's rehearsal of Sacheverell's iniquities continued. The next accusation was that Sacheverell had taken twenty-seven men, armed with swords and bucklers, to a place called Lyncyche, near Desford Wood, where they had stayed all night. Dorset was highly suspicious, thinking that such an action 'can be thought for no good intent nor purpose'. The following day, the armed band had gone into Desford Church, and, finding that Dorset's heraldic arms were displayed higher in the church than Lord Hastings', had torn them down – a great insult to a man who was the king's own cousin. Rather than acting as a 'good and loving neighbour', Sacheverell had failed to reprimand his men.

Nevertheless, Dorset assured Wolsey that, no matter how badly Sacheverell was behaving, he himself would follow Wolsey's orders. Still worried about deer numbers, Dorset assured Wolsey that, if the king needed more deer to stock Birdsnest, now that he owned it, he could let the king have as many as he wanted, for 'there is no deer nor other thing that I have but shall be at his grace's pleasure'.[3] Shortly after this letter was dispatched, Wolsey advised Leonard not to deliver Dorset's earlier letter to the king in which he assured his master of the presence of 3,500 deer, as Dorset's claims were not backed up by the information that the king's commissioners had relayed. Dorset thanked Wolsey for his advice, and asked him to keep the letters until Dorset was able to come to London and show that all he had said was true – 'or at least the more part thereof', stepping back in case he had exaggerated. He was sure that the king's commissioners would 'approve and affirm the same' – or, at the very least, the commissioners would 'think the same to be true'. Wolsey responded to the situation by forbidding Dorset, Hastings and Sacheverell from attending the quarter sessions, to prevent further violence.

Whatever annoyance Henry might have felt with Dorset over the matter of deer numbers and the rows with Sacheverell, it did not result in any long-term breach. In September, Dorset was back with the court, at the newly constructed house at Newhall, otherwise known as Beaulieu, in Essex. Henry had arranged yet another feast to entertain his wife and court. Eight men entered the great hall after dinner, disguised with long, white beards and dressed in cloaks of blue satin, painted with cyphers and powdered with gold spangles. They danced in stately fashion with the ladies, until Katharine snatched off their masks to reveal Dorset, Suffolk and several other men. The chronicler noted, rather unkindly, that the ladies were amused to see such old men masquing, as they were all at least fifty. This was rather an exaggeration, as Dorset was only forty-two, and Suffolk some seven years younger.

Marks of favour continued. In April 1520, Dorset was given a licence to import 20 tuns of wine each year for the use of his household without paying duty, and the next month he took part in the celebrations held at Canterbury to welcome Emperor Charles. Henry had finally agreed the long-planned summit with François, and a nervous Charles was determined to undermine the meeting. He had therefore invited himself to visit his 'dear uncle' en route from Spain to the Low Countries. He brought an enormous train with him, including Queen Germaine, second wife of his late grandfather Ferdinand and his reputed mistress. What Katharine made of the woman who had succeeded her mother as her father's wife is not recorded, but she must have been curious, to say the least. Despite the visit lasting only four days, Henry pulled out all the stops – including a full procession to the cathedral, where the royal party was followed by some 600 courtiers, all draped in gold cloth. At the banquet, Buckingham, Norfolk, Dorset and Northumberland's son presented the various bowls and towels for the sovereigns to wash their hands.

As if this were not enough expenditure on the grand gesture, Dorset left Canterbury as part of the enormous retinue that Henry and Katharine took to France for the meeting with François and Claude, known to history as the Field of Cloth of Gold. Dorset's retinue included forty-five servants, four chaplains and eight gentlemen. Dorset's role was prominent – he rode ahead of the king, bearing the sword of state as Henry made his official visits to the French camp. His gravitas in chivalric matters, derived from many years of involvement in tournaments, resulted in his appointment as one of the judges in the extremely serious matter of the correct placement of the arms of the two kings. In the end, it was decided that the French arms would take the senior side on the right, but that both French and English should be at equal height. He also showed his continuing prowess on the tournament field, taking part in the jousts as one of the king's three aids.

Neither Cecily nor Margaret Dorset were included in the royal retinue, the latter probably owing to pregnancy, but the ladies of the family were well represented by Dorothy Willoughby, Elizabeth, Lord Leonard's wife, and Lord John's wife. One of Dorset's brothers, however, blotted his copybook. He was overheard in conversation with a friend, in which one said, 'If I had a drop of French blood in my body, I would cut myself open to get rid of it', to which the other replied. 'So would I.' On this coming to Henry's ears, the men were arrested, and the Venetian ambassador thought they would fare badly unless François interceded for them. Nothing more is heard of this intriguing incident, but it shows the general English view of France and the French.

While the public purport of the Field of Cloth of Gold was to promote a long-term friendship between France and England, and confirm the treaty with France of 1518 and marriage of Princess Mary to the dauphin, the reality was that, behind the scenes, Henry was again being courted by Charles. At the prior meeting in England, they had agreed a further meeting would take place after that with France, between Henry, Katharine, Charles and Archduchess Marguerite. Dorset had the honour – and no doubt the expense – of providing lodgings for Charles's minister, the Cardinal of Toledo, at his own house in Calais. He himself was present as a councillor at both ceremonial and business meetings. The English court returned to London in July, and a month later Dorset was at Windsor hunting with the king, although Pace wrote to Wolsey that the marquis' legs were 'not so meet for hunting as is his Kendal coat'. Pace thought that Dorset had gout, a recurring malady which may have been what he had alluded to when he mentioned 'his old sickness'. Nevertheless, despite affliction with this extremely painful problem, Dorset's duties continued, with renewed commissions of the peace for various counties.

*

In May 1521, Dorset and his colleagues were shocked, and perhaps frightened, by the arrest of Edward Stafford, 3rd Duke of Buckingham, for treason. Buckingham was closely connected to Dorset – the duke's mother, Katherine Woodville, was Dorset's great-aunt; his brother, the Earl of Wiltshire, was Dorset's stepfather; and Lord Edward and Lord Leonard may have had positions under him. He had been a regular jouster alongside Dorset since the turn of the century, and present at most of the key ceremonies of Henry's reign. He was also Henry's nearest Lancastrian relative. Despite, or perhaps because of, his kinship to the king, Buckingham had never had a particularly good relationship with him – and had a positively dreadful one with Wolsey, whom he considered an upstart. The duke was indicted for treason after it was reported that he had listened to prophesyings about the king's death, in the event of which he would become king, ignoring the rights of Princess Mary.

Buckingham was entitled to trial by his peers, so the court of the Lord Steward was convened, presided over by Norfolk and Lord Chief Justice Fyneux. The duke's immediate family were not required to take part, ruling out Wiltshire, Northumberland, Surrey, Montagu and Westmorland, but Dorset and his brothers-in-law Ferrers and Willoughby de Broke were among the judges. The duke was found guilty, and Norfolk pronounced the sentence of execution with tears running down his face. Henry had shown his ruthless streak before, in the execution of Edmund de la Pole and his father's councillors Empson and Dudley, but the English nobility could easily have understood and approved those decisions. The execution of the last of the royal dukes must have made them more wary of their charismatic king. Whatever Dorset's private thoughts, he benefited materially from Buckingham's death with the grant of former Stafford lands in Warwickshire. Lord Richard also received a grant of one of the duke's Yorkshire manors.

Having dealt with the problem of treason at home, Henry could concentrate on foreign affairs. In August and September 1521, Wolsey presided over an arbitration session in Calais. Some historians have viewed this session as a genuine attempt to resolve the endless war between Charles and François, but others have characterised it as obfuscation and delaying tactics, designed to cover the development of a new alliance between Henry and Charles. Henry agreed to send 6,000 archers to Charles, suggesting Dorset, Shrewsbury or Worcester as the leader of the expedition – showing a trust in his cousin that the 1512 debacle did not necessarily warrant – but Wolsey counselled against the appointment: 'The lord Marquis is valiant and active, but would be more expensive than a lower person.' As well as the expense, Wolsey was concerned that fortune in 'acts martial' had eluded Dorset and thought that his services 'might be forborne at this time'. Henry accepted the advice, and in fact no one was appointed because Wolsey persuaded Henry to delay – it was hardly appropriate to be arbitrating peace while arming for war.

Whatever the original intentions of the parties to the peace conference, what emerged was further warfare in Italy and the Treaty of Bruges between Henry and Charles, which included the betrothal of Charles to Princess Mary. Given that Mary was still officially betrothed to the dauphin, and Henry and François had agreed a treaty of friendship only three years before, this treaty was predicated on the assumption that it would only come into effect if François were deemed by Henry to be the aggressor in the current struggle with Charles. With Henry as his secret ally, the emperor agreed to pay a state visit to England to negotiate further. The trip was organised in the most minute detail and was the most splendid foreign visit of Henry's reign – the Anglo-Imperial equivalent of the Field of Cloth of Gold, although not so expensive! Dorset sailed to Calais on 23 May on the *Michael*. Together with the Earl of Essex, the Bishop of Exeter, Lord de la Warr and the Calais officers, he met Charles at the Burgundian border and conducted him to the city gates, where the Lord Deputy and the Porter of Calais solemnly handed over the keys of the city and the prison. After two or three days in Calais, Charles and his train crossed to Dover, arriving at four in the afternoon of 27 May, where he was greeted by Wolsey, Suffolk and some forty other nobles, prelates and court gentlemen, as well as gentlemen of Kent and Sussex, and conducted to Dover Castle. On 29 May, Henry had the pleasure of showing Charles his best ship, the *Henry Grace à Dieu*, and the various other vessels that lay in Dover Roads, ready for the joint attack on France.

The same day, Henry sent Clarencieux Herald to France to declare war, on grounds derived from the 1518 Treaty of London: first, that Henry believed François to have been the aggressor in the conflict with the emperor; second, that François had broken the treaty by allowing the Duke of Albany to return to Scotland; third, that François had withheld the pension due to England. The next day, the party departed for Canterbury, where Charles saw the massed ranks of the English clergy on either side of the street, as he rode on Henry's right hand to Christ Church, to be greeted by Archbishop Warham and shown the famous tomb of St Thomas Becket, one of the premier tourist spots in Europe. Over the next few days, the two monarchs travelled from Canterbury to Gravesend, where they were met by 'gorgeously apparelled' barges belonging to the king and other nobles. Charles's suite required thirty barges to convey it to Greenwich. All the remaining craft between Greenwich and Gravesend were anchored along the route, with banners and streamers, and ordinance to salute the emperor as he passed.

On the evening of 2 June, they arrived at Greenwich, where Queen Katharine, holding Princess Mary by the hand, was waiting at the palace door to greet her nephew, who knelt to ask her blessing. The entertainment continued with a joust. Henry and the Earl of Devon, clad in cloth of gold and silver with embroidered letters, led one team, while Suffolk and Dorset, dressed in russet velvet with gold knots, led the opponents. Charles and Katharine watched from the stands as the two teams first ran at each other singly, and then en masse. The joust was followed by dancing. As Henry was arming for the next day's tourney, he received a letter from his ambassador in France, Sir Thomas Cheyne, informing him that François denied all of Henry's allegations, and affirming that he had withheld Henry's pension only because he suspected that Henry was preparing to use it to make war on him. Henry immediately sent Sir William Compton to let Charles know, and to request him to join the king. The monarchs read the letter over with great excitement, before proceeding to the tourney, in which both Charles and Henry took part.

On Friday 6 June, Henry and Charles made a splendid entry into the City of London. The City Corporation had been preparing frantically, finding lodgings for the emperor's suite as well as food and wine. A mile outside the city gates, a tent had been set up where the emperor and king rested whilst the procession formed – and a grand spectacle it must have been. Riding sided by side, Henry and Charles were followed by their nobles and households, decked in velvet and cloth of silver. The welcome speech was made by Sir Thomas More. As the procession rode past the prisons of the Marshalsea and the King's Bench, Henry graciously acceded to Charles's traditional request for prisoners to be freed. Tableaux and pageants lined the streets, including one in which

Charlemagne gave the sword of justice to the emperor and the sword of triumphant victory to Henry. Another, which had been arranged by the Italian merchants, showed Edward III and his son John of Gaunt, Duke of Lancaster, with a structure representing a tree, in the branches of which were hung some fifty-five images of kings, queens and nobles, with representations of Henry, Katharine and Charles at the top, showing how they were all of common descent from the House of Lancaster. A similar pageant showed them all descended from Alfonso the Wise, King of Castile. There were scenes from King Arthur and the Knights of the Round Table, and representations of the stars and planets. Eventually the procession reached St Paul's, where Archbishop Warham met them, and the monarchs made offerings at the altar.

Saturday was devoted to tennis. Sunday being Whitsunday, the monarchs went in solemn procession, dressed alike in white and silver, to St Paul's, where Wolsey conducted high Mass. After dinner at Bridewell they went on to Westminster, where Charles was impressed by the size of Westminster Hall. Henry VII's chapel was also part of the tour. The following day, Henry and Charles were the guests of Suffolk at Southwark. Hunting formed the major part of the entertainment as the party moved to Richmond, and thence to Hampton Court. The next stop was Windsor where the monarchs and their councils discussed terms. The treaty provided for the marriage of Henry's daughter, Mary, to Charles when she reached the age of twelve. Unless he had a legitimate son in the meantime, Henry's death would see Mary become queen and England effectively become part of Charles's territories. The only thing that could make this palatable to Henry was the knowledge that he and Charles were about to carve up France. Once all was agreed, Dorset was a signatory to the resulting Treaty of Windsor. Charles took part in a Garter ceremony, wearing his robe and sitting in his own stall, before the monarchs took the Sacrament and swore to the treaty.

From Windsor, Charles, accompanied by Dorset and Spinelly, headed for Southampton, hunting all the way. Arrived at the port, Dorset heard the latest news on events in Italy. François had withdrawn from the peninsula and was about to redeploy his troops to attack Charles's disputed Burgundian territories. Spinelly wrote the report to Henry, with Dorset adding a postscript in spelling that even for the time was remarkably idiosyncratic: 'I trwste youre grase vyle be conten wythe the same, and if note, your plesyr knohyne, I chale fole [follow] the same. The Emperur has byne style in consele, so that I sa hym nott by twys sens I kame to tone.'[4] Dorset remained in attendance until Charles finally departed on 6 July with another 150,000 gold crowns borrowed from Henry.

Spinelly recommended that the emperor be encouraged to invade the Dauphiné (a region in south-west France) with English aid. But Henry was finally coming to see that he had been taken advantage of in the past, and thought that, for the current year, the emperor should pay for his own efforts, especially as the king was now short of money. Thanks to Henry VII's frugal administration and avoidance of war, until the 1520s Henry VIII had been able to conduct his foreign policy through a mixture of his own funds and taxation that Parliament had been reasonably willing to grant. By now, he had exhausted his treasury, and needed an injection of cash before Parliament could be called – even supposing that body would be willing to grant further taxation. The king requested a 'loan' of £2,000 from from the City of London, which was given, although with poor grace, then worked with Wolsey to come up with another solution. The cardinal abstracted a huge grant from the Church (contributing £3,000 himself, while Archbishop Warham was stung for £1,000), and then brought forward a new, or rather very old, scheme for raising funds from the laity – forced loans. Previously euphemistically referred to as 'benevolences', they had been extremely unpopular under Edward IV, and Richard III had initially tried to dissociate himself from them, although he had found that it was almost impossible to keep an army without them.

The first step was to find out how much individuals might be able to contribute, which was to be done under the pretext that it was merely an investigation to assess each man's rate for the 'furnishing of harness', that is, their ability to provide armour or other weapons in case of need. The chief men of the different counties were commissioned in September 1522 to investigate the wealth of all individuals worth over £20 per annum in their districts. Each person was to be questioned under oath – any plea of debt was to be followed up for details, and if the commissioners had reason to suspect the person was giving false information on oath, they were to question neighbours and friends. Only once all the information had been gathered were the commissioners to bring together the local worthies and explain to them the danger the country faced, and the need for the king to borrow money. The suggested loans were progressive, beginning at 10 per cent up to £300 per annum income, then about 16 per cent up to £1,000, with higher amounts to be suggested at the commissioners' discretion. Dorset was assessed at £100, suggesting a net annual income just under £750. This was low, considering his status as a marquis, when the minimum income for an earl was 1,000 marks. Of course, Dorset only had his father's property, which had never been of the usual value attributable to a marquisate; his mother and Wiltshire still being alive, he had no way of getting hold of the Bonville and Harington lands.

Finances were very much to the fore among the Grey family again in December 1522. Cicely's husband, John Dudley, had complained to the king that Wiltshire was withholding his stepdaughter's dowry. Wiltshire's response, written from Cicely's house at Wiscombe, was that Dorset had failed to keep a prior agreement, probably that of 1515, a copy of which he enclosed, requesting that Wolsey compel Dorset to obey. Wiltshire was certainly in dire financial straits himself – at the end of the previous year, he owed £4,407 to the king and had been obliged to ask Wolsey to obtain a longer respite for payments. Wiltshire's troubles were soon to be over – at some time in early 1523, he died, leaving Cecily a widow for the second time. No information exists about Cecily's relationship with Wiltshire, but, although she was married to him for nearly twenty years, she chose to be buried beside her first husband, Thomas I, and Wiltshire did not merit a single mention in her will; he wasn't even included in the prayers for the souls of her family.

Wiltshire's death seems to have led to at least a partial resolution of the arguments over the Grey sisters' dowries, arbitrated by Wolsey. Dorothy's first husband, Robert Willoughby, Lord de Broke, had died in 1521, leaving her one of the executors of his will. Willoughby's death did not change the fact that his estate was still owed Dorothy's dowry, and it was now agreed that Cecily would lease the executors and Dorothy's new husband, William Blount, Lord Mountjoy, the manors of Trelawney and Treggewell, Cornwall, until they had received therefrom the sum remaining due out of Lady Dorothy's £1,000 dowry.

*

Having chiselled some money out of his unwilling subjects, the king turned his thoughts to his northern border, as a proxy for war with France. The Scottish government was still struggling with the conflicting ruling claims of Queen Margaret, her second husband, the Earl of Angus, and the official governor, the Duke of Albany. Thomas, Lord Dacre, Warden of the West March and an experienced commander, was so concerned about Albany's intentions that, working with Margaret, he agreed a truce with the duke, which displeased the king. Henry insisted that the presence of Albany was a provocation by the French, and was implacable in his determination to interfere and promote a pro-English, anti-French faction.

Dorset, having been disappointed of an appointment to undertake war in France, was now to have a chance to prove his military skills on the less glamorous, but more gritty, Scottish border. In February 1523, he was appointed as Warden of the East and Middle March alongside Dacre, while Surrey was appointed as the king's lieutenant, in overall command. Whether as a corollary to this appointment or in a separate mark of the king's confidence, Dorset was also appointed to the Privy Chamber – Henry's inmost circle. By 15 April, Dorset, Surrey and their force had reached Alnwick in Northumberland. Once the anticipated victuals and ordnance had arrived, Dorset would move on to Norham, Surrey would go to Berwick and the rest of the captains to the other English strongholds, Etal and Wark. Among Dorset's men were his brothers Leonard and John, the latter of whom unfortunately 'toke the gowte in the said rode, and never came out of his bed sith'.[5]

Queen Margaret's chief desire was to obtain power in Scotland, and to have control of her son. In 1523, she was still hoping that this would happen with the support of her brother, and she kept Surrey informed, so far as she could, with information about Albany. She also wrote to Dorset, requesting him to spare the abbey of Coldstream from any attack – the prioress there had not only been a good friend to the queen, but was an excellent spy for the English. Dorset suspected that Margaret would come to an accommodation with Albany, who, although he was in France, was courting her co-operation, and let Henry know that the queen had returned to Stirling.

As Wardens of the Marches, Dorset and Dacre were responsible for the reconciliations that needed to be effected between the warring clans on each side, carried out on regular truce days. Dorset wrote that Dacre had undertaken that the men of Redesdale would make reparations for all the robberies they had undertaken since the departure of the Scottish Warden, Lord Ross, while Ralph Fenwick had taken the same commitment from the men of Tynedale, and brought some of them to the king's men as sureties. Surrey had made a proclamation that anyone with a grievance should come and declare it. Unsurprisingly, the presence of such a preponderance of the king's soldiers meant that since '(their) coming hither, strange to say, there have been no offences on either side. Seldom has there been peace so long.' Dorset's conduct pleased the king, and in June, he and Sir Thomas Lovell were granted, in survivorship, the offices of Warden, Chief Justice, and Justice in Eyre, of all royal forests and chases south of Trent, and of Master of the Hunts therein. Dorset also received more of Buckingham's lands in Warwickshire, in tail male.

Surrey made a few forays across the border, taking fortresses, laying waste to the countryside and generally intimidating the peasantry. The weather was dreadful, and he struggled to supply his men, so withdrew to Alnwick to await orders and further opportunities to strike fear into Scottish hearts. In early June, the council sent north the news that Henry intended a serious invasion. Surrey and Dorset were to come south to discuss strategy. Surrey informed his council colleagues that the Scots were becoming disillusioned with Albany and the French alliance because far more aid was promised than ever delivered, and that the French were now holed up in Dunbar Castle, afraid that they might be assassinated, as Albany's deputy had been. Even more pleasing for Henry was the information that there was such poverty and confusion among the Scots that many were willing to throw off Albany and adhere to a pro-English policy, if only one Scots lord were willing to break ranks and show the way. Dorset confirmed Surrey's view, adding that without French aid the Scots would not themselves be able to raise an army, partly because they lacked sufficient funds and partly because they were so divided that they would not be able to proceed effectively. Dacre, however, in his missives to Wolsey, disagreed with Surrey and Dorset's assessment. He thought Albany would command support, and that any invasion by England would be expensive and would not achieve the main objectives.

Surrey returned north, where the situation now seemed to reflect Dacre's view. Surrey had spies everywhere, and was in constant communication with Margaret, enabling him to write to Henry and Wolsey that Albany was due to land in Scotland with some 8,000 troops, intending to invade England in mid-October. The earl requested reinforcements, adding that he regretted the loss of the men commanded by Dorset. Dorset himself he recommended as a 'noble, valiant and painful [painstaking] man'.[6] In response, Dorset was sent back, along with Wolsey's view that there was no possibility that the rumours about Albany's forces could be true. Even James IV, Wolsey pointed out, had never achieved the level of men and supplies that Surrey believed Albany to be commanding in the time he had available. Further, Wolsey and the king thought that François was now so tied up in Italy that the rumour that he was supporting Richard de la Pole was 'nothing but French brags'. If it proved necessary to invade to repel any encroachment by Albany, Dorset should be given command of half the English force, which was to go no further than St Cuthbert's banner might be carried – presumably a reference to the geographic area over which the See of Durham held sway.

Dorset met with Surrey in Newcastle just before 23 October and went to Alnwick the next day with an advance guard. By the 28th, he was at Berwick with 6,000 or 7,000 men. The two sides settled down to a waiting game – each hoping the other would run out of supplies and be obliged to dismiss their men, leaving the border open. In the end, Albany was obliged to withdraw, and the border reverted to its usual state of low-level skirmishing, Henry having decided to concentrate on the French offensive. Lord Leonard acquitted himself well during the campaign, leading a successful ambush in which twenty-five Scots were killed and sixty-one taken prisoner along with their horses, a standard and a 'gyttern' (a guitar-like instrument). This was at the cost of one Englishman dead, and one captured. This feat may have recommended Leonard to the Duke of Suffolk, as he was summoned back from the north to join the duke's invasion force bound for France in the autumn of 1523. Lord Richard remained in the north, while Lord John, perhaps unable to serve because of his gout, was appointed a commissioner for Northamptonshire for collection of the subsidy wrung from a reluctant Parliament. Dorset was granted permission to return south, on grounds of illness.

The French campaign began well. Suffolk infiltrated from the English bridgehead at Calais, taking several castles en route and leaving them garrisoned with Englishmen, appointing Leonard as captain of the captured castle of Bongard. They advanced towards Paris, even capturing the town of Bray, where Leonard, presumably having left a deputy at Bongard, conducted himself valiantly. But Suffolk did not have enough money, men or supplies to take the capital. His men were decimated by cold, hunger and sickness, not to mention disappointment that the promised support from Charles and the Duke of Bourbon was nowhere to be seen. Eventually, Sir William Sandys, who had served with Dorset in Fuenterrabia, returned to England to ask for orders as to how they should proceed. He received the welcome news that Dorothy's new husband, Lord Mountjoy, and Sir Robert Jernningham were being sent with a relief force of some 6,000 men. Disappointingly, before they could arrive, Suffolk had been obliged to retreat because of the lack of supplies and the mutinous soldiers, and many of his men had dashed for home. When the new force arrived, it was too late to bring the whole army together. Suffolk, afraid of Henry's displeasure, remained at Calais until he had news that the king understood that he had no choice but to let the men go, but it was some time before he was received into Henry's presence again.

*

Returning from the Scottish campaign, Dorset took up his usual duties as a member of the council, sitting with Wolsey and others on a panel to appoint men to a commission of searches. He sat with the cardinal and the new Duke of Norfolk (Surrey inherited the dukedom on the death of his father in May 1524) to hear the intercepted letters of de Praet, the Burgundian ambassador, which were somewhat derogatory in tone towards Henry and Wolsey. He busied himself with commissions of the peace and undertook some business for Wolsey in Coventry. He made another land exchange with the king – in return for his manor of Clay-Coton in Northamptonshire, he received the fee simple of Beaumont Lees, in Leicestershire, adjoining the royal park of Frith. This helped with the ongoing consolidation of Grey lands in Leicestershire, extending around Bradgate. There had been a lull in actual violence with Sacheverell, but by 1524, Dorset was complaining to Wolsey that, contrary to orders, Sacheverell, or some of his men, had forcibly ejected Dorset's servants from the town of Leicester, precipitating a riot.

Accusation and counter-accusation of retaining, maintenance and embracery (the corruption of juries) flew until 1526, when the parties were summoned to the Star Chamber. Lord George participated vigorously in this family fracas. In the visitation of his College of St Mary in 1525, the bishop identified friction between Lord George and two of the permanent lay residents of the college – none other than Sir Richard Sacheverell and Lady Hungerford. There were frequent scuffles between George's servants and theirs, and George accused Sacheverell of profiting from the sale to the college of the manor of Ashley in Wiltshire, and of obtaining leases from the college during his own absence, without paying the proper entry fine. The matter was taken to the council, which remitted settlement to Bishop Longland of Lincoln; the judgement is lost but Sacheverell and his wife appear to have gone on living at Newarke until their deaths. George was still on poor terms with some of his canons, so Longland instituted various new injunctions to improve matters. These were successful – no further complaints were made in the visitation of 1528. However, in 1530, George resigned the post of dean – perhaps he was worn out by the endless arguments with his tenants.

11

Darkening Skies

He hath given his empire
Up to a whore

Shakespeare, *Antony and
Cleopatra*, III vi

In March 1524, the precarious nature of the Tudor hold on the crown became apparent when Henry had an accident in the tiltyard. Suffolk was back in favour and he and Henry were to joust, the king keen to try out a new suit of armour made to his own design. Dorset and Surrey were Henry's supporters at one end of the yard, with Suffolk at the other. Suffolk's man told him that the king was ready, to which the duke replied that he could not see him, because his helmet was closed. Dorset handed Henry his spear, and Henry set off, having forgotten to close his visor. The crowd, seeing Henry's bare face, shouted 'hold, hold' but neither combatant heard. Both struck their targets, Suffolk hitting that part of the headpiece that was normally covered by the visor and splintering his spear. Henry's helmet was full of splinters. Dorset was loudly blamed for handing Henry his spear when the king's visor was not down, but Henry, who did not generally blame men for honest mistakes, took all the responsibility himself – he should have lowered his visor. Suffolk rapidly disarmed and raced over to the king, swearing he would never joust with him again – but Henry insisted all was well, and ran another six courses.

Had Henry been killed, it is likely the succession would have gone to his eight-year-old daughter, Mary, probably with the popular Queen Katharine as regent, but Suffolk's own son by the French Queen, Henry, Earl of Lincoln, might have been preferred, or possibly the king's cousin Henry Courtenay, Earl of Devon, or even Lord Montagu, grandson of George, Duke of Clarence. It became clear to Henry that his lack of an unquestionable heir, in the form of a son, was an acute problem.

During the summer of 1524, Dorset was in Devon – probably initially to visit his mother, perhaps to discuss an arrangement that was brokered by Wolsey to resolve the financial difficulties of the family. Cecily agreed that her daughters' dowries would be paid out of her lands rather than the Grey patrimony, that her younger sons would be granted a life interest in various of her properties, and that she would pay 500 marks per annum towards Wiltshire's debt to the king of over £4,400, retaining only 300 marks to live on. This was a significant sacrifice on Cecily's part – her annual income was in the region of £975, or 1,460 marks, so she was allocating nearly a half of it for her daughters and younger sons. While he was in the south-west, Dorset also paid a visit to his aunt Katherine of York, Countess of Devon, at Colcomb, less than 3 miles from Shute. Katherine regaled her nephew with a feast of strawberries and cherries, supplied by Master Motton of Exeter, which cost her 2s 6d. He visited Cecily again in March 1525, when he wrote to Wolsey that the abbot of Forde was refusing to acquiesce to Wolsey's demand that William Parsons be elected abbot of Newenham Abbey, Axminster, which Dorset described as 'my lady my mother's foundation'.[1]

*

Once again, Henry's alliance with the emperor turned to ashes. Charles's lack of support for Suffolk in 1523 might have been forgiven after the emperor scored an overwhelming victory at Pavia on 24 February 1525, when François was taken prisoner, had he then followed up the victory as previously agreed. On hearing the news of Pavia, Henry was ecstatic. Now was the time for Charles and him to dismember France – 'not an hour is to be lost'. The icing on the cake was the news that Richard de la Pole had fallen in the battle, fighting for the French. The jubilant king pressed more wine on the messenger, saying, 'God have mercy on his soul, all the enemies of England are gone.' Of course, money would be needed for Henry and Charles to pursue their advantage, and the king and Wolsey sought funds immediately. The wounds from the loans of 1523 were still smarting, but on 21 March 1525 commissioners were sent scurrying round the country to collect an 'Amicable Grant', to enable the king to seize this golden opportunity. The laity were asked to contribute one-sixth of their income and the clergy one-third. Meanwhile, diplomatic missives were flying back and forth between Henry and Charles, to arrange the details. Henry was beside himself with glee. He would obtain perhaps not the whole of France (he was not greedy, and assured Charles he was willing to compromise on the crown itself) but the ancient territories of Normandy, Guienne and Gascony. Charles would benefit through his marriage to Mary, as one day he too would rule all this additional territory. All that was needed was a plan to organise the actual invasion.

Henry's opening suggestion was for Norfolk to lead a force of 20,000 men, while the king himself brought another contingent. But Henry had counted his chickens too early. Charles prevaricated. He too was short of men and money, and had never had any real interest in dethroning François, just in keeping him out of Italy, Charles's patrimony of Burgundy, and the independent duchy of Savoy. He refused to aid Henry, although not in so many words, and also gave him an ultimatum concerning Princess Mary: the nine-year-old and her dowry had to be sent to Spain immediately for the marriage that was to take place when she was twelve. Otherwise, Charles would look elsewhere for a bride. Henry's house of cards came crashing down. He could not send his daughter to Spain. She was his heir, and could not be allowed to leave the country unless she were to be married immediately, which legally could not happen for three years – and even then, Henry was reluctant to allow a marriage before his daughter was physically mature. Flanked by his council, including Dorset, Henry rejected the demand.

Alongside the evasions of Charles, Henry also received the unwelcome news that his subjects were anything but amicable in their response to the request for money. There were riots, and downright refusals to pay. Archbishop Warham wrote to Wolsey that 'the people sore grudgeth and murmureth and spekid cursedly among theymselves as far as they dare'. He also reported that, although the gentlemen in the counties might be just about able to manage, many of them did not want to ask for more from the commons 'considering their poverty'. Henry, realising that he had crossed a line with his subjects, claimed to have had no knowledge of the demand and reframed it as optional. The idea that a major tax could have been levied without Henry's knowledge is laughable, although the details may have been hammered out by Wolsey and the council. Nevertheless, Wolsey shouldered the blame.

Utterly disgusted with his ally, on 18 June 1525, Henry VIII sent a message to both the emperor and his own wife, for twenty-five years the symbol of Anglo-Spanish friendship, by ennobling his illegitimate son, Henry Fitzroy, as Earl of Nottingham, and Duke of Richmond and Somerset. Dorset took part in the ceremony, holding the sword of state. In the same ceremony, he himself lost his distinction as the only marquis in England, when the Earl of Devon was invested as Marquis of Exeter. It was Dorset's role to usher in the new marquis, Suffolk supporting his other side. Next, Sir Thomas Boleyn was created Viscount Rochford; this was perhaps in recognition of his sterling work as ambassador – although no other functionaries were similarly honoured – or perhaps partially in his capacity as father of Henry's new love interest, Mistress Anne Boleyn.

A grand ducal household was created for Richmond, and Dorset's son Lord Henry Grey, aged eight, became a member of it, wearing Richmond's livery. The new semi-royal establishment was led by Sir William Parr, its chamberlain, with the king's uncle Arthur Plantagenet, Lord Lisle (illegitimate son of Edward IV) as its lieutenant, and Edward Seymour as the Master of the Horse. Other boys selected to be educated with Richmond were Sir William Parr's nephew, another William, around four years older than Lord Henry; Henry Clifford, son of Lord Clifford, the same age as Lord Henry; and Thomas Fiennes, a couple of years older. It was in Richmond's household that Lord Henry was first exposed to the growing anti-clericalism of the times. The duke's Greek tutor, Richard Croke, sent repeated complaints to Wolsey that the clerk comptroller, Richard Cotton, 'allows buffoons to sing indecent songs and to abuse the clergy' in front of the boys, who laughed and were protected by the grooms from punishment.

At the same time as Lord Henry was appointed to Richmond's service, Dorset's daughter, Lady Katherine Grey, joined the household of Princess Mary, now titular Head of the Council for Wales and commonly referred to as Princess of Wales. Dorset himself was appointed as Lord Master of Princess Mary's household, but there is no evidence that he had any day-to-day involvement with it, while his brother-in-law Lord Ferrers was appointed as steward. Another generation of Greys was being trained to continue service to their royal cousins. During August, Dorset was again in Coventry, investigating a riot in which a man had been killed, probably related to further resistance to the Amicable Grant. He went from the town to his home at Astley, and then, in his capacity as constable of both castles, on to Warwick and Killingworth (Kenilworth) by 13 August.

With no hope of completing the conquest of France, Henry had little choice but to seek peace, and a treaty was formalised on 1 September 1525, at Wolsey's palace of The More. As was customary, the French had agreed to pay pensions to suitably friendly English nobles, and Dorset wrote a wheedling letter to Wolsey, requesting that he might be one of the lucky recipients as he had been before, for 'if another were put in his stead, it would seem strange to both his kinsmen in France (the St Pol connections of whom he remained proud) and to his friends in England'. He reminded Wolsey that he had always been ready to 'serve the king to the best of [his] power, and often to [his] great cost'. He hoped that Wolsey would, as promised, 'keep him in remembrance'. His plea was successful – François granted him a pension of 218¾ crowns per annum, not a stretch as he gave 47,368 crowns to Henry and 12,500 to Wolsey. Even Lord Rochford received 262½ crowns. This agreement with France did not prevent the emperor continuing to send pensions to many of Henry's nobles. The Imperial accounts for December 1525, list pensions of 1,000 crowns per annum for Dorset and many of the other English peers, while Wolsey received 6,000 annually.

Dorset had already received two more offices that summer, that of Steward of the lordship of Chellismore, Warwickshire, and Master of the Game there. That the Dorsets were worth cultivating as intimates of the king is reflected in the New Year gifts of Eleanor, Countess of Rutland, who sent a gift to Margaret Dorset among other great ladies – Katherine, Countess of Devon and her daughter-in-law Gertrude, Lady Marquis of Exeter, who was Dorothy's stepdaughter, plus both duchesses of Norfolk.

In February 1526, news came to the English court of a treaty between Charles and François. Dorset and the other councillors could only echo Henry and Wolsey's strangled expressions of delight that Christendom was now at peace. The prospect of war had receded, but money was still tight, so Wolsey made another attempt at reforming the king's household, the retrenchments of 1519 having failed to improve standards or reduce costs. Known as the Eltham Ordinances, copious instructions were issued for the king's employees. Lists were drawn up of those who had the right to lodgings at court and to food at the king's expense. In the first draft, Dorset and his wife were both allocated lodgings on the king's side, but Margaret's name was struck out by the cardinal – presumably, it was thought she could share with her husband. In an indication that Dorset spent most of his time at Henry's side, he, along with Norfolk, Suffolk, the Bishop of London, Exeter and various others, was named as one of the hearers of poor men's complaints, gathered up as the king made his progresses. He was one of the most diligent of Henry's councillors, third highest in his regular attendances, after the second and third dukes of Norfolk.[2] His appointments to the commissions of the peace for Leicestershire, Warwickshire, Northamptonshire, Essex and Staffordshire were also regularly renewed.

That year, Wolsey was embarking on one of his most important ventures: the creation of Cardinal College, Oxford. Dorset was a witness to the foundation charter in May 1526 and provided at least 1,000 oaks from his park at Sheldon for the building. The college was to be funded in part by the suppression of a couple of monasteries, including that of St Frideswide in Oxford itself. Among the men working for Wolsey on the dissolutions was one Thomas Cromwell, who may well have been introduced to Wolsey by Dorset. Wolsey was a genius at identifying good servants – many of the men he trained later moved to the king's household and gave sterling service to the monarch. Not only Cromwell but Gardiner, Audley, Wriothesley and Rich all began their careers in the cardinal's household.

Cromwell had a colourful background – the son of a small businessman in Putney, south London, he had soldiered in Europe, before returning to England in the closing years of Henry VII's reign. During his chequered early career, Cromwell had picked up enough legal knowledge to act as attorney for numerous clients. At some point before August 1522, he entered Dorset's service and remained there long enough for Dorset's arms to be displayed in his house at Austin Friars in the mid-1520s. Cromwell's latest biographer, Diarmaid MacCulloch, has identified that Cromwell was probably introduced to Dorset by Morgan Williams, a member of the Dorset household and Cromwell's brother-in-law.

Cromwell was not just undertaking legal business for the Greys, but more quotidian activities as well. On 14 August 1522, Cecily wrote to him in forthright tones, requesting him to arrange to send her 'the trussing bed of cloth of tissue, and the featherbed with the fustians and a mattress [be]longing to the same with the counterpoint [bedspread]'. She wanted these items sent to her at Bedwell, the home of Dorothy and Lord Mountjoy, suggesting that she was intending to make a protracted stay. It seems that, although the matter of Dorothy's dowry was not entirely resolved, this had not affected the relationship between Cecily and her daughter. Cromwell was also ordered to send all of Cecily's 'tents, pavilions and halls' to Leonard. Given the timing of this request, it may be that the items were to be used by Leonard and his brothers as part of their military campaigns that year.[3]

The following year, Cromwell wrote to Lady Dorset, telling her that he had received a letter from Dorset with information about his 'honourable adventure in Scotland', and that there was also a letter from Lord George.[4] Cromwell is frustratingly vague, but then goes on to say that, if Lady Dorset informs the marquis of the contents of George's letter, it would be 'well taken when he [the marquis] shall perceive that you do and shall continually for the advancement of his honour'. The reference to George, and the hint that Lady Dorset and the marquis might not be on good terms, indicates that the addressee was probably Cecily, rather than Margaret. MacCulloch speculates that this relationship with Dorset may solve the mystery of which parliamentary seat Cromwell sat for in 1523, suggesting Carlisle in Cumberland, or Appleby in Westmorland, based on a draft petition regarding the abbey of Hulm Cultram, which was within Dorset's lands.

Although Cromwell left Dorset's employ to join Wolsey, both Morgan Williams and his son, Cromwell's nephew Richard, were retained by Dorset for a much longer period, and the association with the Greys continued. Lord John wrote to him on 12 January 1526 from Tilty, addressing him familiarly as 'Broder Cromwell' and requesting that Cromwell arrange for him to retain the farm of Tyckford and obtain that of Ranston when Wolsey took the priories of Tykford and Ranston for the new college.[5] He was willing to pay whatever sum Cromwell thought reasonable for the office. Cromwell lent Lord George Grey at least £310. On 14 May 1529, George wrote to 'Fellow Master Cromwell', sending him means to discharge £20 of it: 'The days are longer than I would, but I beseech you make the best of it.'

Dorset's squabbles with Hastings and Sacheverell continued, mainly concentrated on disputes over the management of the royal parks in the county – Beaumont, Frith, Birdsnest, Barne, Toly and Heathely Lodge. The parties were once again brought before the council for a settlement and required in December 1527 to enter a bond for £1,000 to abide by the award of the cardinal, Norfolk, Suffolk, the Bishop of Bath, Lord Rochford, the Chief Justices of the King's Bench and the Common Pleas, the Chief Baron of the Exchequer, Justice Sir Humphrey Coningsby and Sir Thomas More, Chancellor of the Duchy of Lancaster (to which the parks largely belonged). The arbitration was to be made on the day after Ascension Day, 20 May 1528, and the bond recorded the interim arrangements to be made for the management of the disputed parks. Despite this, Dorset remained high in the confidence of both king and cardinal, and his closeness to the centre of power was recognised by others, an example being the Council of the North's query to Wolsey as to whether the Duke of Richmond should give a 1528 New Year gift to the marquis.

*

While none of Henry's courtiers can have been ignorant of the rift between the king and his erstwhile ally and once 'beloved' nephew Emperor Charles, almost no one knew that his dissatisfaction with his wife had gone beyond anger at the miserable behaviour of her relatives, and was now circling in on her inability (in his view, that of his contemporaries and apparently of most modern writers, who still use the phrase, implying a default on her part) to 'give' him a son and heir. Since Henry was utterly convinced of his own virtue and his place high in God's favour, the lack of a son must be attributable to some egregious sin – and it dawned on him sometime in 1525 that that sin was his marriage to his brother's widow. He read, or reread, the verse in Leviticus that forbids a man to marry his brother's wife – transgressors would be childless. He ignored the conflicting verse in Deuteronomy that positively commanded such a marriage, and the fact that he was not childless but had a daughter. He requested Pope Clement VII grant an annulment. To be fair to Henry, although we tend to see his efforts to discard his wife in the light of his desire to marry another woman, he had a very respectable theological case, and, had the politics of Europe been different, the pope might well have granted the annulment he sought, as other popes had accommodated kings before.

The Grey family, like every other noble family at the king's court, was caught up in the years of drama that followed, and some saw their loyalties torn. So far as the evidence goes, Dorset, his wife and his brothers, Leonard, John, Edward and George (Anthony disappears from the records in the 1520s), put their loyalty to Henry above all else. Of the sisters, Mary, Lady Ferrers does not seem to have been involved in court life, but Lady Margaret was in service with Queen Katharine, Dorothy's husband was the queen's Lord Chamberlain and struggled with conflicting loyalties, and Elizabeth, Countess of Kildare became a more open partisan of the queen. Cicely, Lady Dudley had so many troubles of her own that the matter probably passed her by. For nearly two years, few people knew anything of 'the King's Secret Matter', although Dorset may have heard a whisper, as a member of the council and also an early patron of John Longland, Bishop of Lincoln and Henry's confessor, who has been credited – or blamed – for first bringing the issue to the king's attention.

Henry's hopes of a quick resolution to the matter were destroyed when the shocking news arrived in the early summer of 1527 that the unpaid troops of the emperor had sacked Rome, and that the pope was effectively Charles's prisoner. Any leeway that Clement might have been willing to give Henry was now off the table, reinforced by the pope's unwillingness to undermine the power of his office by questioning a predecessor's dispensation in the face of a rising tide of Lutheranism.

During 1528, England was ravaged once more by an epidemic of the mysterious sweating sickness. Henry avoided London, moving whenever someone fell sick, but this merely spread infection, and the sickness followed the court. On 26 September, Sir John Russell wrote to Wolsey from Hertford Castle: 'The king's majesty is much troubled with this disease of the sweat; for at this night there is fallen sick My Lord Marquis, My Lady Marquis, Sir Thomas Cheyne, Mrs Crook. Master Norris and Master Wallop be recovered and Master Poyntz is departed, which Jesu Pardon.' The lord and lady marquis might have been either the Dorsets or the Exeters. Whichever couple it was, they, along with Anne Boleyn and her father Rochford, were among the minority who recovered from this strange illness, while Sir William Compton, a jousting companion of Dorset's, died of it.

If they had been suffering from the sweat, the Dorsets were well enough to attend the customary New Year celebrations at court, their servants receiving the usual gifts from the king. The atmosphere must have been strained. Henry and Katharine were still officially living together as husband and wife, but the 'Secret Matter' was secret no longer. Pope Clement had finally bowed to pressure and agreed to send a legate to sit with Wolsey in a specially convened ecclesiastical court. This visiting legate, Cardinal Lorenzo Campeggio, was a past master at delaying tactics. Both pope and emperor hoped that if the matter were strung out long enough, Henry would lose interest – despite the prescient Wolsey having warned Clement that if Henry were not accommodated, papal authority would be thrown off.

While the ins and outs of the king's annulment case were complex, it could be boiled down to whether Katharine's first marriage, to Prince Arthur, had been consummated. If it had – and Church law assumed consummation unless there were opposing proof – then Henry's contention was that Pope Julius II had exceeded his authority in granting the dispensation for his marriage to Katharine, because it was specifically forbidden by Leviticus. The Church's position was that a pope did have that power, even if the marriage had been consummated. Katharine claimed that since her marriage to Arthur had not been consummated, there was no affinity between her and Henry, and therefore Julius' dispensation was merely belt and braces.[6]

Wolsey had suggested to the king that he pursue a different argument – that Julius had given the wrong kind of dispensation, because he had been misinformed on the facts. This would have been far easier for the pope to accept, but Henry was adamant that his theological point should be the crux of the case.

After months of delay, the public sitting of the court opened on 18 June 1529. It proved a fiasco. Katharine knelt before the king to make a deeply moving personal plea, in which she swore that she had married him as a virgin and been a faithful and loving wife, and asked him to dismiss the case or, failing that, to allow her to appeal to Rome. Henry, mortified, angry and touched in equal parts, would not dismiss the matter but granted her leave to appeal. The queen immediately stood up and departed the court, rejecting its jurisdiction.

Ignoring this setback, the cardinals continued the hearing. Depositions were taken from old courtiers, Dorset among them, about the truth of Arthur and Katharine's marriage. There were twelve questions, which covered four areas: whether Arthur and Henry were brothers; whether Katharine and Arthur had been married, their ages, and whether they had consummated the marriage; the subsequent relationship of Katharine and Henry; and some closing legal points. Dorset confirmed that the princes had been brothers and that he had himself been present at the christening of both boys. He was also at the marriage of Arthur and Katharine, and knew that the prince was just fifteen. He himself had accompanied Arthur to Katharine's bedchamber, where she lay under the covers 'as the manner is of queens in that behalf'. He believed the marriage to have been consummated, Arthur having been of 'a good and sanguine complexion'. He could say nothing as to the marriage ceremony between Henry and Katharine as he had been in Calais at the time (he probably did not welcome this reminder of imprisonment) but knew that they had subsequently lived as husband and wife. He was unable to answer the question as to whether the marriage between the king and queen was legal in divine and Church law, nor whether its legality was dependent on any dispensation. Nor did he have any opinion as to whether the legality of a marriage between Henry and Katharine had been questioned at the time, either by the laity or clergy. He thought it was the case that Henry and Katharine no longer cohabited, and he accepted the jurisdiction of the legatine court. Sacheverell was also deposed, and showed himself slightly more willing to accommodate the king, by deposing that he had frequently heard people say that 'it was not meet' for a man to marry his brother's wife.

Despite these depositions, the court case collapsed when Cardinal Campeggio adjourned it. In theory it was to resume in October with the new law term, but in practice it was closed forever. Henry, more determined than ever to achieve his annulment, turned on Wolsey. The cardinal had long had enemies among Henry's courtiers, envious of his wealth, aggravated by his ostentation and offended by his attempts to apply the law equally to noblemen as well as commoners. Most historians subscribe to the theory that personal animosity from the Boleyns and Suffolk were motivating factors, while others conclude that if Wolsey had been able to succeed in obtaining the dispensation (despite the endless obstacles put in his way by Henry himself running an independent campaign and keeping Wolsey in the dark) the Boleyns would have overlooked their dislike of him. G. W. Bernard argues cogently that, far from there being a long-running anti-Wolsey faction, it was not until Henry himself showed a willingness to move against his minister that others jumped on the bandwagon – although those two positions are not mutually exclusive.[7]

Whether Henry were the prime mover or was nudged into it, on 8 October a charge of praemunire, contrary to the statute of 1399, was brought against the cardinal. The crime of praemunire concerned the relative jurisdictions of king and pope. It was a treasonable offence to try a matter in the ecclesiastical courts which could be heard in the civil courts, or appeal to any higher power than the king. Wolsey was found guilty, but pardoned by Henry, who still had a soft spot for his old friend. The next move against the cardinal was a list of articles, probably prepared by Lord Darcy, outlining Wolsey's supposed offences, that was read in Parliament in November. His iniquities ranged from writing 'I and my king' in letters, rather than putting the king first, via carrying the great seal out of England when on embassy, to 'breathing on the king' despite having the French pox (syphilis). Sadly, despite their long history of co-operation and friendship, it appears that Dorset was willing to go along with the majority and append his name to the long list of accusations. Wolsey accepted the charges and signed his name in token of his guilt.[8]

Around the time the ecclesiastical court was preparing to convene, in May 1529, Cecily died, aged about seventy. Her will, made 31 March 1527, shows the depth of the rift between herself and her eldest son. In accordance with land law at the time, hardly any of Cecily's land could be disposed of by will but descended to her eldest son.[9] He now also took control of those elements of his father's estate that had been assigned to Cecily for the performance of Thomas I's will. The 1503 arbitration had limited what Cecily could do with half of her estate, even during her lifetime, but she had retained the right to assign income from the other half, or grant life interests from it on any terms she chose. Using this power, she made complex arrangements for the profits from many of her manors to be assigned to specific purposes, so that Dorset would only obtain the benefit of them once Cecily's other legacies had been performed. In the 1527 subsidy roll, the annual income from the whole of Cecily's estate had been assessed at £923 19s 4½d per annum – a very comfortable income, although not on the scale of the roughly £6,000 that the Duke of Buckingham had enjoyed, and, as mentioned previously, she had allocated half of it to her younger children and the payment of Wiltshire's debts.

Cecily's will opened conventionally, with various options for her burial, depending on the location of her death. She died at Astley, and so was buried in her preferred location, alongside Thomas I at Astley College. Other options were Westminster Abbey or St George's Chapel, Windsor. Oddly, despite the amount of money and effort she had poured into her college at Ottery St Mary and the abbeys at Newenham, or even Porlock, none of these were listed as potential burial locations. Her funeral expenses were to be paid, including 200 Masses for her soul. She then directed her debts to be paid, in order of age. She bequeathed all the members of her household at the time of her death a year's wages, above and beyond any wages owing. The household was to be maintained for eight weeks, during which all her servants were entitled to bed and board. All her servants who attended her funeral, including her stewards, bailiffs and other officers, were to receive a black gown. Her executors were to provide a suitable monument for Thomas I and herself, over their tomb at Astley, or, if she were buried elsewhere, one each, hers to be of the maximum cost of £100. £30 was to be distributed in alms at her funeral, and a further £20 to poor households within four miles of the place she died.

Next, Cecily turned to the outstanding matters of Thomas I's testament. The £1,000 dowries for her daughters Cicely, Dorothy, Elizabeth and Margaret, or such parts of them as had not been paid, were to be paid out of specified properties. Although Elizabeth had married without the consent of her mother or her father's executors, Cecily forgave her disobedience, and, since the marriage was honourable, 'and I and all her family have reason to be contented with the same', Elizabeth was reinstated in her right to her dowry. In particular, Margaret was to have her £1,000 out of two manors, as she had received nothing so far, never having married.[10] Having dealt with her daughters, Cecily moved on to her younger sons, confirming that an agreement she and Dorset had made for a lifelong manor for Lord Richard should stand. The manors she had granted for life to Lord John and Lord Leonard were also confirmed, and after their lives were to be returned to her estate for the performance of her will. Edward, Anthony and George are not mentioned. We can probably assume that Edward and Anthony were dead, and that George, who was very much alive, was considered adequately provided for with his deanship.

The unpaid bequests from Thomas I to the scholars of Oxford and Cambridge were still to be made, and are listed next. The plate for Astley College that Thomas I had bequeathed had never been delivered either, and Cecily's executors were to make suitable purchases to the value of £200 for the college. All the debts of the late lord marquis that could be proved were to be paid. Prayers were to be said for the soul of the late lord marquis and all of Cecily's ancestors – she did not mention Wiltshire's soul, perhaps an indication that the marriage had been a mistake. After this came the vast debt she owed the king – or rather the £4,473 that Wiltshire had died owing. Only the month before making her will, Cecily had entered an indenture with the cardinal and Sir Henry Wyatt, as the king's representatives allocating profits from specified manors, to the value of 500 marks per annum, to be paid to reduce the debt. Once this huge debt was paid, the income was to go to the performance of her will, until it was completed.

The remainder of the estate was to pass to Dorset, but Cecily was clearly suspicious of his financial motives. In three separate clauses, she anticipated that Dorset might attempt to prevent his siblings receiving their fair shares. Her first stipulation was that any costs or charges incurred by her executors in defending any attempts to upset the will would come from her estates. Second, if any of her sons or daughters were 'disturbed' in their inheritance by her 'entirely beloved son the lord marquis', or by his procurement or assent, then her executors were to compensate the beneficiary from her other lands. The third, even more draconian clause, stipulated that 'if the said Lord Marquis, his heirs or assigns or any other by his assent, procurement or means, hinder, breach or cause my will to be performed in any point or article contrary to the true meaning of the same, that any legacy to him made by me of my said manors be void ... and that my said executors ... shall take ... any profits (from any) ... hereditaments whereof I have power to make a will and dispose (of them) in deeds of charity'. She asked her executors to pay for two 'goodly tokens', worth £20 each, to be given to the king and the cardinal.

To enable this will to be performed, Cecily's list of executors ran into double figures, headed by Henry Courtenay, Marquis of Exeter; her sons-in-law Mountjoy and Sutton; one stepson from each of Dorothy Mountjoy and Elizabeth Kildare; her 'trusty and beloved' grandsons John and Thomas Arundell; Lord Chief Justice FitzJames; Richard Lister, the king's Attorney General; and her 'trusty' chaplain, Walter Coke. The list also included her nephew George, Lord Hastings. Either the family quarrel had subsided, or she had never been part of the row. The will must have made embarrassing reading for the family, but probate was granted in November 1529, to Lord Mountjoy.

It may have been Cecily's possession of Astley during her widowhood that had driven Dorset to relocate to Bradgate, but he and Margaret also had another home that they used regularly – Tilty Grange, within the abbey of Tilty in Essex. It is not known when they began occupation, but in 1529 they took a new lease for thirteen years, at an annual rent of £20. The accommodation was described in the lease as the 'new house over against the [abbey] church with the orchards, hop garden and all other houses as they were accustomed to have hitherto'. A later addition to the deed describes the property as 'the Guest Hall, with Green's house; Byard's chamber, with the new lodging made by the same marquis, and the buttery, pantry, cellars, parlours and kitchen, garden, orchard and cook's garden'. All of this suggests that Dorset spent considerable amounts of money to construct new buildings, and that their house was self-contained and separate from the abbey complex. They did not have total possession of the property, seemingly sharing it with the abbot, to whom they had to give eight weeks' notice if they wanted to use it, nor were they responsible for repairs during any period that the abbot was in residence. Dorset was granted the stewardship of the monastery at the more or less negligible fee of 20s per annum and stabling within the abbey precincts for twenty horses. Why Dorset and Margaret liked Tilty so much is not apparent – although closer than Bradgate, it was not particularly convenient for London, nor to Dorset's other land in the county at Woodham Ferrers, or Margaret's childhood home in Kent. Their steward at Tilty was a man named Henry Sadleir, whose son Ralph became a prominent member of Cromwell's household, and had a distinguished career as a diplomat.

For Dorset, life in 1529 continued as usual after the death of his mother. He spent some time at Bradgate, during which time he was entertained by the Mayor of Leicester.[11] Towards the end of the year, he was involved in arbitrating a difficult case that had set the Duke of Norfolk and the Earl of Oxford at loggerheads, in a dispute that dragged on for several years. In October, he was appointed to carry Henry's cap of maintenance at the opening of Parliament, a great honour, and in December he witnessed the elevation of Thomas Boleyn, Viscount Rochford, to the earldom of Wiltshire.[12] Leonard, too, remained in favour, being granted the manors of Sportely in Yorkshire and Barrow in Lincolnshire.

Despite having spent all his adult life eager to obtain control of his mother's lands, Dorset did not long enjoy them. His name more or less disappears from the records after December 1529, and he died in October 1530. Henry VIII was, we may presume, grieved at the loss of a cousin who, if not the most competent of his soldiers, had always been a devoted subject, a reliable and competent councillor and administrator, and had burnished the name of English chivalry through his tournament success in France in 1514. The king paid the registrar of the Order of the Garter for 1,000 Masses for Dorset's soul.

Dorset's will left his wife, 'well-beloved' Margaret, as his chief executor, and the details of the will suggest he loved and trusted her. He wished her to have 'the guiding of 'all [his] children, sons as well as daughters', and she was left a life interest in much of his estate, including Bradgate. His next concern was for his son and heir, Lord Henry, who was to remain under the care of his schoolmaster, Richard Broke, who was to receive of £20 per annum until such time as the executors could find him a living worth £30. Should Dorset's male line fail, his daughter Mary was to inherit his lands in Cumbria and Lancashire – why she was singled out and why those particular estates were chosen is not revealed. All of the daughters were to have £1,000 for their dowries, provided they married 'by the advice' of their mother, or, after her death, of his executors. His house at Bradgate was to be completed in accordance with a plan already made, as were the tombs of his parents at Astley College, which were to be paid for by a charge in perpetuity on his manors at Bedworth and Packington. This charge was also to support the maintenance of priests at Astley, as willed by Cecily, and the building and maintenance of an alms house for thirteen poor men, who were to receive 12*d* per week each, chosen by Margaret, and then by his heirs. Any spare money from these manors was to be spent on priests and clerks for an annual Mass to be said on the day of the dole. Philip the Hermit was to receive a weekly stipend of 12*d* so long as he remained at Astley, praying for the souls of Dorset, his parents, his wife, and all Christians.

Dorset's other executors were his 'special friends' Cuthbert Tunstall, bishop-elect of Durham, Sir John FitzJames, Chief Justice of the King's Bench, schoolmaster Richard Broke, William Ashby and Margaret's brother Edward Wotton. Various of his manors were assigned for life to his younger sons, Thomas, Edward and John. Contrary to his mother's fears that Dorset would try to deprive his siblings of their living, his sister Cicely Dudley's miserable state was not forgotten – she was granted one of Dorset's manors for life for 'the advancement of her better living'. She was also to be entitled to 'meat and drink' for herself and one man and one woman servant – either at Margaret's table, or by payment of £20 per annum. There is a bequest to a Mary Thomason, who may be Dorset's illegitimate daughter mentioned earlier – she was to have 5 marks per annum.

There follow some other interesting bequests – his best gelding for the king, along with £100 to buy a saddle, and two of his hounds (delivered in July 1532), and a surprising £20 for 'my lady Anne Boleyn'. His old comrades in arms Norfolk and Suffolk were to receive £40, the Earl of Oxford £30, while Sir William FitzWilliam, Sir Henry Guildford (his wife's brother-in-law) and Dr Stephens (Stephen Gardiner) received £20 each. A number of ladies, probably Cecily or Margaret's lady attendants, were bequeathed £10 towards their marriages. £100 at the rate of £20 per annum was allocated to the church at Tilty.

The will, which Margaret proved on 18 November 1531, was costly, as Dorset not only left large bequests of his own but also the majority of Cecily's bequests. The costs of completing Bradgate and the chapel at Astley were considerable, as was the outstanding debt to the king left by Wiltshire – it seems that Dorset had been right to fear that his mother's second marriage would have a materially detrimental effect on his estate. The fulfilling of the will would lead to even more bitter disputes between Margaret and her son Henry than Dorset had waged with Cecily.

Seventy years after Dorset's death, his tomb was opened when major structural damage to Astley College occurred. He was found to have been around 5 feet 8 inches tall, with a broad face, and 'yellow' hair.

Part 4

1530–1547
'Time hath its revolutions'

Family of Thomas, 2nd Marquis of Dorset and Margaret Wotton (1)

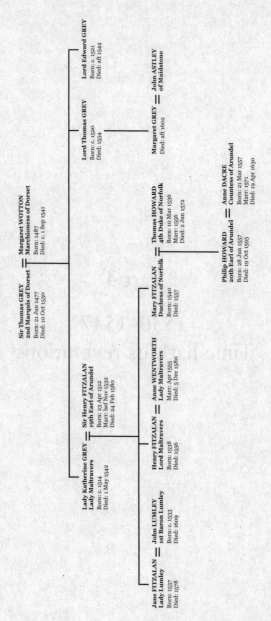

Sir Thomas GREY
2nd Marquis of Dorset
Born: 21 Jun 1477
Died: 10 Oct 1530
= **Margaret WOTTON**
Marchioness of Dorset
Born: 1487
Died: c. 1 Sep 1541

Lord Thomas GREY
Born: c. 1520
Died: 1554

Lord Edward GREY
Born: c. 1521
Died: aft 1544

Margaret GREY
Died: aft 1602
= **John ASTLEY**
of Maidstone

Lady Katherine GREY
Lady Maltravers
Born: c. 1514
Died: 1 May 1542
= **Sir Henry FITZALAN**
19th Earl of Arundel
Born: 23 Apr 1512
Marr: bef Nov 1532
Died: 24 Feb 1580

Henry FITZALAN
Lord Maltravers
Born: 1538
Died: 1556
= **Anne WENTWORTH**
Lady Maltravers
Marr: Apr 1555
Died: 5 Dec 1580

Mary FITZALAN
Duchess of Norfolk
Born: 1540
Died: 1557
= **Thomas HOWARD**
4th Duke of Norfolk
Born: 10 Mar 1536
Marr: 1556
Died: 2 Jun 1572

Jane FITZALAN
Lady Lumley
Born: 1537
Died: 1578
= **John LUMLEY**
1st Baron Lumley
Born: c. 1533
Died: 1609

Philip HOWARD
20th Earl of Arundel
Born: 28 Jun 1557
Died: 19 Oct 1595
= **Anne DACRE**
Countess of Arundel
Born: 21 Mar 1557
Marr: 1571
Died: 19 Apr 1630

Current Dukes of Norfolk

Family of Thomas, 2nd Marquis of Dorset and Margaret Wotton (2)

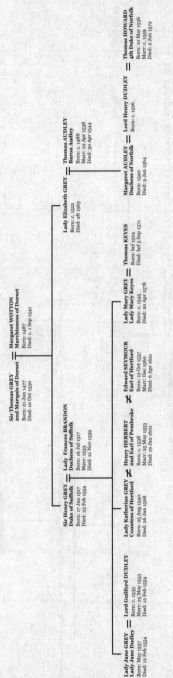

Sir Thomas GREY
2nd Marquis of Dorset
Born: 22 Jun 1477
Died: 10 Oct 1530

= **Margaret WOTTON**
Marchioness of Dorset
Born: 1487
Died: c. 1 Sep 1541

Sir Henry GREY
Duke of Suffolk
Born: 17 Jan 1517
Died: 23 Feb 1554

= **Lady Frances BRANDON**
Duchess of Suffolk
Born: 16 Jul 1517
Marr: 1533
Died: 21 Nov 1559

Lady Elizabeth GREY
Born: c. 1522
Died: aft 1563

= **Thomas AUDLEY**
Baron Audley
Born: c. 1488
Marr: 22 Apr 1538
Died: 30 Apr 1544

Lady Jane GREY
Lady Jane Dudley
Born: May 1537
Died: 12 Feb 1554

= **Lord Guilford DUDLEY**
Born: c. 1535
Marr: 25 May 1553
Died: 12 Feb 1554

Lady Katherine GREY
Countess of Hertford
Born: 25 Aug 1540
Died: 26 Jan 1568

≠ **Henry HERBERT**
2nd Earl of Pembroke
Born: c. 1538
Marr: 25 May 1553
Died: 19 Jan 1601

≠ **Edward SEYMOUR**
Earl of Hertford
Born: 12 Oct 1537
Marr: Dec 1560
Died: 6 Apr 1621

Lady Mary GREY
Lady Mary Keyes
Born: c. 1545
Died: 20 Apr 1578

= **Thomas KEYES**
Born: bef 1524
Died: bef 5 Sep 1571

Margaret AUDLEY
Duchess of Norfolk
Born: 1540
Died: 9 Jan 1564

= **Lord Henry DUDLEY**
Born: c. 1526

= **Thomas HOWARD**
4th Duke of Norfolk
Born: 10 Mar 1536
Marr: c. 1559
Died: 2 Jun 1572

**HM Queen Elizabeth the Queen Mother
& current Dukes of Devonshire**

Current Earls of Suffolk

Family of Thomas, 2nd Marquis of Dorset and Margaret Wotton (3)

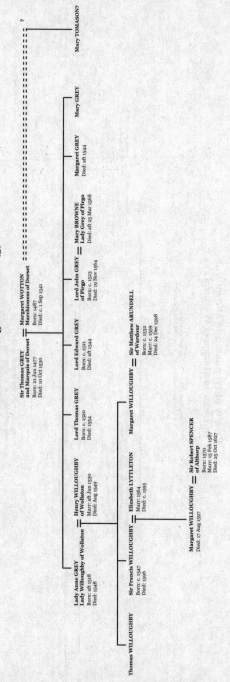

The Grey and Hastings Rivalry (Simplified)

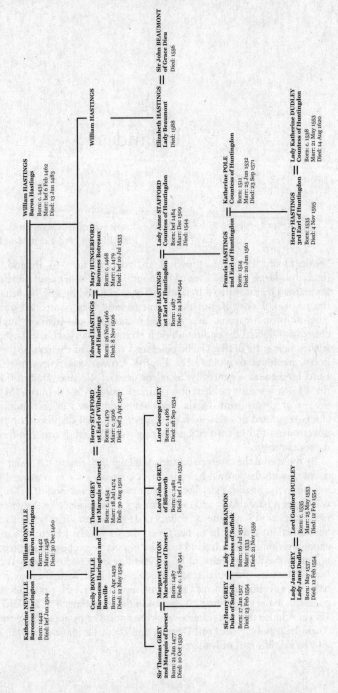

Katherine NEVILLE
Baroness Harington
Born: 1442
Died: bef Jun 1504

William BONVILLE
6th Baron Harington
Born: 1442
Marr: 1458
Died: 30 Dec 1460

William HASTINGS
Baron Hastings
Born: c. 1431
Marr: bef 6 Feb 1462
Died: 13 Jun 1483

Cecily BONVILLE
Baroness Harington and Bonville
Born: c. Apr 1459
Died: 12 May 1529

Thomas GREY
1st Marquis of Dorset
Born: c. 1454
Marr: 18 Jul 1474
Died: 30 Aug 1501

Edward HASTINGS
Lord Hastings
Born: 26 Nov 1466
Died: 8 Nov 1506

Mary HUNGERFORD
Baroness Botreaux
Born: c. 1468
Marr: c. 1479
Died: bef 10 Jul 1533

Henry STAFFORD
1st Earl of Wiltshire
Born: c. 1479
Marr: c. 1506
Died: bef 3 Apr 1523

William HASTINGS

Elizabeth HASTINGS
Lady Beaumont
Died: 1588

Sir John BEAUMONT
of Grace Dieu
Died: 1556

Sir Thomas GREY
2nd Marquis of Dorset
Born: 22 Jun 1477
Died: 10 Oct 1530

Margaret WOTTON
Marchioness of Dorset
Born: 1487
Died: c. 1 Sep 1541

Lord John GREY
of Blisworth
Born: c. 1481
Died: bef 1 Jun 1530

Lord George GREY
Born: c. 1486
Died: aft Sep 1534

George HASTINGS
1st Earl of Huntingdon
Born: 1487
Died: 24 Mar 1544

Lady Anne STAFFORD
Countess of Huntingdon
Born: bef 1484
Marr: Dec 1509
Died: 1544

Sir Henry GREY
Duke of Suffolk
Born: 17 Jan 1517
Died: 23 Feb 1554

Lady Frances BRANDON
Duchess of Suffolk
Born: 16 Jul 1517
Marr: 1533
Died: 21 Nov 1559

Francis HASTINGS
2nd Earl of Huntingdon
Born: 1514
Died: 20 Jun 1561

Katherine POLE
Countess of Huntingdon
Born: 1511
Marr: 25 Jun 1532
Died: 23 Sep 1571

Lady Jane GREY
Lady Jane Dudley
Born: May 1537
Died: 12 Feb 1554

Lord Guilford DUDLEY
Born: c. 1535
Marr: 25 May 1553
Died: 12 Feb 1554

Henry HASTINGS
3rd Earl of Huntingdon
Born: 1535
Died: 4 Nov 1595

Lady Katherine DUDLEY
Countess of Huntingdon
Born: c. 1538
Marr: 21 May 1553
Died: 14 Aug 1620

12

Ireland

Never ... desire to be great about princes, for it is dangerous.
John Blount, 3rd Lord Mountjoy

While Henry Dorset is growing up, we will turn to Ireland, which figured so largely in the lives of his aunt, Lady Elizabeth, and uncle, Lord Leonard. The lordship of Ireland had been claimed by English kings since the reign of Henry II, but the extent of land they controlled under the Anglo-Norman barons, later referred to as the Anglo-Irish or 'Englishry', ebbed and flowed depending on their strength relative to the 'Irishry', the Irishry being the native Gaelic chieftains who ruled the rest of the island in an arcane clan system. The English Crown was represented by the Lord Lieutenant – generally, as in the case of Richard, Duke of York in the 1450s, a senior nobleman – or, more usually, his deputy. '[M]uch of the art of government (by the lieutenants) consisted in ensuring that the chiefs remained at odds with each other and well disposed towards the government and in correctly predicting trouble and drafting in forces for its containment.'[1]

By the end of the fifteenth century, the Englishry controlled about half the country, with the Crown being in direct control of the area around Dublin known as the English Pale. The appointment of English nobles as lieutenants was never a particularly successful strategy – the resident Englishry resented interlopers, and the complex politics of Englishry and Irishry were hard for newcomers to master. In earlier times, the Crown had been able to wring enough revenue out of Ireland to make it a viable proposition to try to rule it, but by the time of Edward IV, expenditure exceeded revenue – a chronic lack of coinage inhibited trade, which, combined with the government's habit of providing for its men by taking supplies from the peasantry without payment, made life for many a misery. In the second reign of Edward IV, the king concluded that governance would be improved by appointing one of the Anglo-Irish nobility as Lord Deputy, and chose the most powerful, Gerald FitzGerald, 8th Earl of Kildare.

Following his appointment, Kildare consolidated his personal position, but also improved governance, and both the Crown and the Englishry were largely content with his performance through the reigns of Edward IV, Edward V and Richard III. With the accession of Henry VII, Jasper, Duke of Bedford was appointed Lord Lieutenant, with Kildare remaining in post as his deputy. Henry sought to meet Kildare, but the earl refused to come to London, although he did agree to a marriage between his daughter and Piers Butler, cousin of Henry's friend, the long-time Lancastrian adherent Thomas, 4th Earl of Ormond. In 1487, Kildare arranged the crowning of Lambert Simnel, and kept courts in the name of Edward VI. The failure of the rebellion gave Henry the opportunity to circumvent Kildare's power by giving concessions to his rival, the Earl of Desmond. In 1492, when Kildare failed to back the king against Perkin Warbeck, Henry replaced him as deputy, first by a joint commission and then by Sir Edward Poynings, whose role was to rearrange the governance of the country to Henry's satisfaction, before a slightly chastened Kildare was allowed to return to office. As a mark of a new relationship with Kildare, the king gave him a second wife in the form of Elizabeth St John, Henry's own cousin. Kildare was also given free rein to encroach on the Gaelic lands, with the promise that he could hold, under the king, anything he captured, and could appoint all officers in Ireland except the Lord Chancellor. Just to make sure Kildare did not forget his loyalty, his eldest son, Lord Gerald FitzGerald, was detained at Henry's court as hostage, until 1505, when he was given another cousin of the king's, Elizabeth Zouche, as wife, and returned to Ireland as Treasurer.

In September 1513, the 8th earl died. His son was elected as Justiciar, and, shortly afterwards, appointed Lord Deputy. But the 9th earl did not have the skills to manage the Irish council as effectively as his father had. Soon, complaints were heard in London, mainly from the English officers who had been appointed to the Irish council, that Kildare was taking too much on himself – treating with the Irish chiefs and making peace or war without consulting the council. The English officers also thought the Englishry were far too close to the Irishry – not surprising, as there was a good deal of intermarriage. Kildare came to London, and Henry VIII, who knew him well from his youth in England, was persuaded of his good intentions and reappointed him.

Shortly after, a row erupted over the earldom of Ormond. On his death in 1515, the 4th earl, the late Henry VII's friend, who had spent most of Henry's reign in England, left two daughters – Lady Margaret Boleyn and Lady Anne St Leger – but no sons. His cousin Piers Butler, Kildare's brother-in-law, claimed the earldom, but Henry VIII wanted the sisters to inherit as they were both married to men he valued. Eventually, the inheritance was split, with the sisters sharing the English lands, and Butler receiving the Irish properties and using – although without formal agreement – the title of earl of Ormond. It was as part of a potential settlement of this dispute that Lady Margaret Boleyn's granddaughter Anne was mooted as a wife for Piers Butler's son James. Despite this settlement, Piers felt that Kildare had failed him and became his brother-in-law's sworn enemy.

In January 1519, Kildare was summoned to court. The king wanted his own council to investigate how Ireland could be 'reduced and restored to good order and obedience'. Unfortunately for Kildare, he was unable to control his temper when his management was questioned, and he quarrelled violently in council with Cardinal Wolsey. To annoy the king's chief minister was an unwise move – the earl was required to remain in England, and the Earl of Surrey was appointed deputy in his place. Kildare was obliged to kick his heels at court, possibly even spending some time in prison. In May 1520, he gave a bond not to travel outside London, probably to cover the king's absence at the Field of Cloth of Gold, and, two months later, another bond to appear in front of the council on demand.

Before he had left Ireland, Kildare had been widowed, and it was rumoured that he would use the trip to England to seek a new marriage. While at court, he seemingly fell in love with Lady Elizabeth Grey, daughter of the 1st Marquis of Dorset. Elizabeth, in her mid-to-late twenties, was past the age when noblewomen usually married. Any efforts Cecily or her brother might have made to find her a match would have been hampered by the difficulties in producing her dowry. Either for love alone, or perhaps the desire to marry a cousin of the king, Kildare agreed to take her without her dowry paid down. For Elizabeth this was a mixed opportunity: Kildare was of similar rank to her father, and was reputed to be extremely attractive, and she may have fancied the adventure of a life in Ireland, while her status would rise as a married woman and a countess. On the other hand, Kildare was under something of a cloud with the king, and her mother had refused consent. Why Cecily refused her permission is not recorded. Perhaps she thought her daughter could do better than a widowed earl from Ireland with a family already, or perhaps she didn't want Elizabeth to leave the country. Perhaps it all came down to inability or unwillingness to find £1,000. If her daughter married without her consent, the obligation in Thomas I's will to pay the dowry lapsed.

Nevertheless, Elizabeth went ahead and married Kildare. This was perilous financially – if she did not bring a dowry Kildare was under no obligation to settle a jointure on her, and if she were widowed she would only be entitled to the legal minimum dower of one-third of his income. She also knew he had at least two sons and two daughters by his first marriage, so she would be unlikely to be the mother of the next earl. There is an indication in a later letter that Henry VIII at least encouraged the match, if he did not specifically mandate it.

By mid-1521, Kildare had been restored to Henry's good graces, having cleared his name of Surrey's imputation that, even though he was absent from Ireland, he was fomenting unrest there. Surrey himself was heartily sick of his post – the expense and the bloody flux were both killing him. He advised the king that unless Henry were willing to pour out the time and money required to undertake a complete conquest of Ireland, subdue the Irishry and entirely reform the government of the country, to have an Englishman as deputy was a waste of the king's time and money. The subjugation of Ireland held little temptation for Henry, once again focused on French conquest, so Surrey was called back to London to explain the situation in detail, while Butler of Ormond was appointed as his replacement in May 1522. Lord Ferrers, Mary Grey's husband, had been put forward as a possibility by Henry, but Wolsey thought that Ferrers too inexperienced. Whilst he was a

> good and right active gentleman meet and able to have the conducting of a good number of men in the wars (where other higher captains having experience shall be governors above him) yet to commit the whole rule and governance of Ireland unto him as your lieutenant, not being expert in weighty matters, sad advice and good counsel, especially amongst such brittle people as they be, in whom is much craft and little or no faith and truth, it is thought dangerous though he were charged nothing to do but by the advice of the council there, and yet in that case he should rather be ruled than rule.[2]

As well as Ferrers' inexperience, the matter of cost had weighed in favour of Ormond. However, he found it as hard to keep order as Surrey had.

In January 1523, Kildare returned to Ireland, taking his new wife with him to settle at his chief seat of Maynooth Castle, where they lived in some state, surrounded by as fine tapestry and furnishings as Elizabeth would have seen anywhere other than at the king's court, and with large quantities of gold and silver plate, a stable of 1,000 horses and a similar number of cattle. Kildare was said to be so enamoured of his wife that whenever he had new clothes made for himself, she had a matching set. The earl began a programme of non-co-operation with Ormond, which culminated in the murder, by Kildare's men, of James Talbot as he was en route to Ormond's castle for Christmas. In revenge, Ormond attacked several of Kildare properties in county Wicklow.

Elizabeth wrote a pleading letter to Wolsey, complaining of Ormond and asking Wolsey to favour Kildare's suits. She was particularly eager that her intercession might help, because 'as yet my said lord and husband hath not had any great profit by me, yet I find him as good and kind unto me always as any man may be to his wife'.[3] Elizabeth was 'in continual fear … of the king's deputy's sore and unfavourable demeanour unto my said lord'. She imputed this to Kildare's refusal to favour Butler's suit for the earldom of Ormond. Butler's exigency to have the earldom was even, Elizabeth accused, causing him to '[maintain] the king's Irish rebels', who, she insisted, had been benefited by the destruction of Kildare's castles.

Kildare had complained to the Irish council, but it would not, or could not, prevent Ormond's actions against him. Elizabeth further assured Wolsey that it was only her husband's respect for him and the king that prevented him avenging himself. She also thanked Wolsey for the recent agreement he had forced her mother and brother into for the payment of her dowry. Elizabeth probably also wrote to Dorset, who is credited with intervening at this point to have the quarrel between Kildare and Ormond investigated in Ireland, rather than requiring the earls to come to England again. A complex reconciliation was arbitrated at Kilkenny Castle: among numerous clauses, the earls were each bound to keep the peace, and to stop encouraging the Gaelic chiefs to raid the other's lands.

Despite royal intervention, the reconciliation failed, and both men continued to complain to Henry and Wolsey. It may have been at this period, or perhaps a year or two later, that Elizabeth wrote to the Earl of Shrewsbury, who was also Earl of Waterford in Ireland. She explained that the 'sinister report' he had heard of depredations among his tenants being committed by Kildare was quite false, nothing but 'forged fables'. Kildare was as tender of Shrewsbury's tenants as he was of his own – although that was purely for the earl's sake, as the tenants themselves were 'people of the most inordinate demeanour that I know in all this land, full of rancour and malice and no perfect love or charity between them and evermore be provoking and stirring war with Irishman', which required Kildare to defend them.[4]

In August 1524, Kildare replaced Ormond as Lord Deputy, but the feud continued. Ormond complained that Kildare had kept monies that should have been paid to him, which Kildare stoutly denied. Kildare followed this up by asking his brother-in-law Lord Leonard Grey, who had come to Maynooth on a combined family visit and tour of inspection on the king's behalf, to take back letters to the king which were, in effect, a long bill of complaint against Ormond. Had Lord Leonard known how this involvement with Ireland would end, he would probably have thrown the documents into the fire! At about the same time, Ormond agreed with the king that he would surrender his title to his cousin Thomas Boleyn, and take the title of earl of Ossory in substitution. This cannot have pleased him, but he was cheered when he saw an opportunity to rid himself of Kildare. Triumphantly, he accused Kildare of secretly warning the Earl of Desmond of his imminent arrest for plotting with Charles V, allowing Desmond to escape.

Furious at this hint of treason, Henry summoned both Desmond and Kildare to London, where they were rapidly imprisoned in the Tower. Kildare had left his son by his first wife, Lord Thomas FitzGerald, in charge, but orders arrived swiftly from London for Lord Devlin to be appointed instead. Determined to prove that only he could manage Ireland, Kildare sent a message to his daughter Alice, wife of the Gaelic chief O'Conor. Delighted at the opportunity to make a stir, O'Conor made 'invasions, roodes and hostilities',[5] which encouraged the Irish council to inform Henry that Kildare's brothers and kinsmen could 'cause more damage than three times as many [men] in other parts of the land'. They therefore requested his return 'for there is none of this land that can do or may do for defence of the same so well as [Kildare]'. A group of Kildare's friends and connections agreed to stand surety for his good behaviour if he were released from gaol. The Duke of Norfolk (who had been Lord Deputy under his former title of Surrey) headed the list, but he was followed by Elizabeth's family – Cecily, Dorset, Lord Leonard and Dorothy's husband, Lord Mountjoy, were all prepared to stand for Kildare, suggesting that their objection to his marriage to Elizabeth had not been personal, or, if it had been, that he had won them over, and that Elizabeth had pleaded for their help.

The plan backfired. Henry was furious – if there was one thing he hated, it was being manipulated. He complained that Kildare 'went fraudulently about to colour that the king should think that he could not be served there but only by him', and clapped the earl back in the Tower. Instead of a single deputy, the king decided to try the expedient of leaving the deputyship empty, while the government was managed by the three chief officers: Archbishop of Dublin and Lord Chancellor John Alen, Treasurer John Rawson and Chief Justice Bermingham. This did not work as well as hoped. Sir William Skeffington, Master of the Ordnance, was sent to report on their progress and soon said they had neither money nor capacity to manage. Elizabeth knew Skeffington well – he was around seventy years old, and had been one of the executors of her father's will. Pleased with Skeffington's diligence, and encouraged by the advice of Norfolk and Rochford, Henry appointed him as Lord Deputy with 250 troops and orders to promote good relations between Kildare, Ossory and Desmond and secure cooperation against the Irish. With this robust officer in place, Kildare was released from the Tower. After serving the king by signing the letter the English nobles sent to Pope Clement VII in favour of the king's annulment suit, he and Elizabeth were allowed to return to Maynooth.

Within months the old rivalry between Kildare and Ossory had broken out, and a new quarrel was in hand between Kildare and Skeffington. Skeffington's problems were exacerbated by a lack of money to pay his troops and the refusal of the Irish parliament that autumn to grant a subsidy. He tried another method of raising funds, levying scutage – that is, a fine on men who refused to answer the king's call to arms. There were plenty who might be required to pay it, as the Englishry were tired of the constant wars with the Irishry on behalf of the Crown, preferring an overall acceptance of the borders with a few skirmishes from time to time.

While Skeffington was scrabbling about for money, in 1531 Kildare was making his own financial arrangements – an elaborate agreement for Elizabeth's jointure. He named various manors from which she was to draw an income of 300 marks Irish per annum – this was to be in full recompense of her dowry, presumably now paid by Cecily's executors.

The rights of Kildare's children by his first marriage and his second were clarified. Elizabeth was to have the use of the manor of Portlester, should she wish to live in Ireland after her husband's death.

*

The politics of London were played out in Dublin. Kildare was supported by Norfolk and Rochford, so Ossory, needing friends, courted Thomas Cromwell, who was rising to prominence with the fall of Cardinal Wolsey. However little Kildare and Ossory liked each other, they were united in their complaints about Skeffington, so in spring 1532, Kildare, Ossory, Lord Justice Bermingham and Rawson were summoned to court yet again. Elizabeth, as always, accompanied her husband. Bermingham and Rawson accused Skeffington of malpractice, partiality and faking musters, while they had no criticism of Kildare, claiming he had been a good servant until provoked by Skeffington's favouritism of Ossory. Ossory concurred – he blamed Skeffington for sowing discord between himself and Kildare. Skeffington was recalled and dismissed, to be replaced with Kildare as Lord Deputy again, and Ossory as Treasurer, while John Alen, the Chancellor, was replaced by George Cromer, Archbishop of Armagh. Immediately, Kildare increased his aggression against the Irishry, during the course of which he was wounded by gunshot.

Kildare had picked the wrong horse on the English council as his patron – Norfolk's influence was declining, while Cromwell's grew. Cromwell wanted a different approach in Ireland – he did not like the traditional, semi-autonomous management of the country, preferring more direct Crown control. A nephew of Archbishop Alen, confusingly also named John, was appointed as Master of the Rolls, and Kildare and Ossory were once again required to attend upon the king in September 1532. Kildare declined, sending Elizabeth to make his excuses – his gunshot wound was failing to heal and he was too ill to travel. Elizabeth arrived in late 1532, or early 1533, and stayed with Lord Leonard at Beaumanor. From there, she wrote to the king, reminding him that she was his 'poor kinswoman' and that he had caused her to be married to his 'true subject' the Earl of Kildare. Since Kildare had 'fair issue' from his first wife, and had settled almost all of his lands on them long before his marriage to Elizabeth, leaving only lands that were of little value as they were 'among the wild Irish', could Henry grant her and her son Gerald several manors in Meath, at the rent he was accustomed to receive?[6] Leonard backed her up with a letter to Cromwell on her behalf. She hoped that Cromwell would 'labour in secret' over the matter, as her husband wanted the same properties for his eldest son by his first marriage.

With Elizabeth safely in England, Kildare began moving royal ordinance to his own properties. Alen and others of Cromwell's appointees came to England to make a formal complaint – so long as either Kildare or Ossory held the deputyship, there could be no resolution of Irish issues. This left Henry and his council in a quandary: no one wanted the job of deputy. The actual Lord Lieutenant was Henry's son, the thirteen-year-old Duke of Richmond, and Cromwell mooted sending him as a figurehead to instil respect for the Crown. Norfolk objected, probably thinking the job would be too difficult and dangerous. Only Skeffington could be tempted to take office again – perhaps eager to revenge himself on Kildare, who had humiliated him in front of his own troops. But for him to be installed, Kildare would have to be ousted. The king wrote again to Kildare, allowing him to appoint a deputy of his own if he would come to England, sending the letters by Elizabeth's servant Robert Reilly, who also carried one from Elizabeth to her husband. Skeffington complained that Reilly was 'making no manner of expedition or haste' and dawdling about until the winds were foul, but the letters eventually arrived, and, after installing his son, Thomas, Lord Offaly, as his deputy, Kildare departed in February 1534 for England.

On arrival, he was questioned by the council. Unable to allay suspicion of treason, he was arrested and sent to the Tower once more, while Skeffington took his place. Kildare, now dying from the effects of his gunshot wound, was able to send a secret message to his son, warning him not to come to England if sent for. Believing a false rumour that his father had been executed, Thomas called a meeting of the Irish council at St Mary's Abbey, Dublin, where, despite pleading from the councillors, he formally withdrew his allegiance from the king, throwing down his sword of state, the silken fringes on his doublet sleeves fluttering so extravagantly that he was nicknamed Silken Thomas ever after. He now rose up in open rebellion, citing Henry's religious policy in hopes of attracting supporters who would hesitate to rebel under normal circumstances. For this, he received some limited help from Emperor Charles and the pope. Confident that Charles would promise more than he would ever deliver, Henry sent a large force to Ireland under Lord Leonard in October 1534, a month after Kildare had died in the Tower. Silken Thomas withdrew to Maynooth. The Englishry were forced to choose between their fellow earl and the king's deputy. Unenthusiastically, they supported Skeffington, who besieged the earl. Thomas slipped out of Maynooth to gather reinforcements, leaving as constable his foster brother, who soon intimated to Skeffington that the castle was for sale. Skeffington accepted the terms, but instead of freeing the garrison, hanged them – an outrage that became known as 'The pardon of Maynooth'. Thomas hid among the Irishry for some time, mounting raids here and there but not attracting the support he had hoped for.

Eventually, having received reassurances from Lord Leonard that he would be pardoned if he surrendered and went to London, Silken Thomas gave in. He wrote to Leonard that

> whereas I have done anything contrary against my sovereign lord the king his mind, came nothing of my own mere motion but only by your Council the which being in your lordship's company now … I …

did nothing but after their mind … Wherefore I heartily desire your lordship to be intercessor betwixt his said grace and me, that I may have my pardon for me and my life and lands the which shall not be undeserved to the uttermost of my power…[7]

If this unrepentant shifting of blame came to the king's eyes, it cannot have encouraged him to feel merciful. Leonard took Thomas to London in person after his surrender on 24 August and received a £200 bonus for his part in bringing Thomas in, as well as £116 for the costs of transporting him. Before departing, Thomas left considerable amounts of his plate with, among others, the White Friars at Kildare, as well as with the Gaelic chief O'Brien, who also took charge of some of Elizabeth's clothes. The hangings from Maynooth Castle and the late earl's parliament robes were left with Thomas's sister, Lady Cicely, the wife of the chief O'Carroll.

On 13 September 1535, Lord Audley wrote to Cromwell about various bills for introduction into Parliament – one of which related to the dispute between Thomas Boleyn, Earl of Wiltshire and father of the new queen, and his Butler cousins regarding the title of Earl of Ormond. He had drafted a commission for Skeffington for holding an Irish parliament there 'after the old custom'. He had heard that that 'arrant, false, traitor, Thomas FitzGerald' had been taken, but that rumour had it that he had been promised, if he submitted to certain conditions, to be allowed to enter the king's presence to explain himself. Audley, sarcastically claiming to be 'a man of very little experience and less wit', confessed he could not believe that anyone could have made such an agreement with so 'cankered a traitor' – especially that he might come to the king's presence a free man. If such an agreement had been made, why had the king's council in Ireland been so busy telling Henry that there could be no peace in Ireland until the 'blood of the Geralds' was 'wholly extinct'? Audley wrote that if his advice were taken, FitzGerald would go straight to the Tower – any other course would be an encouragement to traitors.

Henry agreed with Audley, and Thomas was taken to the Tower when Leonard delivered him in mid-September. Nevertheless, Norfolk prevailed upon the king to honour Leonard's promise, at least in the short term – failure to do so would undermine the credibility of the Irish council and fan the embers of rebellion. Norfolk was no great fan of Leonard, whom he saw as a crony of Cromwell's, but he obviously thought Leonard had given his promise in good faith.

Henry heeded Norfolk's advice. Thomas was released and given freedom to move about the court. Henry even granted him a personal audience, leading him to believe he would be pardoned. Since Cromwell had previously indicated that no pardon would be forthcoming, this graciousness on Henry's part was particularly gratifying. Nevertheless, the Imperial ambassador, Eustace Chapuys, was cynical, sure that once Thomas's uncles, who were still holding out, had been captured, and Ireland reduced to suitable obedience, Henry would find another quarrel with Thomas, despite any pardon, and dispatch him. He also disbelieved the story that Leonard had left hostages in return for Thomas's safety, as he had heard from the wife of one of the English councillors that Thomas had slipped away 'in his shirt' to take advantage of the king's offer of clemency.

Skeffington had protested in 1532 that he was too old to be deputy, but Henry had insisted. Now, Alen, appointed as Master of the Rolls, and Gerald Aylmer, the new Chief Justice, wrote to Cromwell that when they had arrived in the country they had been surprised at the extent of destruction. Similarly, they were astonished to learn that Skeffington had ordered that the Irish should pay for 1,000 'kerne' (native soldiers), together with horses and provisions, for a three-month period. There was no possibility, the men reported, that the country could stand that level of impost – such a demand was bound to produce 'either insurrection, or desolation'. The deputy, roughly seventy years old by now, was in failing health – if he rose before 10 or 11 a.m., he was 'almost dead before noon'. They advised that he be recalled, and that Leonard be appointed deputy in his place, suitably hedged about with orders to do nothing without the council's agreement. Everything should be done in secret as the Irish were accustomed to 'do great hurts' during handover periods.

Having delivered up Silken Thomas, Leonard was sent back to Ireland as Chief Marshal of the Army in Ireland, subservient to Skeffington. He was in high favour with the king, as reported to Lord Lisle:

> My lord Leonard Grey is gone into Ireland again and has with him many gunners and in all things well furnished. The King's Grace gave him in reward v hundred marks sterling in money and a hundred pound land to him and his heirs, beside his former grant of 3 hundred marks ... And also the King's Grace gave him a ship well trimmed and the Queen's Grace gave him a chain of gold from her middle worth a hundred marks and a purse with twenty sovereigns.[8]

Although Skeffington had been a friend of Leonard's father, the two men were unable to work together harmoniously. The king wrote to Skeffington, assuring him that Leonard had been ordered to render him 'reverence and obedience'. Nevertheless, Skeffington was to be mindful of Leonard's rank, and his position as a blood relative of the king, and he was to follow the advice of the Irish Council, especially Leonard, St Loe and Chief Justice Aylmer. He was also taken to task over reported slackness in taking musters. The king thought that, with Silken Thomas safely taken, most of the soldiers could be discharged. He also 'marvelled' that Skeffington had not taken hostages from those Irish lords with whom he had parleyed and come to an agreement. Skeffington was to 'use diligence' to apprehend a number of traitors, including Elizabeth Kildare's brothers-in-law, James, John, Richard, Oliver and Walter FitzGerald, and 'as many of the bastard Geraldines' as the Privy Council 'shall think convenient'. Skeffington was also to send particulars of Kildare's lands, and those of other attainted traitors, as well as the king's revenues.

The Irish council was as fractious as the country, with the Chancellor, Master of the Rolls and Treasurer quarrelling, telling tales, and complaining of each other's bad behaviour. The Treasurer, Sir William Brabazon, was initially the object of internal rancour, although Ossory, Sir James Butler, Aylmer, Alen and Leonard all signed a letter to Cromwell, denying any plot to remove him from office. Brabazon certainly had one strong supporter – Sir Edward Beck wrote a sycophantic letter to Cromwell, praising the Treasurer as doing more work than the others put together. Cromwell was lauded as having 'preserved this land', which would

> never have come to such reformation but for [him]. [He] could not have done a better act in slaying infidels than the bringing of this land from such misery into obedience to law and justice, for the country is in good peace and quiet, and in greater fear of justice than it has been these forty years.[9]

On 31 December 1535, Skeffington died, and Lord Leonard was formally appointed deputy, and ennobled in the Irish peerage as Viscount Grane. Within days, a former servant of Skeffington's, Anthony Colly, wrote to Cromwell with a list of complaints about how Leonard was conducting himself. Leonard was, in fact, following the king's orders regarding the management of the soldiers, but the imposition of strict discipline, following a more relaxed regime, engendered resentment. Leonard had mustered the troops 'in strait and cruel fashion', used 'unfitting words' to Skeffington, menaced the captains and threatened to strike Skeffington's son, his own namesake, Leonard Skeffington, with his dagger. This, in the view of Colly, had so distressed Skeffington that it had shortened his life. With a strong suggestion of a new broom sweeping clean, Leonard had then berated the soldiers at muster for their poor horses, although Colly thought them quite good enough, and felt that not enough consideration had been given to the fact that the troops had not been paid for seven months. Leonard was encouraged in his approach by the Master of the Rolls. It was only the goodness of Treasurer Brabazon that had saved the soldiers significant losses from their wages. Colly was also aggrieved that Leonard had taken control of recruitment, not allowing captains to either retain or dismiss men without his express permission.

Yet another black mark against Leonard was his alleged treatment of Colly's kinswoman, Skeffington's widow, Anne, who, Colly maintained, had been prevented from writing to Cromwell. Lady Skeffington, fearing her post would be intercepted, had felt obliged to seek an unfamiliar messenger to take her letters. Either Lady Skeffington had been paranoid, or her ruse worked – Cromwell received her letter, which contained numerous allegations against Leonard, including that he refused to let her have her belongings from Maynooth Castle unless she gave him 'such parcels as he had a mind to', and had confiscated not one, but two, ships she had hired to send letters home, along with horses she intended to send to the king, the queen and Cromwell. She asked Cromwell to obtain permission for her to send whomever she wished home, and for orders to be issued to the Skeffington faction on the council – the Lord Chancellor, the Treasurer and the Chief Baron of the Exchequer – since Lord Leonard, the Chief Justice and the Master of the Rolls would 'advance all matters cruelly to her vexation'. So incensed was Lady Skeffington that she even wrote directly to Queen Anne, asking her to intercede to ensure Cromwell granted her petition – she and her children had been 'undone' by her husband's service to the king.

The various reports of Leonard can be added up to indicate an avaricious streak – but, of course, it may be that Anne Skeffington was holding onto property that belonged to the office of the deputy, rather than to her personally – or perhaps, since the items were at Maynooth, they actually belonged to Leonard's sister. The ships, too, may have been required for other purposes.

With Skeffington gone, there was a rapprochement with Brabazon, and the council reported Leonard's success in capturing the five FitzGerald brothers. The Irish council, in self-congratulatory mood, described this as 'the best deed ever done for the weal of the king's poor subjects'. Leonard took a short trip to London to deliver the captives, but was back in Ireland by May 1536, and entered into bonds with the O'Neills. Unlike the Anglo-Irish FitzGeralds, the O'Neills were native kings, with their power base in Ulster. Their status had been recognised as late as 1493, when Henry VII referred to O'Neill as Chief of the Irish Kings. Henry VIII's policy, however, was to dominate Ireland by conquering the lands of the Irish chiefs and regranting them to the chiefs as his vassals. The Irish, unsurprisingly, did not like this idea, and were by now in communication with Scotland, where Henry's nephew James V nursed an implacable resentment towards his overbearing and interfering uncle. Leonard wrote that numerous Scots had been sent to join the Irish, and that he was being advised by Brabazon and the others to furnish a ship and lie in wait for the Scots. Cromwell was requested to give Leonard's servant Matthew King licence to levy sailors and mariners for such an expedition. Despite having formally been appointed as deputy, Leonard professed anxiety about derogatory reports that Cromwell might have received about him – presumably referring to Colly and Lady Skeffington's missives – and asked the Secretary to ignore them.

In Leonard's first parliament of May 1536, the Acts of Succession and Supremacy that had been passed in England, establishing the children of Anne Boleyn as the inheritors of the realm, were enacted in Ireland. Embarrassingly, by the time the news that the Acts had been passed in Ireland reached London in June, Queen Anne had been executed, and her marriage annulled. Cromwell immediately ordered that the Acts be stayed – they had, he said, been imperfectly passed. The Dublin parliament did not much care who the king's wife or heir was, so, as soon as Henry VIII's new marriage to Jane Seymour was brought to their attention, the Act of Succession was replaced with a new one, settling the crown on Henry's children by Jane. The act requiring the 'first fruits' of the bishoprics to be sent to the king, rather than the pope, was also accepted, as was an act of resumption against the lands of absentee landlords, in particular the earls of Shrewsbury and Wiltshire (who held the titles of Earl of Waterford and Ormond in Ireland respectively) and the Duke of Norfolk. In return for these approvals, the Irish Parliament anticipated that Silken Thomas would be pardoned and restored, if not to the deputyship, then at least to his accustomed place among the Englishry. However, Henry was not in a forgiving mood and Thomas remained in gaol. Parliament's refusal to grant the king the subsidy he had requested did not help the situation. Further attempts to raise money also failed and may have inclined Henry to the drastic step he took in February 1537, when Silken Thomas and his five uncles were all executed.

Following the death of Silken Thomas, Gerald FitzGerald, Elizabeth's son, was heir to the earldom of Kildare. When his father left Ireland in 1534, the boy had been in the care of his aunt Lady Eleanor, daughter of the 8th earl, who allegedly agreed to marry Manus O'Donnell, one of the chiefs of Ulster, only on condition he protect Gerald. Elizabeth Kildare had remained in England after the death of her husband, dividing her time between the court and Leonard's house at Beaumanor. In July 1537, she arrived at Beaumanor to find her second son, eight-year-old Thomas, accompanied by people she did not know, who would give her no information as to how they had arrived, nor on whose orders they had brought the boy. She begged Cromwell for instructions as to what to do, but hoped she could keep Thomas in her custody 'because he [was] an innocent' whom she wished to see brought up in virtue. It is unclear whether 'innocent' in this context means innocent of any wrongdoing or refers to learning difficulties.

Henry, hoping for an improvement in his finances by a more thorough subjugation of Ireland than any of his predecessors had attempted, was disappointed – the expenses of trying to crush the country were by no means compensated by the little income that could be squeezed out of it. Impervious to financial reality, the king dispatched a stinging letter in 1537, accusing Leonard and the council of lining their own pockets rather than filling the royal coffers. Cromwell appointed a new commission, led by Sir Anthony St Leger and including Brabazon, to enquire into the conduct of the deputy and the council, and find a way to reduce costs.

Leonard's remit may be summarised as reducing costs, raising revenue and keeping the peace, none of which were easy. So far as keeping the peace was concerned, he believed the best way was to emulate his late brother-in-law's armed progresses through the Irishry to extend royal authority. From the point of view of containing the Irishry, he was

Henry VI, whose weakness led to the Wars of the Roses. (Courtesy of Yale Center for British Art)

Above: Astley Castle, the inheritance of Sir Edward Grey, Lord Ferrers. Possibly the married home of Elizabeth Woodville. (© Melita Thomas)

Left: The exterior of Astley Church, burial place of 1st & 2nd marquises of Dorset, and Cecily Bonville, wife of the 1st marquis. (© Melita Thomas)

Above left: The College of Dean and Canons at Astley was founded in 1343, and was a beneficiary of the wills of the 1st & 2nd marquises, and of Cecily Bonville. The painted interior dates from the fourteenth century – this is what the family would have seen. (© Melita Thomas)

Above right: Effigies (r–l) of Sir Edward Grey, his wife, Elizabeth Talbot, Viscountess Lisle, and Cecily Bonville, wife of Thomas I. (© Melita Thomas)

Below: A remnant of Groby Hall, the chief residence of Lord and Lady Ferrers. (© Melita Thomas)

Above: Extended by William, Lord Hastings, Ashby Castle was probably one of the childhood homes of Cecily Bonville, and the home of the Hastings family, rivals of the Greys. (© Melita Thomas)

Below: Kirby Muxloe, another Hastings property, where Cecily spent some of her childhood. (© Melita Thomas)

Above left: Elizabeth Woodville, wife of Sir John Grey, mother of Thomas I and Sir Richard Grey.

Above right: Edward IV, stepfather of Thomas I and Sir Richard Grey. (Courtesy of Ripon Cathedral)

Below: Eltham, where Thomas I and Sir Richard Grey may have spent part of their childhood. (© Melita Thomas)

Above: Ludlow Castle, seat of Council for Wales and the Marches. Both the 1st marquis and Sir Richard Grey spent time here, as members of the council headed by their half-brother Edward, later Edward V. In 1520s, the 2nd marquis was Lord Great Master of the Household of Princess Mary, based at Ludlow, and his daughter, Lady Katherine, was a member of the princess's retinue. (© Melita Thomas)

Below: Remains of mediaeval Thornbury Castle. Buckingham's Rebellion was planned here. (© Melita Thomas)

Above left: Richard III, whose usurpation of the throne ended in the death of Sir Richard Grey and the disappearance of the Greys' half-brothers. (Courtesy of the Rijksmuseum)

Above right: Henry VII. Thomas I supported him in exile, and was left in France as the pledge for a loan. (Courtesy of Ripon Cathedral)

Right: Elizabeth of York, half-sister of Thomas I and Sir Richard. (Courtesy of the Rijksmuseum)

ELISABETH D'YORCK.

Shute Barton Manor Gatehouse. Shute was part of the Bonville estate, extended by Cecily and Thomas I. (© Melita Thomas)

Above: Shute dates from the thirteenth century. The range to the left was built by Cecily. (© Melita Thomas)

Below: Thomas I began the house at Bradgate in the 1490s. It was the childhood home of Lady Jane Grey. (© Melita Thomas)

Right: Cardinal Thomas Wolsey. Thomas I was his first patron.

Below: Ottery St Mary church. (© Melita Thomas)

Inset: Built by Cecily, the Dorset aisle inside the church was modelled on the ceiling of St George's Chapel, Windsor. (© Melita Thomas)

Above left: Henry VIII. Thomas II was the king's devoted friend, subject and jousting companion. (Courtesy of the University of Florida)

Above right: Katharine of Aragon. Elizabeth, Countess of Kildare was a staunch defender of the queen, and Dorothy, Lady Mountjoy's, husband was her Lord Chamberlain. (Courtesy of Ripon Cathedral)

Below: The Field of Cloth of Gold, at which Thomas II was a key member of Henry VIII's jousting team.

Above: Kenilworth Castle, of which Thomas II held the constableship. (© Melita Thomas)

Below left: Anne Boleyn in a portrait by Holbein. Thomas II left Anne £20 in his will. (From A. L. Baldry's *Drawings of Holbein*, 1906)

Below right: A Holbein sketch purported to represent Margaret Wotton, Marchioness of Dorset. Thomas II's trusted wife, she quarrelled with her son over money. (From A. L. Baldry's *Drawings of Holbein*, 1906)

Ightham Mote,
which was owned
by Richard Haute,
cousin of Thomas I,
who was executed
with Sir Richard Grey.
Later, Margaret
spent long periods
here during her
widowhood.
(© Melita Thomas)

Ightham Mote
Courtyard.
(© Melita Thomas)

A Holbein sketch purported to depict
Lady Elizabeth Grey the Younger, Lady
Audley. Daughter of Thomas II and
Margaret, she married Lord Chancellor
Audley when she was about sixteen.
Ancestor of HM The Queen. (From A.
L. Baldry's *Drawings of Holbein*, 1906)

Above: The remains of Sudeley Castle's Mediaeval Great Hall. Jane lived here with Queen Katherine Parr. (© Melita Thomas)

Below: Sudeley Church, where Katherine Parr is buried. Jane was chief mourner at the funeral. (© Melita Thomas)

Above left: Heinrich Bullinger. Suffolk and Jane corresponded with this leading Protestant. (Courtesy of Zentralbibliothek Zurich)

Above right: John Knox, the radical Protestant preacher at the court of Edward VI. (© Melita Thomas)

Edward VI, whose 'Devise for the Succession' was an attempt to divert the crown from his Catholic half-sister, Mary, to the Protestant Jane Grey. (Courtesy of the University of Florida)

Right: Charterhouse, where Suffolk, Frances, Katherine and Mary stayed after Mary I entered London. (© Melita Thomas)

Below: Following his arrest, Suffolk may have entered the Tower by the Traitors' Gate. (© Melita Thomas)

Tomb of Francis Hastings, Earl of Huntingdon, and his wife, Katherine Pole, at Ashby Church. Huntingdon had been Suffolk's friend, but led his capture in 1554. (© Melita Thomas)

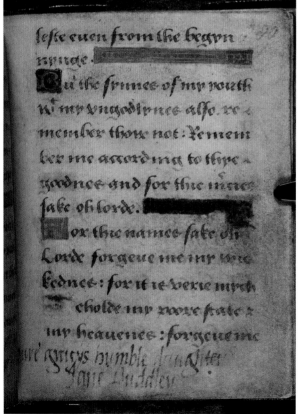

Jane's last message to her father. (© British Library Harleian MS2342)

successful – he broke down a bridge built by O'Brien that had been a bone of contention, destroyed the O'Connor castle at Dangan and recaptured the castle of Athlone. In 1538, he attacked the MacMahons, invaded Offaly and made a second military tour through Galway. Once he had brought them to heel, he imposed harsh terms on the Gaelic chiefs, such as the arrangement he made with Brien O'Connor. O'Connor was to be released from his previously imposed sentence of making amends for damage he had done along with Silken Thomas before Skeffington had been appointed as deputy, but was to restore any prisoners or cattle he had taken and pay a fine of 800 cows for action taken after Skeffington's arrival. He was also to account for the late Earl of Kildare's possessions that he was holding, and was to allow the king's subjects, the deputy and the army to pass through his country, and support the army with horse and foot if required.

This conspicuous efficiency in imposing English rule brought the Irish chiefs to combine against Leonard, and to look to Scotland, France and the Empire for help. An alliance was formed between O'Neill, O'Donnell and several O'Connor and O'Brien chiefs to invade the English Pale in August 1539. Leonard successfully chased them out, and when news of his victory reached Henry, the king was delighted, thanking God that traitors were never successful against him.[10] Leonard followed up his victory, and by February 1540 even managed to get to the O'Neil heartland of Dungannon.

Leonard's task with his Irish opponents was straightforward, simply a war of territorial aggression. His real problems were at his back. Leonard believed, as did most of the deputies appointed from the English nobility, that the Anglo-Irish were an obstacle to the good governance of Ireland – naturally interpreting good governance as that acceptable to the English Crown. The Anglo-Irish, he thought, were far too ready to make common cause with the Gaelic chieftains, and they kept large retinues in defiance of the statutes on livery and maintenance. This attitude, together with his conduct of the campaigns against the Irishry and his high-handed insistence on doing things his way, created resentment. Lord Butler complained that 'my lord deputy is the Earl of Kildare newly born again'.

Leonard's enemies saw their opportunity when his nephew Gerald Kildare was successfully smuggled out of the country. A whole slew of complaints was made against him, while, in retaliation, he charged Lord Chancellor John Alen with numerous infractions. We need look no further than the murder of Alen's uncle, the Archbishop, by two of Silken Thomas's men to find the root of Alen's enmity. In April 1540, both men were required to return to England to face an investigation by the council. Leonard's accusers deposed that he refused to take account of his council's advice, saying he would 'not be bridled', that he surrounded himself with his own advisors who were 'geraldines' and that his conduct of business was antagonistic: 'When contradicted in the council, he falleth in fury with menacing words and great oaths, laying his hand on his dagger or sword, saying, "if he were not in that authority, he would shortly be even with them"; so they must suffer him to talk out his pleasure and so consume the day.'[11] He had even threatened to strike one of the councillors, and called 'those whom the king willed him to consult most, as the Chancellor, Treasurer, and Chief Justice ... knaves'.[12] Another flurry of charges related to his conduct of the raids against the Irishry, but the chief complaint was that he had aided and abetted the hiding of Gerald FitzGerald from the English government and connived at his escape.

On 25 June 1541, Lord Leonard was tried by his peers, and found guilty of treason. Three days later, he was executed. Stowe recorded Leonard's last moments:

> He ended his life very quietly and godly. And as he was come of high lineage, so was he a right valiant and hardy personage, having in his time done his Prince and his country good service both in Ireland, France and other places, although now his hap was to lose his head.[13]

Leonard has been portrayed as a rash and quarrelsome deputy who was resented not just by the incumbent Anglo-Irish lords but also by his own councillors. This view has been challenged by Irish scholar Ciaran Brady, who contends that Leonard, faced with intermittent support from home and the political instability of Ireland, made a reasonable fist of the job. His execution in 1541 can be considered the result of the fall from power of his friend and patron Thomas Cromwell. If Leonard was, as charged, using his office to line his own pockets, the evidence was quickly removed. Henry, under the impression that Leonard had 'a good substance both of money and other things, as plate, apparel, household stuff etc', ordered an inventory to be taken, and for his goods to be put in safe custody and delivered to his replacement as deputy, Sir Anthony St Leger. The inventory is not extensive for a man of his rank. Interesting items within it are a pair of mustard querns, a saffron shirt, vestments of purple velvet, a horse covering of tawny velvet, five pairs of coarse sheets and another five 'of no value', seven pairs of socks, seven featherbeds, a quilt with a hart, and twenty-five old horses and geldings.[14]

With her husband and brother both dead, and her son Gerald in exile, Elizabeth Kildare had no desire to return to Ireland. In July 1541, she surrendered her jointure lands in return for an annuity of 200 marks English. Unfortunately, the annuity was not regularly paid – on 28 August 1546, she had to petition the king for payment of arrears. The new deputy, Sir Anthony St Leger, confirmed that 121 marks 8s 6d had been retained in Ireland 'for more necessary affairs', and Elizabeth received a warrant from the king for the amount. As well as this income, she regularly received wages from the various queens' households, at a rate considerably higher than most of the ladies-in-waiting. Her daughter Elizabeth FitzGerald was placed first in the household of Henry's elder daughter, Mary, then in that of Katheryn Howard, and finally joined the entourage of the king's younger daughter, Elizabeth. At the age of about thirteen, she was immortalised by Henry Howard, Earl of Surrey, in his sonnet to 'Fair Geraldine'. 'Geraldine' married Sir Anthony Browne in 1543, and both the king and Princess Mary attended her wedding. She was widowed in 1548, and next married Edward, Lord Clinton. Lady Clinton was a leading light of the Edwardine court and remained one of the Lady Elizabeth's closest friends. After the accession of Elizabeth I, Lady Clinton was a prominent member of the court until her death in 1590.

As for Gerald FitzGerald, he remained abroad with his distant kinsman Cardinal Reginald Pole, although his aunt Eleanor O'Donnell was granted a pardon by the king in 1545.[15] Elizabeth continually begged for her son to be pardoned and allowed to return home. In January 1548, she succeeded in persuading Protector Somerset to issue a pardon, and she wrote to Gerald, telling him of her long battle to gain his pardon:

> God knoweth what sorrowful days I have led ... and still do and by what means I have studied to devise some good means for your relief and comfort ... Son, it cannot be excused but yours hath been the fault and therefore to deserve grace ... make demonstration of humble submission to the king's majesty's mercy ... therefore, good son, I pray and charge you of my blessing that you fail not to follow my advice ... [your pardon will be] one of the most joyous tidings that may come to me...[16]

Gerald heeded the maternal advice, submitted humbly to the protector and the king, and was pardoned. In 1551, he was restored to some of his lands, and in March 1554, after his support during Wyatt's Rebellion, Queen Mary reinstated him as 11th Earl of Kildare, with his full patrimony. He soon married Mabel Browne, whose sister, Mary Browne, was the wife of Lord John Grey. Kildare's adherence to the old faith made life under Elizabeth difficult, although she protected him for his sister's sake, and he died exiled from his lands in Ireland.

13

A Thankless Child

How sharper than a serpent's tooth it is
To have a thankless child!
Shakespeare, *King Lear*, I iv

Whether Margaret Dorset mourned her husband must be a matter of conjecture. If she did, there was certainly enough to distract her from her grief in the execution of her husband's will and the management of her eight children, all still underage. The Grey daughters, ladies Katherine, Elizabeth, Anne and Margaret, would need husbands, and the younger sons, Thomas, Edward and John, would need careers and wives – preferably wealthy ones. Margaret had all these costs to contend with from an estate seriously depleted by the wills of Cecily and Thomas II. The offices Thomas II had held now lapsed, further reducing the family's income. The thirteen-year-old marquis, Henry, would be taken care of by his guardian, if the king appointed someone other than Margaret, and he also had a post in the household of the Duke of Richmond, which would stand him in good stead, especially if Henry VIII declared Richmond his heir – an unlikely, but not impossible, scenario in 1530. Richmond's separate household in the north had been broken up by 1530 and the princeling lived at court. Henry Dorset and his schoolmaster may well have been with him – it was the custom for royalty to be brought up with other children. The king himself had childhood companions in his cousin Courtenay, now Marquis of Exeter, and Sir Edward Neville. Lady Katherine was similarly provided for in the household of Princess Mary, still treated as Princess of Wales, despite the ongoing annulment case.

Before his death, Thomas II had contracted with the Earl of Arundel for Lord Henry and Lady Katherine to marry two of Arundel's children – confusingly with the same names – Lady Katherine FitzAlan and Henry, Lord Maltravers, the earl's heir. Margaret was shocked and angry when Dorset, following his fourteenth birthday in January 1537, refused to honour the betrothal. This was a most unusual proceeding – although it was the law that upon reaching marriageable age a child could repudiate any prior marriage arrangement, it was rarely done.

Why Dorset did not like Katherine FitzAlan is not recorded. Had his father still been alive, he might have been more amenable to parental pressure; as it was, the king stepped in, and indicated to the young man that he should honour the commitment, but then Lord Arundel decided that, his daughter having been spurned by Dorset, he was no longer interested in maintaining the arrangement, but would require Margaret to pay the substantial damages agreed in the contract. Margaret had to bear both the disgrace of her son's behaviour and its cost – 4,000 marks payable in annual instalments of 300 marks. This was a severe blow to her finances, and Margaret was to plead poverty for the remaining eleven years of her life. While the tone of her letters suggests she may have been one of those people who are always complaining of lack of money, she certainly had some heavy financial burdens. At least half of the total family income was now accounted for in repayment of the debt to the king left by Wiltshire and the payments to Arundel.

Unsurprisingly, Dorset became concerned about finances, and disinclined to spend money. On 16 December 1531, Henry Sadleir, the steward at Tilty, wrote to his son Ralph, now one of Cromwell's clerks, asking for help in finding another post, either at the Tower or near London, despite his many years of service to the Greys. The new marquis, Sadleir complained, would give him only 'fair words' and no money. Further, Dorset was planning to dismiss many of his yeoman to go to court at Christmas, to cut costs. Whilst money might be tight, Margaret still needed to put on a good show, and for New Year 1532, she gave the king a buckle and pendant of gold, receiving plate in return.

In April 1532, Margaret was staying at Ightham Mote in Kent, the home of Sir Richard Clement, the husband of Margaret's sister-in-law Anne, widow of Lord John Grey, who died sometime after 1527. Ightham Mote is not far from Margaret's childhood home at Boughton Malherbe, so the families may already have been connected. She addressed a letter from Ightham to Cromwell, in very different tone from that employed in Cecily's letter to 'my son's servant' ten years before. Now, Margaret was the one courting favour as Cromwell climbed the greasy pole. By 1532 he was Master of the Jewel House, and involved in all aspects of the king's government, as well as the ongoing campaign to secure the king's annulment. The purport of Margaret's letter was a request for her son's schoolmaster to obtain the benefices of Bosworth, Leicestershire and Eston in Essex. The latter, which she thought belonged to the prior of Tilty, now her usual abode, was being claimed by the Bishop of London. If she could obtain these benefices for the schoolmaster, Margaret wrote to her 'only succour', not only would she have fulfilled the direction in Thomas II's will, but the schoolmaster would be able to attend Dorset daily at court.

A month later, Lord Leonard, at this early stage far from the headsman's block, was sending his own requests for help to Cromwell. His wife, Elizabeth Arundell, had died, and he was looking for a new alliance. He wrote from Kyme in Lincolnshire, where he had enjoyed 'very good cheer' with the widowed Lady Tailboys. Such good cheer, in fact, that he would rather marry her than 'any other lady or gentlewoman' living. But this might not be straightforward, as Lady Tailboys was none other than Henry VIII's former mistress Elizabeth Blount, and such a marriage would make Leonard the stepfather of Richmond. Since Henry clearly had no problem with Elizabeth being married, he might well have considered his loyal cousin Leonard as suitable. Leonard asked Cromwell to put in a good word for him with both the king and the Duke of Norfolk, whose daughter Lady Mary Howard was betrothed to Richmond. Leonard enclosed a 'blank' – that is, a signed paper, on which either Cromwell or his colleague Anthony Budgegood, another former servant of the Greys, could write the letter to Norfolk. Rather unsubtly, Leonard apologised for not sending a horse he had promised to Cromwell – the beast had not 'prove(d) well', so £5 was enclosed for Cromwell to choose his own mount.

While Leonard's motives in courting Lady Tailboys probably had worldly advantage as their origin, another letter to Cromwell, six weeks later, from his own home at Beaumanor, suggests that his interest was at least partly motivated by personal attraction. He would rather marry the lady than 'be made lord of as much goods and lands as any nobleman within this realm ... I promise you, at this hour my heart is not in my governance, nor I ruler thereof'. Unless the king disapproved of the match (which Leonard was sure he would not), Leonard's 'wretched carcass will suffer more pains in obtaining this matter than other folks would think for'. He hoped that Cromwell would help him to obtain the lady 'which [he] would fainest bring to pass of anything in this world'. Cromwell must help him 'now or never'. What Lady Tailboys thought of the matter is not recorded, but if the king were not unwilling for the marriage to take place, she must have refused Leonard. She married Edward, Lord Fiennes de Clinton at some time before 1535. Personal attraction may have been involved in her choice – Leonard was probably around the same age as Elizabeth, or a few years older, whereas Clinton was about ten years younger.

In June, still at Beaumanor, Leonard wrote again to Cromwell. This time it was about business, not romance. It is apparent from the frankness of the letters that the two were on good terms. Leonard had received an order from Henry to attend him with a retinue of twelve at the forthcoming meeting with François of France at Calais. This summit, which took place in autumn 1532, was Henry's last-ditch attempt to persuade the French to support his annulment. Just as Henry had taken his queen to France in 1520, this time he was planning to take Anne Boleyn, in the hope that the French would recognise her as his intended wife and help smooth their path. The affair was not on the lavish scale of the Field of Cloth of Gold, but Henry and Anne still needed to cut a dash, and numerous courtiers were commanded to attend. Leonard was worried about the expense and hoped that Cromwell would remind the king of the land that had been promised him.

Leonard then moved onto ecclesiastical matters relating to St Mary de Pratis Abbey, Leicester, a house of Augustinian canons, which, being close to the Grey estates, was of interest to the family. Leonard had heard that Bishop Longland of Lincoln, who was responsible for the regular visitations to monitor the conduct of the abbey, was likely to dismiss the abbot, Richard Pexall, and also the prior of nearby Ulverscroft, which was of even more concern to the Greys as the burial place of the Ferrers barons of Groby. Following the visitation of 1528, Pexall had been disciplined for financial impropriety and poor conduct of his house – he seldom attended services, kept excessive numbers of hunting dogs who roamed the abbey precincts, and when he did attend services, he was accompanied by his jester. The boys in the abbey school were not being educated properly, and, with such a poor example, the canons were ill disciplined: drunk, philandering, and frequently outside the abbey precincts. Leonard had assured Pexall that if he would 'order himself as Cromwell thought good', then he, Leonard, would ensure that Cromwell would 'be his (the abbot's) friend'. Both Pexall and the prior of Ulverscroft reported themselves happy to abide by Cromwell's direction. Leonard and Cromwell's support for Pexall (paid for by handsome presents out of the abbey's fast-dwindling resources) made it almost impossible for the bishop to act against him. Leonard's willingness to write on behalf of a wayward abbot, and to buy and sell ecclesiastical offices, indicate that he had little of the piety of his mother and that he, like Cromwell, had imbibed the anti-clericalism of the age.

The Greys, like many others, were increasingly financially indebted to Cromwell. When one of Cromwell's clerks drew up a list of money owed to his master in September 1532, the late marquis, lady marquis Margaret, Lord Leonard and Lord George were all listed. Margaret was struggling to keep up her repayments. She wrote in November from Tilty to 'my very loving friend, Mr Cromwell', asking him 'out of [his] kindness to [her] and [her] late lord to accept payment of the £116 13s 4d, due at Christmas, at the following Ladyday instead', because she was so pressed for money that quarter. A couple of weeks later, still at Tilty, she sent her son George Medley with another letter to Cromwell, bemoaning her lack of money and the problems that disrupted the calm of the abbey. Following the last visitation in 1530, the abbot had been deposed. Cromwell had then undertaken some unspecified action to 'quiet the poor house of Tilty, which otherwise would have been destroyed' and she hoped he might intervene again. So far as her financial woes were concerned, Cromwell had obviously declined her request to postpone payment. She sent him £40 of her debt but hoped he would help her with reducing her annual costs by interceding for her with the king, to persuade the Earl of Arundel to accept an annual payment of £100, instead of the 300 marks due. She thought this was reasonable on two counts, first because Arundel had refused to accept Dorset after the king had persuaded him to go ahead with the match, and second because the corresponding arrangement for the marriage of Lord Maltravers and Lady Katherine had had a penalty clause of only 3,000 marks.

Three days later, Margaret wrote yet again, this time on behalf of Tilty Abbey, which was, she wrote, too poor to pay some unspecified pensions. Cromwell's response was to increase Margaret's problems by sending her the servant of a skinner named Addington who was pressing for payment of a bill to the late marquis. Margaret refused. Addington had impounded the late marquis's crimson velvet creation robes, and she would not pay him until they had been restored. Once again, she flattered Cromwell, urging that 'no one has more need of your help than I'. Hopefully, the king's gift of plate for New Year 1533 eased her financial situation – although it may not have been acceptable to melt down a royal gift, other than in the most dire circumstances, and of course she had to send the king regular presents to remain at the forefront of his mind. In July 1532, she sent him two hounds and two geldings. She was also attempting to collect money owed to the estate: Lord Lisle, Thomas I's stepbrother, owed £150 and she was pressing him for payment.

Regardless of the cost of the trip to Calais, Leonard had to obey, funding the trip by pawning plate to Cromwell, redeemed in July 1533. Another attendee was his niece Katherine's husband, Lord Maltravers. It was after their return from Calais that Henry VIII and Anne Boleyn were secretly married, even though the status of the king's marriage to Katharine remained unresolved. Princess Mary continued to live as Princess of Wales and in March 1533 was residing at Knole, where Margaret and Lady Grey (probably Lord John's widow, still entitled to that title, as her second husband was of lower rank) visited her. Margaret dined with the princess again in April, together with Katherine Maltravers and two of her other daughters. That Lord Maltravers had gone to Calais with Henry and Anne while his wife was still attached to her old mistress is an indication of how difficult these years were for Henry's courtiers. The following month, Thomas Cranmer, Archbishop of Canterbury, finally declared the king's marriage to Katharine of Aragon to have been invalid from its inception. The king's marriage to the now pregnant Anne Boleyn was therefore declared legal, and Queen Anne's coronation was planned for 1 June.

It may have been in connection with the coronation that the king sent his secretary, Brian Tuke, to Margaret with a letter. After reading it, she told Tuke that she must beg to be excused from doing what the king had requested. Tuke forwarded Margaret's response to Cromwell. It is possible that Margaret was hoping to avoid the coronation of Anne. She was evidently close to Princess Mary, and she had respected Katharine as queen for twenty-four years so may well have been reluctant to involve herself in the coronation of her supplanter. Alternatively, she may have wished to be excused because of the costs involved. Indeed, the letter may have been on some other matter entirely – as we have seen, Thomas II had been on good enough terms with Anne to remember her in his will.

Dorset, now sixteen, began to play a role in court ceremonial. He served the king at dinner on 29 May 1533 and the following day was dubbed a knight of the Bath as part of the coronation ceremonies. Thomas Arundell (second son of Lady Eleanor Grey) was similarly honoured. On 31 May, Anne processed through the City of London, from the Tower to Westminster, clothed in white, with a circlet of rich gems on her loose hair. Behind her were seven ladies, dressed in crimson and gold, and then a chariot containing the Dowager Duchess of Norfolk and Margaret – if she had wished to avoid involvement, she had been disappointed. The next day, Anne was crowned in Westminster Abbey. Dorset bore the sceptre on the queen's behalf as she approached the altar for the crowning. With the ceremony complete, the queen, the nobles and the clergy returned to Westminster Palace for the feast. A week later, Margaret again dined with Princess Mary, this time with Dorset as well as one of her daughters. While this is indicative of Margaret's sympathies regarding the annulment, it is not hard proof.[1] There were many who were willing to support the annulment, even if not enthusiastically, but who continued to see Mary as the heir to the throne. It does, however, show the continuing tie between the royal family and the Greys.

The king's annulment is likely to have caused some distress for Lady Dorothy. Her second husband, Lord Mountjoy, had been Queen Katharine's chamberlain since 1509, and her stepdaughter Gertrude, Lady Marquis of Exeter was one of Katharine's ladies.[2] In May 1533, Mountjoy was given the unenviable task of informing his mistress that her marriage had been annulled by Cranmer, and that the king had contracted a valid marriage with Anne. Hence, Katharine was no longer to be called queen, but treated as Dowager Princess of Wales. Katharine had deliberately avoided her chamberlain to put off receiving the news, but on 3 July, Mountjoy managed to gain access to his mistress. He and the other commissioners found her bedridden – she had hurt her foot by treading on a pin and was also troubled with a cough. There followed the now famous confrontation, during which Mountjoy was constrained to inform Katharine that her marriage had been invalid, and that Henry was married to Anne, but that if she accepted the situation then she could enjoy her income and possessions. To this Katharine replied that she was Henry's true wife; that no court had competence in the matter, other than that of Rome; that the king's subjects must act as they chose, but that conscience would not permit her to accept the annulment; and, as for possessions, they were irrelevant to the matter. She would not disobey

God or her conscience. Regarding her servants, she would not respond to any who did not call her by her right title.

Mountjoy brought out Henry's direst threat – that her stubbornness would lead him to withdraw his affection from their daughter. Disdaining this emotional blackmail, Katharine merely replied that she hoped her daughter would grow into an honest woman, and that, as she was the king's true-begotten daughter, he must do with her as he saw fit. Katharine also pointed out that, if she were the king's wife, then she was indeed his subject, but if she were not, then 'she came not into this realm on merchandise' but to be his wife and not otherwise his subject, and would not, therefore, be bound by English law. She harangued the commissioners further on the topic, and when they said that she must move from the relative splendour of the palace at The More, she said was content to accept the king's command. The location chosen was the castle at Ampthill, where she and Henry had frequently stayed in the past.

Despite his efforts, Mountjoy soon received a rebuke from the king, transmitted by Cromwell. It had come to the royal ears that many of Katharine's attendants were continuing to refer to her as queen. Mountjoy wrote his defence, obviously in despair and wishing to wash his hands of a matter that had brought him into 'high displeasure'. He had twice proclaimed the king's will in the matter of how Katharine was to be addressed, but her household had heard the rumours that the pope had finally declared in her favour and he did not see that he could be 'a reformer of other folks' tongues'. He did not want to accuse her servants, whom he believed to be true to the king, and nor did he wish to 'vex or unquiet her' since the king himself had caused him to swear allegiance to her so long as she was true to the king, which he believed her to be. He had received harsh words from his mistress when he relayed the king's orders – every time he addressed Katharine as 'princess', she would claim that he bore false witness, contrary to the Ten Commandments. Thus, he would rather serve the king in any other capacity than this, no matter how dangerous. Please could Cromwell find a replacement so that he could resign? He wrote from Stondon, not far from Ampthill, where he, and presumably Dorothy, had been obliged to absent themselves from Katharine's house since he was quite unable 'to accomplish the king's pleasure herein'.[3]

*

In March 1533, Margaret came to an arrangement with Charles, Duke of Suffolk, Thomas II's old comrade in arms, for Dorset's wardship and marriage. Suffolk paid 2,000 marks for the wardship and a further £1,000 for royal consent for a marriage between Dorset and Lady Frances Brandon, his eldest daughter by the French Queen. This was an excellent match, reinforcing the Greys' relationship with the royal family – future generations would be cousins to the Tudor dynasty through both their royal and non-royal blood. It would also be of great benefit for Dorset to be part of the circle around Suffolk, still the king's closest friend. Under the agreement, Suffolk was to be responsible for Dorset's 'finding' until he reached his majority. Accordingly, Margaret stopped paying her son any allowance, and he spent much of his time either at court or with his betrothed and her family in Suffolk.

There, Dorset not only became acquainted with Frances and her sister, Eleanor, but also with her two half-sisters and their husbands. The elder, Anne Brandon, had served at the court of Marguerite of Austria at the same time as Anne Boleyn and was married in about 1525 to Edward, Lord Grey of Powis. Anne's marriage was deeply unhappy. Her husband had been unfaithful, and she had retaliated by having an affair with a man named Ralph Howarth. Her husband had broken into their lodgings and beaten her lover, then cast off Anne. Suffolk, working with Thomas Cromwell, had forced Lord Grey to continue to maintain his wife, and chiselled a settlement of £100 per annum out of him. There was considerable sympathy for Anne, enabling her to rise above the scandal and continue to frequent the court. The second half-sister, closer in age to Frances, was Mary Brandon, who married Lord Monteagle, once suggested as a husband for one of Dorset's own sisters.

When the French Queen died in June 1533, Dorset was one of the mourners at her funeral, along with his brother Edward, who seems to have had a place in the Suffolk household, as the previous Lord Edward Grey once had. Another member of the household was the fourteen-year-old Katherine Willoughby. Katherine, a considerable heiress, had originally been intended as the bride of Frances's brother Henry, Earl of Lincoln, but within weeks of the French Queen's death Suffolk snapped the girl up for himself, perhaps aware that his son had not long to live, and that if he wanted to capture the Willoughby inheritance he would need Katherine as his own bride – or perhaps because he wanted to marry a nubile girl. Queen Anne Boleyn had already accused him of an unhealthy interest in his daughter (presumably Anne meant Katherine – his intended daughter-in-law – rather than one of his actual daughters). Katherine, having lived in the Suffolk household for some time, was on excellent terms with Frances and was soon a friend of Dorset, too.

Despite the long friendship between the families, Suffolk, often short of money himself, reneged on his promise to pay for Dorset's keep. In July, a complaint was made to the king's council, by Dorset or perhaps by Cromwell on his behalf, that Margaret was not supporting her son. The council decided, despite her heated protests about the agreement with Suffolk, that Margaret was failing in her duty, and ordered her to pay for her son's maintenance. Not satisfied with the ruling, Margaret directed a stream of letters of complaint to both Suffolk and Cromwell, to which the duke responded on 28 July 1533 from his London home at Southwark:

> I understand ... that upon my promise made to you 'to find my lord your son' and discharge you thereof, you are much disquieted at being bound to find him by the Council, and think me unkind that I have not

discharged you. I fully intend to keep my promise, and that you shall be discharged; and if my daughter die before their marriage, 'then I to dispose and sell him to my pleasure'. Next term, when the king and I shall be thoroughly at a point, I will request the king to discharge you, and when the time comes, considering my charges, you shall show yourself a loving mother to your son and augment his estate.'[4]

Guilt over the trouble he had caused Margaret may have prompted Suffolk to help her brother-in-law Lord Richard Grey. Sometime after 1523, Lord Richard had married Florence Pudsey, the widow of Henry, 10th Lord Clifford. Florence was a widow with a daughter when she married Clifford as his second wife, but she had been much younger than her husband. As part of the marriage settlement, he had settled five manors in Westmorland on her, but by the early 1520s there was 'unkindness and strifes begun between my lord and my lady', and she had been obliged to sue for the return of her conjugal rights. After Clifford's death in 1523, her stepson, who was created Earl of Cumberland in 1525, rented the manors of her jointure from her for 225 marks per annum. This made her a very suitable partner for Lord Richard, and the king himself arranged the match, summoning her to court to hear his commands, 'wyche sall ryght well satisfye, content and plese [her]'.

Unfortunately for Florence and Richard, Cumberland turned out to be a slow payer. Lord Richard wrote to him, pushing for payment, requesting sums to be remitted to Richard's agent, the lawyer Robert Aske of Gray's Inn. Getting little satisfaction, Richard turned to his friend Suffolk, who wrote to the earl:

My very good lord, in my right hearty manner I commend me unto you. And so it is that my lord Richard Grey hath shewed me that ye owe him divers sums of money as in the right of my lady his wife concerning her dower and jointure, whereupon resteth and dependeth a great part of his living. And forasmuch as my said lord is content at my desire no further to open this matter against you, I pray you my lord to see him paid as speedily as ye conveniently can so that he have no further cause to complain against you. And thus the Holy Trinity have you, my very good lord in his keeping. At the king's manor of Greenwich the 14th of January, Yours assured Charles Suffolk.[5]

Clifford paid up at this time, but in the mid-1540s, after Lord Richard's death, Florence was obliged to go to law for her money.

By the end of August 1533, Dorset, presumably with Frances, was staying at Astley.[6] In the first evidence of him taking an interest in the management of the Grey estates, Dorset wrote to Cromwell regarding a dispute between the priory of Nuneaton and the tenants of Lord St John's estate at Coton. Unsurprisingly, as steward of the Nuneaton house, he thought it had been wronged and asked Cromwell to intervene. Soon after, Dorset and Frances headed back to Greenwich, where, on 7 September, Queen Anne bore a daughter, who was christened Elizabeth. As might be expected from their rank, the Dorsets took prominent parts in the ceremony. Dorset carried the salt, which would be sprinkled as part of the baptism itself, and Margaret was godmother, along with the Dowager Duchess of Norfolk.

The spat over Dorset's keep obviously had not injured Margaret materially with the king, for the same month she was granted custody of Thomas II's lands in England, Wales and Calais during Dorset's minority, for an annual rent to the king of £333 6s 8d (500 marks). She was also, as custodian of the Dorset estates, keeper of the royal parks at Tilty and Dunmow, and bailiff of the latter, although combined the posts gave an annual income of less than £10. The total income of the Astley, Ferrers, Bonville and Harington inheritances, based on the subsidy returns and a visitation of Cecily Dorset's estates undertaken in 1525, was about £2,000 per annum or 3,000 marks, less the amounts attributable to the manors Cecily had granted to her younger sons, which may have equalled 200–300 marks in total. From the remaining 2,700 marks, Margaret had to pay 400 marks per annum to Arundel, 500 marks to cover the outstanding debts to the king and a further 500 marks to the king for the custody of the lands during Dorset's minority, along with paying the bequests of Cecily and Thomas II, maintaining herself and her younger children, and paying her daughters' dowries. It is not surprising she was strapped for cash. Mindful of the help that Cromwell had given her, she wrote to him, thanking him both for the pains he had taken on her behalf, and also for action he had taken in regard to the abbey of Tilty, where another abbot had been deposed for his 'unthrifty' management of the house. She requested that he might also be good to '[her] poor sister [Mary] Guildford', whose husband, Sir Henry, had recently died.

As well as financial problems, Margaret was worried about Dorset, who was not, she feared, behaving as well as he ought. She hoped that Cromwell would keep an eye on him. If Cromwell were to see Dorset in 'any large [gambling] or great ... swearing or any other demeanour unmeet for him to use, which I fear me shall be very often, I pray you, for his father's sake to rebuke him, and if he has any grace, he will be grateful to you when he grows older'.[6] Margaret went on to explain in what straitened circumstances she found herself – she was aware that many thought her means to be far greater than she admitted. In particular, she was worried about the maintenance of Dorset and Frances, as Suffolk, despite his earlier promise to pay for Dorset's maintenance (which she enclosed for Cromwell's information), was now requesting her to bear part of the costs of Dorset at court and Frances in the country – or else to have Frances and her retinue live with Margaret. Margaret assured Cromwell that the level of debts left by Thomas II already meant there was little left for her to maintain herself and her younger children. This was the reason she 'did stick so much to be discharged for the finding of [her] son the marquis' when the council was considering the matter.

Margaret also anticipated future problems – once Dorset and his wife were of age, she would be responsible for their maintenance. Still, 'that no one may judge [her] as an unnatural mother, [she would] help his advancement more than any other of [her children]'. There was no place better for him than the court, and if he were to do well it would be of help to his siblings. Once again, Margaret was staying at Ightham Mote – perhaps a way to reduce her own expenses! She was still pursing Lisle for his debt in the Court of Common Pleas, but Lady Lisle's nephew John Grenville managed to have the matter stayed.

Although Dorset does not appear to have had any reluctance to accept Anne as queen, his aunt Elizabeth Kildare, who had been close to Queen Katharine, was one of a circle of disaffected courtiers who dined with Chapuys regularly and complained to him of the 'disorder' of affairs. Grumbling under her breath was one thing, but outright defiance of the king was completely different, and there is no reason to suppose that Elizabeth or any of the Greys made the smallest fuss about accepting either the Act of Supremacy, making Henry Supreme Head of the Church in England, or the Act of Succession, which vested the crown in Henry's children by Queen Anne.

By early 1535, Cromwell seems to have tired of Margaret's constant pleas for help. She wrote again, thanking him for his kindness to her son but worrying at his message that he thought she 'impaired' the abbey of Tilty. Cromwell must have been misinformed by some 'sinister rumour', and she hoped that he would not give it any credence until she could explain matters to him. In the meantime, to help him maintain his good opinion of her, she gave him £10 and a silver-gilt standing cup, previously received from the king. The problem discussed may have related to Margaret's plan to take a sixty-year lease of an extended property at Tilty – not just Tilty Grange, but also the abbey guest house, the vineyard, the demesne lands and the manor of Tilty for George Medley. Monasteries with an annual income below £200 were being dissolved, with the monastic buildings and lands becoming the property of the Crown. It is possible that the payment of the rent of £60 to Tilty for the new lease took the house over the limit, thus keeping the abbey out of the king's hands. If that were the problem, Margaret either explained herself to Cromwell, or ignored his displeasure – the lease was completed on 6 October 1535.

*

Henry had moved heaven and earth to marry Anne Boleyn, but, unfortunately, the marriage was not turning out as he had hoped. The birth of Elizabeth had not, as he had confidently predicted, been followed by that of a son, and when Anne miscarried in January 1536 (not long after the death of Katharine of Aragon), her situation looked grim, especially as Henry was making eyes at one of her maids of honour, Jane Seymour. The court was always a hotbed of gossip, and in late April 1536, Elizabeth Kildare, the

Marquis of Exeter and Lord Montagu dined with Chapuys, passing on the news that Cromwell and Anne had fallen out.[7] The ambassador was not surprised – he already knew that they were on bad terms and that Anne had told Cromwell she would like to see his head struck off. By the end of that month, Cromwell had collected enough explosive material to have the queen arrested. Within a month, she was tried and executed for adultery, incest and treason. Among Anne's twenty-six judges was Lord Maltravers, but Dorset was not selected for the panel, nor was Richmond, although the duke attended Anne's execution. If Dorset accompanied his friend and witnessed the terrible sight of the execution of a queen, he failed to heed the warning. Ten days later, Henry VIII married Jane Seymour.

Despite not yet having received livery of his lands, Dorset was summoned to the parliament that opened on 8 June 1536 and attended diligently. On 30 June there was a first reading of the new succession bill, declaring both the king's daughters illegitimate and conferring the succession on Henry's as yet unborn children by Jane Seymour. Given his presence in the capital, Dorset was probably one of the courtiers who rode from Whitehall to Westminster Abbey behind Henry and Jane at the great Corpus Christi festivities. A month later, the court had the unpleasant memories of the spring wiped away with an elaborate triple marriage at the nunnery of St John the Baptist, Shoreditch, adjoining the Earl of Rutland's house. The earl's eldest son, Lord Ros, married Lady Margaret Neville, daughter of the Earl of Westmorland, while Rutland's daughter Lady Anne Manners married Westmorland's eldest son, Lord Neville, and Westmorland's eldest daughter, Lady Dorothy Neville, married the Earl of Oxford's eldest son, Lord Bulbeck. Dorset and Suffolk led the new-made Lady Neville out of the church. The wedding was followed by a grand feast, with 'great dishes', 'delicate meats' and 'subtleties', eaten to the accompaniment of music. Henry's taste for disguisings, which had characterised his early court, had not entirely left him, and after dinner he arrived with seven masked companions, all dressed in Turkish fashion in gowns embroidered with gold, with black velvet hats embellished with white feathers.[8] It seems possible that the company feigned more surprise than they felt when his identity was revealed.

Less than three weeks after these celebrations, Dorset lost his boyhood companion when Richmond died at St James's Palace, aged just seventeen. Henry did not react as might have been expected, with a grand funeral for his bastard, although he had been an affectionate father. Instead, Norfolk was given responsibility for proceedings, and the young man was quietly buried at Thetford priory, the Howard mausoleum in Suffolk, and later transferred to St Michael's, Framlingham.

In September 1536, Cromwell sought some recompense from Margaret for his help in the past, requesting her to give the office of Steward of Whitwick, Leicestershire, to John Babington, whose father had previously held the position. Unfortunately, John Beaumont, one of Margaret's council, had requested it within days of Babington senior's death and Margaret had already confirmed him in the post. She was probably disappointed that she could not oblige Cromwell so easily, but wrote hopefully that, since Beaumont was Babington's friend and kinsman, perhaps he would not mind too much. The letter was sent from Tilty, where she appears to have been almost permanently in residence, while Dorset was usually at court. He was named in the household roll beginning 1 October among those who were to attend upon the king, alongside Lord Maltravers and his old colleague from Richmond's household, Edward Seymour, the brother of Queen Jane, now Viscount Beauchamp and soon to be Earl of Hertford.

The parliament of summer 1536 had voted the king a new subsidy.[9] This was the last straw for many of Henry's subjects – taken with other economic and social factors and the massive dislocation caused by the continuing dissolution of the religious houses, the subsidy provoked rebellion in Lincolnshire in October 1536. Although Suffolk was immediately sent to Lincoln, and managed to put down the insurrection there, it soon spread across the Humber into Yorkshire. Known as the Pilgrimage of Grace, this rebellion was probably the greatest threat the Tudor Crown ever faced. The rebels 'persuaded' many of the gentry of the north to join them – some no doubt more willingly than others. Norfolk was in charge of the king's forces, backed by the Earl of Shrewsbury. Dorset does not seem to have had any role. The rebellion was suppressed, mainly because Henry made extravagant promises of redress to the insurgents, and, with a notion of honour far greater than the king's, was taken at his word by the rebels' leader, Robert Aske, the lawyer who had previously acted for Dorset's uncle, Lord Richard. The rebels were persuaded to lay down their arms and return home. Another rebellion broke out in February 1537, and although it was disowned by Aske and the others, it gave Henry the opportunity for revenge on them all. Two men who had been pressed to join the rebels, lords Darcy and Hussey, were tried by a panel of their peers, with Dorset and Maltravers both on the jury. Unsurprisingly, the men were found guilty and executed. This left a Garter stall empty, and Dorset was nominated. Henry, however, decided that his faithful secretary, Cromwell, should be appointed instead.

*

In late 1536 or early 1537, nineteen-year-old Frances prepared for childbirth, probably at the family's town house in the Strand, rather than at the family seat in Bradgate.[10] As the daughter of a queen, Frances may have followed, so far as the couple's straitened circumstances allowed, the conventions drafted by her great-grandmother Lady Margaret Beaufort for a queen's lying-in.[11] According to these ordinances, the whole birthing chamber was to be hung with arras, except for one window, where the hangings were to be arranged to allow in a little light if the mother required it. The chamber was to contain two beds – a pallet for the actual birth, and the main bed for the happy mother to show off her baby. The sideboard was to be covered with matching tapestry, and loaded with gold and silver plate. Dorset probably sent his servants scurrying around all his properties, gathering up every article to grace the birthing chamber. The requisite sheets of fine lawn they probably had, but the cloth-of-gold counterpanes suitable for queens were undoubtedly absent, and tapestries might have proved a problem, unless those bequeathed by Thomas I to Thomas II in 1501 were still in the family home.

Whatever the level of grandeur that surrounded her, Frances produced a healthy daughter. There are no records of the baby's baptism, but her name, Jane, indicates that the queen was her godmother, either in person or by proxy. Other family and friends who might have attended the ceremony include Frances' father and stepmother, the Duke and Duchess of Suffolk, and, depending on when the event took place, Frances' cousin, formerly 'princess' but now 'lady' Mary. Mary had returned to her father's court in early 1537, having been browbeaten into accepting the annulment of her parents' marriage. She and Frances had been friends since childhood, along with their cousin Lady Margaret Douglas, daughter of the Queen of Scots.

Between six months and a year after Jane Grey was born, another birth caused the whole country to celebrate. King Henry had a male heir at last. The baby was born about two in the morning on 12 October 1537, at Hampton Court, and news was sent immediately to London. By eight o'clock the bells were ringing and *Te Deums* were being in sung in every parish. An hour later, Dorset and all the great and the good of the realm who were in London assembled at St Paul's. The bishops of London and Chichester and the deans of St Paul's and Westminster were there, all in their mitres, while the mayor, aldermen, sheriffs and guilds of London were robed in their liveries. Another *Te Deum* was sung, as was the anthem of the Trinity, and the great guns of the Tower fired a salute. God willing, the kingdom would now be safe in the hands of a male. The baby was christened Edward with as much pomp and circumstance as could be arranged.

Henry was extremely cautious as to the baby's health. The loss of his first son, Henry, Duke of Cornwall, in 1511, at a mere six weeks, had rendered the king paranoid about infection. No one who had been in contact with any illness was allowed near the baby, which meant that the Grey family was excluded en masse from the christening. Margaret had been staying with the Maltraverses in the vicinity of Croydon, where contagious sickness had broken out. Maltravers warned Sir William Fitzwilliam and Sir William Paulet, Lord St John, two of Henry's chief councillors, that three or four people were dying every day and two of the household were sick of an unknown illness. He and his wife and mother-in-law intended to leave to escape infection. The king, hearing the news, forbade them all to come to the christening, and included Dorset and Frances in the ban, even though neither of them had been anywhere near Croydon, or the rest of the family. He had gone from London to Stebbing in Essex, and she to stay with Lady Derby. Despite this, Henry conveyed his thanks but would 'spare them' from coming to Hampton Court on this occasion. Similarly, the mayor and aldermen were not to come from plague-ridden London. Two days later, Margaret wrote to Henry, expressing her delight at receiving the queen's official announcement of the birth. She was thrilled that Henry had originally asked her to carry the baby to the font,

> ... and much it grieveth me, that my fortune is so evil, by reason of the sickness here in Croydon to be banished Your Grace's presence, this time at which I would most gladly have done service and since my chance is such that I may not be there, I shall, according to my bounden duty, daily pray for the preservation of Your most noble Grace by whom it hath pleased Almighty God to have this your whole realm in his remembrance...[12]

Rejoicing turned to mourning when Queen Jane died within a fortnight of her son's birth. To honour his wife, Henry arranged an elaborate funeral, echoing that of his own mother. Dorset was one of the senior peers present and he, along with the Suffolk and the earls of Surrey, Westmorland, Wiltshire and Sussex, accompanied the entourage to Windsor. His aunt Dorothy's stepson Lord Mountjoy bore one of the banners. The chief mourner was the king's elder daughter, the Lady Mary, and immediately behind her came a carriage containing Frances and several countesses; the second carriage contained a Lady Margaret Grey, probably Thomas II's still unmarried sister. After the funeral, Frances received some of Queen Jane's jewellery.

In January 1538, Margaret made arrangements for one of her younger sons, Lord Thomas, to join Cromwell's household:

> ... as for my son Thomas whom at this time I do send to your lordship, I reckon myself much bounded to you that it pleased you to accept him; praying you my good lord in the honour of God and for my lord my husband's sake (whose soul Jesu pardon) to be a very father to my said son, who of his part shall not have my favour but as he, with his diligent attendance and suit to you may deserve yours; according as I have to him declared at his departing from me. Concerning his finding and charges, I would be glad, my lord, he should in his youth learn to live according to the portion limited and assigned to him by my lord his father's will. Howbeit if that at any time do not suffice, I will from time to time, as by you shall be thought meet for causes reasonable, aid him farther, and depart to him of mine own. I have appointed to wait upon him one Clement Charyd an old servant of my lord my husband's because my son is young and has need to have one honest sad man to be with him: to whom I pray you, my lord, it may please you to be good lord unto. I doubt not but you will like him well.[13]

Once again, Margaret wrote from Ightham. Either her sister-in-law was exceptionally fond of her, or she was outstaying her welcome!

*

While the younger Greys were beginning their careers, one member of the previous generation was encountering difficulties, for which she too sought Cromwell's help – little knowing that he had been contributing to her problems. Thomas I had agreed to the marriage of his daughter Cicely to John, son and heir of Lord Sutton of Dudley, before his own death in 1501, although the couple were still only children at the time. The marriage probably took place towards the end of Henry VII's reign. Confusingly, the family are sometimes referred to as Lords Dudley, and sometimes as Lords Sutton. Cicely's father-in-law, the 2nd Lord Sutton,was Lord Chamberlain in the household of Princess Mary in the Marches. He died in 1531, leaving John as the 3rd Lord Sutton of Dudley.

John Sutton was not, to put it mildly, a man with any business sense, and became laden with debt. This was at least in part the work of his cousin, another John Dudley, son of Henry VII's councillor Edmund Dudley. This Sir John Dudley was a rising man. A friend of the Earl of Hertford, and an associate of Cromwell's, by the 1530s he was vice admiral, and had the task of protecting merchant ships in the English Channel alongside his colleague Sir Thomas Seymour, another of Queen Jane's brothers. Sir John Dudley was one of the most rapacious and acquisitive men in an age which was notable for greed. It is clear from the complex land exchanges, court cases, debts and counter-claims that he deliberately ensnared his cousin, Lord Sutton, and also indulged in what might at best be called sharp practice against his own stepfather, Lord Lisle, aided and abetted by Cromwell and Hertford.[14]

To clear his father's debts, Lord Sutton mortgaged land to Dudley for £2,000, repayable at the rate of £400 per annum, although he was adamant that he only ever received £1,400 from his cousin. He then borrowed a further £6,000 from Dudley, giving his remaining lands as surety. Dudley pressed for payment, so Sutton begged Cromwell to ask the king to lend him £1,400 to repay Dudley, in return for which the king would have a parcel of his land for twenty years on the death of Lord Sutton's eighty-six-year-old grandmother. (Lady Sutton was probably nearer seventy-six in fact, but her age may have been exaggerated to make the offer more tempting. She did not die until 1539.) Sutton's pleading letter to Cromwell closed with the information that Lord Sutton could not ask him in person as he dared not come to London since 'Sir John Dudley lays wait for me in the city of London to keep me afore the days of payment'. Despite the promise of £10 per annum that Lord Sutton made to Cromwell if he could obtain the loan from the king, Cromwell either could not or would not help.

Lord Sutton, obviously unaware of the close connection between Dudley and Cromwell, asked Cromwell himself to pay the annual £400 owed to Dudley, in return for Lady Sutton senior's jointure lands, but he pleaded in vain. By the end of 1537, Sutton of Dudley had lost his patrimony, including his share of Powis Castle, sold to his nephew, and the family seat of Dudley Castle, sold to John Dudley. Cicely's two elder sons, Edward and Henry Sutton, were serving with their uncle Leonard in Ireland, but she and her younger children were rendered homeless and were obliged to take refuge at the priory of Nuneaton, which, as mentioned above, was under the protection of the Grey family. Cicely, clearly unaware that he had been aiding and abetting cousin John, wrote to Cromwell to plead for the convent at Nuneaton to be spared dissolution:

> ... glad to hear of your good health. Your lordship knows that by means of my lord my husband, I and mine are utterly undone unless the king take pity of us. I have little above £20 a year which I have by my lady my mother, to find me and one of my daughters, with a woman and a man to wait upon me, and unless the good prioress of N[un]eaton gave us meat and drink of free cost I could not tell what shift to make ... And besides that, whensoever any of my children comes hither to see me they be welcome unto the prioress as long as they list to tarry, horse meat and man's meat, and cost them nothing, with a piece of gold or two in their purses at their departure ... If ought should come to the house of Nuneaton I stand in a hard case. I thank you for your goodness to my son Edward ... especially in his suit to my lady Berkeley, in which you wrote and procured the king's letters as if for your own son. Nevertheless he has not been successful; which has been to his great cost and hindrance, as he has been this great while living on me and other friends. I see he has been bold to come to dinner and supper with your lordship by your goodness, which I beg you will continue.[15]

Edward Sutton's suit, which Cicely mentions, was his plan to marry the widowed Anne Savage, Lady Berkeley. He had written to Sir Thomas Wriothesley, one of Cromwell's colleagues and another man rising fast in the king's service, to request both the king and Cromwell to write to Lady Berkeley, recommending him. Before her marriage, Lady Berkeley had been one of Queen Anne Boleyn's maids of honour, and the king appears to have been fond of her. Although she was much trammelled with the usual problems of widows – the difficulty in having her jointure assured, and the reluctance of her husband's family to work with her – Lady Berkeley was still a good match for an impoverished man like Edward Sutton. The lady, however, was not willing. She told Edward that she 'was not minded to marry', and would in due course answer the king. Edward saw this as mere delaying tactics. He thought her not unwilling as she had previously 'entertained [him] most lovingly, showing she would suffer [him] to lie in her lap', although since receiving the king's letters suggesting the marriage, she had greeted him more coldly. He wanted the lady to be commanded by the king, in which case he thought she would acquiesce.

While Edward paid lip service to the idea that he wished to marry Lady Berkeley for love, his economic motivation was quite obvious. 'My heart,' he wrote, 'is so assured to her it is impossible to remove it, and though my suit has been expensive, yet if it were worth £1,000, I would spend it for her sake.' He wrote from the Dorset house of his aunt Dorothy, Lady Mountjoy, and it was Dorothy who was the bearer of his letter to Cromwell, since Edward was unable to travel, for lack of money. Lady Berkeley persisted in her refusal: 'I cannot with my heart bear fair unto Mr [Sutton] ... my stomach cannot lean there, neither as yet to any marriage.' Concerned that her refusal would annoy the king, she asked Cromwell to speak to him on her behalf, 'so I may stand in no displeasure with his grace'.[16]

14

Reformation

A wise ruler ought never to keep faith when by doing so it would be
against his interests.

Niccolò Machiavelli

In January 1538, Dorset turned twenty-one. In July, he was granted livery
of lands as son and heir of the deceased Thomas, Marquis of Dorset,
together with all the 'portion in possession, reversion, or otherwise, of
the possessions whereof Margaret marchioness of Dorset, his mother,
was seised for her own or another's life, or whereof Sir John Dudley,
Lord Dudley and Cicely his wife are seised in right of the said Cicely, or
Margaret, Lady Grey, for life, or Lord Richard Grey, for life, or Lord
Leonard Grey, for life'. Margaret had sent George Medley to search out
all of the documents Dorset would need, but the relationship between
mother and son was still strained. Once again, the council felt obliged to
intervene.

Margaret wrote to Cromwell that she was 'trouble[d] not a little' by
the rumours of her 'unkindness' to Dorset. She thought them especially
unfair considering 'what a good mother [she had] been to him, what pains
[she had] sustained and what bonds [she had] brought her friends into
for his sake, since … his father's death'. She was sure the council would
not believe these stories, and hastened to add that she was always willing
to supplement the 'little portion' that was his by law, from those parts of
the late marquis's lands that were managed by her to fulfil his will. She
hoped that Cromwell and Lord Chancellor Audley would refrain from
diminishing her jointure – obviously this was an idea under consideration
to provide Dorset with an income more suited to his position. She thanked
Cromwell and Audley for their good offices in effecting a reconciliation
between her and her son 'although there was nothing between [them they]
could not end [themselves, they] were both glad to comply, especially
considering the good heart borne by [Cromwell] to [her] late husband'.
Part of the agreement may have been for her to leave Bradgate for the

younger generation, although, as we have seen, she spent most of her time at Tilty or Ightham anyway. She again referred to Cromwell's kindness to her son Thomas – he was to 'call sharply' on the young man for diligent service, which would do him more good than 'the little living' left to him by his father.[1]

Lord Chancellor Audley was taking an interest in the Grey finances because he was betrothed to Margaret's daughter, Elizabeth, and was eager to receive the dowry. The marriage took place on 22 April 1538, giving a likely birth date for Elizabeth of around 1522. Doubtless Margaret was pleased to have another child well settled. Although Audley was not of particularly distinguished birth, he was riding high in royal favour, and was growing rich. It is unlikely Elizabeth was as pleased – Audley was around fifty years old, and widowed, but while her brother had been able to reject a proposed match, such defiance was much harder for a daughter. Another daughter, Lady Anne, married Sir Henry Willoughby of Wollaton, although the date of the marriage is unknown.

Despite having come into his inheritance, Dorset still had money worries. On 15 April 1538, Kenilworth Abbey, another house of which he was steward, surrendered, owing him his half-year fee. He was also still encumbered with the costs of his refusal to marry Lady Katherine FitzAlan. A ruling had been made by the chancellor that damages were to be paid out of various Grey lands in Leicestershire and Warwickshire. George Hynde, Margaret's receiver and bailiff at Lutterworth, had been ordered to allow fees from the estates to be remitted directly to Katherine FitzAlan's receiver, Roger Elis. When Hynde refused to let Elis fulfil his duties, Arundel asked for an injunction from Audley against both Hynde and Dorset. Dorset still hoped to relieve the pressure by persuading Katherine to remit 500 marks of the debt. In a letter of July 1538 to Cromwell, Katherine refused:

> … it were a great thing to remit, considering that it is as well the whole thing that I must trust unto, and the long and continual suit that I have had therein to my great cost and charges … trusting therefore that your lordship would not that I should remit so great a sum to so much my hindrance and almost my utter undoing. For more than that only, I think I shall never have, neither of my lord my father nor of my other kin…[2]

On this occasion, Cromwell listened to the lady's plea, and she sent him a letter of thanks.

While hoping to be forgiven part of his debt to Katherine FitzAlan, Dorset was proving a hard creditor to Lord Lisle. Lisle's man of business, John Hussey, tried to negotiate with Dorset, who was insisting on the money being paid back at the rate of £40 per annum, which Lisle could not afford. Hussey tried to persuade him to accept £20, but the young marquis would not be moved. This was a case where the many family connections made no difference to Dorset's determination to have his money.[3]

Money worries were slightly eased when Suffolk entered into a complex arrangement with Audley to alienate to the latter some five manors that Suffolk had been granted out of the estate of the late Duke of Buckingham. As part of the purchase price, Audley forwent the remaining £900 of Elizabeth Grey's dowry. It is not clear whether Margaret would be obliged to pay Suffolk the money, or whether it was to be balanced against Frances's dowry.

*

The 1530s were a time of religious ferment. During the first phase of the Reformation, the doctrinal debate had centred around 'justification by grace through faith alone' versus 'justification by faith and works'. That is, whether salvation was granted by God, purely through His grace to all those with faith, or whether individuals played a part in their own salvation by their conduct. Luther had espoused the former doctrine – historically, an acceptable belief in the Catholic Church. Where Luther fell foul of the authorities was in his criticisms of Church hierarchy, the use of indulgences and the promotion of 'works' – that is, prayers or Masses as well as charitable deeds – in a way that was becoming perilously close to the idea that salvation could be bought. For Luther, the only sure means of salvation was faith in Christ, and an adherence to the Word of God, as revealed in the bible.

Luther's criticisms found a willing audience among many believers who wanted reform – usually referred to as 'evangelicals' – and the two sides could, perhaps, have been reconciled. Unfortunately, the Church reacted with hysterical condemnation of any criticism. Among the evangelicals had been Anne Boleyn, who had encouraged the aspiration for the Bible to be available in English. She had patronised men such as Thomas Cranmer, Archbishop of Canterbury, Hugh Latimer, Bishop of Worcester, and Nicholas Shaxton, Bishop of Norwich, who would become progressively more radical, moving towards what was, from the late 1540s, called Protestantism, which questioned the nature of the Eucharist and the role of priests, and, in some groups, accepted the idea of pre-destination to salvation or damnation. Another early evangelical Anne welcomed to the court in 1535 after he had suffered religious persecution in France was Nicholas Borbonius. He later became one of the teachers of Jeanne III of Navarre, leader of the French Huguenots, but remained in contact with leading English reformers, including Cranmer, Latimer and Dudley.[4]

In 1536, the Act of Ten Articles was passed by the Convocation of Clergy. This took the English Church down the first steps of doctrinal reform. Instead of the seven sacraments (so vigorously promoted by the king in his own book in 1521) only three were confirmed as necessary for salvation. Faith was essential to justification, but 'works' were also important. In support of traditional Catholic belief, the Act was very clear that the doctrine of transubstantiation was to be accepted – that the bread and wine of the Eucharist become, in some real, physical sense, the Body and Blood of Christ. Encouraging to the evangelicals was the emphasis on the Bible as the source of Christian truth, playing down, although not negating, the pronouncements of the Church. The Act was followed up by a set of injunctions, promulgated by Thomas Cromwell, as Henry VIII's 'vice-gerent' of the English Church. These injunctions removed some of the traditional saints' days, and undermined traditional practices around the veneration of relics and images, which had too often slipped into idolatry. While the Virgin and other saints could still be prayed to and invoked for aid, superstition must be avoided.

The concept that would most have affected the external demonstration of faith was in the Articles' pronouncements on the doctrine of purgatory, and the benefit, or otherwise, of prayers for the dead. The late mediaeval Church has been described as a cult of the dead – significant amounts of time and money were devoted to prayers for those in purgatory, a place of pain and punishment that was neither heaven nor hell, but reserved for those who were neither so sinful they were instantly condemned to eternal fire, nor so virtuous that their souls could immediately enter heaven, thus accounting for most people. Prayers, Masses or indulgences could reduce the amount of time the soul spent in purgatory. This belief is readily seen in the wills of the Grey family that we have come across – 1,000 Masses were requested by Cecily, and Thomas II asked for prayers for three years. The Act of Ten Articles, while not condemning the doctrine, was rather half-hearted about it – purgatory's existence could not be proved by scripture, but prayers for the dead might help them.

By the late 1530s, many of the younger members of the court were evangelicals. It is impossible to pinpoint when Dorset questioned the traditional teaching he had no doubt received – perhaps as early as the late 1520s in the anti-clerical atmosphere of Richmond's household, or perhaps during the early 1530s, when he spent considerable periods with the Suffolks in East Anglia, an area that had been at the forefront of the new doctrines since the 1520s. John Bale, prior of Ipswich, was a leading light among the evangelicals, and, having secured a living in the gift of Dorset's father-in-law, was causing controversy – he had not only married (still an offence in Henry's Church of England) but was loudly proclaiming new doctrines. Katherine, Duchess of Suffolk was moving away from traditional beliefs, and she and Dorset may have influenced each other. They were both friends with others who would later be considered Protestants, such as Sir John Dudley, the Earl of Hertford and his wife, Anne Stanhope, and Dorset's uncle, Sir Edward Wotton. In September 1538, a correspondent informed the Swiss reformer Heinrich Bullinger that Wotton had received one of his books 'with the greatest satisfaction, and [was] diligently engaged upon it'.

It is certainly likely, therefore, that Dorset would have been interested in the debate that was held in Westminster Hall on 16 November 1538. A man named John Lambert had publicly declared his disbelief in the doctrine of transubstantiation, and Henry had decided to question the man personally. The king, a good amateur theologian, took his self-appointed role as Supreme Head of the Church of England extremely seriously, and piqued himself on his knowledge of the scriptures. He entirely trounced Lambert – at least to his own satisfaction. Lambert was condemned by both Archbishop Cranmer and Cromwell as a heretic and burnt at Smithfield. This was the start of a swing back towards traditionalism on Henry's part, reflected in the 1539 Act of Six Articles, known to reformers as 'the whip with six strings'. Attitudes began to harden, with reformers and traditionalists beginning to see each other as 'heretics' or 'papists', rather than fellow Christians.

At about the same time as Henry was debating the finer points of theology with Lambert, the court was rocked by the arrests of the Marquis of Exeter, friend and jousting companion of Thomas II, and Lord Montagu, son of the Countess of Salisbury and brother of Cardinal Reginald Pole, on charges of treason. Henry saw Cardinal Pole as his greatest enemy – intellectually gifted, Pole had been supported financially by Henry, first at Oxford and then at European universities. Henry had been eager for Pole's approval of the annulment, even dangling the archbishopric of York as an incentive for him to interpret the Bible correctly. Pole, after hinting that he might stand with Henry, had published an extraordinarily offensive broadside, likening Henry to Nero and encouraging the emperor to invade England. Henry was incandescent with range, and now, although there was no compelling evidence of conspiracy, there was enough loose talk among the Pole family for there to be some excuse for Henry to be nervous. Exeter had been one of Henry's closest companions in his youth, but the annulment of the king's first marriage had come between them – while Exeter had accepted change, he was not enthusiastic, and his wife, Gertrude, had been an outspoken defender of Queen Katharine. Once again, Henry's other nobles, including Dorset and Maltravers, were empanelled to try their fellows on 3 December 1538, and once again they pronounced a verdict of guilty. Both Montagu and Exeter were beheaded on Tower Hill.

The attempts that Cromwell and Audley had made earlier in the year to reconcile Dorset and his mother failed. Margaret wrote again to Cromwell, complaining that her son would not allow her to have her own goods removed from the house. Dorset presumably felt that, whatever agreement they had come to for him to occupy Bradgate, even though it had been allocated by his father as part of Margaret's dower, he was also entitled to the furnishings. That they were now disputing the pots and pans shows just how entrenched both had become. Margaret was sure that 'few mothers alive' had been so mistreated by their sons. In a further line that certainly suggests she was more than frugal, she complained that the cost of the men, horses and carts sent to collect her goods was mounting up, while they were not allowed to perform their orders. She wanted Cromwell to order Dorset to allow the men to collect the items. She added that, what with her 'years and sickness', her 'aches and pains', she was unlikely to be keeping her son out of his inheritance for much longer, and begged Cromwell, as a nobleman and knight of the Garter, to help her. She felt this especially as, although Dorset had now taken possession of the lands of his late father and his grandmother Cecily, he was refusing to pay any of the debts owed, and the creditors were hounding Margaret, which she, in her 'old age', found hard to bear. She wrote from Christchurch, the Audleys' home in London, excusing herself from attending on Cromwell, owing to age and infirmity. The saga does not show either of them in a particularly attractive light: Margaret penny-pinching and determined to hold what was hers, and Dorset treating his mother disrespectfully, scrambling for dead men's shoes, but unwilling to take on the concomitant responsibilities.

*

On coming of age, Dorset might have expected to become one of Henry's councillors and partake in public affairs. That he was a man of some talent is indicated in the following account of Henry's nobles, written in the second half of 1538 (before the death of Exeter), which gives a fascinating insight into Henry's advisors, although the ages are wildly out. The writer does not seem to have thought particularly highly of many of Henry's nobles, thus his praise of Dorset is surprising. 'Power' in this context may be taken to refer to extent of property and numbers of retainers, while 'experience' relates to military prowess.

> The Duke of Norfolk, 72 years, the chief and best captain. The Duke of Suffolk, of the same age, a good man and captain, sickly and half lame. The Marquis of Exeter, 36, lusty and strong of power, specially beloved, diseased often with the gout and next unto the Crown of any man within England. The Marquis Dorset, 26, young, lusty, and poor, of great possessions, but which (?) are not in his hands, many friends of great power, with little or no experience, well learned and a great wit. The Earl of Oxford, of 66 years, a man of great power and little experience. The Earl of Arundel, 60, a man of great power, little wit, and less experience; his eon, young and lusty, of good wit and like to do well. The Earl of Shrewsbury, of great power, young and lusty, and little wit and no experience. The Earl of Derby, the greatest of power and land, young, and a child in wisdom, and half a fool. The Earl of Cumberland, a man of 50 years, of good power, without discretion or conduct. The Earl of Westmorland, of like age, of a great power, without wit or knowledge. The Earl of Rutland, of like age, of great

power, with small wit and little discretion. The Earl of Essex, an old man, of little wit and less experience, without power. The Earl of Sussex, of 50 years, of small power and little discretion and many words. The Earl of Wiltshire, of 60, of small power, wise, and little experience, Queen Anne's father. The Earl of [South]Hampton and Admiral of England, made by the king; wise, active, and of good experience; one of the best captains in England. The Earl of Bath, old and foolish. The Earl of Worcester, young and foolish, and of great power in Wales. The Earl of Hertford, young and wise, of small power, and brother unto the last Queen deceased. The Earl of Huntingdon [Thomas II's cousin, George Hastings], of 60 years, of great power, little discretion and less experience.[5]

In late 1538, the king was disturbed by a rare outbreak of peace between François I and Emperor Charles. After many years of war and destruction, devastating the economies of their nations, Chapuys informed Henry's councillors that France and the Holy Roman Empire were now in 'perfect friendship'. The councillors, including Dorset, had no answer to make, 'seeming stupefied'. They might well have been astonished, given the history of the previous thirty years. Their main concern, however, was the risk this rapprochement presented of Charles and François joining forces to forcibly return England to allegiance to Rome. Henry's strategy was to undermine the peace by coming to a separate agreement with either party for the marriage of the Lady Mary to one of their relatives; alternatively, he would ally with the Imperial duchy of Cleves, which had a long-running dispute with Charles.

This ominous reconciliation gave Dorset his first opportunity to prove himself, with his appointment in early 1539 as a commissioner to take musters in Northamptonshire. The risk of invasion by either France or the Empire was growing, and the country was being put on a war footing. Although war with the Empire was feared, the niceties of court etiquette required Henry to order suitable obsequies to be observed on the death of Empress Isabella, the lady whom Charles had married after jilting Henry's daughter. A 'great and solemn obit' was held in St Paul's Cathedral in her memory in late June. A huge hearse was set up in front of the altar, draped in black velvet and hung with the arms of Charles and Isabella. Lord Audley represented the king as chief mourner, followed, as he traversed the cathedral to the altar, by Norfolk, Suffolk, Dorset, Cromwell and numerous other lords, all dressed in mourning robes and hoods. They knelt and sang the dirge in front of the hearse, then repaired to the Lady Chapel where, along with the Imperial and French ambassadors, they consumed wine and spices.[6]

A source from November 1539 offers a rare insight into domestic life, showing how, despite the claims and counter-claims for money, families, particularly the women, attempted to keep the channels of communication and kinship open. Sir Thomas Wharley wrote to Lady

Lisle that he had received thanks from Lord Chancellor Audley and his wife for the puncheon of French wine and the hogshead of Gascon wine that she had sent them, 'and as for your conserves they say they never eat better and so said the old and young lady Marquis and commend you highly for the making thereof'. Despite Lady Lisle's best efforts with her jam jars, Dorset would not be moved on the Lisles' debt.

Soon after this, the court was agog with the news that the king's new bride (his fourth!) was en route from her home country of Cleves. Henry, strongly advised by Cromwell, had entered a treaty with the Duke of Cleves to marry the duke's sister, Anne, as a defence against the Franco-Imperial alliance. The Duke of Cleves, like Henry, was doctrinally Catholic, but had rejected papal supremacy and was aligned with the Schmalkaldic League – a group of imperial princes who had espoused the Lutheran Confession of Augsburg and were a permanent thorn in the side of Charles. By allying with this group, Henry might hope to spur them into causing trouble for Charles and distract him from thoughts of invading England. The Lady Anne of Cleves was twenty-five years old, and Henry had been utterly charmed by the portrait of her that his court painter, Hans Holbein, had created. Widowed now for two years, the king still hoped that he might have more sons. Prince Edward was hale and hearty, but infant mortality was too high not to want an insurance policy.

The Lady Anne set out on her long journey across Europe, arriving in Calais in December, where she remained trapped by contrary winds for a fortnight. Eventually, the weather was calm enough for her flotilla to set sail, but it was a rough crossing, and Anne was stricken with seasickness. While she was recuperating at Rochester, watching a bear-baiting from an upstairs window, a group of merchants entered the room, the largest of whom attempted to engage her in conversation, and even kiss her. Shocked and appalled, and quite unaware of the chivalric tradition of a bridegroom 'accidentally' happening on his bride and love being instantly kindled, Anne coldly rejected the merchant's attempts to befriend her. This was either the greatest mistake, or perhaps the greatest good fortune, of Anne's life. The merchant was none other than the king in disguise. He was deeply affronted by her failure to recognise him as her heart's desire, and no amount of submission and gracious apology on her part could ever undo the damage done by this unfortunate meeting. Henry took against Anne immediately – he did not wish to go through with marriage, he thought she was nothing like as attractive as her portrait, and he quickly conferred with Cromwell to find a way out. But it was impossible for him to wriggle free. Charles and François were still on the warpath: sending the lady back to her family as inferior goods would be a gross insult, and leave Henry and England isolated. There was nothing for it but to go through with the match. Extensive and elaborate celebrations had already been planned, reminiscent of the state visit of the emperor in 1522. Dorset and his wife were, of course, among those drafted in to honour the new queen.

On Saturday 3 January 1540, Anne arrived with her retinue at Shooter's Hill, near Blackheath, south of London, where she was greeted by the great ladies of the court, including Frances, and Elizabeth Audley. Anne withdrew into a tent to change her clothes and partake in a banquet. Informed of her arrival, the king's cavalcade set out to meet her. Preceded by his trumpeters, it consisted of his council, his legal officers and the gentlemen of his Privy Chamber; next came the barons, bishops, earls and dukes, including Dorset's brother-in-law Lord Maltravers, his wife's brother-in-law Lord Clifford, and Lord Ferrers, whose wife, Thomas I's daughter Mary, had died in 1534. Dorset followed, bearing the sword, with the king himself directly behind him. On either side of the king's route his gentlemen pensioners were lined up, among them Sir Thomas Arundell, Dorset's cousin. Arundell, although a younger son, was doing well. More vigorous and ambitious than his only brother, John, he had joined Wolsey's household in the 1520s and was now building up a substantial estate in the West Country, focused on Wardour Castle and comprising swathes of land purchased from the king that had once belonged to abbeys of Shaftesbury and Cerne. His half-sister Mary was in attendance on Jane Seymour, before marrying Sir Robert Radcliffe in 1537 to become Countess of Sussex. Arundell was now appointed receiver general to Anne of Cleves. Neither Frances nor any of Dorset's sisters were given a permanent role in Anne's court, although Katherine Suffolk was named as one of the 'great ladies' who would attend the queen on ceremonial occasions.

In early 1540, we can infer that the Dorsets were in favour with the king. For New Year, Frances had given her uncle a gift of 'a linen and two cellars, the turrets gilt', and Dorset had given a leash of greyhounds. In return, Frances received a gold cup with a gold cover, while Dorset received a gilt glass (a mirror) with a gold cover. These pleasing exchanges may have led Dorset to hope for appointment to the Garter that year, when he was nominated by his uncle Lord Ferrers, but he was again disappointed – the vacant stalls were granted to his brother-in-law Audley and Sir Anthony Browne. Had Dorset shown the talent for jousting that his father and grandfather had once displayed, the king might have looked more warmly on his aspirations to knighthood, but, although we cannot be sure as the lists are incomplete, he does not seem to have been involved in the tournament held at Westminster to celebrate May Day 1540. Since the king himself no longer jousted, there were fewer tournaments than in the first half of his reign, but this particular event was of some consequence, taking place over several days. The challengers were led by Sir John Dudley, seconded by Sir Thomas Seymour, while the leader of the defenders was Henry Howard, Earl of Surrey.

Dorset asked the parliament that sat in April 1540 to vary the terms of his father's will, in so far as it made provision for his brothers. He wanted to retain the principle, but alter the specific properties that the younger brothers were to receive. Inferring from the names of the places in question, he wished to allocate them manors located in the south-west – part of the Bonville inheritance, rather than his core lands in Leicestershire and Warwickshire. The exception is the manor of Bosworth, which was to pass to Lord Thomas after the death of Anne, widow of Lord John Grey of the previous generation. During her lifetime, Lord Thomas was to have several manors in Wiltshire. Since these are all to be surrendered for Bosworth, we can infer that the latter was a particularly valuable manor. The bill was carried on 29 May 1540, the same day as that for Queen Anne's dower.

We do not know what Dorset or Frances thought of Queen Anne, who was only a couple of years their senior. Most people spoke well of her, and even the king liked her; he just was not physically attracted to her. As the spring progressed, it became obvious that the royal marriage had no future – especially as Henry now had his eye on one of Anne's maids of honour, Katheryn Howard. Politically, this was not promising for Dorset's family. Miss Howard was the niece of the Duke of Norfolk, whose rivalry with Suffolk for influence in East Anglia had grown over the years. Norfolk, and by extension his niece, were considered to be religious conservatives, and for Dorset and the other reformers, their rise jeopardised religious progress. Henry, of course, was in no way concerned about the opinions of anyone around him. His marriage to Anne of Cleves was annulled, and he married Katheryn Howard. As part of the fallout, Thomas Cromwell, on whom the Grey family had so frequently relied for help, and who was a religious reformer, was executed. Elizabeth Grey's husband, Lord Chancellor Audley, quickly distanced himself from his former colleague, and over the following year received a series of grants, including the position of Lord Steward of all the monasteries in the king's hands north of the Trent.

Lord Maltravers was also on the up. He was appointed as Deputy Lieutenant of Calais in 1540, and proved active and successful in the role. If Katherine went to Calais with her husband, she did not remain there. She was in London in May 1542, when she died – given her age, the probable cause is childbirth. She had already borne three children – the ladies Jane and Mary, and Lord Henry. The young FitzAlans were prodigiously well educated. Lady Jane FitzAlan, later Lady Lumley, was to become one of the most distinguished scholars of her generation, translating Isocrates and publishing the first known drama in English written by a woman. Lord Henry died young, leaving Jane and Mary as co-heiresses to their father's ancient earldom.[7] Working alongside Maltravers from November 1540, as Treasurer of Calais, was Margaret's brother, the evangelical Sir Edward Wotton.

Compared with his brother-in-law's career, Dorset's was distinctly lacklustre. He missed out on the Garter again in 1541, first when Hertford received the stall that had been Cromwell's and then when three more fell vacant that year, eventually being granted to the Earl of Surrey, Sir Anthony Wingfield and Sir John Gage, despite Dorset having been sponsored by Audley. He was, however, required to sit on a jury in an unusual case in June 1541, when Thomas Fiennes, Lord Dacre of the South, was indicted for murder. Generally, when a nobleman was involved in an affray that led to murder, they would be punished more lightly than a common man and were usually pardoned by the king – as in the case of Edmund de la Pole, Earl of Suffolk, mentioned previously. In this case, however, the killing of a witness to Dacre and a band of his friends hunting illegally in the king's park was not overlooked. Dacre was persuaded to change his original plea of not guilty and throw himself on Henry VIII's mercy. Unfortunately, the advice was bad – he was not only convicted, but hanged, rather than given the much swifter death of execution by beheading, which peers were generally granted. Chapuys reported on the case in some mystification – apparently, the jurors begged the king for Dacre's pardon, but Henry refused, even though one of the other men accused with him was pardoned, although it was not his first offence – one wonders if there were more to the story than is now known.

Shortly after this salutary hanging, Henry went on a formal progress to Yorkshire, accompanied by his elder daughter and the delightful little wife upon whom he fawned, to the amusement of ambassadors. To pacify the Pilgrimage of Grace, five years before, Henry had promised that a parliament would be held in the north, and hinted that his queen of the time, Jane Seymour, would be crowned there. Neither of those events had come to pass, and there had been further disturbances in the north at the beginning of that year. Henry's progress had two purposes – to strike awe into his northern subjects, and to meet his nephew James V, King of Scots. James had not confirmed a rendezvous with his uncle, but Henry chose to take vague statements as cast-iron promises. The court made a leisurely journey up the Great North Road, pausing for a few days at Grimsthorpe Castle, the home of Suffolk and Katherine, then at Gainsborough Hall, before crossing the Humber to Hull. During the court's absence, in late August or early September, Margaret Dorset died at Elizabeth Audley's home in London. The Lord Chancellor wrote to the king, saying he planned to withdraw from London to his home at Terling, Essex, in case Margaret's illness had been infectious (suggesting she did not die of more recognisable causes such as stroke, heart attack or cancer). The king ordered Audley to remain in London until the court returned, although he could go to either the king's house or Cromwell's vacant property if he feared infection. Margaret's death released her dower lands to Dorset, and her lease of Tilty to Medley.

The court returned south with the king in a foul mood – James V had failed to come to York, so Henry had looked a fool, waiting for a visitor who never arrived. His temper was anything but assuaged when a scandal erupted that made him look like something worse – a cuckold. Queen

Katheryn Howard was accused of a lack of chastity before her marriage and of the intention, if not the fact, of adultery subsequent to it. Unlike her cousin Anne Boleyn, Katheryn was not tried in open court, and Dorset can have been in little doubt, as he carried the cap of maintenance in the opening ceremony for the January 1542 parliament, that it would be called upon to dispatch the unhappy girl by act of attainder. The queen, although by no means a political intriguer herself, was widely considered to have been pushed into the king's bed by the religious conservatives, led by her uncle Norfolk, and Bishop Gardiner of Winchester. Dorset, as a keen advocate of reform, may well have been pleased at the queen's downfall, although we can hope he pitied her plight. Thomas Arundell's feelings were probably quite the opposite – in around 1530 he had married Katheryn's older sister, Margaret, and had at least five children by her. Consequently, he was probably disappointed that Katheryn did not remain as queen, and perhaps have a child by the king, to be cousin to his own offspring, although Margaret Arundell was not close to her sister – in 1540, when she and Thomas visited London, they had stayed with Sir Richard Rich, rather than being allocated space at court.

The pressing business of the condemnation of the queen out of the way, the session also settled Frances's jointure, a generous £1,015 3s 3d per annum. The properties were drawn from across all of Dorset's inheritance and included the family seat at Bradgate. When Cicely Dudley died, the manor she had been left by her mother was to be included. Nevertheless, the estates were still encumbered by debt. Sir Brian Tuke wrote to Sir Thomas Wriothesley about arranging repayment for a loan made to the king – rather than ready cash, the notes of debts owed to the king were to be passed on, and the people in question were all, according to Tuke, 'good payers'. They included the late Cecily Dorset's estate, still owing £666 13s 4d, and Dorset, owing £200. The estate was further enhanced in July 1542 when Dorset finally obtained undisputed possession of the Beaumont lands in Leicestershire that Elizabeth Scrope, Dowager Countess of Oxford, had been holding for thirty years. He had to surrender Marston in Sussex, and Harlington in Bedfordshire, as well as paying £14 13s 4d, but it was worth doing – it increased the estate around Bradgate.

*

James V's failure to meet his uncle at York in the autumn of 1541 had enraged the king. Quite unmoved by the knowledge that his nephew had lost two sons and his mother during that year, Henry continued his assaults on the northern kingdom, determined to make the Scots bend to his will. Seventy-year-old Norfolk was still the king's chief soldier but was less enamoured of campaigning than he had once been. He wrote from Newcastle on 12 October 1542 to Wriothesley and Bishop Gardiner, begging them to intercede with the king on his behalf – he was worried that he would once again be posted as Warden of the Marches. He was too old, he said, and another winter anywhere north of Doncaster would kill him – unless, possibly, he could live at Leconfield, where 'the air [was] nothing so vehemently cold as it is here'. He reminded them that, twenty years before, Thomas II, Warden at the time, had been excused on the grounds of health when winter came, and Norfolk had been required to take on Thomas II's job as well as his own. That Henry was still relying on his old warhorse, despite the scandal of Katheryn Howard, suggests that he thought the younger generation not as capable of war. He certainly did not seem in any way eager to promote Dorset, who had undertaken nothing more than ceremonial duties and the low-profile commissions of the peace – and even those he did not have in so great a number as his father had.

Norfolk's pleas fell on deaf ears. Suffolk was also sent north, with Lord Edward Grey among his men. The war came to a head in November 1542 when James led a disastrous raid into England at Solway Moss, about 10 miles north of Carlisle. The Scots were caught by an incoming tide as they crossed back into Scotland and sustained heavy losses, including the capture of some 1,000 men. James, mindful of his father's death at Flodden, did not fight himself but was close enough to the army to catch one of the common diseases of soldiers – dysentery or similar. He returned to Linlithgow, where his wife, Marie of Guise, was awaiting the birth of their third child, then rode on to Falkland where he died in mid-December 1542. Queen Marie's child was a girl, named Mary, who now became Queen of Scots, under the governorship of the Earl of Arran.

The news of James's death pleased Henry immensely. He had been depressed since the beheading of Katheryn Howard, but now he shook off his morose mood, and invited his daughter Mary to come to Hampton Court 'with a great repair of ladies' to celebrate Christmas and the New Year. He cheered up even further in spring 1543 when he began to see more of one of Mary's friends, the recently widowed Katherine Parr, Lady Latimer, who was already being courted by Sir Thomas Seymour. Initially reluctant to accept Henry's proposal, Lady Latimer was persuaded that she had been called by God to marry the king, and the wedding took place on 12 July 1543. The new queen's closest companions were her friend – now stepdaughter – Lady Mary; her sister, Anne, Lady Herbert; Jane, Lady Lisle (wife of Sir John Dudley, who had become Viscount Lisle on the death of his stepfather); Anne, Countess of Hertford; and Katherine Suffolk. With the exception of Lady Mary, all of these ladies were soon known to be strong supporters of the reformed religion.

Shortly after becoming queen, Katherine Parr appointed John Parkhurst as her chaplain, taking him from the Suffolk household, where he had been chaplain for only a year. Parkhurst, a graduate of Merton College, had been ordained by Nicholas Shaxton, Bishop of Salisbury and Almoner to Queen Anne Boleyn. Shaxton was at the radical end of the religious spectrum during the 1530s, and Parkhurst was in sympathy with him. By 1542, his reformist credentials would have been well known to the Suffolks, so his appointment as chaplain must have been a conscious decision, probably by the duchess, to promote reformist preaching in the household. His time there was short, but his influence on Katherine Suffolk and the Dorsets was strong, and now he would influence Katherine Parr. The queen was well educated and of an intellectual turn of mind. Before long, she was learning Latin and Spanish, and there was an air of debate and intellectual curiosity at her court that had not been seen since the downfall of Anne Boleyn.

Now happily married again, Henry returned his thoughts to his earlier preoccupation – pressing his claim to 'overlordship' of Scotland, which he intended to reinforce by the marriage between of the Queen of Scots and Edward, Prince of Wales. In spring 1543, Audley, along with Norfolk, Gardiner, Lord St John and Sir John Gage, was commissioned to treat with Arran. Arran, flirting with religious reform, was willing to follow a pro-English policy, as was the Earl of Angus, Henry VIII's brother-in-law. Initially, Arran persuaded his fellow peers to accept the marriage plan, and in March 1543 it was agreed. However, not everyone in Scotland liked the idea of subjection to England, and there was a strong party, led by Cardinal Beaton, with the support of the dowager queen, Marie of Guise, which preferred the traditional French alliance.

While the Reformation had made little headway in Scotland before the death of James, who had resisted his uncle's encouragement to throw off his allegiance to Rome, the new ideas now began to spread. This put some weight in the English side of the scales, but not enough. Over the course of 1543, the Scots nobles became disenchanted with the idea of their queen marrying the English prince, and in December 1543 the treaty was rejected in favour of a French alliance. Henry, furious, sponsored a long military campaign to bring the Scots to heel, largely led by his brother-in-law Hertford. Hertford was a very successful general, and the years between 1543 and 1547 were a time of constant war, named the Wars of the Rough Wooing some three centuries later by Sir Walter Scott. Dorset had no part in either the negotiations or the war. Although he was again appointed to commissions of peace in Somerset, Wiltshire and Devon, he had no role in council or foreign affairs. Perhaps because he had little to do in an official capacity, Dorset spent more time in scholarly pursuits and the education of his daughters. Parkhurst's friend John Aylmer was appointed as Jane's tutor.

15

End of an Era

Rulers, in the fullness of their power, are apt to think right that which
suits their pleasure.

John Fisher, Bishop of Rochester

On Sunday 23 December 1543, after the king had heard Mass, he
entered his presence chamber and seated himself upon his throne,
beneath the cloth of estate. The doors opened, and Dorset and the Earl
of Derby led in the queen's brother William Parr. Behind them came
Lord Lisle, carrying the king's sword, and Garter king-of-arms holding
a patent of nobility. Parr knelt in front of the king while the patent
was read, creating him Earl of Essex, the title formerly held by Parr's
father-in-law, before briefly resting on Cromwell. The queen's uncle was
ennobled as Baron Parr of Horton. Both men were known to Dorset
from Richmond's household, and both were zealous reformers. The
king's council was beginning to split along religious lines: Hertford,
Lisle, Cranmer, Lord Russell and Essex were on the reformist side, with
Norfolk, Gardiner, Wriothesley and Rich defending traditional religion.
Dorset was nowhere – still not on the council, and passed over yet again
for the Garter, despite nominations from almost all the other knights,
even Norfolk. Henry ignored them and chose Sir John Wallop, a man
who had previously been pardoned for treason, in what must have been
a humiliation for Dorset.

At last, the opportunity came for Dorset to prove himself. In March
1544, with the peace between Charles and Francois in tatters, Henry was
planning yet another invasion of France. Lists were drawn up of the men
and horses that each of his peers ought to be able to provide. Against
Dorset's name are listed 60 horse and 290 foot, armed with bills, pikes
and other weapons. He was to serve, along with Suffolk and his brother-
in-law, who was no longer Lord Maltravers but Earl of Arundel, in the
king's division. Arundel was in favour with the king. He was appointed
Lord Marshal for the campaign, and soon after received the Garter.

Also in the king's army were Dorset's cousins Sir John and Sir Thomas Arundell, together with Sir John's son, another John. Dorset's brother Lord Edward had been part of Suffolk's retinue, but during 1544 was appointed, at the duke's recommendation, as one of Henry's Gentlemen Pensioners, under the captaincy of Sir Anthony Browne, the king's Master of the Horse, and so would have been involved in the campaign. Lord Thomas and Lord John are not listed.

While preparations for war continued, Lord Audley found himself so ill he could not carry out his duties as Lord Chancellor. He returned the Great Seal to the king, and died a few days later. Although Audley and Elizabeth had a daughter, Margaret, who was her father's co-heir along with her elder half-sister, Mary, Elizabeth was not appointed as an executor of his will. The wardships of the sisters were granted to reformers – Margaret's to Sir Anthony Denny, and Mary's to Sir William Herbert, the queen's brother-in-law. Both men received £50 per annum out of the Audley lands for their trouble. Audley was succeeded as Lord Chancellor by Sir Thomas Wriothesley, a traditionalist.

On 3 July 1544, Dorset and Suffolk put to sea, along with Sir Anthony Browne, who had recently married Dorset's cousin Elizabeth FitzGerald. The men sailed for Calais, a flag of St George in the top, and were soon joined by the ships of Lord Admiral Lisle, and the Admiral of Flanders, with a further thirty vessels. They remained in Calais for two nights, then camped in various locations within the Pale, and even on French territory, skirmishing all the while with the French. On 14 July, the king himself arrived at Calais. The following day, Suffolk and Dorset, leading some 1,100 men, set out to besiege Boulogne. Meanwhile, Norfolk was besieging Montreuil, 20 miles further south. Norfolk was well aware that this was labour and men wasted – the town was too well defended for the English to have any hope of capturing it – but Henry had insisted. Strategically, Henry's plan made sense – an outpost of the English army at Montreuil kept the French from a concerted attack on the attackers at Boulogne, the real English target. Boulogne surrendered to Suffolk after two months, enabling the king to enter in state on 18 September, with Dorset bearing the sword before him. The king 'tarried a space' before returning home to be feted as a conquering hero. The king was suitably grateful to his old friend Suffolk, for whom he declared the 'special love, and good affection which [he bore] towards [him] before others'.

True to form, Charles and François concluded a peace behind Henry's back. He could not, or would not, understand that for his fellow monarchs England was peripheral – their contest in Italy was of greater importance to both of them. The French advanced, isolating Boulogne before the English army could join Norfolk, who had no option but to withdraw and lead the remnants of the army back to England in a sorry state. All that Henry had to show for the vast cost in men and money was the continued holding of Calais, with an outpost of English troops at Boulogne. Predictably, the king was furious, but Suffolk was able to calm him down. The king's trust in his old friend was so great that Suffolk was appointed as his Lieutenant for the South, with responsibility for raising troops to fend off the anticipated French counter-invasion which now seemed a real threat. The country was again put on a war footing. With more faith in the man than the king apparently had, Suffolk appointed Dorset to lead the Sussex and Hampshire troops, alongside Sir Anthony Wingfield. War was no cheaper than it had ever been – in fact, it was becoming even more expensive as the coinage was debased by the reduction of silver content, and inflation took hold. Parliament had granted a subsidy in 1543, which was to be payable over three years, but Dorset, along with Francis Hastings, the new Earl of Huntingdon, was sent to 'persuade' people to pay by 1 July 1545, sooner than the money was due. The burghers of Leicester not only had to put up with the marquis pressing them for cash, but had to expend 6*d* for sugar, almonds and cake to entertain him while he did so.[1]

As the summer progressed, the fear of French invasion increased – the fleet patrolled the English Channel, and it was feared the enemy would land on the Isle of Wight. There were running naval battles in the early weeks of August, during which the *Mary Rose* sank. Lisle, in command of the fleet, proved a capable seaman. He was eager to chase the French, but Henry, sensibly, preferred a defensive strategy, allowing the treacherous currents and winds of the Channel to take their toll, and protecting the English fleet using cannon positioned high on the cliffs above Portsmouth. By 18 August, the French fleet retired. In the meantime, the proxy war with France in Scotland continued. Hertford was in charge of operations there, whilst Suffolk was appointed to take reinforcements to Boulogne. Serving under the duke were to be Surrey, in charge of the vanguard, Dorset, who was to lead the rearguard, and Arundel, who was to be marshal. The plans were rapidly altered in August, when Suffolk died. Dorset and Arundel were both discharged, and Henry sent Surrey to lead some 5,000 troops by himself – an extraordinary vote of confidence in a man who had shown excellent promise but was still of limited experience.

The death of his father-in-law came as a huge blow to Dorset. Suffolk had held a far higher opinion of him than the king, and had been a well-regarded man: he was 'almost of all estates and degrees of men, high and low, rich and poor, heartily loved'.[2] The king's esteem for Suffolk was so great that he caused him to be buried at Windsor, his own intended place of interment. Dorset was chief mourner at the funeral, with Arundel as second mourner. Frances and Eleanor Clifford received £200 worth of their mother's plate, but the title and property passed to Henry Brandon, eldest son of Suffolk and Katherine.

In January 1546, commissioners of musters were appointed to gather more troops. Dorset was charged with raising 500 men in Leicestershire, along with Huntingdon, Lord Cromwell (Gregory, Thomas's son),

Sir Ambrose Cave and Sir Richard Manners. Sir Thomas Arundell was responsible for finding 100 men in Dorset. Henry's aim, according to Sir William Paget, who was becoming his most confidential councillor, was to put 30,000 men in the field. Paget's correspondent was Christopher Mont, a native of Koblenz, naturalised as an Englishman in 1531, and once one of Cromwell's men. Mont was employed in the 1540s on various diplomatic embassies for Henry VIII, particularly to Germany, where he became friends with the reformer Melanchthon. Paget continued with the information that Hertford had been appointed lieutenant, with Dorset captain of the forward, and Surrey the rearward. His description of all three as 'favourers of God's Word' – code for reformers – provides Dorset's first definite association with the reformers. Paget praised Lord Lisle as 'God's own knight'.

Dorset was to bring his men to Dover to support the fleet that Lisle was about to take to revictual Boulogne, the French having already captured fifteen or sixteen vessels. It may be that Lisle overstepped the mark in retaliating – in early April the council received a complaint from the emperor that his subjects' shipping was being attacked in the Channel. Orders were sent to the chief gentlemen in the southern coastal counties, including Sir Thomas Arundell, to detain all 'men of war, adventurers' who were in port, and to recall any at sea, and there were follow-up orders to restore goods. This was perhaps a welcome excuse to ease back from hostilities. The Imperial ambassador, van der Delft (Chapuys had retired), wrote home that he thought the English in general were unenthusiastic about the war – it was only the king's determination to hold Boulogne that kept it going. The conflict rumbled on, and Henry continued to need money to prosecute it. In May 1546, Dorset, along with other Leicestershire gentlemen, was required to assess the 'loving contribution' that the people of the county ought to be willing to make to the king, for the necessary defence of the realm against the French king. If Dorset hoped that his fairly limited war efforts to date would finally recommend him to the king for the award of the Garter, he was yet again to be disappointed. Despite him being nominated by all of the knights present on 3 May 1546, the king, after deliberating for some days, decided not to appoint anyone.

While Dorset was busy collecting his men, he received a present from Anne, Lady Cobham, whose husband, George Brooke, had replaced Arundel as Lord Deputy in Calais. Lady Cobham's servant, John Wilkins, reported that Dorset had promised to 'do his best to content [her]' when she returned to England. The Cobhams were at the centre of not one but two scandals at Henry's court. Lord Cobham's sister Elizabeth was the wife of the poet Sir Thomas Wyatt, but had been cast off by him for adultery. It was not until Wyatt was under suspicion of treason in 1541 that he was forced to capitulate to the Cobhams' demands for him to maintain his wife, in return for a pardon. One of Lady Cobham's daughters, another Elizabeth, had been living in open adultery with Dorset's friend Essex since 1543. Essex had thrown over his previous mistress, Lady Cobham's younger sister Dorothy Braye, to take up with the niece. The Cobhams were part of the reformist circles that constituted Dorset's friends.

*

War was not Henry's only preoccupation – the succession and religion were of continuing concern. Archbishop Cranmer was quiet but persistent in his pursuit of further reform. Henry was never going to succumb to the archbishop's desires entirely, but his personal affection for Cranmer meant that he was protected from the efforts of the conservative faction to remove him. One indication of creeping reform was the passing of the Chantries Act of 1545. This Act claimed that a significant proportion of chantry chapels, such as that of the Grey family at Astley, were misappropriating funds intended for charitable purposes. The Act did not forbid chantry foundations, but authorised the king to set up commissions of investigation into their governance. Poorly managed ones were to be dissolved, and, in theory, the funds diverted to proper charitable purposes – in practice, that often meant the pockets of the king and his courtiers. Given the timing of the Act, we may infer that it was motivated more by financial concerns than by religious ones. Henry needed gentry and nobles who could afford the costs of war.

The queen's inner circle, of which Katherine Suffolk was a member, continued its Bible studies, and the dowager-duchess patronised the radicals Hugh Latimer and John Bale. Bale, who had left England for Antwerp on the fall of Cromwell, wrote in 1547 that Katherine Suffolk was an example of a 'Godly woman' – the term 'Godly' being widely used among early Protestants for each other. Such encouragement of reform by the queen and her friends had political repercussions, particularly as Henry VIII declined. The traditionalist and reformist factions at court were jockeying for power. No one thought Henry would live to see his son achieve maturity, so who would control the administration during Edward's minority?

The traditionalists were appalled by rumours current in the early months of 1546 that Henry was looking about for a new queen – the novelty of his marriage to Katherine Parr had worn off, and she had shown no signs of pregnancy. The lady whom the gossips named was none other than Katherine Suffolk. That the rumours existed is certain; that Henry had any such intentions is not. He liked witty women – wit had been Anne Boleyn's chief charm – so an attraction to Katherine is quite likely, but that is a long step from marriage. Nevertheless, the rumours may have been a catalyst for those traditionalists, led by Bishop Gardiner of Winchester, who wanted to oust Katherine Parr – and her heretical friends with her. It would be vital to remove Katherine Suffolk as well – had Henry married her, the traditionalists would have been out of the evangelical frying pan and into the Protestant fire.

The method of attack was through a Lincolnshire woman named Anne Askew, whose unhappy marriage to Sir Thomas Kyme led her to seek fulfilment elsewhere. Anne became increasingly outspoken in proclaiming her beliefs, which were, according to the law as it stood, heretical. In 1543, she returned to the house of her brother Francis, who was sympathetic to her views. The following year found her in London, where a third Askew sibling, Edward, had a place in Henry VIII's Privy Chamber, and the husband of a fourth was a lawyer in Katherine Parr's household. Anne was also connected to the radical John Lascelles, whose information against Queen Katheryn Howard had led to the queen's execution. While in London, Anne lodged at The Temple, very close to the Dorsets' town house, and it was probably there that she met fellow reformers Katherine Suffolk, Lady Hertford and Lady Denny. Anne became something of a celebrity – she had an amazing knowledge of the Bible and facility in quoting it – and the strong personality which shines from her writings gave her influence. An early trial for heresy collapsed for lack of the requisite number of witnesses willing to testify against her. Released, no doubt with dire warnings, she returned to Lincolnshire, but was arrested again in a major onslaught against heretics in May 1546. Anne and her estranged husband were brought before the council, ostensibly to discuss their marriage. Kyme was dismissed, but Anne was detained and questioned on her beliefs. She prevaricated so far as she could, and was dispatched to Newgate gaol. She was later questioned by Lisle and Essex, whom she accused of hypocrisy, knowing them to hold similar opinions. Anne was tried at the Guildhall and condemned for heresy.

The matter, however, did not end there. Sir Richard Rich, Chancellor of the Court of Augmentations, and Lord Chancellor Wriothesley took a hand, hoping to implicate the queen and her ladies, and thereby their rivals on the council. Anne was taken to the Tower, and was submitted to harsh questioning, including torture on the rack, but no amount of brutality could persuade her to implicate anyone else. She answered only that if she were to say anything against the queen or the other women it could not be proved. She did admit that Lady Hertford and Lady Denny had sent her money. The lieutenant of the Tower, appalled at the torture of Anne, went personally to the king to have it stopped, but investigation into the queen's ladies and their reading matter continued. Frances is not mentioned among these ladies – probably because she was not always in attendance at court, although she had an official position as one of the ladies of the queen's household alongside her cousins Mary, Elizabeth and Lady Lennox, and her own sister Lady Clifford. Frances's absence from court could have had any of a variety of causes: perhaps she and Dorset did not want to spend much time together, or maybe she did not get on with the queen, or disagreed with her religious views. She may have simply preferred to stay with her children. Cost may well have been a factor, too.

According to John Foxe (the only source of this widely believed anecdote), Queen Katherine, upon hearing that she was being investigated, ordered her ladies to hide the banned books, and circumvented the threat by appealing to the king personally, knowing his tendency to pardon those who were able to enter his presence. Accompanied by her sister Anne Herbert and cousin Lady Lane, the queen went to Henry's chambers, where she persuaded the king (who was eager to be reconciled) that she had only argued with him on religious points to learn from him and distract him from his pain.[3] Thereafter, the queen kept a low profile in religious matters, as did her friends. Anne Askew had not been so fortunate. She was burnt for heresy. Her example was not lost on Dorset's daughter Jane, now aged about nine. Jane probably came to court with her mother from time to time. If she did, she would have been influenced by the evangelical tone of the queen's household, particularly the outspoken radicalism of her step-grandmother, Katherine Suffolk. The martyrdom of Askew had a profound effect on the little girl, and her later writings reflect some of Askew's works.

The queen's encouragement of scholarship and religious reform emboldened Dorset in his educational programme for Jane and his younger daughters, Katherine and Mary, born in around 1540 and 1545 respectively, and growing up at Bradgate. Given the spacing of their births, it is likely that Frances suffered miscarriages or early infant deaths as well. The Grey family valued education – witness Thomas I's will granting legacies to scholars, the description of Dorset as 'well-learned and a great wit' – and now Dorset's daughters benefited from the great leap forward in female education that occurred in this period. As well as the traditional education of upper-class women in household and domestic management, plus the courtly skills of music, dancing and hunting of various sorts, the girls received an academic education that included Latin, Greek and, for Jane, Hebrew. Whether or not Frances's convictions were as strong as her husband's, at the centre of the girls' education was the Reformed faith. The tutor in the Grey household was John Aylmer, who had been patronised by Dorset for some years. The other men involved in the education of the Grey sisters were the family's three chaplains – John Haddon, a Fellow of Trinity College, Cambridge; Thomas Harding, holder of the Regius Chair in Hebrew at Oxford; and John Willock, a former Dominican friar. All four of these men were, by the mid-1540s, convinced reformers. (Harding later returned to the Catholic fold and was treated to an excoriating written attack from Jane.)

Meanwhile, Dorset struggled with the same arguments with landowners in Leicestershire that had dogged Thomas II. In June 1546, John Beaumont, the king's Receiver of the Wards, complained to the council that Dorset had 'used threats' against him at the recent quarter sessions in Leicester. Sir William Turville had intervened to protect Beaumont. All three were brought before the council at Greenwich, and Dorset was ordered to leave Beaumont alone. While Beaumont appears to be the victim on the face of the information furnished thus far, there may be more to this than meets the eye. Beaumont's second wife was Elizabeth Hastings, granddaughter of Cecily's mother, Katherine Neville, and therefore a protagonist in the long-running Grey/Hastings dispute. This hearing was not the end of the matter. On 4 July, the council delved further into the dispute. Beaumont was asked to produce evidence of Dorset's threatening behaviour, which the council concluded was insufficient to fully substantiate his charge. Dorset was bound over to keep the peace with Beaumont, and Beaumont, as well as being bound in the sum of 500 marks not to leave London without the council's licence, was given a severe 'lesson to know in better sort his superiors' – he should not complain of a nobleman without cause.

*

All sides, Imperial, English and French, were tired of the war, and negotiations began for a truce. Lisle, Paget and Dorset's uncle Dr Nicholas Wotton were the English negotiators. The matter hinged on Boulogne. The French were willing to pay up to 200,000 crowns for its return. Lisle and his team pointed out that it had cost 8 million crowns to capture. If the French would repay that, and all the arrears of the numerous pensions and payments due to the English Crown, at reasonable dates, then Boulogne would be returned. The terms finally agreed were complex, but in summary, the French would be able to redeem Boulogne after eight years, on payment of 2 million crowns, plus arrears of pensions and so forth. The Treaty of Camp was proclaimed on 13 June. Once again, despite his high rank and relationship to the king by both blood and marriage, Dorset had no part in affairs.

However little Henry thought of Dorset's military or political ability, he was happy to use him for ceremonial. Along with other senior peers and courtiers, he was required to take part in the ceremonies surrounding the visit of the Lord Great Admiral of France, who came to London in July 1546 to ratify the treaty. The ambassador was treated with almost as much reverence as his master would have been. The peers were each required to supply a horse for the ambassador's retinue, trapped with a footcloth, while the mayor and corporation of London were persuaded that a generous present should be forthcoming. They presented the admiral with a cup of gold and silver and silver-gilt flagons, filled with hippocras wine, and a selection of 'marchpanes, sugar-loaves, sucketts, wafers and spices' for his table, to the value of £100. Since man does not live by sugar alone, the city also provided six dozen capons, and a firkin of fresh sturgeon, among other delicacies. Dorset attended the official reception, and was chosen to stay for the dinner. The very highest-ranking ladies – the queen, the ladies Mary and Elizabeth, and the Lady Anne of Cleves – withdrew, leaving the king's niece Lady Lennox,[4] his daughter-in-law the Duchess of Richmond, Katherine Suffolk, Lady Audley and the other ladies to dine.

Dorset and Frances also continued to receive financial favours from the king. In August 1546, they were granted the lands of the dissolved chantry colleges of Astley and Newenham, previously patronised by Cecily. Dorset now had the pleasure of admiring the monuments of his forbears, without the inconvenience of paying priests to pray for their souls. It was becoming a widely accepted view among the reformers that prayers for the dead were not just pointless but sinful, so both Dorset's conscience and his pocket were happy. That the lands were granted in tail, rather than tail male, indicates that it was not anticipated that the couple would now have a son. Dorset was also allowed to buy the manor of Atherstone in Warwickshire for £377 11s 8d, and the former monastery of the Blackfriars in Leicester. In 1547, the Harington chantry at Porlock was granted to Lord Thomas.

Part 5

1547–1554
Woe to the kingdom, whose prince is a child

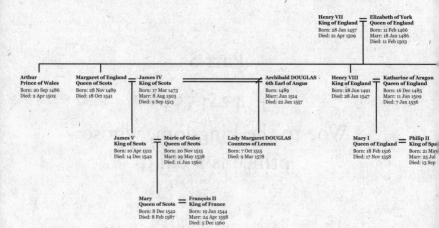

**The Tudor Royal Family
(simplified)**

**Henry VII
King of England**
Born: 28 Jan 1457
Died: 21 Apr 1509

**Elizabeth of York
Queen of England**
Born: 11 Feb 1466
Marr: 18 Jan 1486
Died: 11 Feb 1503

**Arthur
Prince of Wales**
Born: 20 Sep 1486
Died: 2 Apr 1502

**Margaret of England
Queen of Scots**
Born: 28 Nov 1489
Died: 18 Oct 1541

**James IV
King of Scots**
Born: 17 Mar 1473
Marr: 8 Aug 1503
Died: 9 Sep 1513

**Archibald DOUGLAS
6th Earl of Angus**
Born: 1489
Marr: Jun 1514
Died: 22 Jan 1557

**Henry VIII
King of England**
Born: 28 Jun 1491
Died: 28 Jan 1547

**Katharine of Aragon
Queen of England**
Born: 16 Dec 1485
Marr: 11 Jun 1509
Died: 7 Jan 1536

**James V
King of Scots**
Born: 10 Apr 1512
Died: 14 Dec 1542

**Marie of Guise
Queen of Scots**
Born: 20 Nov 1515
Marr: 29 May 1538
Died: 11 Jun 1560

**Lady Margaret DOUGLAS
Countess of Lennox**
Born: 7 Oct 1515
Died: 9 Mar 1578

**Mary I
Queen of England**
Born: 18 Feb 1516
Died: 17 Nov 1558

**Philip II
King of Spa**
Born: 21 May
Marr: 25 Jul
Died: 13 Sep

**Mary
Queen of Scots**
Born: 8 Dec 1542
Died: 8 Feb 1587

**François II
King of France**
Born: 19 Jan 1544
Marr: 24 Apr 1558
Died: 5 Dec 1560

16

Sibling Rivalry

> No prince's revenues be so great that they are able to satisfy the insatiable cupidity of men.
>
> Elizabeth I

Throughout the autumn of 1546, as Henry's health declined, his councillors jockeyed for position. Their division into religious 'traditionalists' and opposing 'reformers' is valid but simplistic – much of the rivalry was personal. Hertford treated Wriothesley to 'vain and injurious words', and Lisle even went so far as to physically assault Bishop Gardiner during a council meeting. While Hertford and Lisle were characterised by the Imperial ambassador, van der Delft, as 'great stirrers of heresy', Surrey, although he leant towards the Reformed faith himself, objected vehemently to the growing prominence of the Seymour family, whom he saw as upstarts. Surrey was his own worst enemy, so it was not difficult for Hertford and his faction, aided by the conservative Lord Chancellor Wriothesley, to engineer Surrey's execution for treason, and the dispatch of his father, Norfolk, to the Tower.

Henry VIII died early in the morning of 28 January 1547, comforted by his old friend Archbishop Cranmer, who claimed that Henry had squeezed his hand when he was asked if he died in the faith of Christ. This signal could assure the deceased king's subjects that he repented of his (very few!) sins and could be ushered straight into heaven. Before he died, Henry had given great thought to how the country should be governed during the minority of his nine-year-old son, now proclaimed as Edward VI. It would be at least five years before the king could realistically be involved in decision making, before attaining his majority at eighteen.[1]

According to Henry's instructions, Edward was to be ruled by the advice of the whole council, including in the matter of his matrimony, with no single individual having supreme authority. Most of the members of Henry's Privy Council had been nominated: Hertford, Paget, Lisle, John, Lord Russell, and Cranmer. Dorset's uncles Sir Edward Wotton and

Dr Nicholas Wotton were included, and were also executors. Another dozen men were appointed as assistants to the council. These included Arundel, Essex, and Hertford's brother Sir Thomas Seymour. Conspicuous by their absence were Queen Katherine, even though she had been regent during Henry's absence in France in 1544; the Duke of Norfolk, whose execution for treason had only been forestalled by Henry's own death; Bishop Gardiner of Winchester, whom Henry had dropped because 'no man could rule him'; and Henry's nearest male relative, Dorset.

But even Henry could not control events from the grave. Happy that the king they had so recently praised for his wisdom and benevolence was now safely winging his way to the pearly gates, his council immediately disobeyed his detailed, considered and sensible arrangements. His death was kept secret for several days while Hertford, supported by his crony Paget, persuaded the other councillors that, as the new king's oldest uncle, he should be installed as Lord Protector. The other councillors, by and large, accepted this suggestion – either genuinely convinced of the arguments or, more likely, afraid to stand up to Hertford.

The other instance in which Hertford and Paget interpreted Henry's will very freely was their implementation of the 'unfulfilled gifts' clause. Henry directed that any gifts he had made or promised during his lifetime should be fulfilled. In itself, this was not an unusual clause, but a week after Henry's death, Paget suddenly remembered that Henry had recently asked his advice on promoting a whole swathe of councillors to new titles, and on the distribution of the lands of the attainted Norfolk. The councillors were delighted to hear how Henry had intended to honour them, and accepted his favour with alacrity. Hertford became Duke of Somerset; Lisle, Earl of Warwick; Wriothesley, Earl of Southampton; Essex, Marquis of Northampton; Sir Richard Rich, Baron Rich of Lees; and finally, Thomas Seymour became Baron Sudeley as well as being confirmed in his position as Lord Admiral. While there has been plenty of understandable cynicism about the convenience of these gifts, Lipscomb argues cogently in *The King Is Dead* that there is good evidence Henry did intend to effect at least some of these creations.[2] Somerset's other significant appointee was William Cecil as secretary to the council. Cecil's grandfather had been a servant of Lady Margaret Beaufort, and his father had been a page to Henry VIII.

The young king's sisters were placated during Somerset's usurpation of power through land grants, which they received instead of the cash income that Henry had intended. The Lady Mary, now heir to the throne, a position she had lost in 1533, received an enormous estate, immediately translating her into one of the greatest landed magnates in the country – a decision that many councillors would live to regret.

Van der Delft thought he had the measure of the council. Somerset and Warwick would have the whole management of it, while Paget and Wriothesley would do the donkey work and 'each one will strive his best for his own advancement'. He was right about the principle, if not the detail. By the end of February, those left out in the cold were complaining. Bishop Gardiner, no doubt thoroughly annoyed at being left off the council, accused Sir William Paget of having overstepped his authority. That Gardiner was anticipating a change in religious tone – Somerset being a known reformer – is evident from Paget's reply that he bore the bishops in general no ill will and Gardiner none in particular.

Two men were not happy with Somerset's new role. Lord Chancellor Wriothesley, or Southampton as he now was, complained vociferously about Henry VIII's instructions being ignored. This incensed Somerset, who was not just angry that Southampton had questioned his right to be protector but offended because he had used 'unfitting words to me, the said protector, to the prejudice of the king's estate'. As Lord Chancellor, Southampton could not easily be side-lined, so a pretext was quickly found to unseat him. Managing all the Lord Chancellor's business required a prodigious amount of work, and Southampton had delegated some of his legal duties to four senior lawyers. This was pounced upon by Somerset, who on 5 March accused Southampton before the rest of the council of 'manifold abuses' in his conduct of the chancellorship, and relieved him of it. The other man who resented Somerset's usurpation of power was his brother Sir Thomas Seymour. Seymour's objection was less one of principle than of personal ambition. He claimed that, as another of the king's uncles, he should have an important role – preferably Guardian of the King's Person. The protector refused his brother's demands, but appointed him to full membership of the council, rather than just assistant. Still unsatisfied, Seymour was soon hatching grandiose schemes to accrue power.

Dorset, too, was displeased – there was no new title for him, as Somerset did not want any other new dukes to upstage him, and the Imperial ambassador opined that the elevation of Essex to the marquisate of Northampton had been granted 'more for the purpose of degrading the other marquis, who has hitherto been the only one, than of exalting this one'.[3] Dorset's only reward was the bestowal, at last, of the Garter.

Within weeks, Henry's will was overthrown in a more determined manner: Letters Patent were issued which conferred upon Somerset the right to exercise monarchical powers beyond those given to previous protectors, and to appoint or dismiss councillors. To give Somerset's rule further force, on 21 March, a royal commission in Edward VI's name appointed one 'trusty personage … our said uncle as Governor of our person and Protector of our realm', and everything done by him would be ratified by the king. Seventy-four years before, when Edward V, a few years older, had been left in a similar position, his throne had been usurped by his uncle, but there was no risk of that in this case. Somerset, although he had drops of royal blood like any noble, was so far from the throne that there could be no possibility of him trying to take it. All he had to do was to keep on good terms with his nephew, becoming his indispensable and most trusted adviser, without offending the other nobles too much, and he could look forward to a long and honourable life. Unfortunately, as is often the case, Somerset's ambition outstripped his ability. He was one of the best military commanders of his generation and, so far as can be told from his actions, he had a genuine religious faith and tried to implement at least some of the tenets of Christianity in regard to the treatment of his fellow man, but he lacked emotional intelligence and struggled to get on with his colleagues. His pride in his own position and the arrogance he displayed became defining characteristics of Somerset's protectorship – he even addressed the King of France as 'brother', only to receive a rebuke from the offended monarch. This attitude eventually led to the rest of the council becoming thoroughly sick of his pretensions. But that was for the future.

Meanwhile, two ceremonies had to be completed – the burial of Henry VIII, and the coronation of Edward VI. Henry's body lay in state at Westminster for two weeks, embalmed and encased in a huge lead-lined coffin, surrounded by the banners and escutcheons of his royal arms, lit by eighty huge candles, while Masses for his soul were sung. Early in the morning of Monday 14 February, the vast coffin was heaved onto a chariot and began its long trundle to Windsor. Dorset rode immediately behind as chief mourner – the old king's nearest male blood relative other than Edward himself. Behind came the other mourners, all in black, riding horses trapped in black velvet. They rode for five hours, before depositing the coffin at its appointed overnight stop, the old abbey of Syon, which had been dissolved in 1539. The next morning, after more Masses had been performed, the procession continued, arriving at St George's Chapel during the afternoon. The coffin was set down to wait overnight within the 35-foot hearse, surrounded by enough candles to consume 4,000 pounds of wax. On Wednesday 16 February, at 6 a.m., the Mass was performed, followed by the funeral service, with Bishop Gardiner making the oration. The grave containing the remains of the late Queen Jane was opened, and Henry's coffin lowered in by sixteen heroically strong yeomen warders, using five linen bands to distribute the weight. The officers of his household, led by Lord St John, Great Master of the Household, broke their staves of office, and threw them into the grave. The stone covering the tomb was replaced, and Henry was left to eternity, while his officers ate dinner.

Three days later, on Saturday 19 February, the court changed from mourning robes to best clothes as Edward made his formal procession through the City of London from the Tower to Westminster for his coronation. The lower ranks were at the front, gentlemen, esquires and knights, then the clergy, foreign ambassadors and councillors, walking in pairs. Archbishop Cranmer was paired with van der Delft, but declined to speak to him. Dorset rode immediately in front of the king, in the role of Constable of England, carrying the upturned drawn sword. Edward was flanked by Somerset and Warwick, and directly behind rode Sir Anthony Browne. The route was decorated with tapestries, painted cloths and banners hanging from the windows. The different guilds set up entertainments – the king was delighted to see an Aragonese acrobat slide down a tightrope from the battlements of the steeple of St Paul's to the deanery gate.

The Monday following, Edward was dressed in his velvet coronation robes, furred with ermine, while his nobles donned their scarlet velvet parliament robes. The whole phalanx walked to Westminster Hall, where more of the royal household was waiting, to form the procession to the abbey. Once again, Dorset carried the drawn sword of state. Edward walked under a canopy supported by the barons of the Cinque Ports, his train carried by Warwick, Northampton and Sir Thomas Seymour. To the right was the Earl of Shrewsbury, whose role was to hold the king's right glove and help him with the sceptre, and to the left was Cuthbert Tunstall, Bishop of Durham – a religious conservative, but a man who largely avoided politics. The coronation differed from any previous coronation of an English king – it was shorter, and the coronation oath had been altered by Archbishop Cranmer, to the detriment of the rights of the people. Instead of the congregation being asked if it would accept Edward as king, it was asked if it would 'serve' the king. Perhaps not hearing the difference, or not comprehending how this changed the monarchy from something based on public support to something imposed from on high, the congregation responded with the customary 'Yea, yea, yea, King Edward'. The king's own oath, rather than promising peace and concord to people, Church and clergy, and to observe the laws 'chosen by your people', excluded the clergy entirely and gave the king's role as law-making and the people's as obeying. Although probably only Cranmer, Somerset and a few chosen councillors realised the import of these changes, they converted the English monarch from a leader ruling by consent, to one with the powers of a tyrant.

The oath sworn, Dorset and his young brother-in-law the Duke of Suffolk stood to either side of Edward, helping him support the sceptre and orb. At the coronation feast in Westminster Hall, Dorset, clad in cloth of gold and carrying a staff of silver, rode in as Constable of England, with Arundel, similarly clad, as Marshal. Under their supervision, the other nobles with offices to perform entered, and the king's table was laid.[4] The next day, the new knights of the Garter were installed – Dorset received the fourth stall on the emperor's side, empty since the death of his father-in-law, and was later promoted to the third stall on the emperor's side, replacing Norfolk. Two days later, Dorset's brother Lord Thomas Grey was dubbed knight.[5] The following Sunday, celebrations continued with a joust in which Lord John took part.

One aspect of Henry VIII's will may have been welcome to Dorset. The Succession Act of 1544 had confirmed Edward's right to inherit under the normal process of the law of inheritance, unaffected by statute. Similarly, he was to be followed by any other legitimate children Henry might have. The statute then departed from common law by naming Henry's daughters, Mary and Elizabeth, as potential heirs should Edward have no children, despite the sisters being illegitimate according to the law of England. In another departure from common law, the Act also gave Henry power to nominate Elizabeth's successor, in the event of her dying without children. Henry was to identify these putative heirs, either by Letters Patent or by his will, signed 'by his gracious hand'. Henry did so nominate (although his will was not actually signed 'by his gracious hand', which led to some dispute as to its legality later). Under the generally accepted rules of inheritance, his heirs were the descendants of his elder sister, Margaret, Queen of Scots – that is, Mary, the young Queen of Scotland, or Margaret, Lady Lennox. But Henry designated the 'heirs of the Lady Frances', daughter of his younger sister, the French Queen, instead. Should Lady Frances have no heirs, she was to be succeeded by the heirs of her sister Lady Eleanor, Countess of Cumberland. Henry ignored both Frances and Eleanor themselves, moving straight to their children, despite that fact that neither had a son. Frances had three daughters, and Eleanor had one. None of these younger girls was married – the eldest, Frances and Dorset's daughter Jane, was only ten.

Henry gave no reason for passing over Frances and Eleanor, but it clearly cannot have been gender based. Instead, one is left to conclude that he did not think much of the competence of either the ladies themselves, or their husbands. Eleanor was occasionally at court, but is thought to have spent most of her time in and around the Clifford strongholds in Cumberland. Her husband, Henry Clifford, had inherited the earldom on the death of his father in 1542 but was never given office by Henry VIII. In later life, he became involved with the Rising of the Northern Earls under Elizabeth I – during which rebellion he completely failed to cover himself in glory. Henry VIII was an excellent judge of character in his ministers – if he passed over Clifford, it was for good reason, and we can similarly assume that Dorset's failure to achieve any meaningful post in Henry's reign was a reflection of Henry's assessment of his talents.

While Dorset might have been pleased on Jane's behalf by a vague claim to the throne that might accrue if three siblings all died without heirs, it was a weaker feeling than his disgruntlement at the rash of new titles. Previously, with the Duke of Norfolk in prison, he had been outranked only by his wife's half-brother Suffolk. Now, he had Somerset ahead of him, and Northampton on the same rung. Lord Admiral Seymour, seeking support in his drive to increase his influence, found Dorset a willing tool in his mission to rival his brother. Seymour's bid to have himself appointed as guardian of the king's person having failed, he put out feelers towards marrying one or other of the late king's daughters but did not pursue this. Instead, he reverted to an old plan – marriage to the dowager queen, Katherine Parr. Seymour reasoned that this would give him a level of prestige and influence at court and with the king that would make it hard for him to be side-lined. To marry Katherine too soon was risky. What if she should fall pregnant within such a space of time that Henry might feasibly be the father? But to delay might mean the whole scheme would miscarry – Seymour was well aware that Somerset and the other councillors would attempt to block any such marriage. Seymour therefore sought to make the king his ally – something easier said than done, for Edward was carefully surrounded by Somerset's appointees at all times.

It was not easy for the admiral to gain access to the boy, so he resorted to bribing the king's servant, Fowler, and the king himself, by sending him pocket money. The rather austere Somerset saw no need to give the king any ready cash, which was making Edward's life difficult – one of the marks of royalty with which he had been brought up was to be generous with his friends and servants. Fowler had the task of persuading Edward to suggest a marriage between Seymour and Queen Katherine, so that, when it came to light that they had already married, the admiral would be able to point to the king as the instigator of the plan, and Somerset would have to put a good face on it. Anticipating success, Seymour and Queen Katherine were secretly married before 17 May. Katherine had been left very comfortably off by the king, with dower properties at Chelsea and Hanworth, and it had been agreed that her younger stepdaughter, the Lady Elizabeth, thirteen at the time of her father's death, would reside with her. This was excellent from Seymour's point of view – he had already given thought to whether he might marry one of the king's daughters, and now, with the younger under his roof, he could devise a strategy to influence her. But Elizabeth was not the only girl named as a potential inheritor of the crown – there was also the ten-year-old Jane Grey.

The Dorsets were living at their London house, and Jane came to the palace with other young people during Edward's rare hours of recreation, reading, dancing or playing with him. That Edward and Jane got on well set Seymour thinking – perhaps a marriage between the two might be of advantage to him? He had already convinced himself that the protector was planning to marry the king to his own daughter, Lady Jane Seymour, if the match to the Scottish queen did not materialise, although there is no evidence of this other than in Seymour's jealous imaginings.[6] Far better for the king to marry Jane Grey – there should be no difficulty bringing her into his sphere of influence. He opened his campaign by sending one of his men, Sir John Harington, to Dorset with the information that he 'was like to come to great authority and that being the King's Majesty's uncle … might do [Dorset] much pleasure advising [Dorset] therefore to resort unto him and to enter a more friendship and familiarity with him'.[7] This was followed up by Harington's assurance that if Dorset placed his daughter with the admiral he would arrange her marriage to the king. Dorset's ears pricked up at this, and within the week he was at the admiral's house, Seymour Place, talking terms. The men rapidly came to an agreement for Jane's wardship and marriage to be bought by the admiral for £2,000. Dorset believed that his daughter, being of royal blood on her mother's side and being firmly inculcated with the Reformed faith, would be a very suitable bride, should the king choose an English-born wife, as his father had done four times.

Jane, accompanied by her tutor, John Aylmer, moved to Seymour Place. It is surprising that Frances was persuaded to allow the anomalous situation of a young girl residing in the household of an apparently unmarried man, but perhaps Jane's youth made the point seem minor – or the Dorsets may have been let into the secret of his marriage to Katherine, and thought the situation temporary. It is also possible that the admiral's mother, the widowed Lady Seymour, acted as chaperone. Seymour today has a reputation as a man attractive to women and something of a philanderer, yet I can find no contemporary evidence that the admiral had any such reputation, other than relating to the events that were to unfold over the next year. Prior to his interest in Katherine Parr on the death of Lord Latimer – which must have been genuine as there was no great fortune involved – the only other lady he was ever connected with was the Dowager Duchess of Richmond, who refused to entertain the idea of marrying him. His morals, in this regard at least, may have been unfairly traduced.

When Seymour and Katherine's marriage became common knowledge, the court was shocked, even though the king had been inveigled into approving the match. The general feeling was that Katherine Parr had demeaned herself by marrying so quickly from motives of personal affection, and there was a consequent loss of respect for her. Katherine Suffolk certainly saw the funny side, naming her new stallion and mare Seymour and Parr. The marriage gave the Lord Protector's wife, once Queen Katherine's lady-in-waiting, an excuse to try to claim precedence of the queen. On one occasion the duchess even jostled the queen out of a doorway, so that she could pass through first. A running battle ensued over the queen's jewels, left to her by Henry. Somerset impounded them, but they were then seen draped over Duchess Anne's bosom.

Jane frequently visited Queen Katherine and Lady Elizabeth, although her official home was still Seymour Place. In January 1548, William Grindal, the Lady Elizabeth's tutor, died. Refusing the advice of Katherine and Seymour, she appointed Roger Ascham to replace him. Ascham had been brought up in the household of Sir Humphrey Wingfield, a member of the Suffolk affinity, before becoming a Fellow at St John's College, Cambridge, where many of the radical reformers of the mid-sixteenth century were educated. Jane was at least three years younger than Elizabeth, so is unlikely to have shared lessons with her, but she did become acquainted with Ascham. For Jane, it was a golden year. She soon came to love Katherine, and the atmosphere in the household was gentler and happier than in her own parents' household. While there is no evidence on which to base an informed opinion of Dorset and Frances's marriage, the lack of any pregnancy following the birth of their youngest daughter, Mary, in 1545, and Frances's continued friendship with Lady Mary, perhaps suggests incompatibility. Ten years later, Frances had no difficulty conceiving by her second husband, so lack of more children cannot be imputed to infertility on her part.

Somerset was not satisfied with the religious changes of Henry's reign. He was eager to move from the reformed Catholicism of Henry to an openly Protestant stance. Change became visible in churches in the summer of 1547, when, as well as reinforcing the requirement for an English Bible and a copy of the translation of Erasmus' *Paraphrases on the Gospels* to be in every church, the parish clergy were exhorted to remove anything that could tend to idolatry or image worship, while radical preachers, who would have risked being burnt under Henry VIII, now had licence to preach.[8] In this atmosphere of reform, Katherine Parr, encouraged by Katherine Suffolk, published her religious work *Lamentations of a Sinner* in November 1547. *Lamentations* was plainly Protestant, in that Katherine espoused the doctrine of justification by faith alone, but she said nothing against the Mass, and nor did her work openly embrace the Calvinist doctrines to which Dorset was drawn.

Soon after, one of the ambitions dear to the heart of the reformers was enacted – the clergy were instructed to administer communion in both kinds to the laity. Catholic services only administered the bread to the laity, with the wine reserved for the priest. Not everyone was happy with these religious changes. One of the most outspoken critics was Gardiner, who objected strongly to such changes being made before Edward VI reached his majority. Somerset sent William Cecil to try to persuade the bishop to conform to government policy but met with no success. Gardiner preached a very public sermon, condemning the changes. Between 25 September 1547 and 30 June 1548, Gardiner was repeatedly brought before the council, until he was eventually committed to the Tower. With the different religious atmosphere under Somerset, the Marquis of Northampton, whose marriage to Lady Anne Bourchier had been annulled in 1543 by Act of Parliament because of the lady's adultery, requested Somerset to implement a commission of enquiry to decide if he could marry again. He and Elizabeth Brooke were still lovers, and he wanted to marry and have an heir. Despite the favourable report of the commission, Somerset decided against allowing the union, and the couple were supposed to remain separate. Thus did Somerset make another enemy, as if the country did not have conflict enough.

*

Edward VI inherited a kingdom still at war with its northern neighbour and clinging to a fragile peace with France. François had outlived his old sparring partner, Henry VIII, by a mere couple of months. His successor, Henri II, was determined to regain Boulogne, and also to promote the Franco-Scottish alliance. He was an affectionate friend to the Scottish dowager queen, Marie of Guise, and eager for the marriage of Mary, Queen of Scots to his son, the dauphin, rather than to King Edward. Somerset remained determined to force through the marriage of Edward and Mary, and he lost no time in mobilising to continue the Scottish war. Commissioners for musters were ordered to have men and matériel ready for 29 May, with the intention of mounting a full-scale invasion, to be undertaken by Somerset himself, supported by Warwick, now

Lieutenant-General of the North. Ralph Sadleir was appointed Treasurer for the war.

Somerset left London on 22 August, and the main English force crossed the border at Berwick on 1 September. Keeping close to the coast, he captured and destroyed Dunglas, Innerwick and Thornton castles. He burnt the town of Tranent and then encamped at Prestonpans. At some point (the sources differ as to whether it was before or during hostilities), Somerset sent an overture of peace to the Scots – although the purport of it was merely to reiterate the demand for a marriage between Queen Mary and Edward VI, possibly sweetened with an offer to pay compensation for the damage done during the campaign. The offer was rejected. This led to the Battle of Pinkie Cleugh, which was an overwhelming victory for England. The slaughter was terrible – up to 8,000 Scots were killed, and 1,000 prisoners taken. English casualties were far lower, something up to 500 men in total. Following the battle, Warwick laid siege to Edinburgh. With the English ships at Leith, the way seemed open for a complete conquest of Scotland. Somerset, however, retreated; perhaps he was aware that the cost in money and men to hold the country was too great.

On 1 October, the Privy Council instructed Norroy Herald to 'declare to the queen-dowager and council of Scotland the causes that moved his grace the protector to enter their country with an army. That God had shown his power in giving his grace the late victory over those that withstood principally God and this godly purpose.' He was then to press Marie and the Scottish council 'to deliver the young queen to the protector to be suitably nourished and brought up with her husband, as a queen of England—as [the protector] promises to do on his honour, failing which, that he will use all means to bring it about by force'. The Scots refused to be browbeaten, and mounted counter-attacks on English shipping. French aid was requested, and on 19 January 1548 the English council questioned two captured Scotsmen – it was rumoured that seven ships had arrived from France, one carrying the exiled Gerald, Earl of Kildare, Dorset's cousin, who was supposedly planning to marry the Queen of Scots and mount a double-pronged attack on England. Hostilities continued, but the Scots managed to smuggle their queen out of the country to France in July 1548. It was not until England and France made peace in 1549, followed by the Treaty of Norham in June 1551 between England and Scotland, that hostilities finally ceased.

*

Around the new year of 1548, Queen Katherine fell pregnant. Perhaps preoccupied with the joy and trepidation of becoming a mother for the first time at the age of thirty-six, she at first failed to notice the outrageous flirtation (to put it no higher) that her husband was conducting with her fourteen-year-old stepdaughter, Elizabeth. Dressed only in his nightclothes, he would rush into the girl's bedchamber before she was up, and leap on her bed to tickle her. Elizabeth was both outraged and thrilled by his actions, and would burrow into the bedclothes. Feeble remonstrances from her governess, Katherine Astley, made no impression on the admiral, so eventually Astley had no alternative but to complain to the queen. Should any breath of scandal touch her charge, Astley would be blamed, and Elizabeth's prospects permanently damaged. Katherine dealt with the situation by joining in the 'fun', on one occasion holding Elizabeth while the admiral slashed the girl's gown to ribbons. It was not until she came upon her husband embracing Elizabeth that the scales fell from Katherine's eyes, and she realised that her charge was in danger.

Quite what Seymour was thinking is unclear – his wife was healthy, so he could not be contemplating marriage, while to seduce the king's sister would be an outrage so flagrant that the two of them might well end up shorter by a head. It may have been a way of putting the young girl in thrall to him, so that in any future position she held, either in England or abroad, she would value him, and perhaps give him a powerful role. Nowadays, we tend to be more outraged by his advances towards Elizabeth on account of her youth, considering it child abuse, but at that time many girls of fourteen were married – they were not perceived as children. Contemporaries were more shocked by advances to a girl of high rank.

We have no idea what, if anything, Katherine said to her husband, but Elizabeth was told, firmly and clearly, that such conduct was unseemly and could damage her reputation for life. She was sent to the household of Astley's sister and brother-in-law, the Dennys, at Cheshunt, while Katherine herself, accompanied by Jane, retired to the admiral's property at Sudeley in Gloucestershire. Seymour, apparently unabashed by the trouble he had caused, remained in London, but wrote the queen affectionate letters, urging her to take care of her health. She was to keep the 'little man' small, to ease her childbirth. He hoped the child would live to revenge their wrongs – the insults she had suffered at the hands of the arrogant Duchess of Somerset, and his own exclusion from power. On 19 July, Fowler, the king's personal servant, smuggled out a note from King Edward to Seymour, and also informed him that Duchess Anne had just borne a son. He hoped the queen would be as fortunate.

Sadly, Queen Katherine was not so lucky as her sister-in-law. On 30 August, she gave birth to a healthy daughter, named Mary for her elder stepdaughter, but the queen herself died of childbed fever – crying out in her delirium that she had not been well treated by those she loved. Jane was chief mourner at the funeral – the first funeral of an English queen that was at least partly Protestant, conducted in English, with candles only to honour the deceased's memory, and no prayers for the departed soul. The preacher was Miles Coverdale, whose translation of the Bible into English was at the core of the Great Bible, instituted for reading in all English churches by Henry VIII in 1539. Subsequently, he had gone into exile in Strasbourg, returning in March 1548 and joining Queen Katherine's household. While abroad, he had engaged actively in the debate on transubstantiation, coming down firmly on the Reformed position.

Within a few days of the queen's death, the admiral wrote to Dorset and Frances that he would send Jane home as her father was the person who would be most 'tender on her'. The ink was hardly dry on this letter before he had second thoughts, writing on 17 September to Dorset that right after the queen's death he had thought he must break up his household, but that he had since decided he would be able to maintain his house, keeping the queen's ladies of the Privy Chamber, as well as the maids, and the household at large, although they all had the month off. He apologised for perhaps giving the impression in his previous letter that he was trying to rid himself of the burden of Jane, and assured Dorset of his affection for him, and his goodwill towards Jane, whom he proposed should remain in his care. Lady Seymour would preside over the household, and would love Jane as her own daughter, while he himself would be 'half a father' to her, and all in his house would 'be as diligent about her' as Dorset could wish.

Dorset responded to this letter with thanks, acknowledging the admiral's affection. Nevertheless, considering the state of his daughter, and her 'tender years ... wherein she shall hardly rule herself as yet without a guide, lest she should for lack of a bridle take too much the head and conceive such opinion of herself that all such good behaviour as she heretofore has learned by the queen's and your most wholesome instructions should altogether be quenched in her or at the least much minished', it would be better for her to be in her mother's care. While the admiral's 'good mind' towards her education could not be bettered by Dorset, she needed one who could 'correct her as a mistress, and monish her as a mother'. He hoped Seymour would agree, and was at pains to point out that he was not going back on their agreement for Seymour to have control of Jane's marriage; it was just that, in her young years, Dorset needed to address Jane's mind to 'humility, sobriety and obedience'. Frances, too, wrote a flowery epistle to Seymour from Bradgate on 19 September:

> Although good brother, I might be well encouraged to minister such counsel unto you as I have in store, for that it has pleased you not only so to take in worth that I writ in my Lady of Suffolk's letter, but also to require me to have in readiness such good advice as I shall think convenient against our next meeting, yet considering how unable I am to do that hereto belongeth, I had rather leave with that praise I had gotten at your hand than by seeking more, to lose that I had already won.[9]

She finally went to the heart of the matter, offering her hope that he would be happy to give Jane back into her care and promising she would take his advice in all things, particularly in the matter of Jane's marriage. The admiral, faced with the demands of both parents, had little choice but to send Jane back to Bradgate. But he did not give up. He wrote to

Jane personally (a letter that is known only from her reply), to which Jane responded on 1 October. Her letter, probably supervised by Frances, says absolutely nothing in a dozen lines – a perfect example of polite and meaningless letter-writing by sixteenth-centuries ladies:

> Thinking myself so much bound to your lordship, for your great goodness towards me from time to time, that I cannot by any means be able to recompense the least part thereof, I purposed to write a few rude lines to your Lordship, rather as a token to show how much worthier I think your Lordship's goodness than to give worthy thanks for the same, and these my letters shall be to testify unto you, that like as you have always become towards me a loving and kind father, so I shall always be most ready to obey your godly monitions and good instructions as becometh one upon whom you have heaped so many benefits…[10]

At the same time as he addressed Jane, Seymour must have written to her parents, suggesting he come to Bradgate to discuss Jane's place of abode. Frances responded with the hope that, by discussing the matter, they could conclude an arrangement by which '[he] shall be satisfied and [she] contented'.[11] Within days, Seymour and his associate Sir William Sharington arrived at Bradgate. Sharington was master of the mint at Bristol and had used his office to indulge in a spot of counterfeiting, to the benefit of the admiral and himself, although his nefarious activities were as yet undetected. They used the classic tactic of divide and conquer – Sharington worked on Frances while Seymour took Dorset, the more easily persuadable. Eventually, the couple were worn down. The admiral was 'so earnest with [Dorset] in persuasion', and Sharington similarly with Frances, both using the temptation of a marriage with the king once the admiral had him 'at liberty' from Somerset's overzealous protection.

Frances having given in, Dorset 'could not but consent'.[12] Dorset later admitted that he had been so 'seduced and inveigled' by the admiral that he had sworn that, excepting his duty to the king, he would spend his life and blood on the admiral's part against all men. His devotion to the admiral was probably enhanced by production of £500 of the £2,000 originally promised, to be made without any kind of IOU or 'gage', other than the person of Jane. Dorset thus took Jane back to London, stopping en route to receive a gift of wine from the borough of Leicester. Jane took up residence at Seymour Place, under the elderly eye of Lady Seymour, who, fifty years before, as Margaret Wentworth, had been feted as a beauty of Henry VII's court.

Perhaps his grief at the loss of his wife overcame such sense as Seymour had. He became completely uncontrollable in his attempts to wrest power from his brother, and plotted to marry Elizabeth. Dorset, too, however intelligent and learned he might have been in an academic way, had no grasp of the realities of politics. While some members of the council might be murmuring against Somerset's arrogance, there was no possibility that Seymour was ever going to attain power. Even the admiral's servants were concerned at the course events were taking. Not long after Queen Katherine's death, one of them, William Wyghtman, had a conversation with Sir Nicholas Throckmorton in which they commiserated Seymour's great loss but agreed that it would, in the end, benefit him, by turning him from thoughts of 'worldly goods' to standing in 'fear and awe of God'. Throckmorton hoped that Seymour's loss would also make him more 'humble in heart and stomach' towards Somerset. A reconciliation might now be easier, as the queen's passing meant the argument between her and the duchess over precedence and the royal jewels must necessarily be over.

Further, Throckmorton hoped that Seymour would mend his ways, for people were already talking of his 'slothfulness to serve' and 'greediness to get'. Sharington expressed sorrow that his master was so spoken of and hoped his misfortunes would reform him. Throckmorton advised Sharington to urge the admiral to drop any 'perilous' plans he might be hatching, to marry one of the king's sisters. Sharington assured his friend that he would indeed counsel against a course that could only end in destruction. If Seymour were so foolish as to make such a match without the council's consent, that would be treason; if he did it with consent, he should never be allowed within 10 miles of the king. Sharington later swore that he continually aimed to control Seymour's self-destructive behaviour with regard to various legal disputes, but it was in vain; once Seymour had an idea in his head, said Sharington, 'neither lawyer nor other could turn him'.

With Seymour and Jane settled at Seymour Place, Dorset was a frequent visitor, spending convivial evenings there along with his second cousin Francis, Earl of Huntingdon, and Sharington. The quarrel between the Greys and the Hastings seems to have subsided by this time, perhaps because these two representatives of the families now saw eye to eye on religious matters. In December 1548, the admiral became convinced that Parliament was planning some new legislation that would harm him. 'If I be thus used, they speak of a black parliament. By God's Precious Soul, I will make it the blackest parliament that ever was in England,' he shouted to his deputy, Lord Clinton. Clinton replied, 'If you speak such words, you will lose my Lord (Somerset) and undo yourself.' The admiral, enraged, responded, 'I would you should know, by God's Precious Soul, I may better live without him, than he without me.' He then added, 'Whosoever shall go about to speak evil of the queen, I will take my fist from the first ears to the lowest.' Dorset intervened to keep the peace: 'My lord, these words need not; for I think there is no nobleman that would speak evil of her for he should then speak evil of the king that dead is; wherefore you have no cause to doubt therein, and I trust all shall be well, and you friends again.'

Seymour continued to be argumentative and irrational. He told Dorset that he would refuse to pay the newly granted subsidy of 2*d* per sheep. Dorset asked why Seymour objected, considering it was less harm than a subsidy on land. But Seymour stubbornly affirmed he would not pay it. He continued to attack Somerset's office, claiming there was no need for any protector because the king, being 'wise and well-learned', ought to rule himself, perhaps with Somerset as head of the council. Although the admiral knew he could not make the change he wished immediately, he swore he would bring it about within three years. Seymour began to talk even more wildly, hinting at rebellion – Dorset was not to worry too much about the gentlemen of the counties, who 'had somewhat to lose', but to be on good terms with the franklins (loosely, yeomen farmers with the franchise), who were able to command the commons. He wanted Dorset to move to Warwickshire, to build up his networks there, as a bulwark against the Earl of Warwick, who was still working closely with Somerset. Dorset objected that his house in Warwickshire (Astley) was almost a ruin, which he could not afford to repair. Seymour offered to send a man there at Christmas to make a plan for repairs, for he thought that Dorset must have plenty of stone, brick and timber. Dorset agreed he had, but suggested that he was perfectly well placed at Bradgate, which was only 15 miles from Warwick. Despite agreeing this to be a negligible distance, Seymour was still insistent on Dorset moving, proving Sharington's point about him sticking to his own notions, regardless of rational argument.[13]

Seymour's violent words and angry temper undid him. His final act of insanity was to break into the king's apartments in an attempt to take control of the king. Disturbed, he panicked and shot one of the king's dogs. On 8 January 1549, Sharington's house was raided by order of the council, and evidence of his counterfeiting activities discovered. But that was not the purpose of the raid – an attack on Seymour was the motivation. Sharington quickly sang like the proverbial canary. Next to be hauled in was the young Earl of Rutland, who admitted that Seymour had talked to him about building relationships with yeomen.

Seymour, warned of Rutland's interrogation, put a brave face on matters. He attended Parliament on 17 January 1549, and then he, Dorset and Lord Thomas Grey dined at Huntingdon's house. Seymour continued to bluster that he would refuse to obey any summons from the council, but Lord Thomas advised him to throw himself on his brother's mercy. Later that night, Seymour was arrested and taken to the Tower. Within days, his friends and associates were being questioned – including Dorset and the Lady Elizabeth. Dorset was interviewed by Somerset himself, and agreed that Jane, rather than being put forward for a match with the king, would instead marry Somerset's son. He did not want to put the agreement in writing, but would confirm it verbally, if necessary. In March 1549, Seymour's death warrant was signed by his brother and he was executed. This act, although it seemed necessary to Somerset at the time, was looked upon with horror and surprise. Even the hardened men of the Tudor court were uncomfortable with fratricide. The French ambassador's view was that the Earl of Warwick had encouraged Somerset to take drastic measures, and another observer believed that if Warwick hadn't created the quarrel between the brothers, he had certainly fomented it.

17

Religion and Rebellion

Serfs you are, and serfs you shall remain...
King Richard II

During the summer of 1548, as Jane walked and talked and studied with Katherine Parr, the country underwent a religious revolution. The Chantries Act of 1547, which came into force in 1548, went further than the Act of 1545. It disbanded the religious guilds that had been such an important feature of mediaeval life, that mixture of civic duty and religious devotion that had built the churches and cathedrals, and instituted a whole system based on belief in the doctrine of purgatory. Now, prayers for the dead were outlawed as pointless and irreligious, use of the rosary was forbidden, and statues of the saints, long-venerated holy relics and even stained-glass windows were torn down and destroyed. Since the Dorsets and Katherine Parr had long eschewed such practices, Jane would not have personally been affected, but she would have been delighted that the poor, benighted souls of the general population were now prepared to be saved. Jean Calvin, the leading continental Reformer, was unimpressed by Somerset's efforts. He wrote to him in October 1548, urging him to new reforms. Somerset was eager to reconcile with the traditionalists as much as was possible without compromising his beliefs, so slow and steady change remained his plan.

In November 1548, the Act of Uniformity introduced the new Book of Common Prayer, which was to be the only legal service from the following Pentecost. Largely written by Archbishop Cranmer, the Prayer Book was still Catholic in its theology, based on the traditional Sarum rite of the English Church. Much of the ceremonial of the Catholic Church was retained, including the wearing of vestments. Nevertheless, the Book of Common Prayer was ground-breaking in that it was in English, rather than Latin, and undermined, without explicitly denying, the doctrine of transubstantiation. For the more radical clergy, the 1549 Book did not go nearly far enough. Bishop Hooper of Gloucester claimed that it was 'very defective ... in some respects manifestly impious'. This was a view shared by the European Reformers in England – Martin Bucer and Peter Martyr, who were Professors of Divinity in Cambridge and Oxford, and John Laski, who was Superintendent of the Stranger (foreign) Churches in London. It was probably a view that Dorset espoused. But for the more conservatively minded (the majority of the population outside London and East Anglia, where Protestantism flourished), it was unacceptable.

In Cornwall, where many people did not speak English, the imposition of the Book of Common Prayer was deeply resented. They rose up, determined to protect their faith, bearing the banner of the Five Wounds of Christ from the Pilgrimage of Grace. The rebels advanced into Devon, and joined up with a separate group, inspired by the resistance of the parish of Sampford Courtenay to the new Prayer Book. The local gentry were divided, with many sympathising with the rebels' desire to adhere to the old ways while others, like Sir Peter Carew, wanted to come down harshly on the insurgents. Somerset sent a small force under Lord Russell to contain the rebellion. The insurgents, not thinking strategically, made no attempt to bypass the small government force and march for London, but remained in the west, where Exeter was besieged. Over the following weeks, Russell did what he could with minimal forces, eventually relieving Exeter. The rebellion culminated at a confrontation in Okehampton in mid-August, where up to 4,000 of the rebels were killed.

Murmuring against religious changes was enhanced by 'a dearth of provisions' across the country, which the council sought to investigate in December 1548. Among other measures, a bill was drafted to prevent enclosing, a process by which open, arable fields, strip-farmed, dotted with farmsteads and owned by the manor, with the tenants having ancient rights and duties, became enclosed pasture land or a single arable expanse, considered as being in the sole possession of the lord of the manor. Enclosing had begun when the Black Death of 1348–49 and the ensuing waves of plague reduced the population of the British Isles by more than a third. The consequent scarcity of labour obliged landowners to find new ways to make economic use of land. The answer was sheep-farming. The land that had taken twenty men to plough, sow and reap could run a flock that needed only a shepherd and a dog to tend. It soon became apparent that sheep-farming was vastly more profitable than subsistence agriculture had been, and the economy of those areas where wool could be produced, and the sea ports whence it could be exported to the weavers of the Low Countries, boomed.

When the population began to grow again towards the end of the fifteenth century, conflict arose between the need for food and employment for the poorer members of society (not everyone had access to the skilled trades involved in the cloth industry) and the opportunities for profit from sheep-farming. Enclosure continued, earning widespread condemnation as those who had previously occupied and worked the land lost their employment and, if their cottages were pulled down, were also evicted. The Crown's objection to enclosure (although it was heavily dependent on the taxes and duties from the wool industry that formed the majority of peacetime Crown income) was a mixture of genuine concern about unemployment and the resulting 'vagrancy', which terrified an establishment that saw stability of people within their home villages as fundamental to good order, and the risk of becoming dependent on foreign food imports – starving men are dangerous. A welter of parliamentary acts and royal proclamations had attempted to limit enclosure, but were ignored, suggesting that the economic benefits of sheep-farming outweighed any fear of real punishment. The Greys had undertaken their share of enclosing – at Astley, 30 acres of demesne land around the castle had been enclosed in the early years of the century, then a 'great park' was formed, enclosing 18 acres at Astley, and another 90 acres at the neighbouring manor of Arley.

In 1548, Somerset instituted a further commission to identify illegal enclosures, although he quickly granted pardons to guilty landowners. Simultaneously, disaffected countrymen who had uprooted the hedges in anticipation of the commission findings were first condemned, then forgiven. Warwick was particularly disgruntled when one of his parks was ploughed up and planted by angry commons. By 1549, rampant inflation and a growing population brought anger against enclosure to a head. Somerset wrote to Dorset and Huntingdon on 11 June, instructing them to issue proclamations against the assembling of 'lewd persons' to throw down the enclosures, and to keep themselves in readiness to suppress any rebellion. Dorset had already experienced the tearing down of fences at Bradgate, and the situation deteriorated over the summer. In August, Dorset's request for the council to send his brother Lord Thomas to help maintain order was refused. Dorset was thanked for the quietness of Leicestershire and Rutland, but Thomas could not be spared. He had been sent to Newhaven (Ambleteuse) with 200 men as reinforcements for another Grey brother, Lord John, who had been appointed as Deputy Lieutenant of this outpost of English occupation in France. Henri II, aware of the difficulties of the English government at that juncture, had taken the opportunity to attack the Calais Pale.

Dorset's fears of further disturbances were instigated by the rebellion that was emerging in East Anglia, under Robert Kett, at the same time as the Prayer Book Rebellion. The two insurgencies were very different. The East Anglian men had no objections at all to the Prayer Book – in fact, among them were far more radical thinkers who even, to the horror of the authorities, believed in the early Christian ideal of holding all goods in common. Their complaints were economic and they were, initially at least, far more conciliatory in tone than the Cornish rebels.[1] The Marquis of Northampton was sent to suppress them, but the rebels were too strong: they had encamped on Mousehold Heath, and taken control of the city of Norwich. The marquis retired in ignominious defeat. On 7 August, after much discussion in council, Warwick was appointed as Lieutenant General against Kett and his rebels. He marched on Norwich with perhaps as many as 5,000 troops. Pardons were offered to all except Kett, but before negotiations could be completed, one of the rebels, described as a 'boy', pulled down his breeches and insulted the king's herald. Warwick's men responded by shooting him. Kett offered to meet Warwick to negotiate, but was prevented from doing so by his men. Warwick immediately attacked the city and captured it, hanging forty-nine of the rebels out of hand. The rebels withdrew from Mousehold Heath to Dussindale, where they were attacked by Warwick's army. Kett and the other leaders fled, but between 2,000 and 3,500 of the rebels were killed. Kett was captured and brought to London, where he was condemned, before being returned to Norfolk to be hanged from the walls of Norwich Castle.

*

Somerset's poor handling of these crises lost him the confidence of his colleagues – most dangerously, it lost him Warwick's faith. It was rumoured that a disaffected group consisting of Warwick, the religiously conservative earls of Southampton and Arundel, and Lord St John, would send to the Lady Mary, to test her appetite for becoming involved in a plot to unseat the Lord Protector. The princess prepared herself to decline involvement – she had no desire to be involved in the schemes of men she deemed a pack of disloyal upstarts – but, in the event, no approach was made. Warwick's resentment was exacerbated when Somerset refused to grant lands or offices to Warwick's nominees and failed to pay the wages of the men who had marched against Kett. While the protector was absent from London on a visit to Hampshire, the council took the opportunity to plot against him. Warwick gathered several hundred troops at Ely Place, his residence in Holborn, where he was joined by the earls of Shrewsbury and Derby and Lord Rich, as well as Southampton and Arundel.

By 4 October, the Lord Protector was aware of the attempts to undermine him and raced back to Hampton Court to secure the person of the king. He announced that Warwick and the other lords were attempting to overthrow him to install the Lady Mary as regent, and hinted that Edward's own life was in danger. Without the backing of the City of London, it would be hard for Warwick and the other lords to depose Somerset, so the mayor and aldermen were invited to Ely Place. They were lukewarm about involving themselves in a spat between noblemen, especially as Somerset had the support of many, particularly the lower classes, who thought of him as 'the good duke'. They had welcomed his efforts, futile though they were, in the matter of enclosures, and his apparent concern for grievances of the poor – seemingly untroubled by the duke's own extravagant lifestyle, particularly the construction of the enormous palace of Somerset House. The Londoners agreed that they would defend the king, if necessary, but would not attack Somerset.

Despite sending his man, Edward Wolfe, racing to London, Somerset was unable to secure the Tower of London, and, with Hampton Court indefensible, retreated to Windsor Castle, still holding the king. The armies which had been gathered to suppress the Prayer Book Rebellion under the command of Lord Russell and Sir William Herbert had not yet been paid off, and for a short while there seemed to be a risk of civil war, but Russell and Herbert urged the necessity of surrender on Somerset. The protector gave in. He made an official submission to the king, who wrote to Warwick and the others, requiring them to make a 'friendly determination' with his uncle, pointing out that no one was blameless and suggesting that if they treated Somerset's errors with rigour then the same sternness might be visited on them. Cranmer and Paget, too, pleaded for Somerset's life. The duke wrote to Warwick, once his dear friend,

> ... I cannot persuade myself that there is any ill conceived in your heart ... against me; for that ... seemeth impossible that where there hath been from your youth and mine so great a friendship and amity betwixt us ... now so suddenly there should be hatred ... I never meant worse to you than to myself...[2]

Nevertheless, when the king was brought back to London, Somerset came under armed guard, before being stripped of the office of Protector and sent to the Tower.

With Somerset out of the picture, there was the usual struggle for control. At first it seemed that the conservative Southampton might rise to the highest place, and traditional Catholic observances suddenly became fashionable again. But Warwick had managed to manoeuvre four of his closest allies, including his brother Sir Andrew Dudley, into positions as Gentlemen of the Privy Chamber, close to the king every day. He thus came to understand Edward's thinking, and particularly his desire for religious reform to continue. Despite being only twelve years old, Edward was showing signs of a deep intellectual and emotional commitment to Protestantism, which accorded with Warwick's own political views – although the king's faith was stronger than that of his minister.

Nevertheless, Southampton continued to be courted. He assured the Imperial ambassador that the Lady Mary, who at the personal suit of the emperor had been permitted to continue hearing Mass in the old form, rather than adopting the Book of Common Prayer, would be allowed to maintain her traditional worship. Feelers were put out to Mary to make a bid for the regency, which she rejected – probably as much from conviction that the whole plan would go horribly wrong as from any desire to eschew the office, as it would have been an opportunity for her to halt the Protestant march. Meanwhile, Warwick managed to block the appointment of another conservative to the council, and engineered the appointment of a Protestant bishop, Thomas Goodrich, while Dorset finally gained a seat. Always looking for someone to follow, Dorset now hitched himself firmly to Warwick's wagon. The appointment of Goodrich and Dorset led one commentator to note that 'all honest hearts [were] in good comfort for the good hope that they have of the perseverance of God's Word'.[3] The opposite view was taken by the Imperial ambassador:

No mention has as yet been made of restoring religion, and those who desired to see this step taken have been displeased to see that the Marquis of Dorset and the Bishop of Ely both of them entirely won over to the new sect, have recently been admitted to the Council, which may well have been done by the Earl of Warwick in order to strengthen his party.[4]

Southampton hurried to mount a counter-offensive. Together with Lord St John and Arundel, he visited Somerset in the Tower to conduct his examination on treason charges. Somerset insisted that he had done nothing without Warwick's advice. Southampton, seeing his moment to be rid of both of his rivals, confided to Arundel that 'I thought ever we should find them traitors both [Somerset and Warwick] and both are worthy to die'. The day Somerset was condemned, he continued, Warwick would be sent to the Tower. Unfortunately for Southampton, his words were reported to Warwick by St John.

The next day's council meeting was held at Ely Place, as Warwick claimed to be too ill to leave his bed. When Southampton mooted that Somerset be condemned for treason, Warwick leapt from beneath the covers, and, brandishing his sword, accused Southampton of seeking the death of Somerset and himself. Southampton was placed under house arrest, dying from natural causes in June 1550, while Arundel was dismissed from his office of Lord Chamberlain, and, in a rather bizarre episode, accused of stealing locks and bolts from royal residences, for which he received the swingeing fine of £12,000. Given that Dorset's relationship with his brother-in-law had always been uneasy, it is unlikely that he made any objection. Sir Thomas Arundell, who had worked with Somerset despite being a religious conservative, was also sent to the Tower. By the end of 1549, Warwick was the most influential man on the council and the pace of religious reform stepped up. A proclamation on Christmas Day confirmed the requirement to use the Book of Common Prayer and impounded Catholic books of worship. Warwick's supporters on the council were rewarded with new titles – Russell became Earl of Bedford, and Lord St John became Marquis of Winchester. Another reformist councillor was appointed – Lord Ferrers, widower of Lady Mary Grey, and now Viscount Hereford. Northampton, by way of reward, was permitted to marry Elizabeth Brooke.

In the fighting at Mousehold Heath, Dorset's brother-in-law Sir Henry Willoughby had been killed, leaving three orphaned children – Dorset's sister Lady Anne had died the previous year. The eldest son, Thomas, came to Bradgate as Dorset's ward, while the younger siblings, Margaret (who was later to marry the son of Sir Thomas Arundell) and Francis, although under the guardianship of Dorset's half-brother George Medley, spent a good deal of time with the Grey sisters. As well as gentry cousins, the Greys had far more impressive relatives, and in November 1549 Frances took her children to Beaulieu in Essex for a visit to Lady Mary. The two had been friends all their lives, but now, the hardening of religious lines was driving a wedge between them. Nevertheless, Lady Mary showered gifts upon the three girls.

According to Foxe, during this visit the precocious twelve-year-old Jane asked why Mary's lady-in-waiting had curtseyed in the chapel despite the princess not being present, and was told that the lady had curtseyed to the consecrated Host – her 'maker'. Jane replied, 'How can He be there that made us, when the baker made Him?' Men and women had been burned for less in Henry VIII's reign, but if the story is true, and Mary heard of it, she made no change in her treatment of her young cousin. After leaving Mary, the family went on to spend Christmas at Tilty with George Medley and his wife, Mary Danett. In another example of the way the lives of the nobility were interwoven, Mary Danett had been one of Princess Mary's household in Wales in the 1520s, along with Mary Browne, now the wife of Lord John Grey, who was shortly to arrive for Christmas with her husband, children, brother-in-law Lord Thomas and twenty-one servants.

Jane's attitude towards her cousin's continued adherence to the old faith was indicative of the radical religion now espoused by the English government. On 14 January 1550, the Imperial ambassador wrote home of his concerns that Mary would be forced to accept the Prayer Book unless the emperor intervened again:

> for Warwick is proving himself not merely unstable, but evil and cruel too. The Marquis of Northampton, who has two wives, and the Marquis of Dorset, a senseless creature, belong to his crew; and they are all of them Sacramentarians, as they publicly declared in Parliament quite lately ... The Lady Elizabeth is more of their kidney.[5]

The reformers, of course, saw Dorset very differently. Hooper, Bishop of Gloucester, who had spent much of the 1540s in exile in Zurich with Heinrich Bullinger, suggested that for Bullinger to dedicate one of his works to Dorset would be a worthwhile action, for Dorset was 'pious, good and brave and distinguished in the cause of Christ. You will not a little advance the glory of God by giving encouragement to him and others by your writings.'[6] Similarly, John of Ulm, another follower of Bullinger, thought Dorset and Warwick were 'the shining lights ... of the church of England: for they alone have exerted, far more than the rest, all their power and influence in the restoration of the church'. He was particularly struck by their magnanimity in restoring the king's uncle 'from being in the utmost danger of his life, out of darkness into light and life'.[7] John of Ulm was studying at Oxford, and Dorset had granted him a pension – he was perhaps an unworldly man, and saw Dorset and Warwick's action as entirely motivated by their faith. So far as Dorset was concerned, that was probably true, but Warwick's outlook was distinctly more devious.

With no recent precedent for a man who was not a member of the royal family acting as regent, Warwick needed to make use of established offices to consolidate his power, rather than taking the title of protector or regent. He was Lord President of the Council, holding the authority to dismiss and appoint councillors, and Lord Great Master of the King's Household, controlling Edward's servants and all those who came into contact with him. In particular, the king's security and education were carefully monitored. No opinions contrary to those espoused by Warwick were introduced to Edward. As well as the rigorous Protestant education that he was receiving, Edward was encouraged by Warwick to practise the martial arts of kingship – riding, hunting and training in the use of weapons – and the more relaxed pastimes popular at the Tudor court, such as bear- and bull-baiting. Dorset's seat on the council led to a clutch of honours and offices being granted to him: Steward of the King's Honours and Constable of Leicester Castle, lands in Leicestershire, Warwickshire, Rutland, Nottinghamshire, and the Duchy of Lancaster. He commanded 100 horse in Warwick's new guard, for which he received £2,000 per annum. At last, the recognition that had eluded him under Henry VIII had been granted. To facilitate his presence at council, the family resided mainly in London, at Dorset House near the Temple, or at the old Sheen Priory.

Confident that the council was now packed with his own men, Warwick could afford a reconciliation with Somerset, who was restored to a place on the council by the end of April – perhaps to lend his authority as the king's uncle to the new state of affairs, or perhaps Warwick was genuinely willing to build bridges with his old friend, provided he remained in charge himself. Peace with France and Scotland was agreed in April 1550. The price was the restoration of Boulogne, for which the only recompense was the slight prospect of a marriage between Edward and Elisabeth, daughter of Henri II, now that Mary, Queen of Scots was irrevocably promised to the dauphin. The following month, Dorset, along with Northampton, Paget and the Lord Privy Seal, went by barge to collect the French ambassadors and bring them to court for the signing of the treaty by the king.

Despite the cessation of war, and the religious divisions on the council having been more or less healed with the purging of the conservatives, the country remained volatile. The economy was in dire straits, with inflation rampant and poverty rife everywhere, exacerbated by the return of soldiers from France, and it was feared during the summer of 1550 that there might be a repeat of the previous year's rebellions. While Warwick and Somerset were now on sufficiently good terms for them to arrange a marriage between Somerset's daughter Anne and Warwick's eldest son, John, Warwick scented trouble when Somerset tried to effect a rehabilitation of Gardiner, still in the Tower. Somerset persuaded the bishop to accept the Prayer Book, but Warwick wanted an abject confession of guilt, which Gardiner would not give, angering the king as well. The bishop remained in the Tower. In 1550, various parliamentary acts swept away what was left of the traditional rites and rituals, and Protestant bishops were appointed. Some of the peers were restive at this rate of change – the earls of Shrewsbury and Derby, like Gardiner, wanted Henry VIII's religious settlement strictly observed until Edward came of age.

In the late summer of 1550, Edward fell gravely ill, but even this threat to their position did not prevent Warwick and Somerset from clashing again. The king recovered and the two men calmed down, but matters between the two rivals were permanently soured. King and council now had to contend with the problem of the Lady Mary's refusal to accept the religious reformations. She was adamant not only that she had been promised personal exemption by Somerset, but also that no changes in religion were legal during the Edward's minority. It was widely known, however, that her objections were religious rather than political. She attended court that Christmas, and she and Edward argued on the matter until both dissolved in tears. But Edward was determined that his sister should obey his laws – apart from anything else, tolerating her defiance would set a bad example to other subjects. The council, bolstered by Edward's stance, refused to countenance further disobedience. Warwick informed the Imperial ambassador that the exemption from the law given to Mary previously was now superseded by Edward's growing maturity.

Mary remained intransigent. She made a bold display of wealth, power and determination, riding to London, accompanied by her household and retainers, all ostentatiously brandishing the forbidden rosaries. She came before the council, in the presence of Edward and Warwick as lord president. A vigorous exchange of views followed, in which Mary pointed out the council's infractions of Henry VIII's will, and Warwick countered that she sought to show the council in a bad light to the king. The meeting ended in stalemate, but soon after, Mary won a victory of sorts when the emperor threatened to back up with warships his requests for her to be allowed the Mass. The council, quite unable to risk either civil or international war, folded. Unfortunately, Edward had taken on all of the praises of him as a young king in the biblical mould, the saviour of his people, and refused to accept their advice. More shuffling with the emperor took place, and some of Mary's chaplains were imprisoned for holding Mass without her being present. Mary herself contemplated escaping to Imperial territory, but changed her mind at the last minute.

Unable to coerce Mary, the council concentrated on disobedient members of the lower orders. Tempers ran high on both sides of the debate – many resisted the changes, while others, eager for the country to embrace the new faith, were willing to accuse their neighbours. The Imperial ambassador reported in February that

> several peasants [were] brought into court at Greenwich before two or three of the bishops that ordinarily preach in London. Some of the peasants were accused of having disobeyed the king's ordinances on religion, whilst the others were their accusers. One after the other, they were all examined by the council, and the accused were roughly handled and had such loud and violent words addressed to them as to be heard by all those who were near the chamber. Afterwards they were conducted to prison by the king's guard, and the accusers were heartily

received and given drink from the king's cellar before everybody. And among the councillors who shouted loudest, the voices of my Lord of Warwick and the two marquises (Dorset and Northampton) were recognised.'[8]

The Imperial ambassador was, of course, biased against the new religious laws, but there is no reason to doubt his representation of Dorset as one of those most eager to implement them. Dorset was present in March when a servant of the deposed Bishop Bonner of London was examined over an allegation that he had smuggled in a barrel of 'most false and detestable books from Paris'.[9]

Dorset now had the opportunity to show himself not just as a warrior for the faith, but a warrior for the king. He was appointed as Lord Warden of the Marches and sent north to carry out the same military duties as his father had had in 1523, with three local wardens under him, as well as a small force of horsemen and his favourite preachers. However, it does not appear that Dorset was terribly keen on his new role. He was commissioned in February, but by 9 April had advanced no further than Bradgate. He was still there ten days later, writing to Somerset's brother-in-law, Sir Michael Stanhope, requesting the latter to extend various leases of George Medley's at the monastery of Lenton. Stanhope no doubt proved eager to comply with this request from the newly influential marquis.[10]

A month later, Dorset was finally at Berwick, but wrote to Cecil (once an acolyte of Somerset's, but now glued to Warwick), that he had written to the council for the backpay of the garrison, to assuage their 'lamentable complaints'. He longed to hear from Cecil 'as they that are in hell would gladly hear how they do that be in heaven'.[11] Clearly Dorset was an office man, not a soldier. The king noted in his journal that Dorset, 'grieved much with the disorder of the marches towards Scotland, surrendered the wardenship thereof to bestow where I chose'.[12]

One cheerful note during Dorset's exile from the heaven of the court was the arrival of John of Ulm with a copy of the new instalment of Heinrich Bullinger's *Decades*, dedicated to Dorset. He received the work with enthusiastic thanks and praise, echoed by the Bishop of Norwich, whom John describes as 'on the most intimate terms with our marquis'. This is odd, as the Bishop of Norwich in May 1551 was Thomas Thirlby, who had voted in Parliament against the Act of Uniformity, and, although he conformed to the law, was later elevated under Mary, and rejected the Oath of Supremacy under Elizabeth – hardly the marks of a man of the same 'kidney' as Dorset. Returning south, John of Ulm stopped at Bradgate to visit Frances and Jane. He passed the time agreeably with 'those excellent and holy persons, Haddon and Aylmer', then wrote to Bullinger in paroxysms of delight about both father and daughter – he was the 'thunderbolt and lightening of the papists' and she was 'pious and accomplished beyond what can be expressed'.[13]

A passage from Roger Ascham's book *The Schoolmaster* has given rise to the belief that Dorset and Frances were abusive parents, certainly in relation to Jane. Ascham reported (years later) that Jane complained, in effect, that nothing she could do pleased her parents, who punished her with nips and pinches. A biographer of the sisters, Leanda de Lisle, puts this plaint into context, citing more contemporary accounts that suggest that Jane was no more harshly treated than any of her contemporaries, and also pointing out that Jane was a teenager – an age recognised even in the Tudor period as one when rebellion against parental authority was normal, although they believed it had to be firmly nipped in the bud, as indicated in Dorset's letters to Seymour in 1548, quoted in Chapter 15. There are no records of how Jane's younger sisters felt about the strict regime of study, but they were not destined for greatness like Jane (whom Dorset still fondly believed might one day marry Edward VI) and were not required to be the paragon of learning that their older sister was. Whether this is a reflection of the differing intellectual capacities or tastes between the girls or just the high ambitions set for Jane cannot be known. Certainly, Jane was exceptionally intellectually gifted in an age that valued detailed knowledge of texts and formal logic, rather than critical thinking. Had Jane been brought up in the old faith, rather than the new, it seems likely she would have been equally passionate about it – it seems to have been her nature to be wholehearted and embrace a cause.

While at Bradgate, John heard that Jane was still the intended bride of the king. Given that the peace with France had included the marriage of Edward to Elisabeth of Valois, this was an unlikely dream on the part of Dorset and Frances. In an effort to bring some meaning to the Anglo-French peace treaty, the Garter was bestowed on Henri II and the Marquis of Northampton led the embassy to France for the formal ceremony of investiture at Chateaubriand on 20 June 1551. A final request for the hand of the Queen of Scots was refused, but the marriage with Princess Elisabeth was agreed and celebrated with a midnight picnic and deer hunt. One of the upsides of the agreement with France was the isolation of Lady Mary. With England and France in alliance, the emperor would be far less likely to interfere on behalf of his cousin, so Warwick took the opportunity to pass a resolution in council to prohibit the celebration of Mass in Mary's household. He brought the Catholics Arundel and Derby to the meeting, although they were not generally allowed anywhere near the government, to make them complicit in the decision, their only other option being open rebellion. The emperor's continued threats were met by Warwick's statement that Edward, now old enough to take part in business, was adamant. Somerset, continuing to argue for Mary to hear the Mass, was confronted by an outburst: 'The Mass is either of God or of the Devil. If it is of God, then it is but right that all our people should be allowed to go to it; but if it is not out of God ... why then should not [it] be proscribed to all?'

This last was too much for Somerset, who began discussing with Arundel the possibilities for removing Warwick. Sir Thomas Palmer, changing his allegiance to Warwick, claimed that Somerset was planning to have Warwick and Northampton assassinated. Warwick bided his time before striking, gathering more support through another round of title and honours. Shortly before, in July 1551, family tragedy had struck Frances – her two half-brothers, Henry, Duke of Suffolk and Lord Charles Brandon, died within hours of each other during an epidemic of sweating sickness. While their mother was distraught, and presumably the whole family mourned the passing of two promising boys who were only in their mid-teens, their loss was now Dorset's gain. On 11 October 1551, in a ceremony at Hampton Court, the dukedom of Suffolk was recreated for Dorset. In the same ceremony, Warwick was elevated to the dukedom of Northumberland. William Herbert, brother-in-law of the late Queen Katherine Parr, and another evangelical, became Earl of Pembroke, and William Cecil was knighted. A few days later, the former protector was arrested, and the new Duke of Suffolk signed the warrant for his removal to the Tower – probably the most important document he had ever signed. It seems more likely that he felt the thrill of power than any compunction about sending a man who had once been his friend to prison, and probably execution. Perhaps he saw it as revenge for the death of Seymour. With Norfolk and Somerset both in the Tower, the two new dukes were at the top of the noble tree.

During 1550–51, Marie of Guise had been in France, visiting her daughter, the Queen of Scots. Now, Henri II requested a safe-conduct for Marie to travel home through England should her convoy need to take refuge in any English ports. In October, this proved necessary when Marie's flotilla of ten vessels ran from storms into Portsmouth. The Captain of Portsmouth, Sir Richard Wingfield, gave her the option of re-embarking for Scotland or travelling through England. Having had enough of an autumn sea journey, Marie elected to travel overland. The local nobles went to pay their respects, and orders were sent from the council to the grandees of the counties between Portsmouth and London to give her appropriate hospitality.

It took Marie several days to reach London. A mile or so from Hampton Court, she was met by Northampton and Elizabeth Brooke, officially accepted as his wife, although the act confirming the marriage was not passed until March of the following year. Marie stayed at Hampton Court, spending the evening 'in dancing and pastime', then travelled to London by barge to stay at the Bishop of London's palace, Baynard's Castle. The mayor sent presents of veal, mutton, swine, beer, wine coals and even a sturgeon to make her stay more pleasant. On 5 November, Suffolk was the chief of the lords sent to wait upon her, accompanied by the new Earl of Warwick (Northumberland's son), Huntingdon, Lord Russell, Lord Stourton, Lord Willoughby and Lord Wentworth. The day after, the ladies of the court, led by Marie's sister-in-law Margaret, Countess of Lennox, the duchesses of Northumberland and Suffolk, the Lady Jane Grey and the Countess of Pembroke, together with some hundred noble- and gentlewomen, accompanied her to court. The king's sisters, ladies Mary and Elizabeth, had declined their invitations.

The king met Marie in the entrance at Whitehall, and she was conducted to the queen's side of the palace where she dined on the left hand of the king, under the cloth of state, with Frances in the place of honour to her left. The room was decorated with the king's best plate – a sideboard with four shelves of gold utensils and one of six shelves of 'massy silver'. Having recently met the young man her daughter was contracted to marry, Dauphin François, Marie now had the opportunity to compare him with the alternate suitor, a boy of similar age. According to the Protestant John Knox, who treated Edward VI as a Protestant hero, Marie said that 'she found more wisdom and solid judgement in the young King of England than she should have looked for in any three princes of full age then in Europe'. After dinner, which finished at around 4 p.m., Marie returned to Baynard's Castle, where she rested for another day. Before she left, Northumberland, Winchester and other lords paid her a final visit to present her with gifts from the king – two 'nags', and a ring with a diamond. Messages were sent to the sheriffs in the counties she would pass through, to meet her and pay her the appropriate honours.

*

The public was sceptical of the claims that Somerset intended to take control of London and the Isle of Wight – believing, despite his inept rule, that he had genuinely cared for the good of the commons against the nobles. The majority, according to the Imperial ambassador, put his arrest down to Northumberland's 'covetousness'. Northumberland examined Somerset himself before the formal trial, which took place on 30 November 1551. Northumberland, Suffolk and twenty others sat as judges. Northumberland protested against any charges involving threats to himself being taken as treason. Rather than seeing this as magnanimity, commentators thought it a ploy to garner sympathy. Astonishingly, in an age when few treason trials resulted in acquittals, the peers found Somerset not guilty of treason, although he was condemned to death for lesser crimes. In time-honoured fashion, Somerset asked forgiveness from Northumberland and others and requested that his family be taken care of. Northumberland, perhaps concerned at the level of support Somerset had found among both nobles and commons, hesitated to take the final step. The 100 men-at-arms previously appointed to Somerset were now appointed to Suffolk, and Somerset was sent to the Tower while Northumberland considered his next move.

Having cogitated over Christmas, Northumberland resolved to dispatch his former greatest friend, and now greatest rival, once and for all. Edward signed the death warrant, and Somerset was executed on 22 January 1552. If the king had any compunction about the treatment of his uncle, it is not apparent from his journal, although the Imperial ambassador reported that he was 'grieved' about it. Northumberland took the opportunity to have some of Somerset's supporters executed, ensuring the jury was locked in until it returned guilty verdicts on four men, including Sir Michael Stanhope and Sir Thomas Arundell. Paget was side-lined, accused of corruption and appropriation of public funds. It would have been difficult to find a member of Edward's council not guilty of having his hands in the royal coffers!

Christmas 1551 was celebrated by the Greys at Suffolk House. It was a low-key affair, as Katherine Suffolk joined them, still desperately mourning her sons. Walter Haddon, brother of the family chaplain, wrote a eulogy for the dead boys, and a similar volume of praise for them by their tutor Thomas Wilson was dedicated to Suffolk. Mourning was not the only reason for a subdued Christmas. Traditional revelry was now being frowned upon by the Protestants, and a more puritanical regime was introduced. Playing cards was prohibited, at least for the servants, and Suffolk's daughters were discouraged from music. Plainness of dress was also becoming all the rage among the 'Godly' in contradistinction to conservatives such as Lady Mary who continued to dress resplendently. Ascham reported that Jane, on receiving a magnificent dress from Lady Mary, refused it with an insolent message – asking why she would follow the Lady Mary against God's Word, rather than the Lady Elizabeth who observed it. Elizabeth's new-found modesty had more to do with living down the Seymour scandal than religious fervour, but Jane was not to know that.

With the death of Frances's half-brothers, all the Brandon lands not entailed on a male heir became the inheritance of Frances and, possibly, her half-sister Anne, Lady Grey of Powis (Eleanor Clifford and Mary Monteagle were both dead). Lady Powis had always been of dubious legitimacy, as well as being mired in scandal, although she had married her lover immediately after her husband's death in 1551. By his will, Lord Powis left everything to his illegitimate children, so Anne had no income at all. This induced her to begin a case for possession of lands she said her father had willed to her. She found a willing accomplice in John Beaumont, the man who had previously quarrelled with Suffolk, and who was now Master of the Rolls, the second most senior judge in the court of Chancery. She and Beaumont agreed that he would rule in her favour, and in return she would sell him the land. As well as being willing to commit the offences of champerty and embracery, Beaumont went further, forging Charles Brandon's signature.[14]

The collusion between Anne and Beaumont to defraud Suffolk and Frances was surely driven, at least on his part, by personal vendetta. Anne may have had no particular animus against her brother-in-law, just a need for money – although it does indicate that Suffolk and Frances were not willing to help her half-sister, and is consistent with Suffolk's hard dealings over money. Perhaps they were also taking a strict line on Anne's adultery. On 9 February 1552, Beaumont was arrested and imprisoned. He confessed to the charges, along with others relating to misuse of public funds. By 4 June, he had surrendered all his lands and possessions to the king in compensation, although Anne appears to have escaped punishment.

*

In spring 1552, Northumberland was ill. His symptoms were those of severe stress – stomach ailments, depression and sleeplessness. As so often with those who strive for power, it proved less attractive in the reality than it had seemed in the prospect. Discontent with his position was never far from the surface. He also discovered that he had created a monster, in his supporters' constant demands for money and land. The country was close to bankruptcy and could not even raise debt in the money markets of Flanders at an interest rate of 16 per cent. Edward, too, fell sick in April. He recovered sufficiently to resume his normal routine, but modern medical theory suggests that whatever the illness was, it fatally undermined his health. He was well enough to go on his first progress outside London in May, and Suffolk accompanied him, commanding twenty-five men-at-arms. By 23 July, the court was at Petworth, where the king was informed that the dearth of food in the neighbourhood made it necessary to curtail his train – Suffolk's contingent was reduced by ten men, and others faced a similar reduction. The progress continued to Cowdray, home of Sir Anthony Browne, brother-in-law to Lord John and stepson of Lady Elizabeth FitzGerald.

Northumberland's influence over Edward grew. He persuaded the king to overrule the Earl of Cumberland's refusal to permit the marriage of his daughter Margaret Clifford (Frances's niece) to his own son Lord Guildford Dudley. Edward wrote to the recalcitrant earl on 4 July 1552, 'desiring him to grow to some good end forthwith in the matter of the marriage of the Lord Guildford to his daughter'. Either Cumberland still refused, or Northumberland changed his mind, as the marriage did not take place. Another huge influence on Edward was the powerful Scottish preacher John Knox, whom Northumberland, impressed by hearing him preach at Newcastle, introduced as a royal chaplain in August 1552. Knox (who never liked to admit that he had once been a Catholic priest) was a Calvinist, and utterly unwilling to compromise with anything he saw as deviating from religious purity. What he had to say shook the court. Cranmer had revised the 1549 Prayer Book into a more Protestant version, clearly denying transubstantiation, but commanding Communicants to kneel as a sign of respect. Knox claimed this was idolatry, infuriating the archbishop. Cranmer became even more enraged when a body of evangelical preachers, including Knox, was engaged by the council to review his Prayer Book.

While these religious controversies were raging – and we can be confident that Suffolk would have sided with Knox – the duke was worried about Frances. On 22 August, he wrote to Cecil from Sheen that Frances was so ill she might die. There is no information as to what ailed the thirty-five-year-old duchess, but whatever it was, it did not prove fatal.

18

'Jane the Quene'

Oft expectation fails, and most oft there where most it promises...
Shakespeare, *All's Well that Ends Well*, II i

In early February 1553, perhaps sensing that Edward's health was not as robust as it had once been, the council sought a rapprochement with the Lady Mary, who rode to her house at Clerkenwell, accompanied by 200 horse. On the 10th, accompanied by all the great ladies, including Frances, she went down Fleet Street to Whitehall, where she was met by Suffolk and Northumberland and the rest of the council, who treated her with an honour and respect she had not received since the mid-1520s when she had been called Princess of Wales. Edward was bedridden for some weeks with a cold, and there were reports of fever and breathing difficulties, but he recovered sufficiently to open Parliament on 1 March, after which he went to Greenwich, in the hopes of recuperating.

Edward's commitment to the Reformed faith was deep and sincere, and his great fear was that Mary would undo all his good work. Perhaps suspecting that he was dying, and anxious to preserve his legacy, Edward drew up a document that he called his 'Devise for the Succession'. In it, he sought to overturn both the Act of Succession of 1544 and his father's will, by expunging his half-sisters from the succession on the grounds that they were not only illegitimate but might risk the kingdom by marrying outside of it. Mary's religion, too, was a bar. Gender was more complex – the idea of female rulers was even more unpopular with the Reformers than it had been with Catholics. Bible study dwelt a good deal on the wickedness of women and their duty of obedience. A particular scourge of womankind was Knox, later to write his *First Blast of the Trumpet against the Monstrous Regiment of Women*, excoriating female rulers. In January, Knox had also proclaimed that there were secret traitors, poised to bring back the old religion.

The king's Devise, therefore, named as his heir the heirs male (not yet born) first of Frances, then of her three daughters, then of Frances's niece Margaret Clifford. In the event of a minority, the putative boy's mother was permitted to be regent, provided she did everything her male councillors advised. If no males had been born by the time of the king's death, Frances was to be regent until a boy was born. As initially drawn, the Devise was unworkable. What would happen if a younger sister had a son, and then an older sister did? But Edward, although clever, perhaps had as little understanding of political reality as Suffolk.

Yet even more important than gender was religion. Edward had a perfectly serviceable male heir, had that been the only criterion – Margaret, Lady Lennox, his first cousin, had an eight-year-old son, Henry Stuart, Lord Darnley. Darnley had been born in England, and there was every reason to believe he was as intelligent and gifted as any of the Tudor children, as well as being descended from the older, rather than the younger, sister of Henry VIII. But Lady Lennox, although she conformed to the law, was suspected of Catholic sympathies, so she and her family were passed over entirely. She had also been passed over by Henry VIII, despite him being personally attached to her. One can only presume it was, again, distrust of her husband.

Whether any of Edward's councillors took the Devise seriously in the spring is a moot point. But it did mean that there were four young women available to be snatched up as matrimonial prizes, by whom the councillors could potentially make their sons father of a king. Lady Mary Grey and Lady Margaret Clifford, both aged eight, were too young for marriage, so this left the two older Grey girls, Jane and Katherine. Later, it was said that Elizabeth Brooke, now Marchioness of Northampton, devised the marital arrangements that were finally made. Lady Northampton definitely did not want to see Mary as queen. She could be fairly certain that the act legalising her marriage would be reversed, especially as Northampton's first wife, Lady Anne Bourchier, was a friend of Mary's. Elizabeth therefore mooted possible alliances to her friend Pembroke, who discussed the idea with Northumberland, who then broached the matter with Suffolk and Frances. The suggestion was that Katherine Grey should marry Pembroke's son, nephew of Katherine Parr; Jane Grey should marry Northumberland's eldest unmarried son, Guildford; while Northumberland's daughter, another Katherine, would marry Henry Hastings, heir to the Earl of Huntingdon. As well as being a cousin and friend of Suffolk's, Huntingdon was a great-grandson of Margaret, Countess of Salisbury, and thus carried royal York blood. According to Sir Robert Wingfield, who wrote about the events of 1553–54 almost contemporaneously, Suffolk and Frances took some persuading – the younger son of Northumberland was rather a comedown in expectations from a marriage to the king. Wingfield described Suffolk as an 'illustrious and widely-loved nobleman of ancient lineage, but lacking circumspection'.

Suffolk, as I freely allow, feared the fierce nature of the man (Northumberland) more than he ought to have done on the two particular grounds that Northumberland was believed to be dangerous and that he seemed to be like Phoenix in his companionship with the king and second in authority to none. The timid and trustful duke therefore hoped to gain a scarcely imaginable haul of immense wealth and greater honour of his house from this match and readily followed Northumberland's wishes, although his wife Frances was vigorously opposed to it, but her womanly scruples were of little avail against the opponents of such wealth and power.[1]

Before accepting this description of events too readily, we should note that, after the event, Mary and her government were eager to thrust all of the blame onto Northumberland. What would not have suited Mary was any representation of Suffolk as driven by zeal for the Reformed religion – the attempted coup was always cast as an ambitious power-grab.

The betrothals were common knowledge by 18 April, when the Imperial envoy, Scheyfve, commented on them as boding no good. The renowned Professor Ives suggested in his book *Lady Jane Grey: A Tudor Mystery* that these marriages were no more than the usual bartering among nobles. In particular, he believes the marriage of Katherine and Herbert was a routine aristocratic arrangement, and that, far from Pembroke being Northumberland's crony, the two men did not get on well. The counter-argument might be that Pembroke was given the second prize of Katherine, in order to gain his support for the marriage of Jane to Northumberland's son, and certainly observers at the time assumed that Northumberland, even if he did not encourage Edward in his Devise with the possibility of such a marriage in mind for his son, certainly leapt at the opportunity when it was presented. Three other matches completed the arrangement – the last Dudley brother, Henry, to Margaret Audley, Frances's niece; Margaret Clifford, whom her father had refused for Guildford, for Northumberland's rather elderly brother Sir Andrew Dudley; and Lady Mary Grey to the old warhorse Lord Grey of Wilton. Fortunately for Margaret and Mary, these marriages did not take place.[2]

If Suffolk and France had held out initially against the match for Jane, in hopes of her finally snagging the king, it was soon obvious that that could never happen. Edward was too ill to attend any of the ceremonies, contenting himself with sending presents of 'rich ornaments and jewels'. The weddings took place on 25 May 1553 at the Northumberland residence, Durham House. It was a day of traditional celebrations – feasting, jousting and masquing. Jane and Guildford did not immediately cohabit, possibly because of recent illness on Guildford's part, but soon did. Katherine, although too young to consummate her marriage, went to live at the Pembroke's London home, Baynard's Castle, together with her fifteen-year-old husband. There were rumours in London, faithfully reported by Scheyfve, that Northumberland had his eyes on the throne. Gossip, of course, is not fact, and Northumberland might not have contemplated any of the dastardly plans attributed to him – that he would arrange for his eldest son, Warwick, to marry the Lady Elizabeth, or that he himself would divorce, or even poison, his wife to marry Elizabeth and take the crown. The rumours are important not for their exact content but for what they tell us about the public view of Northumberland's ambition, and their demonstration that it was widely believed Edward did not have long to live.

On an unknown date, Edward made another change to his Devise. Chris Skidmore, in *Edward VI*, dates this alteration to after the marriage of Lady Jane. In a heart-breaking admission for a boy of fifteen, the king had to accept that he would be dead before a son could be born to any of his female relatives. He therefore bequeathed the throne to 'Lady Jane and her heirs male'. On 12 June, Lord Chief Justice Montagu and the other judges were invited to attend a council meeting to give evidence as to the legality of changing the succession without an Act of Parliament. They were presented with Edward's Devise and ordered to turn it into a legal will. Surprised, and not a little alarmed, the judges retired to consider their position. Edward was a minor – in law, he could not make an enforceable will, even if the Crown could be left by will, which itself was debatable. Henry's freedom to nominate heirs came from a specific Act of Parliament, relating to what would happen after the death of his heir-at-law. The other option was Letters Patent – that is, executive letters from a king. But there was no precedent for a king trying to overturn an Act of Parliament (the 1544 Act) by will or by Letters Patent.[3]

The judges refused to obey the king, citing the danger of committing treason. The 1544 Act had stipulated that any attempt to subvert it would be treasonous, and this was echoed in the 1547 Treason Act. Northumberland exploded in fury, accusing Montagu of treason and threatening personal violence. That there was more to the issue than religion was apparent, when Northumberland angrily spurned the suggestion that Mary's rights could be preserved on condition she agreed to maintain the current religious settlement. Edward, too, was incandescent with rage. Denial was never going to be music to a Tudor king's ears – even a fifteen-year-old king. Two days later, he summoned Montagu again, and ordered him to do as he was told and draw the Devise into legal form. Montagu resisted as long as he could, trying to persuade Edward to call Parliament to make the changes required, but the king was not willing to wait, so, bullied and threatened with dire consequences, Montagu capitulated, first requesting a pardon under the Great Seal.

Letters Patent were drawn up giving effect to the King's wishes. The document was signed repeatedly by Edward, and, over the following week by at least 100 of his councillors, nobles and officials, including, of course, Suffolk. There was a second document, binding its signatories to uphold Edward's wishes 'unto death'. Support was not unanimous. Archbishop Cranmer initially refused, but was talked around on the promise that the further religious reforms he advocated would be implemented, while Judge Sir John Hales refused absolutely. Arundel, while signing the Letters Patent, refused to be party to the undertaking of support. The earls of Shrewsbury and Bedford and the Marquis of Winchester were similarly reluctant. Time was running out. There was little possibility that Edward would live to have a new succession bill ratified by Parliament – even if that body proved willing to change the succession. If there were to be any hope of a smooth transition of power to Lady Jane (no doubt to be ably guided by her experienced father-in-law and father), then more powerful allies were needed.

Henri II of France was very willing to see the succession subverted away from the cousin of his nemesis, the emperor, and encouraged Northumberland to think a treaty was within his grasp – the price would be war with the Empire. The duke, unwilling to go so far alone, insisted that the rest of the council be involved in negotiations. He also informed his daughter-in-law that Edward had nominated her as his heir. Jane is unlikely to have welcomed the news – she would have been delighted for Mary to be legally replaced so that the Reformation could continue unchecked, but in a society where obedience to parents was next only to obedience to God, she would have questioned the passing over of her mother. So ingrained was the habit of obedience that, even though she had just been told she would soon rule all, she still felt she had to request permission from her mother-in-law to visit Frances – although she was not so docile that she accepted the duchess's refusal. She made the visit anyway, travelling by barge to see Suffolk and Frances at Suffolk House. That Jane turned to her parents in moments of emotional crisis surely gives the lie to the notion that they bullied her and that she was terrified of them. The dates of these events are unknown, so it is unclear whether Frances's visit to Edward on 14 June was to remonstrate with him about the position he had put her daughter and herself in, or whether she was summoned by Edward to be informed of his plans.

Rumours that Edward was on his deathbed were everywhere. He was helped to stand at a window at Greenwich to be seen by the public, but few were fooled as to his state of health and there was even talk that Northumberland had poisoned him. Such an idea is scarcely credible – apart from anything else, Northumberland desperately needed Edward to live, either to preserve the duke's current position or to change the succession by Act of Parliament. No doubt the entire council was praying for the king to live long enough for Parliament to relieve them of the taint of treason which clung about them. It was reported that Suffolk and Northumberland, attended only by one servant, went out late on the night of 22 June to visit the French ambassador, and were questioned by the watch.[4]

Edward died on 6 July 1553, giving his councillors the choice of following the law or committing active treason by supporting Jane as his heir. His death was kept secret while they made their plans. Messengers were sent to convey Jane by barge from Chelsea Manor, where she and Guildford had been enjoying (or not!) married life, to Syon House, Northumberland's home. There, she was informed that Edward had died and she was now queen. According to her own account of events,

Jane protested vigorously, affirming that the true heir was the Lady Mary. Eventually, overcome by her parents, her in-laws and the council, she accepted the great office now thrust upon her. Once her resistance had been overcome, Jane became convinced that her queenship was a God-given opportunity to carry Protestantism to victory. Perhaps she remembered Queen Katherine Parr's similar reservations about marriage to Henry VIII, which were then overcome by Katherine being genuinely persuaded that it was God's will.

While Jane was coming to terms with her destiny, requests were sent to Mary and Elizabeth to visit their dying brother, with a view to capturing both women. Elizabeth succumbed to one of the convenient bouts of sickness that always prevented her doing anything she did not want to do, and stayed at home in bed. Mary set out for London, reaching her manor of Hunsdon in Hertfordshire. She was cautious, having been forewarned that Northumberland and the council were plotting against her. When the news arrived late at night that Edward was already dead, she left the house under cover of darkness and galloped for her manor of Kenninghall in Norfolk, where she arrived in the early hours of 8 July, before her pursuers, led by Northumberland's son Lord Robert Dudley, could catch her. She immediately had herself proclaimed queen to her household officers and tenants, and wrote a letter to the council in London, demanding that she be proclaimed queen in the capital. She knew exactly what they had been up to, she continued, but would overlook their misbehaviour if they returned immediately to their allegiance.

This was the moment of truth. Northumberland could have accepted Mary's offer, but he had rolled the dice, and his track record of military prowess and calculated risk-taking probably suggested to him that he would easily win a confrontation – his opponent a woman, and the power of government behind him. Suffolk would go where Northumberland led. On 10 July, Jane was brought by barge from Syon to the Tower, and installed there as queen. The next day, the council received Mary's letter, which apparently caused Frances and the Duchess of Northumberland to 'lament and weep'.[5] Jane was made of sterner stuff. A reply, calculated to inflame Mary with its references to her as illegitimate, was swiftly dispatched, along with a circular, signed by 'Jane the Quene', ordering the lords lieutenant and commissioners of the peace for the shires to proclaim Jane and to stand in their allegiance to her, to ignore the 'slanderous reports' being circulated by the Lady Mary 'bastard', and to keep the realm 'out of the dominion of papists and strangers'.

Since it was apparent that Mary would not meekly submit to being deprived of her rights, it was agreed that an armed force should be sent to capture her. Initially, Suffolk was to lead it. Jane was sure that she could have 'no stronger defence than her own loving father'.[6] Frances, knowing that Suffolk had no skill as a military leader, and perhaps mindful of how, if the coup failed, she might have to explain his actions to Mary, persuaded him to decline the role on a plea of illness – it may well have been a genuine excuse, at least in part. Jane directed the council to send someone else. With a lack of volunteers for the tricky command, there seemed no choice but for Northumberland to do it himself. He made his preparations, then reminded the council that they were all in it together and that they should 'use constant hearts, abandoning all malice, envy and private affections'. They assured him that if he did not trust his colleagues he was mistaken, 'for which of us can wipe his hands clean thereof?'

Not entirely convinced of his colleagues' loyalty, Northumberland left London on 14 July, supported by his son Warwick and son-in-law Hastings, and with a force of around 600 men, who had been paid a month's wages in advance. He noted bitterly that there was not one person in the watching crowd to bid him 'God-speed'. The same day, there was an argument in the Tower when Jane resolutely refused to accept her husband as her king consort, insisting that he would be no more than a duke. Her mother-in-law was incensed, giving colour to the suspicion that the Northumberlands were behind the nomination of Jane to bolster their own position, rather than to satisfy the demands of their religion. Suffolk's cousin Sir Henry Dudley (son of Cicely Grey), who was also Northumberland's cousin, was sent to France to request practical help should Charles intervene to support Mary. While the French were thrilled with the notion of preventing Mary reaching the throne, Henri II's real aim, as the Imperial ambassador pointed out, would be to see his daughter-in-law Mary, Queen of Scots as Queen of England rather than the Protestant Jane. Nicholas Ridley, Bishop of London, preached at St Paul's Cross, promoting Jane's virtues and Protestantism. Half of the crowd had never heard of Jane and needed to have her claim spelt out. Even then, they were underwhelmed.

Meanwhile, Mary had left Norfolk, accompanied by the Earl of Sussex and his son and a growing number of gentlemen and commons, and travelled to her vast castle at Framlingham in Suffolk. This had two advantages – it was practically impregnable, and, should worst come to worst, would give her access to escape by sea. Before long she had a sizeable army. A Lincolnshire man, Richard Troughton, wrote to the council, 'Her grace should have her right, or else there would be the bloodiest day ... that ever was in England.'[7] By 15 July, events were moving against Jane. Norwich had come down on Mary's side, and sent money and men, as had Coventry and Gloucester. Perhaps most depressing of all for Suffolk and Jane, the six ships that had been sent to patrol the waters off the coast of East Anglia defected to Mary (although perhaps more because they had not been paid than for philosophical reasons). Their guns were taken to Framlingham. Lord Wentworth, a major Suffolk landowner, renounced his previous oath to Jane, and defected to Mary.

The councillors in the Tower were becoming restive, and some tried to leave. Suffolk gave orders for the gates to be locked, and the keys handed over to Jane in person, but it was impossible to contain them. Arundel and Pembroke departed for Pembroke's house, on the pretext of receiving the French ambassador. Shrewsbury, Bedford and others joined them, and Arundel persuaded them to abandon Jane and Northumberland. Any who were worried about breaking their oath to Jane should consider the danger of civil war. Now one of them had broken ranks and was prepared to lead, the rest of the councillors could follow in their usual sheep-like fashion. They agreed to proclaim Mary, and a delegation hurried to meet the mayor at Cheapside. Mary was duly proclaimed queen on 19 July, following which the full Latin *Te Deum* was once more heard in St Paul's Cathedral. London went wild with joy.

Even as these events were unfolding, Suffolk and Jane were agreeing to stand as godparents to the son of Edward Underhill, a minor court official. Jane, represented by Lady Carew, named the baby Guildford. The remainder of the council having made their decision, they headed for the Tower, accompanied by a force of armed men. They informed Suffolk that his daughter was no longer queen, and that Mary had been proclaimed. He was then required to proclaim Mary queen from Tower Hill and to undertake the disagreeable task of breaking the news to Jane. Suffolk dismissed the guards and told his daughter that her reign was over, taking down the cloth of estate with his own hands – she must content herself with a private life. Her ladies were also free to leave. In perhaps the most reprehensible act of their entire lives, Suffolk and Frances left Jane to her fate with her husband and mother-in-law in the Tower. As he left, Suffolk asked the Marquis of Winchester to try to obtain a pardon for himself and his family. Winchester had no good reason to think Mary would look particularly favourably on him, but promised to help if he could.

Immediately after causing Mary to be proclaimed, Arundel and Sir William Paget hastened to Framlingham, arriving shortly after Mary had finished reviewing her troops and watching a cavalry charge. They submitted themselves to her mercy and told her that she was now acknowledged as queen. She accepted their grovelling and pardoned them. Orders were sent for Suffolk to be arrested and returned to the Tower.

Northumberland had headed for Bury St Edmunds – the nearest town to Framlingham. He went via Cambridge, whence he wrote to the council, requesting reinforcements, but none were sent. Lord Rich, sent to raise troop in his Essex territory for Jane, headed for Framlingham to support her rival. Given that Lord Rich had shamelessly betrayed both Sir Thomas More and Cromwell and made sure always to be on the winning side, this could have been taken by the council as a certain indication of the end. Despite the exhortations of 'Jane the Quene', the gentry of Sussex declared for Mary. The Earl of Oxford, too, headed for Framlingham. Defeated, Northumberland personally proclaimed Mary's title in the marketplace at Cambridge, there being no herald to hand. He hoped for mercy, but was assured by a bystander that, even if Mary were disposed to forgive him, the new council (that was the old council in a new guise of Marian loyalty) would kill him. The duke shortly received a command to lay down his arms, disband his troops and wait for further orders. The next day, he was treated to the sight of Arundel approaching to arrest him. Northumberland told his erstwhile colleague that he had done nothing without the consent of the whole council. Arundel, whether he felt any shame, or only the pleasure of revenge on the man who had once sent him to prison, responded that he was merely obeying the queen's commands. Northumberland was taken directly to the Tower on 30 July, with only the guards' orders protecting him from the wrath of the furious mob.

The same day, Jane was charged with treason. The Duchess of Northumberland, who had been allowed to leave the Tower, was refused audience by Mary, who was sure that she intended to plead for mercy for her husband and sons. Frances was more fortunate. She raced to intercept Mary at Beaulieu, arriving at two in the morning, and cast herself down in front of her cousin, begging her forgiveness and placing as much blame as she could on Northumberland, pleading that Suffolk had been coerced and poisoned by the duke. Mary, who was of a forgiving nature (leaving religion aside), pardoned Frances and allowed Suffolk to remain under house arrest at Charterhouse, where his younger daughter, Katherine, had been returned by Pembroke as unwanted goods. Mary was only dissuaded from pardoning Jane by the urgings of the Imperial ambassador. Suffolk was too ill to revel immediately in his lucky escape – suffering from colic and 'the stone', he was prostrate for a couple of weeks.

By early August, Mary was on her way to London to claim her crown, and to meet a council that had suddenly discovered that it had supported her all along. Her policy from the beginning was to accept the grovelling from the councillors and let them pin the blame on Northumberland and his two closest allies. She wanted the whole matter treated as a political issue, rather than broaching any discussion of religion – Mary was utterly convinced that Protestantism was still a fringe pursuit of radicals, and that the vast majority of her new subjects would welcome a return to the old faith. On 3 August, as she prepared to enter the capital, she was joined at Wanstead by Elizabeth, miraculously recovered from the mysterious illness that had prevented her sending so much as a word of support to her sister. Dressed in purple velvet and cloth of gold and followed by a huge train of peers and their ladies, as well as by the mayor and a choir of children, Mary rode to the Tower. She was greeted with jubilation as she passed through the streets, church bells rang out and banners reading 'Vox populi, Vox Dei' (the voice of the people is the voice of God) were displayed.

Arrived at the Tower, Mary found a couple of relics from her father's reign: Thomas Howard, 3rd Duke of Norfolk, and Gardiner, whom she named as Lord Chancellor. Mary also found Edward Courtenay, who had been imprisoned since the Exeter Conspiracy of 1539. Aged twenty-six, he had spent all of his youth incarcerated. His mother, Gertrude Blount, Lady Marquis of Exeter, and stepdaughter of Lady Dorothy Grey, had always been one of Mary's warmest supporters. These prisoners were freed, but Northumberland, Jane and Guildford Dudley remained in the Tower, transferred from the royal apartments to respectable lodgings rather than dungeons. The Duchess of Northumberland received a pardon. The French were worried by Mary's victory, and quickly denied having given any support to Northumberland, while the emperor hastily rewrote history by telling his ambassador to inform Mary that he had been in the very midst of sending her aid when the good news of her bloodless succession had arrived, even though, in truth, he had been preparing an accommodation with the new regime. Pembroke sought to distance himself from the Greys, arranging for the marriage between Katherine and his son to be annulled. The young couple, who had become attached to each other, swore that despite her youth they had consummated the marriage. Even if that were true, which is unlikely, no-one was prepared to listen to them.

While Mary, for reasons both personal and political, was prepared to pardon most of the conspirators, even Suffolk, there was no reprieve for Northumberland. He was tried on 18 August, with his son John, Earl of Warwick, and the Marquis of Northampton. Presiding was the old Duke of Norfolk, enjoying a cold dish of revenge against the men who had conspired in the accusations of treason that had killed Norfolk's son. Northumberland, having pointed out that almost all of his judges were as guilty as he, confessed and sought mercy. At the very least, he requested that he be executed as a nobleman, by beheading rather than the hanging, drawing and quartering that commoners suffered. All were found guilty, and three others were condemned the following day: Northumberland's brother Sir Andrew Dudley, Sir John Gates and Sir Thomas Palmer. Before the execution, arranged for 21 August, could be carried out, Northumberland publicly declared his renewed adherence to the Catholic faith, saying, 'The plague that is upon the realm and upon us now is that we have erred from the faith these sixteen years.'

On the scaffold on Tower Hill, Northumberland faced a huge crowd. Admitting his guilt, he maintained that he was not the only one responsible for the attempted coup, but he did not name anyone else. He reaffirmed that he had been led astray by 'seditious preachers and teachers of the new doctrine', before he knelt for the axe. His embracing of the old faith at the time of his death may have been calculated to benefit his children, with whom he had an unusually warm relationship for the time, or perhaps he sought comfort in the familiar faith of his youth. If he hoped for reprieve, he was disappointed. Gates and Palmer were also executed, but the other condemned were eventually pardoned. Northumberland was buried in the church of St Peter ad Vincula in the Tower, near the Duke of Somerset. Jane was shocked and disgusted by her father-in-law's apostasy, condemning him utterly:

> ... like as his life was wicked and full of dissimulation, so was his end thereafter, I pray God I, nor no friend of mine, dies so. Should I who am young ... forsake my faith for the love of life? Nay, God forbid! Much more he should not whose fatal course, although he had lived his just number of years, could not have long continued...[8]

Jane was prepared for martyrdom, but she wanted it to be clear that the martyrdom she anticipated would be for her religion, not for base motives of ambition to steal her cousin's crown. She had already written to Mary that, although she knew she had done wrong in allowing herself to be persuaded, she had never sought Mary's crown. Mary, determined to protect her cousin, accepted that Jane had been overwhelmed by others, and refused to countenance her death, despite the urging of many, particularly Renard, the Imperial ambassador, who, having done nothing to help Mary, now sought to control her. Eventually, Jane and Guildford were tried at the Guildhall on Monday 13 November, along with Archbishop Cranmer. All three were found guilty, but there was no move to have the sentences carried out. The terms of Jane and Guildford's confinement were relaxed somewhat, and they were allowed to receive visitors and take exercise. All might have been well, and the couple eventually released, if Suffolk had not drawn attention to himself, first by disagreeing with Mary's policies in Parliament, and then embroiling himself in another rebellion.

*

The new queen had two overwhelming ambitions: to restore the religious and social world to the lost Elysian Fields of her childhood, before her father had questioned his marriage to her mother; and to have an heir of her own. Both of these ambitions were within the realm of the possible in 1553, but there were serious obstacles to their easy achievement.

To take the religious question first, the majority of the population, other than a small, but very vocal group in London and the south-east, were still Catholic in their religious habits and inclinations. The situation as left at the death of Henry VIII was essentially one of Catholic practice, shorn of some of the more superstitious practices around relics, purgatory and the saints, and with an English Bible, under the headship of the monarch, rather than the pope. Almost immediately, the banned altars and relics that had been hidden reappeared, and a Latin Mass was sung in London. This was not universally welcome in the capital, and a number of Protestant preachers began to incite rebellion. Mary was, of course, according to law, the Supreme Head of the Church and could mandate religious practice. However, she did not use this power to reintroduce Catholicism immediately. Instead, she announced that, while she herself would not deny her own faith, there would be no compulsion in religious matters until Parliament had been called. When convened later that year Parliament was happy to unravel the religious legislation of Edward's reign, reflecting the opinions of the majority of the population. Suffolk, showing the courage of his religious convictions, tried to muster resistance in the Lords, but failed. Renard noted, 'The Duke of Suffolk is doing bad work in connection with religion, and the queen is angry with him for his manner of abusing her clemency and good nature.'[9] The very same actions that annoyed the queen were considered praiseworthy by

Haddon, Suffolk's old chaplain, who wrote to Heinrich Bullinger that 'the duke holds to the true God despite ... the devil whose agents are striving with all their might to lead his lordship astray'.

The second item on the queen's agenda, the bearing of an heir, was just about practicable had she been in good health, but Mary was not robust and was over thirty-seven when she became queen. She needed to find a husband, get married and conceive in very short order to have any hope of an heir. There was no shortage of candidates for her hand, and Mary's councillors and subjects expected her to marry as soon as possible, not just because an heir was required but because received wisdom was that women were not suited to ruling. This was not, of course, the day-to-day experience of most people, as, in all classes of life, women took an active part in managing businesses, arranging marriages, acting as their husband's partners and deputies and functioning independently when widowed. But although individual women were recognised as perfectly capable of managing affairs, the theory was rather different.

To clarify Mary's position as a female sovereign, it was enacted in her first parliament that she had exactly the same authority as a male sovereign, and this was an understanding of her role from which Mary never deviated. But what would the position of her husband be? For other female heiresses, upon marriage the husband immediately took ownership of all her personal goods and possessions, and had a life interest in her lands. Similarly, it was thought that a queen's husband would be king, for at least as long as she lived. That had certainly been Northumberland's thinking, so far as Guildford was concerned – although Jane had seen the matter very differently. For Mary to marry one of her subjects would therefore cause enormous friction as one noble was elevated above the others, while many thought that if she married a foreign prince he would whisk her abroad and England would be devoured by his country.

Mary had two, or possibly three, marital options at home – the aforementioned Courtenay, who was the nearest male blood relative of the royal family of age to marry. But Courtenay had spent so much time in the Tower that he lacked the maturity and experience that Mary needed in a husband. Once the idea was mooted, he 'put on a pride so odious and insufferable to the whole Court, and particularly to the Council, that he has lost credit and is not as well thought of as he was at the beginning'.[10] The second home-grown candidate was Cardinal Reginald Pole, who, despite being a cardinal, was not an ordained priest, and, being the grandson of George, Duke of Clarence, had a useful strain of Yorkist blood. Pole had been in exile since the 1530s for his opposition to Henry VIII. Renard mentioned a third name: Lord Thomas Grey, 'who is a courtier, popular, a man of wit and in favour with the queen, and so outshines Courtenay that Courtenay dares not show himself when the other is present. My Lord (Thomas) has told a friend of mine that every one is disgusted with Courtenay...'[11] The idea cannot be taken very seriously, but it is intriguing to wonder what reaction Suffolk would have had to such a match – and if Lord Thomas would have been willing to forgo his Protestant convictions to be the queen's husband.

Mary's heart was set on a marriage with a foreign prince, partly for reasons of prestige and also because she wanted to reintegrate England into the Catholic Christendom of Europe. Like every English monarch before her, Mary saw France as the enemy she needed to guard against. France had put its eggs in the basket of the alliance with Scotland through the betrothal of the dauphin to Mary, Queen of Scots, whom many saw as Mary's legal heir, discounting Elizabeth on the grounds of illegitimacy. After five centuries during which English history has perceived Spain as the enemy in the sixteenth century, it is hard to remember that Spain had been an ally against the French until the reign of Elizabeth, and so for Mary to look to Spain for alliance was not surprising. Charles V ruled himself out. He was tired, gouty and looking forward to abdicating. Instead, he put forward his son Philip, twenty-seven years old, widowed and with a son. Mary accepted him with alacrity, despite misgivings among her councillors – although none of them was so averse to the match that he couldn't be bought with a pension. Philip was heir to Spain and the Low Countries, and the marriage treaty provided that any heir Mary bore would inherit England and the Low Countries – this would have brought huge economic benefits had it come to pass. Mary also made it clear that she would remain as sole monarch even after marriage, and would not permit her husband to take any official part in government, although it is probable that most men doubted her on this.

A deputation from Parliament, tipped off by Gardiner, who supported a match with Courtenay, requested an audience with the queen, in which they begged her not to marry a foreigner lest he try to either take her abroad, or, in the event of her death, usurp the throne. Mary was outraged by this interference with her royal prerogative, and sent them off with a flea in their collective ear. Meanwhile, Parliament considered the legitimacy of the royal family. The marriage between Henry VIII and Katharine of Aragon was confirmed as legal. Logically, therefore, his marriage to Anne Boleyn could not have been, so Elizabeth was implicitly confirmed as illegitimate. The other girls who might have been astonished to learn that they were illegitimate were Jane, Katherine and Mary Grey. The old betrothal of Suffolk to Katherine FitzAlan was dragged up, and confirmed as a bar to the legitimate union of Suffolk and Frances. This was intended primarily to bar Frances's daughters from the succession, and perhaps to allow Frances to separate from Suffolk.

Such a distancing from the royal family may have exacerbated Suffolk's fears for the future, and for his faith. In a moment of weakness, he and Huntingdon (according to Renard) made their 'confession as to religion'; that is, they accepted the Catholic faith. In return, Mary apparently waived the enormous fines that had been levied on them as punishment for the enthroning of Jane.[12] While Renard is the only source for either of these events, he was kept up to date by the queen, so can probably be relied on. It does not seem that Jane heard anything about her father attending Catholic services – the vigour with which she denounced her former tutor, Dr Thomas Harding, for reconciling himself to the Catholic Church leaves no doubt as to her opinion on such matters: she had thought Harding to be a 'lively member of Christ, but now the deformed imp of the devil'.

Mary decided to marry Philip. The terms were good, and most of her councillors were won over, but a vocal minority of lords objected – among them Lord Thomas Grey, and Huntingdon. They were not the only objectors – fear of foreigners was rife, and a group of Protestant gentry, led by Sir Thomas Wyatt, plotted rebellion. According to Wyatt, there was no desire to depose Mary, merely to prevent the marriage with Philip, but most at the time took his ultimate aim to be the installation of Elizabeth as queen, married to Courtenay. Some also thought that Jane's restoration was a possible motive, but that seems unlikely – she had not commanded support previously, and would be unlikely to do so now. Suffolk, perhaps ashamed of his accommodation with Catholicism, joined in with the plotting, and has been widely condemned for it since. He could surely appreciate that there was a good chance that Jane would be executed if the rebellion were to fail. The only explanation for his behaviour is that he believed, and knew that his daughter also believed, that to risk martyrdom for the sake of their faith was a noble and glorious act, and that they would meet again among the Elect in paradise. Unfortunately, however high-minded Suffolk's motives might have been, he was as politically inept as ever, throwing in his lot with men who were too loose-tongued ever to succeed.

The plans were finalised on 22 December. On Palm Sunday, 18 March, Sir Peter Carew and Courtenay were to rise in Devon, Suffolk in Leicestershire, Sir James Croft in Herefordshire and Wyatt in Kent. Rumours soon spread, and Carew refused a summons to court. On 21 January, Gardiner winkled the truth out of Courtenay. Lord Thomas rode to Sheen to warn Suffolk, and bade him either begin the uprising immediately or at least go to Bradgate: '[A]mongst his friends and tenants, who durst fetch him?' While Suffolk was still debating his course of action, Carew ran for France, and Mary gave Suffolk the opportunity to prove his loyalty by leading her men against Wyatt. Suffolk assured her messenger that he was heading to see the queen: 'Marry, I was coming to her Grace. You can see I am booted and spurred, ready to ride. I will but break my fast and go.'[13] He gave instructions for the man to be well wined. Taking 100 marks, which was all the cash he had, he headed for Bradgate, having arranged to meet lords Thomas and John at St Albans. These two had also been summoned by the queen, and all three were branded traitors when they failed to show up. Bad weather prevented the rendezvous at St Albans, but they finally caught up with each other at Lutterworth, where they stayed for two nights, hoping to provoke rebellion locally by instilling fear of the Spanish marriage.

While Suffolk and the others were heading north, on 22 January 1554, the council distributed the queen's proclamation against 'false and seditious rumours' about the marriage. The advantageous articles of the treaty were to be declared to the people, and the 'rebellion raised by the Duke of Suffolk' was to be suppressed – his fulminations against the marriage were nothing but a smokescreen for his real motive of putting Jane on the throne.[14] Over the next couple of weeks, the proclamation was read across the country, and had arrived in Leicester before Suffolk reached Bradgate on 28 January. Suffolk sent out his own proclamations and offered 6d per day to any who would march with him to oppose the Spanish marriage. He was helped by Francis Cave, who wrote a letter to the queen, justifying the revolt. For all his efforts, the duke collected few followers, although the town of Kegworth sent £500 in support.

Nevertheless, on the 29th, Suffolk armed himself – nervous enough to cuff the clumsy servant who hurt his leg – and called on his men to do the same. They entered the city of Leicester and closed the gates. Meanwhile, the queen had sent the man whom Suffolk thought was his friend, the Earl of Huntingdon, to arrest him. Suffolk, as politically naive as ever, assumed that Huntingdon, rather than being in pursuit, would join him, and sent word of his movements. Wingfield, however, notes that Huntingdon's family 'harboured perpetual enmity for the family of the Greys of Dorset', and that the earl 'most willingly took on the task partly to cancel out his previous blame incurred in Northumberland's conspiracy and partly to avenge the injuries done to the ancient family of Hastings by the duke's ancestors'.[15]

In Leicester, things were falling apart. The mayor, having heard the proclamation against the marriage, asked Suffolk to confirm that nothing was intended against Queen Mary herself. Indeed not, Suffolk assured him, saying, 'He that would her hurt, I would this sword,' slapping his weapon, 'were through his heart.' Despite these assurances, by the end of the day, as he rode for Coventry, Suffolk's band of 140 consisted mainly of his own retainers, including Jane's tutor, John Aylmer, and his own half-brother George Medley. He had sent his secretary, Thomas Rampton, on to Coventry, but this was a miscalculation. Less than a mile outside the town, he was warned that the gates of the city had been closed against him. Confused, and once again displaying the lack of talent or decisiveness necessary to be a great leader, Suffolk turned for Astley, where he and his brothers removed their armour and tried to disguise themselves in coats of ordinary cloth. Concerned for his followers, Suffolk divided the little money he had between them, and told them to flee the country. The four brothers hid, but two were flushed out by Huntingdon with a pack of dogs: Suffolk in an old oak tree, and John under a covering of hay. Thomas escaped as far as Wales, but was picked up there. Medley too was apprehended.

Although isolated, Wyatt went ahead, and marched on London from Kent with a sizeable army. Mary called out her troops and, refusing to flee in the face of rebels heading for her capital, rode to the Guildhall and made an impassioned speech, rallying overwhelming support. The rebels were defeated. Shortly after, the queen signed death warrants for Jane and Guildford, but still resisted their immediate implementation. Even at this late stage, Mary hoped to save her young cousin, both body and soul, and delayed the execution in the hope that Jane could be converted to the Catholic faith. She sent a priest of her own, Dr Feckenham, to try to persuade her. Jane was steadfast in her religion, and, glorying in martyrdom as only a sixteen-year-old idealist can, accepted her fate. One of her last actions was a gift to her sister Katherine of her Greek New Testament, with a message written on the blank leaves. The letter exhorted Katherine to put away the things of the world and be prepared for death at any time:

> I have here sent you, my dear sister Katherine, a book, which although it be not outwardly trimmed with gold ... yet inwardly it is of more worth than all the precious mines that the vast earth can boast of. It is the book, my only best and best-loved sister, of the Law of the Lord. It is the Testament and last will ... which shall lead you to the path of eternal joy and if you with a good mind read it, and with an earnest mind do purpose to follow it, it shall bring you to an immortal and everlasting life ... It shall teach you to live, and shall learn you to die ... My good sister, once more again let me entreat you to learn to die; deny the world, defy the devil, and despise the flesh, and delight yourself only in the Lord. Be penitent for your sins, and yet despair not; be strong in faith, yet presume not; and desire with St Paul to be dissolved and to be with Christ, with whom, even in death, there is life ... Now as touching my death, rejoice as I do, my dearest sister, that I shall be delivered of this corruption, and put on incorruption: for I am assured that I shall, for losing of a mortal life, win one that is immortal, joyful and everlasting ... I pray ... [that you may] die in the true Christian faith, from the which (in God's name) I exhort that you never swerve, neither for hope of life nor for fear of death ... Fare you well, good sister, and put your only trust in God, who only must help you.[16]

She and Guildford were permitted by the Lieutenant of the Tower, Sir John Brydges, to pass a prayer book between themselves. Both Jane and Guildford wrote Suffolk farewell messages inside. Guildford inscribed, 'Your loving and obedient son wisheth unto your grace long life in this world, with as much joy and comfort as I wish to myself, and in the world to come, life everlasting. Your humble son to his death. G Dudley.' Jane's was similar: 'The Lord comfort your grace and that in His word wherein all creatures only are to be comforted. And though it hath pleased God to take away two of your children, yet think not, I most humbly beseech your grace, that you have lost them, but trust that we, by leaving this mortal life, have won an immortal life. And I for my part as I have honoured your grace in this life, will pray for you in another life.

Your grace's humble daughter, Jane Dudley.' This last, heartfelt, message seems finally to negate any idea that Jane and her father had anything but the closest and most affectionate relationship. The other letter attributed to Jane, casting the blame for her death on Suffolk, has been widely identified as a fake.

Guildford was the first to die, on the morning of 12 February, on Tower Hill. He refused a priest, faithful, like his wife, to the Reformed faith. Jane was led out to the private surroundings of Tower Green. In the prayer book, which she had carried to the scaffold, she wrote a final message for Brydges, who had treated her as kindly as he could:

> Good Master Lieutenant ... I shall as a friend desire you, and as a Christian require you, to call upon God to incline your heart to his laws, to quicken you in his way, and not to take the word of truth utterly out of your mouth. Live still to die, that by death you may purchase eternal life ... For, as the preacher saith, there is a time to be born and a time to die, and the day of death is better than the day of our birth. Yours as the Lord knoweth, as a friend, Jane Dudley.[17]

On 17 February, Suffolk was tried at the Guildhall, charged with levying war in the county of Leicester, posting proclamations against the queen's marriage and for 'compassing the death and final destruction of the queen'. He pleaded not guilty on the grounds that it was not wrong for a nobleman to defend his country from 'strangers'. But his protestations were not accepted. Two of his adherents, John Bowyer and Thomas Rampton, had already been questioned and admitted to aiding the duke in treasonable activities. Arundel, the brother-in-law with whom he had shared a strained relationship for nearly thirty years, delivered the death sentence. Suffolk was taken back to the Tower, with a face 'heavy and pensive'. On climbing from his barge, he asked the men to pray for him. He wrote out a full confession and prayed for 'mercy not justice' from the queen. Having already abused the grant of the former, on this occasion he received the latter. Mary still hoped for the salvation of the soul of the cousin she had known all her life. She sent two priests to try to persuade him to accept the Catholic faith, but as with his daughter 'they were in no wise able to move him'. On the morning of 23 February, he was executed, and, in the words of Sir Robert Wingfield, occasioned the 'permanent ruin of the ancient house of Grey of Dorset'.

Aftermath

Time takes away the grief of men.

Erasmus

Frances was left to salvage what she could from the ruin of her husband's mixture of ambition, religious zealotry and political ineptitude. The Suffolk estates were forfeit to the Crown, but within a couple of months Queen Mary had regranted Beaumanor. Lord Thomas followed his brother to execution on 24 April, although Lord John was eventually granted a pardon, as was George Medley.

Frances and her remaining daughters were welcomed at Queen Mary's court, and the following year Frances remarried. Her husband was Adrian Stokes, who had been a colleague of Lord John's at Newhaven before becoming Frances's Master of Horse. None of her pregnancies by Stokes resulted in a living child. Queen Mary did not succeed in bearing an heir either, and the throne passed to Elizabeth, who loathed her Grey cousins. Lady Katherine secretly married the Duke of Somerset's son, and bore two sons of her own before being placed under house arrest with Lord John, dying in 1567, probably of anorexia or a similar stress-induced illness. Lady Mary also made a secret marriage, to the Sergeant Porter of one of the royal palaces, and even this match was still too dangerous in Elizabeth's eyes. The couple were separated, and, although Mary was partially rehabilitated, she died childless in 1578. Lord John Grey's son was granted the barony of Grey of Groby, and his great-grandson was created Earl of Stamford. This earl was a signatory to the death warrant of Charles I. Both titles became extinct for lack of male heirs in 1976.

The descendants of the Grey sisters of the different generations include HM The Queen, and most of the peerage of England, Scotland and Ireland – so the ancient and illustrious house of Grey of Dorset lives on.

Appendix 1

The Descent of the Greys of Ruthin

The man from whom the various branches of the Grey family devolved was Henry de Grey (1155–1219), granted lands in the area still known as Grays Thurrock in Essex by Richard I in 1194. Henry, a friend and intimate of King John, and his wife, Isabel Bardolf, had at least three sons: Sir Richard, who inherited his mother's portion of the Derbyshire Codnor estates, and founded the line of barons Grey of Codnor; Sir John of Shirland, whose descendants became barons Grey of Wilton, of Ruthyn and of Powis; and Sir William Grey of Sandiacre, whose descendants were less exalted. By another marriage, Henry de Grey had Sir Robert, ancestor of the barons Grey of Rotherfield.

By the early fourteenth century, Henry's grandson Reginald (c. 1230–1308) was well established in the favour of the kings of England. He married Maud de Longchamp, heiress of the barony of Wilton, and was first Justice, then Sheriff of Chester. Reginald played a major part in the brutal conquest of Wales by Edward I in the 1280s, after which the English Crown took control of the heartlands of Wales. As a reward for his support, Reginald received the old cantrefi of Tegeingl and Dyffryn Clwyd, which contained one of the few castles built by the Welsh princes – that of Ruthyn.[1]

Reginald died in 1308, and was succeeded by his son John, 2nd Baron Grey of Wilton. John had a far less amicable relationship with his king, Edward II, than Reginald had with Edward I. Edward II, considered to be in thrall to his favourites, Sir Piers Gaveston and Hugh le Despenser, did not enjoy the respect of his peers but Grey drew the line at open rebellion. He had been appointed by Edward as Justice of North Wales, and Constable of Caernarfon Castle in 1315, and in 1322, when Thomas of Lancaster led a group of frustrated barons against the king, John supported his monarch. John de Grey died in 1323, and the barony of Wilton passed to his son Henry, born of his first wife, Anne Ferrers. By John's second wife, Maud Basset, he had another son, Roger de Grey, who inherited the de Grey lands in Wales and was summoned to Parliament in December 1324 as Baron Grey of Ruthyn. Shortly after that, Edward II's reign came to a sorry close when he was overthrown by his wife, Isabella of France, and her lover, Roger Mortimer, who, with the backing of Parliament, set up Prince Edward as Edward III.

Roger de Grey's career was steady, but not spectacular. He married Elizabeth Hastings, the daughter of John, 1st Lord Hastings and Lord Bergavenny. Like his fellow barons, Roger was obliged to take part in the king's wars, first in Scotland and later in France as Edward III claimed the French throne. He accompanied the king on the successful campaign of 1346, which included the famous victory at Crécy. Roger died in 1351, to be succeeded by his son Reginald as 2nd Lord Grey of Ruthyn, who does not appear to have done anything remarkable before his death in 1388. He married Alienor Le Strange, by whom he had at least two children, Ida de Grey – among whose descendants were Anne Boleyn, Jane Seymour and Katheryn Howard – and Reginald, 3rd Lord Grey of Ruthyn. This third Reginald Grey played a far greater part on the political stage than had his father. He inherited aged about twenty-six, and before long he was also claiming the Hastings inheritance on the death of John Hastings, 3rd Earl of Pembroke, his second cousin once removed. Unsurprisingly, this claim was contested by other descendants of Reginald's great-grandfather, who had been 1st Lord Hastings. The case took nine years to settle, after which Grey was permitted to bear the arms of Hastings, quartered with Grey of Ruthyn, and to take possession of various Hastings estates, including lands in Ireland. Reginald served Richard II in Ireland, including a brief period in 1398 as acting Lord Deputy. It is unknown what part, if any, Reginald played in the deposition of Richard II, but he was soon a member of Henry IV's council, advising the king to put to Parliament the question of renewing the war with France.

We might have heard little of Reginald were it not for his part in the momentous events of the early 1400s that convulsed Wales. For many years, he had been feuding with his neighbour in the Welsh Marches, a Welsh gentleman by the name of Owain Glyndwr, a descendant of the native princes of Wales. The dispute escalated – Reginald accused Glyndwr of raiding his lands, while Glyndwr laid a very serious charge against Reginald: that he had deliberately withheld a summons from the king to Owain to fight in the Scottish wars, thus making Glyndwr guilty of the treasonable offence of failing to answer a summons. This dispute between neighbours intensified to become a full-scale insurgency in Wales. Given his personal grievances against Glyndwr, it is not surprising that Reginald advocated strong measures to Henry IV, and in 1401 a series of severe penal laws was enacted against the Welsh. Undeterred, Glyndwr fought on and captured Reginald in an ambush in 1402. Unlike the king's cousin Edmund Mortimer (whom many thought the rightful King of England), also captured by Glyndwr, Reginald refused to join the insurgents, but agreed to pay a ransom of 10,000 marks, with his son John to be handed over as security. Henry IV permitted Reginald to sell various manors, and also contributed to the ransom, as he valued Reginald as a 'valiant and loyal knight'. The sum paid, Reginald was released. The cost of the ransom hit him hard, and, although he took up the fight against Glyndwr again in 1409, he played a less prominent part in Henry's council thereafter.

Henry IV died in 1413, to be succeeded by Henry V, whose all-consuming ambition was the capture of the crown of France. This dream had a terrible human cost, and was disastrous in the long term for England, but it did have the advantage of bringing together the English nobility in a common cause after the disruption of Richard II's deposition. Reginald was appointed to the regency council set up in 1415 under Henry V's brother John, Duke of Bedford to govern England in the king's absence. Before long, it was decided that Reginald's military experience made him suitable for a front-line position, and he served in France in 1421, in the campaign that led to the death of Henry V. He was there again in 1425, although by that time the high-water mark of English success in France was receding, despite Bedford's valiant efforts to retain control for his nephew, the new king, Henry VI. Reginald appeared in the parliament of 1426, but no more is known of him until his death in 1440.

Reginald married twice – his first wife was Margaret Ros, by whom he had a daughter, Margaret, who married Sir William Bonville of Chewton, and a son, John. Like his father, John served in Henry V's French campaigns, including at Agincourt. A soldier of considerable skill, he was elected as a Knight of the Garter, and appointed Lord Deputy of Ireland in 1427–28. John married Lady Constance Holland, widowed Duchess of Norfolk and a great-granddaughter of Edward III. By her, he had two sons: Edmund, born October 1416, and Thomas, later Lord Richemount Grey. John died before his father, and so, in 1440, the Ruthyn lands and title passed straight to the grandson Edmund, now 4th Lord Grey of Ruthyn. Reginald's second wife was Joan, daughter and heiress of Sir William Astley and Joan Willoughby. Her first marriage, to Sir Thomas Ranley of Farnborough, was childless, so on her death in 1448 her inheritance of Astley, in Warwickshire, passed to her eldest son by Reginald, Edward Grey.

Appendix 2

Timeline of the Attempted Coup

Sources are not consistent, so this timeline is partially conjectural.

1544	Third Act of Succession
30 Dec. 1546	Henry VIII makes his will
28 Jan. 1547	Henry VIII dies
9 Feb. 1547	Edward VI crowned
Early 1553	Edward VI draws up first 'Devise for the Succession'
	Edward VI amends 'Devise'
9 Feb. 1553	Edward VI visited at Westminster by his half-sister the Lady Mary
	The Duke of Northumberland, as Lord President of the Council, authorises the Lady Mary to use the royal arms as she had prior to the annulment of her parents' marriage
Late Apr. 1553	Marriage agreed between Lady Jane Grey, daughter of the Duke and Duchess of Suffolk, with Lord Guildford Dudley, son of the Duke of Northumberland
24 Apr. 1553	Royal warrant for wedding clothes for Lady Jane
25 May 1553	Lady Jane and Lord Guildford married
	Lady Katherine Grey married Henry Herbert, son of the Earl of Pembroke
	Lady Katherine Dudley married Henry Hastings, son of the Earl of Huntingdon
12 Jun. 1553	Judges of the King's Bench summoned to give effect to the Devise
14 Jun. 1553	Judges refuse to implement the Devise
15 Jun. 1553	Edward insists Letters Patent are drawn up to give effect to 'Devise'; judges assent, under threat and promise of a pardon under the Great Seal
21 Jun. 1553	Edward's Council signs the Letters Patent

1 Jul. 1553	Edward's last public appearance, in the window of the palace at Greenwich
4 Jul. 1553	Imperial ambassador hears a rumour that Edward is dying and that Lady Jane Grey has been named his successor
5 Jul. 1553	Council sends request to ladies Mary and Elizabeth to visit their dying brother
6 Jul. 1553	Edward VI dies
c. 7 Jul. 1553	Mary warned that Edward is already dead; leaves Hunsdon for Sawston, Cambridgeshire.
	Lady Jane Grey leaves Chelsea for Syon House where she is told of Edward's death and that she will be queen
8 Jul. 1553	Lord Mayor and thirty-one City burgesses sign Edward's 'Devise'
	Mary reaches Kenninghall, Norfolk, and proclaims herself queen
9 Jul. 1553	Mary writes to the council demanding they proclaim her as queen
10 Jul. 1553	Lady Jane travels by river to the Tower of London
	Jane proclaimed as queen in London
11 Jul. 1553	Jane and Council receive Mary's letter and respond, affirming Mary's illegitimate status
	Both Mary and Jane proclaimed separately in Norwich
12 Jul. 1553	Mary arrives at Framlingham Castle, Suffolk
13 Jul. 1553	Northumberland accepts commission to raise troops and to capture Mary; reminds his colleagues on the council that they have all agreed to Jane being proclaimed queen
	Jane and Council issue orders for troops to be raised
14 Jul. 1553	Northumberland sets out from London with around 600 troops, later rising to around 3,000
c.	Jane informs Guildford that he will not be king, only a duke
15 Jul. 1553	Royal ships sent to prevent Mary escaping to the Low Countries declare in her favour; artillery taken to her at Framlingham
16 Jul. 1553	Nicholas Ridley, Bishop of London, preaches at St Paul's Cross, declaring Mary and Elizabeth illegitimate
18 Jul. 1553	Earl of Oxford declares for Mary
	Northumberland advances from Cambridge towards Bury St Edmunds but turns back

Timeline of the Attempted Coup

19 Jul. 1553	Council, led by Arundel and Pembroke, has Mary proclaimed queen at St Paul's Cross and writes to Northumberland to stand down
	Suffolk informs Jane she is no longer queen and proclaims Mary on Tower Hill
20 Jul. 1553	Mary reviews her troops at Framlingham
	The Earl of Arundel and Sir William Paget arrive at Framlingham to seek pardon
	In Cambridge, Northumberland receives the letter from the council and proclaims Mary as queen
21 Jul. 1553	Northumberland arrested by the Earl of Arundel
24 Jul. 1553	Mary leaves Framlingham for London
28 Jul. 1553	Suffolk arrested and taken to the Tower
30 Jul. 1553	Northumberland brought to London
c. 30 Jul. 1553	Frances, Duchess of Suffolk pleads for her husband
c. 31 Jul. 1553	Suffolk released to house arrest at Charterhouse
3 Aug. 1553	Mary enters London
8 Aug. 1553	Edward VI buried in a Protestant ceremony
c. 10 Aug. 1553	Jane writes to Mary, declaring her unwillingness to be proclaimed as queen
c. 13 Aug. 1553	Mary receives Jane's letter
18 Aug. 1553	Northumberland tried and found guilty
21 Aug. 1553	Northumberland's execution delayed so that he can see a priest; returns to the Catholic faith
22 Aug. 1553	Northumberland executed
1 Oct. 1553	Mary crowned at Westminster Abbey
13 Nov. 1553	Lady Jane, Lord Guildford and Archbishop Cranmer tried and found guilty of treason
Nov. 1553	Lady Jane writes to her former tutor, castigating him for being reconciled to the Catholic faith
17 Dec. 1553	Lady Jane allowed to take exercise in the Tower
22 Dec.	Rebels plans finalised
21 Jan. 1554	Courtenay confesses to Gardiner
22 Jan.	Suffolk, Thomas and John head north, ignoring royal summons; Council issues proclamations against Suffolk
28 Jan.	The Grey brothers reach Bradgate
29 Jan.	The brothers enter Leicester and seek support
30 Jan.	Gates of Coventry closed against the rebels
2 Feb.	Suffolk arrested
8 Feb.	Dr Feckenham visits Lady Jane in the Tower
10 Feb.	Suffolk brought to the Tower
12 Feb.	Lady Jane and Lord Guildford executed
23 Feb.	Suffolk executed
24 Apr.	Lord Thomas Grey executed

Notes

Preface

1. Although I cannot find the exact descent, Anchetil de Grey was granted lands at Rotherfield Greys in Oxfordshire which were held by the Greys of Thurrock in the thirteenth century, so the link is probable.
2. The Welsh spelling of the town is Rhuthun, and the pronunciation is RITH-in. It has been anglicised as Ruthin or Ruthyn. The latter spelling is that used to refer to the barony, which still exists, although in abeyance.

Prologue

1. An account of Suffolk's death is contained in Foxe.
2. Quoted in J. G. Nichols, *The Chronicle of Queen Jane and Two Years of Queen Mary*, p.57n.

1 A Failed State

1. Some genealogies give the date of Reginald and Joan Astley's marriage as 1415, giving a birth year of *c.* 1416 for their eldest son, while others give the marriage as 1406, making Edward around twenty-five at the time of his marriage. The latter seems more likely, given Joan's first husband died in 1404.
2. As predicted by Gloucester, Orléans failed to pay his ransom, and did little to negotiate peace.
3. Lander in *The Crown and Aristocracy 1450–1509*, relates that between 1448 and 1455, no less than one-sixth of the peerage were imprisoned for varying periods for 'disreputable conduct'.
4. *An English Chronicle of the Reigns of Richard II., Henry IV., Henry V., and Henry VI.*
5. If male primogeniture were the only rule, then Edmund, Duke of Somerset was first in line, as the grandson of Henry VI's great-grandfather John of Gaunt, third son of Edward III. But John of Gaunt's Beaufort children had been born before he married their mother, Katherine Swynford. The children had been legitimated by the pope, and subsequently by Parliament, but Henry IV had attempted to bar them from the throne by Letters Patent. Although it was debatable whether Letters Patent were sufficient to change an Act of Parliament, the Beauforts' claim was considered dubious. If the Beauforts were barred, the next male heir was Richard,

Duke of York, great-grandson of Edward III's fourth son, Edmund of Langley. But strict male primogeniture was not the rule in England. There was no bar on women inheriting, and certainly no objection to claims being passed through the female line as the Empress Maud had passed her claim to her son Henry II, and female transmission was the whole basis of the English claim to the French crown. So the descendants of the female members of the house of Lancaster could be considered. Henry IV's sister Philippa, Queen of Portugal had descendants, but they were now ruling the various Iberian kingdoms, and there was no desire for a foreign-born king, even if the law allowed inheritance from one not born in the realm – another debatable point. Philippa's sister Elizabeth of Lancaster had borne a son in England – John Holland, 2nd Duke of Exeter. Exeter could therefore claim to be Henry IV's heir general. But, if female rights were acknowledged, there was a stronger claim than either Exeter's or Somerset's – and perhaps, it was occasionally whispered, stronger than the king's own. Richard, Duke of York was descended in the female line from Edward III's second son, Lionel of Antwerp. York's great-uncle Edmund Mortimer, Earl of March, had been nominated as heir by the childless Richard II, before Richard had been overthrown by Henry IV.

6. Records of the Borough of Leicester vol. 2.
7. Quoted in Johnson, *Duke Richard of York*.
8. Quoted in Jones, *The Hollow Crown*.
9. The spellings are various – Widville, Wydeville, Wydville and Wodeville. Woodville has been the accepted spelling by most historians for many years.
10. See Higginbotham, *The Woodvilles: The Wars of the Roses and England's most infamous family* for discussion of the birth order of the Woodville children. Since it was customary to name children for their parents, and Jacquetta Woodville's marriage to Lord Strange was arranged in 1450, I would suggest that Jacquetta was actually the eldest.
11. The lands in question were Nobottle and Brington, a group of small parishes in Northamptonshire, not far from Daventry, and Woodham Ferrers in Essex. The properties were enfeoffed by Lord and Lady Ferrers in 1456, to Robert Iseham, William Wales, William Fielding and others, in connection with the marriage of John and Elizabeth.
12. Eleanor of Aquitaine was regent for Richard I, Isabelle of France for her son Edward III, and Philippa of Hainault for her husband, Edward III.
13. For more on lovedays and arbitration, see Powell, *Settlement of Disputes by Arbitration in Fifteenth-Century England*.
14. From the inquisition into the matter, quoted in Scofield, *The Life and Reign of King Edward IV*.
15. See Laynesmith, *Cicely, Duchess of York*, for reasoned refutation of the allegation that Cicely was personally assaulted or raped.
16. *The travels of Leo of Rozmital through Germany, Flanders, England, France, Spain, Portugal, and Italy, 1465–1467*.

2 The Triumph of York

1. Commynes, *The Universal Spider: The Life of Louis XI of France*.
2. See Higginbotham for a discussion of the probable dates.
3. Laynesmith, *Cicely, Duchess of York*.
4. Dame was the title used for a knight's widow.
5. Quoted in Waurin, ed. Dupont II, pp. 327–83.
6. Mancini, trans. Armstrong, *The Usurpation of Richard III*.
7. Ross, *Edward IV*.
8. Brown & Webster, *The Movements of the Earl of Warwick in the Summer of 1464 – A Correction*.
9. Quoted in article by Edward Kennedy as Thomas & Thornley (eds), *Great Chronicle of London*.
10. Steel, *The Receipt of the Exchequer*.

11. Lander, *Marriage and Politics in the Fifteenth Century: The Nevilles and the Wydevilles*.
12. He died in 1463, allowing the earldom to be granted to Grey of Ruthyn.
13. Savoy was an independent duchy within the Holy Roman Empire, and Philippe, known as 'the landless', was only one of a number of claimants.
14. Sir William Herbert, Earl of Pembroke, was one of Edward's closest friends and now his brother-in-law. Fogge had earned Warwick's enmity as part of a group of Kent landowners who had challenged Warwick's jurisdiction as Constable of Dover Castle. He was married to Queen Elizabeth's niece, Alice Haute.
15. Case identified by Susan Higginbotham – she quotes TNA KB27/836 m. 61d.
16. Acheson, *Gentry of Leicestershire*.
17. There were several lords Scrope with multiple wives and widows. This Lady Scrope was probably born Elizabeth St John, and was the half-sister of Lady Margaret Beaufort – Lady Margaret Stafford at this time.
18. The general reluctance of the nobility to get involved in the wars is covered in detail in Lander's *Crown and Aristocracy*. In 1460, thirty-two or possibly thirty-seven nobles fought for Henry VI, and around twenty for York, although they were generally of lower rank, and were not motivated to crown Richard of York. Seven families were never reconciled to York. In 1471, ten peers fought for Lancaster, and eight for York. In 1485, nine turned out for Richard III and three (probably) for Henry Tudor.
19. Queen Margaret was enrolled in 1475, along with Lady Vaux, née Katherine Penistone, who had been her most faithful companion, and later went into exile with her.

3 The Queen's Sons

1. CPR Edward IV 1474 m. 6.
2. Elizabeth Courtenay's first husband, John Harington, 4th Baron Harington, was the half-brother of another of Cecily's great-grandfathers, 5th Baron Harington.
3. Bookman, *The Hastings Hours*.
4. He had been created Prince of Wales soon after his birth on 26 June 1471, followed by a confirmation in Parliament on 3 July 1471, that he was recognised as heir apparent. Investiture was the ceremonial bit.
5. Quoted in Dalton, *The Collegiate Church of Ottery St. Mary: being the Ordinacio et Statuta, Ecclesie Sancte Marie de Otery, Exon*.
6. Quoted in Evans, sourced from Owen & Blakeway, *Shrewsbury*.
7. Commynes, *The Universal Spider: The Life of Louis XI of France*.
8. See Ramsay, *The Strength of English Armies* for realistic estimates, rather than chroniclers' exaggerations.
9. Rymer's *Foedera*, Vol. 12; also Commynes.
10. The manors of Rochford, Leigh, Paglesham and Foulness in Essex; Thorpe Waterville, Aldwinkle, Achurch, Chelveston and Caldecote in Northamptonshire; Ardington in Berkshire; and Barford St Martin in Wiltshire.
11. The earldom of Norfolk was heritable by females, but the dukedom was not. It was the argument over whether the lands went with the earldom or the dukedom that would cause problems with the Mowbray heirs.
12. CA, M3 fol. 12, spelling modernised.
13. Black, *Illustrations of ancient state and chivalry from manuscripts preserved in the Ashmolean museum*.
14. Clarence and his duchess, Isabel Neville, had two children, Lady Margaret of Clarence, and Edward. The latter was permitted to take his grandmother's title of Warwick.
15. I have seen quoted in several places, that later Edward had said 'Oh, unfortunate brother, for whose life no man in this world would once make request', but there is never any citation of a contemporary source and has the air of an eighteenth- or nineteenth-century dramatization.

16. These arguments, quoted in Commynes, are from a draft letter of Louis, rather than one definitely delivered.
17. Green, *Lives of the Princesses of England* Vol. 3.
18. The Stonor Letters, no. 285.
19. The Stonor Letters, no. 306.
20. CPR Edward IV 1483 m. 16.
21. CPR Edward IV 1476–85 p. 212.

4 Turmoil

1. Hicks, *Richard III*.
2. More, *History of Richard III*.
3. Mancini.
4. Pronay (ed.), *The Crowland Chronicle Continuations: 1459–1486*.
5. ibid.
6. ibid.
7. ibid.
8. Mancini.
9. Sir John was the widower of Lady Ferrers.
10. The de Bohun male line failed in 1373 with the death of Humphrey, 7th Earl of Hereford, 6th of Essex and 2nd of Northampton. This rich inheritance was shared between his daughters, Eleanor and Mary, who were married to Edward III's son Thomas of Woodstock and grandson Henry Bolingbroke respectively. Henry Bolingbroke went on to become Henry IV, although by the time he took the crown in 1399, Mary was dead. Her inheritance passed to her son Henry V and grandson Henry VI. On the death of that king, and his son, Prince Edward of Lancaster, the de Bohun inheritance should have passed to the descendants of Eleanor, of whom the senior was Buckingham.
11. The Stonor Letters, no. 330.
12. I cannot find the family link between Richard's friend Sir Richard Radcliffe and Dorset's friend Sir Robert Radcliffe.
13. Mrs Shore was soon imprisoned herself. She must have chuckled when Richard III's own solicitor proposed marriage.
14. Pronay (ed.), *The Crowland Chronicle Continuations: 1459–1486*.
15. Stonor letters, no. 333.
16. BL Harleian Horrox Vol. 2 25.
17. Quote from Rous Roll in Dockray & Hammond, *Richard III from Contemporary Chronicles, Letters and Records*.
18. Richard III paid £2 6s 4d for the funeral costs.
19. Harris, *English Aristocratic Women*.
20. See Lander article. The law was that a man's whole estate, including that held to his use was forfeit, as was the wife's common law dower. The wife's own inheritance, and her jointure were exempt. But she could only reclaim her inheritance when her husband died, and she was no longer femme couvert, although she could hold the jointure.

5 Exile

1. Text of *Titulus Regius* as reproduced on Richard III Society website.
2. Vergil, trans. Sutton, *Anglica Historia*.
3. ibid.
4. Jones, *Essay from The English Experience in France*.
5. Davies, *Bishop John Morton, the Holy See, and the Accession of Henry VII*.
6. Vergil.
7. Jones.
8. A date of 24 May used to be given, but recent scholarship has indicated 27 May as the correct date.

9. The evidence in favour of it being an impersonation of Warwick: 1. Irish coins, inscribed Edward; 2. The statute of 10 Henry VII c 14 cancelled all statutes passed in the parliament of 'Edward VI' and ordered them destroyed. While no copies of this statute exist, it is not true that they were destroyed as a ploy on Henry's part to obliterate all references to the matter – a copy of the statute remained in Ireland, until its physical destruction in the Irish Civil War of 1920–22. Its contents live on in the work of Professor M. Hayden, who handled the original and referred to it in Haydon, *Studies: an Irish Quarterly Review, Vol. IV No. 16* pp. 622–638, December 1915. There are also traces in the Exchequer records – see 'New evidence for Edward VI's reign in Ireland?' in *The Ricardian* and Janic Markys, *Dublin and the Coronation of Edward VI.*

10. Bennet, *Henry VII and the Northern Uprising.*

6 Royal Service

1. Since Anne's marriage to Maximilian had been by proxy only, it was easy to annul.

2. BL Add MS 7099 folio 6 (Payments) Chamber Books.

3. Joan Rivers (!) is never mentioned in genealogies, but is named in CPR Henry VII 1497 m. 154.

4. e.g. Anne Holland, née Montacute, Duchess of Exeter, made the same stipulation in 1457.

5. Elizabeth, born July 1492, died September 1495 – perhaps named for her recently deceased grandmother.

6. Details are quoted in Strickland, Lives of the Queens of England, from BL Arundel MS 26.

7. Rymer's Foedera with Syllabus Vol. 12, ed. Thomas Rymer (London, 1739–1743), pp. 494–505. British History Online.

8. Lord Harington was an honorary title, the senior of Cecily's baronies.

9. Gairdner (ed.), *Letters and Papers illustrative of the Reigns of Richard III and Henry VII.*

10. Margaret did not take her famous vow of chastity until 1499, by which time she had been married to Stanley for twenty-five years.

11. E101/414/6 f. 117v Obligations from Chamber Books.

12. E101/413/2/2 f. 60v (Receipts) Chamber Books.

13. The lady is sometimes named as Elizabeth, but it is Eleanor on her grave. Dorset's daughter Elizabeth long outlived her sister, and married the Earl of Kildare.

14. CCR – 972.

15. Dorset's mainprisor in September 1496 was Sir James Audley of Audley. As the original Audley family had died out, to be replaced by a collateral line with the surname of Tuchet, I can't be sure that they are the same person, but the Christian name and the designation as 'of Audley' suggests they were.

16. An alternative provenance for Leonard's name might be Cecily's stepfather – Lord Hastings' father's name was Leonard, and if, as is possible if Leonard Grey were born before 1483, Hastings was his godfather, he may have named him.

17. BL Add MS 59899 f, 133r Obligations from Chamber Books.

7 Marriages and Money

1. *Letters and Papers Illustrative of the Reigns of Richard III and Henry VII,* p. 410. Guildford's sister-in-law, Elizabeth Pympe, née Pashley, was Elizabeth Woodville's first cousin.

2. Leland Collectanea.

3. Sean Cunningham discusses the death in detail in *Prince Arthur*, and concludes a local infectious epidemic was responsible.

4. Quoted in Hayward, *The Great Wardrobe Account of Henry VII and Henry VIII* E101/433/11 no. 54 14 June 1503.

5. Quoted in Harris, *English Aristocratic Women*.
6. CCR Henry VII Vol. 2.
7. BL Add MS 59899 f. 157v, Obligations from Chamber books.
8. CCR Henry VII Vol. 2 478.
9. Quoted in Penn, *The Winter King*.
10. Grey v. Alday C1/312/98.
11. CCR Henry VII Vol. 2 580.

8 A New Dawn

1. Hall's Chronicle.
2. The inheritance of Leonor was riddled with poisonings, betrayals and murders – and that was just within the royal family.
3. The whole series of letters that follows may be found in L& P, Vol. 1 pp. 552–648.

9 The Golden Years

1. Gunn, *Charles Brandon: Henry VIII's Closest Friend*.
2. Scarisbrick, *Henry VIII*.
3. On the death of Charles VIII, a childless Anne had hoped to return to her duchy as sovereign, and escape French control, but she was given little alternative but to accept Charles's successor, Louis, as her husband. They had two daughters – Claude, later Queen of France, and Renée, later Duchess of Ferrara.
4. France practised Salic Law, debarring Louis' daughter, Claude from inheriting. François of Angoulême was the son of Louis' cousin Charles, Count of Angoulême. Claude did inherit her mother's duchy of Brittany, but her marriage to François was intended to subsume it into the French Crown.
5. L & P Vol. 1 3416.
6. Lady Ravenstein was a descendant of Dorset's great-great-grandmother, so Don Diego could claim a visit was merely a family affair.
7. Hall.
8. L & P Vol. 2 1935.
9. Giustuinian, *Four Years at the Court of Henry VIII: A Selection of Dispatches. 1515–1519* Vol. II.
10. CSP Venice II 1509–1519.
11. L & P Vol. 2 3588.

10 Local Politics

1. E36/215 f. 676 (obligations 1513) Chamber books.
2. L & P Vol. 3 48.
3. L & P Vol. 3 309.
4. L & P Vol. 3 2368.
5. L & P Vol. 3 2955.
6. L & P Vol. 3 3039.

11 Darkening Skies

1. L & P Vol. 4 1228.
2. Miller, *Henry VIII and the English Nobility*.
3. Wood, *Letters of Royal and Illustrious Ladies* Vol. 2 I.
4. Calendared as 1527 in Merriman, but the reference to Scotland indicates an earlier date.

5.   Farm in this context means the right to collect the rent, and retain part as a fee.
6.   For a more than exhaustive discussion of the theological points, see Scarisbrick.
7.   G. W. Bernard, *The Fall of Wolsey Reconsidered*.
8.   Hall, pp. 767ff.
9.   Land owned in fee simple (usually only urban land) could be alienated by will, and this is the land that Cecily refers to as that which she has the power to dispose. Her manors etc. would have been held for knight's service.
10. Some genealogies list Margaret as married to Sir Roger Wake of Blisworth, but I can find no evidence for this, and she is not mentioned on his tomb. She was certainly neither married nor widowed by March 1527 when Cecily made her will.
11. Records of Borough of Leicester.
12. Cecily's stepson had died young.

12 Ireland

1.   Ellis, *Ireland in the Age of the Tudors*.
2.   SP I p. 72.
3.   Wood Vol. 1. CI.
4.   Wood Vol. 2 XXVII.
5.   Quoted in Leinster, *The Earls of Kildare, and their ancestors: from 1057 to 1773*.
6.   Calendared in L & P as 1523, but the reference to more than one child, and the letter accompanying it to Cromwell from Lord Leonard, make 1533 the more likely date.
7.   SP III p. 272.
8.   Lisle Letters.
9.   L & P Vol. 9 1054.
10. SP II p. 616.
11. L & P Vol. 13, Pt 1 1303.
12. Ibid.
13. Quoted in Pinkerton, *An Inventory of the Household Effects of Lord Deputy Lord Leonard Grey, in 1540*.
14. ibid.
15. FitzGerald and Pole were both descendants of Richard Neville and Alice Montacute, Earl and Countess of Salisbury.
16. Wood Vol. 3 XCVI.

13 A Thankless Child

1.   L & P Vol. 4 1540.
2.   Dorothy was Mountjoy's fourth wife. Gertrude's mother, Inez de Venegas, had been a close friend of Queen Katharine, having come with her from Spain in 1501.
3.   L & P Vol. 6 1252.
4.   L & P Vol. 7 153.
5.   Camden Miscellany XXX. Hoyle (ed.), *Letters of the Cliffords, Lords Clifford and Earls of Cumberland c.1500 – c. 1565*.
6.   Wood Vol. 2 XLVII.
7.   CSPS Vol. 5 Pt 2 43. The naming of Dorset as being a guest at this dinner party is likely to be mistaken – he was of a different generation from the others, and not part of their circle – confusion is caused by Chapuys' habit of referring to 'the young marquis', by whom he meant not Dorset but Courtenay of Exeter.
8.   Wriothesley's Chronicle, Vol. 1 pp. 50.
9.   The Dorsets' comparative poverty is confirmed by their assessment. While Norfolk was assessed to pay £100, and the earls of Huntingdon and Essex

around £44 and £21 respectively, Dorset was only assessed at £14, while his aunt Dorothy Mountjoy, who had been widowed in 1534, was assessed at £9.

10. See both Lisle and Tallis for detailed argument on Jane's birthdate.
11. Nicols, *A Collection of Ordinances*.
12. SP II pp. 570.
13. Wood Vol. 2 CXLI.
14. There is copious evidence of Dudley's sharp practice in the Lisle Letters, in other correspondence in L & P, and the connivance of Hertford and Cromwell is clear.
15. Wood Vol. 3 XXXVI.
16. Wood Vol. 3 XXXV.

14 Reformation

1. Wood Vol. 3 XLVI.
2. Wood Vol. 2 CXLII.
3. Lord Lisle was the stepbrother of Thomas I, and the stepfather of the Sir John Dudley who was making Cicely Sutton's life a misery, while Lady Lisle's sister Katherine Grenville had married Sir John Arundell on the death of Lady Eleanor Grey – making her stepmother to Dorset's cousins John and Thomas Arundell.
4. L & P Vol. 15 534n.
5. L & P XIII p II p. 280. The writer is unknown, but the description was found in the Archivio di Stato in Rome.
6. Wriothesley's Chronicle, pp. 98.
7. Lady Mary died aged only seventeen, having already married the 4th Duke of Norfolk and borne a son, Philip Howard, who eventually inherited the earldom, which continues to this day as the junior title of the dukes of Norfolk.

15 End of an Era

1. Records of the Borough of Leicester.
2. Hall, quoted in Gunn.
3. Lady Lane is sometimes mis-transcribed as Lady Jane – that is, Dorset's daughter.
4. Lisle Sisters – the prayer book is cited as Queen's College Oxford MS 349.

16 Sibling Rivalry

1. Legal majority for a man was twenty-one, but both Edward IV and Henry VIII had taken full regal power at eighteen, and Henry VI a little younger.
2. Lipscomb, *The King is Dead*.
3. CSPS Vol. 10.
4. Haynes, ccxcvi.
5. Haynes, ccci.
6. Calendar of the Cecil Papers at Hatfield House I, p. 70.
7. Tytler I, p. 138i.
8. Ironically, the chief translator of the Paraphrase on the Gospel of St John was none other than the Lady Mary, an accomplished Latinist.
9. This series of correspondence is in Haynes, *A Collection of State Papers*, pp. 74.
10. CSPD V – quoted in Tallis.
11. Haynes, pp. 76.
12. ibid.
13. ibid, pp. 68.

17 Religion and Rebellion

1. For a detailed exposition of the issues in Kett's Rebellion, see *Tudor Rebellions*.
2. Quoted in Skidmore, *Edward VI, The Lost King of England*.
3. Quoted in MacCulloch, *Cranmer, A Life*.
4. CSPS Vol. 9.
5. CSPS Vol. 10.
6. Original Letters I p. 77.
7. ibid.
8. CSPS Vol. 10.
9. Quoted in Tallis.
10. 'Cecil Papers: 1551', in *Calendar of the Cecil Papers in Hatfield House: Volume 1, 1306–1571*. *British History Online*: http://www.british-history.ac.uk/cal-cecil-papers/vol1/pp82-94 [accessed 18 April 2019].
11. ibid.
12. Nichols (ed.), *Literary Remains of King Edward VI Vol. 2*.
13. Robinson (ed.), *Original Letters Relative to the Reformation*.
14. Champerty was the offence of bargaining to buy or sell land not owned, and embracery was the illegal support of a case by a judge.

18 Queen Jane

1. Wingfield, trans. MacCulloch, *Camden Miscellany*, *Vita Mariae Angliae Reginae*.
2. The birth order of Northumberland's sons is uncertain. While Guildford is usually referred to as the youngest, it seems likely that Henry was younger, otherwise he would have been the husband selected for Jane. Henry Dudley died young, and Margaret married the Earl of Derby.
3. The Letters Patent of Henry IV limiting the Beauforts family's right to inherit the throne did not overturn the previous Act, but sought to limit it – the Letters were always considered of doubtful legality, and were certainly ignored by the parliament that accepted Henry VII as king.
4. CSPS Vol. 11.
5. CSPS Vol. 11.
6. Wingfield.
7. Quoted in Whitelock.
8. *Chronicle of Queen Jane*.
9. CSPS Vol. 11 Nov. 1553.
10. CSPS Vol. 11 Oct. 1553.
11. CSPS Vol. 11 Oct. 1553.
12. CSPS Vol. 11 Nov. 1553.
13. Chronicle, p. 37.
14. CSPD Mary, Vol. 2.
15. Wingfield.
16. *Literary Remains of Lady Jane Grey*, p. 41.
17. Ibid.

Appendix 1

1. A cantref was an administrative area.

Bibliography

Abbreviations

BL: British Library
CSPD: Calendar of State Papers, Domestic
CSPS: Calendar of State Papers, relating to Spain
CSP, Milan: Calendar of State Papers, relating to Milan
CSP, Venice: Calendar of State Papers, relating to Venice
SP I–III: State Papers published by HM Commission, 1830
TNA: The National Archive
WM: Westminster Muniments

Books

Andreas, Bernard. *Historia Regis Henrici Septimi: A Bernardo Andrea Tholostate Conscripta, Necnon Alia Quædam Ad Eundem Regem Spetantia*. Longman, Brown, Green, Longmans, and Roberts, 1858
Backhouse, Janet. *The Hastings Hours* London British Library 1997
Bateson M., Chinnery, G. A., Stevenson, W.H., Stocks, J. E., Stocks, H. *Records of the Borough of Leicester; Being a Series of Extracts from the Archives of the Corporation of Leicester*. London: C. J. Clay, 1899.
Bell, Henry Nugent. *The Huntingdon Peerage, a Detailed Account of the Recent Restoration of the Earldom; to Which Is Prefixed a History of the House of Hastings*, 1821
Bernard, G. W. *The Tudor Nobility*. Manchester University Press, 1992
Black W. H. (ed) *Illustrations of Ancient State and Chivalry from Manuscripts Preserved in the Ashmolean Museum*
Bradley, Stuart. *John Morton: Adversary of Richard III, Power behind the Tudors*. Stroud, Gloucestershire Amberley, 2019
Breverton, Terry. *Henry VII: The Maligned Tudor King*. Stroud, Gloucestershire: Amberley, 2016
British Museum. Department of Manuscripts *A Catalogue of the Harleian Manuscripts in the British Museum. With Indexes of Persons, Places, and Matters* London, G. Eyre and A. Strahan, 1808
Byrne, M. St Clare. *The Lisle Letters* Chicago, University of Chicago Press 1981
Commission, Great Britain Record. *State Papers: Pt. I. Correspondence between the King and Cardinal Wolsey, 1518–1530.*

————. *State Papers Pt. II. Correspondence Between the King and His Ministers, 1530–1547*. J. Murray, 1830.

————. *State Papers: Pt. III. Correspondence between the Governments of England and Ireland, 1515–1546*. J. Murray, 1834.

Commynes, Philippe de. *The Universal Spider: The Life of Louis XI of France*. Translated by Paul Kendall. Folio Society, n.d.

Corbet, Dr Anthony. *Edward IV, England's Forgotten Warrior King*. iUniverse, 2015.

Cox, Thomas. *Gloucestershire – Lincolnshire*. 1738

Crawford, James Ludovic Lindsay, and Robert Steele. *A Bibliography of Royal Proclamations of the Tudor and Stuart Sovereigns and of Others Published under Authority, 1485–1714*. Oxford, Clarendon Press, 1910

Cunningham, Sean. *Prince Arthur* Stroud, Amberley 2017

Dockray, Keith, and P. W Hammond. *Richard III: From Contemporary Chronicles, Letters and Records*, 2013

Dunleavy, Bryan. *The Woodville Chronicle: The Story of the Woodville Family of Grafton in Northamptonshire*, 2017

Edward, John Gough Nichols. *Literary Remains of King Edward the Sixth: Edited from His Autograph …* Burt Franklin, 1857

Evans, H. T. *Wales and the Wars of the Roses*. Stroud, Gloucestershire: A. Sutton Pub, 1995.

Flenley, Ralph. *Six Town Chronicles of England*. Oxford, Clarendon press, 1911

Fletcher, Anthony, and Diarmaid MacCulloch. *Tudor Rebellions*. Rev. 5th ed. Seminar Studies in History. Harlow, England; New York: Pearson Longman, 2008

Foxe, John, Stephen Reed Cattley, and George Townsend. *The Acts and Monuments of John Foxe: A New and Complete Edition: With a Preliminary Dissertation, by the Rev. George Townsend …* London, Pub. by R. B. Seeley and W. Burnside

Gairdner, James. *Letters and Papers Illustrative of the Reigns of Richard III and Henry VII* : 1828–1912

Giustinian, Sebastian. *Four Years at the Court of Henry VIII: A Selection of Dispatches. 1515–1519*. Translated by Rawdon Brown. 2 vols. London: Smith, Elder & Co., 1864

Green, Mary Anne Everett. *Lives of the Princesses of England from the Norman Conquest*. Vol. 5. London: Henry Colbourn, 1854

Grey, Lady Jane, and Sir Nicholas Harris Nicolas. *The Literary Remains of Lady Jane Grey: With a Memoir of Her Life*. Harding, Triphook, and Lepard, 1825

Grummitt, David. *The English Experience in France c.1450–1558: War, Diplomacy and Cultural Exchange*, Routledge 2018

Guaras, Antonio de, and Richard Garnett. *The Accession of Queen Mary: Being the Contemporary Narrative of Antonio de Guaras, a Spanish Merchant Resident in London*. London, Lawrence and Bullen, 1892

Gunn, S. J. *Charles Brandon: Henry VIII's Closest Friend*. Stroud: Amberley, 2015.

Gwyn, Peter. *The King's Cardinal: The Rise and Fall of Thomas Wolsey*. London: Barrie & Jenkins, 1990

Harris, Barbara J. *English Aristocratic Women 1450–1550: Marriage and Family, Property and Careers* OUP 2002

Hayward, Maria, ed. *The Great Wardrobe Accounts of Henry VII and Henry VIII*. London Record Society Publications 47. London. Boydell & Brewer, Inc, 2012

Hicks, M. A. *Richard III*. Gloucestershire: History Press, 2011

Higginbotham, Susan. *The Woodvilles: The Wars of the Roses and England's Most Infamous Family*. Stroud, Gloucestershire: The History Press, 2013

Horrox, Rosemary, ed. *BL Harleian MS 43 Vol. 2* 25 England, Signet Office

Horrox, Rosemary. *Richard III: A Study of Service* Cambridge University Press, 2010

Ives, E. W. *Anne Boleyn*. Oxford, Blackwell, 1986

James Gairdner. *The Houses of Lancaster And York*, 1870.

James, Susan E. *Catherine Parr: Henry VIII's Last Love*. Stroud: Tempus, 2008.

Johnson, Lauren. *Shadow King* Head of Zeus, 2019

Johnson, P. A. *Duke Richard of York, 1411–1460*. Oxford Historical Monographs. Oxford : New York: Clarendon Press ; Oxford University Press, 1988

Jones, Dan. *The Hollow Crown: The Wars of the Roses and the Rise of the Tudors*. London: Faber and Faber, 2015

Jones, Michael K, and Malcolm G Underwood. *The King's Mother: Lady Margaret Beaufort, Countess of Richmond and Derby*. Cambridge: Cambridge University Press, 1999

Lander, Jack R. *Crown and Nobility: 1450–1509*. London: Arnold, 1976.

Laynesmith, J. L. *Cecily Duchess of York*. London; New York: Bloomsbury Academic, an imprint of Bloomsbury Publishing Plc, 2017

Leinster, Charles William Fitzgerald. *The Earls of Kildare, and Their Ancestors: From 1057 to 1773. By the Marquis of Kildare*. Dublin Hodges, Smith, 1858

Leland, John, and John Chandler. *John Leland's Itinerary: Travels in Tudor England*. Stroud, Gloucestershire; A. Sutton, 1993

Letts, M. H. I., Tetzel G. and Bírkova, V. *The Travels of Leo of Rozmital through Germany, Flanders, England, France, Spain, Portugal, and Italy, 1465–1467*. Cambridge Published for the Hakluyt Society at the University Press, 1957

Lipscomb, Suzannah. *The King Is Dead: The Last Will and Testament of Henry VIII*. London: Head of Zeus, 2015

Lisle, Leanda de. *The Sisters Who Would Be Queen: The Tragedy of Mary, Katherine & Lady Jane Grey*. Paperback ed. London: Harper Press, 2009

———. *Tudor: The Family Story*, 2014

Louis XII, King of France, and Pre-1801 Imprint Collection (Library of Congress) DLC. *Lettres du roy Louis XII, et du cardinal George d'Amboise. Avec plusieurs autres lettres, mémoires & instructions écrites depuis 1504 jusques & compris 1514*. Brusselle, F. Foppens, 1712

MacCulloch, Diarmaid. *Thomas Cranmer: A Life*. Revised edition. New Haven: Yale University Press, 2016

Macdougall, Norman. *James Iv*. S.l.: John Donald, 2015

Mancini, Dominic. *The Usurpation of Richard III*. Translated by C A J Armstrong. Gloucester, 1984

Miller, Helen. *Henry VIII and the English Nobility*. Oxford [Oxfordshire] ; New York, NY, USA: B. Blackwell, 1986

Mueller, Janel, ed. *Katherine Parr: Complete Works and Correspondence*. London: Univ Of Chicago Press, 2014.

Neillands, Robin. *The Wars of the Roses*. London: Brockhampton, 2003.

Nichols, J.G. *The Chronicle of Queen Jane and Two Years of Queen Mary* The Camden Society, London Longmans, Green etc. 1838

Ottery St. Mary (England), and John Neale Dalton. *The Collegiate Church of Ottery St. Mary : Being the Ordinacio et Statuta, Ecclesie Sancte Marie de Otery, Exon. Diocesis A.D. 1338, 1339, Ed. from the Exeter Chapter MS. 3521, and the Winchester Cartulary Vol. 1. Part Ii.Ff.98–114, with Plans, Photographs, Introduction and Notes*. Cambridge University Press, 1917

Paul, John Dennis. *Bradgate House and the Greys of Groby: A Sketch of the Their History*. Leicester: J & T Spenser, 1899

Penn, Thomas. *Winter King: The Dawn of Tudor England*, 2012.

Pierce, Hazel. *Margaret Pole, 1473–1541: Loyalty, Lineage and Leadership*. Cardiff: University of Wales Press, 2014

Pocock, Nicholas. *Records of the Reformation; the Divorce 1527–1533. Mostly Now for the First Time Printed from Mss. in the British Museum, the Public Record Office, the Venetian Archives and Other Libraries*. Oxford, Clarendon Press, 1870

Pole, Sir William. *Collections Towards a Description of the County of Devon: By Sir William Pole, ... Now First Printed from the Autograph in the Possession of His Lineal Descendant Sir John-William de La Pole, Bart. ...* J. Nichols; and sold by Messrs White and Son ... Robson ... Leigh and Sotheby; and Payne, junior, 1791

Pronay, Nicholas, ed. *The Crowland Chronicle Continuations: 1459–1486*. London: Richard III and Yorkist History Trust, 1986

Raine, Angelo. *York Civic Records*. Vol. 1. Yorkshire Archaeological Society, 1939

Robinson, Hastings. *Original Letters Relative to the English Reformation: Written During the Reigns of King Henry VIII., King Edward VI., and Queen Mary: Chiefly from the Archives of Zurich*. University Press, 1846

Tytler, Patrick Fraser *England Under the Reigns of Edward VI. and Mary: With the Contemporary History of Europe*. R. Bentley, 1839

Ross, Charles Derek. *Edward IV*. London: Book Club Associates, 1975

Royal Commission on Historical Manuscripts. *The Manuscripts of His Grace the Duke of Rutland...Preserved at Belvoir Castle*. Eyre & Spottiswoode for HMSO, 1905.

Samuel Haynes. *A Collection of State Papers Relating to Affairs In the Reigns of King Henry VIII, King Edward VI, Queen Mary and Queen Elizabeth From the Year 1542 to 1570*. Bowyer, 1740

Santiuste, David. *Edward IV and the Wars of the Roses*. Barnsley, South Yorkshire: Pen & Sword Military, 2011

Scard, Margaret. *Edward Seymour: Lord Protector: Tudor King in All but Name*. Stroud, Gloucestershire: The History Press, 2016

———. *Tudor Survivor: The Life & Times of William Paulet*. Stroud: History Press, 2011

Scarisbrick, J. J. *Henry VIII*. Yale English Monarchs. New Haven: Yale University Press, 2012

Seward, Desmond. *The Wars of the Roses: Through the Lives of Five Men and Women of the Fifteenth Century*. 1st American ed. New York, N.Y., U.S.A: Viking, 1995

Shaw W. A. *The Knights Of England Vol. 1 1906*

Shirley, Evelyn Philip. *Stemmata Shirleiana*; Westminster: Nichols and Sons, 1873.

Skeel, Caroline A. J. *The Council in the Marches of Wales; a Study in Local Government during the Sixteenth and Seventeenth Centuries*. London, H. Rees, Ltd., 1904.

Society of Antiquaries of London. *A Collection of Ordinances and Regulations for the Government of the Royal Household, Made in Divers Reigns: From King Edward III to King William and Queen Mary, Also Receipts in Ancient Cookery*. London: Printed for the Society of Antiquaries by John Nichols 1790

Steel, Anthony. *The Receipt of the Exchequer, 1377–1485*. Cambridge: Univ. Pr, 1954.

Stevenson, Joan. *The Greys of Bradgate*. 2nd ed., 1977

Stone, J M. *The History of Mary I: Queen of England*. Sands & Co., 1901

Tallis, Nicola. *Crown of Blood: The Deadly Inheritance of Lady Jane Grey*, 2016

Wadmore, James Foster. *Some Account of the Worshipful Company of Skinners of London, Being the Guild or Fraternity of Corpus Christi*. London, Blades, East & Blades, 1902

Waller, J G. 'The Lords of Cobham'. *Archaelogia Cantiana* 12 1878

Waurin, Jean de. A Collection of all the Chronicles and Ancient Histories of Great Britain, now called England. Tr. E. Hardy, London: Longman, Green etc. 1864

Weightman, Christine B. *Margaret of York, Duchess of Burgundy, 1446–1503*. Gloucester: A. Sutton ; St. Martin's Press, 1989

Whitelock, Anna. *Mary Tudor: England's First Queen*. Penguin 2016

William Maziere Brady. *The Episcopal Succession in England, Scotland and Ireland, A.D. 1400 to 1875*. Tipografia Della Pace, 1876

Wilson, Derek. *The Uncrowned Kings of England: The Black Legend of the Dudleys*. London: Constable, 2005.

Articles

Armstrong, C. A. J. 'The Inauguration Ceremonies of the Yorkist Kings and Their Title to the Throne'. *Transactions of the Royal Historical Society* 30 (1948): 51–73.

Armstrong, E. Review of *Review of Charles le Téméraire et la Ligue de Constance*, by E. Toutey. *The English Historical Review* 17, no. 68 (1902): 782–84.

Bibliography

Attreed, Lorraine. 'An Indenture between Richard Duke of Gloucester and the Scrope Family of Masham and Upsall'. *Speculum* 58, no. 4 (1983): 1018–25.

Attreed, Lorraine. 'Friends in Need or in Deed? Anglo—Portuguese Relations in the Fifteenth Century'. *Mediterranean Studies* 8 (1999): 143–56.

Behrens, Betty. 'The Office of the English Resident Ambassador: Its Evolution as Illustrated by the Career of Sir Thomas Spinelly, 1509–22', *Transactions of the Royal Historical Society* 16 (1933): 161–95.

Bellamy, J. G. 'Justice under the Yorkist Kings'. *The American Journal of Legal History* 9, no. 2 (1965): 135–55.

Bennett, Josephine Waters. 'The Mediaeval Loveday'. *Speculum* 33, no. 3 (1958): 351–70.

Bennett, Michael J. 'Henry VII and the Northern Rising of 1489'. *The English Historical Review* 105, no. 414 (1990): 34–59.

Bernard, G. W. 'The Fall of Wolsey Reconsidered'. *Journal of British Studies* 35, no. 3 (1996): 277–310.

Bohna, Monte. Review of *Review of The Battles of Barnet and Tewkesbury*, by P. W. Hammond. *Albion: A Quarterly Journal Concerned with British Studies* 23, no. 2 (1991): 301–3.

Brereton, Wyllyam, George Dublin, Robert Cowley, and W. Pinkerton. 'Inventory of the Household Effects of Lord Deputy Lord Leonard Grey, in 1540'. *Ulster Journal of Archaeology* 7 (1859): 201–13.

Brinkmann, Bodo. 'The Hastings Hours and Master of 1499'. *The British Library Journal* 14, no. 1 (1988): 90–106

Brown, A. L., and Bruce Webster. 'The Movements of the Earl of Warwick in the Summer of 1464 – A Correction'. *The English Historical Review* 81, no. 318 (1966): 80–82.

Bryson, Alan. 'The Ormond–St Leger Feud.: A 'New Departure' in mid-Tudor Ireland? *History Ireland* 26, no. 3 (2018): 16–20

Bühler, Curt F. 'A Letter from Edward IV to Galeazzo Maria Sforza'. *Speculum* 30, no. 2 (1955): 239–40.

Camden Society (Great Britain). *An English Chronicle of the Reigns of Richard II., Henry IV., Henry V., and Henry VI*. London Longmans, Green etc. 1838

———. *The Chronicle of Calais in the Reigns of Henry VII and Henry VIII to the Year 1540*. London Longmans, Green etc, 1838

———. *Troubles Connected with The Prayer Book of 1549*. London Longmans, Green etc. 1838

Clarke, Peter D. 'English Royal Marriages and the Papal Penitentiary in the Fifteenth Century'. *The English Historical Review* 120, no. 488 (2005): 1014–29.

Currin, John M. 'Persuasions to Peace: The Luxembourg-Marigny-Gaguin Embassy and the State of Anglo-French Relations, 1489–90'. *The English Historical Review* 113, no. 453 (1998): 882–904.

Davies, C. S. L. 'Bishop John Morton, the Holy See, and the Accession of Henry VII'. *The English Historical Review* 102, no. 402 (1987): 2–30.

Dunham, William Huse. '"The Books of the Parliament" and "The Old Record," 1396–1504'. *Speculum* 51, no. 4 (1976): 694–712.

———. 'The Members of Henry VIII's Whole Council, 1509–1527'. *The English Historical Review* 59, no. 234 (1944): 187–210.

Edwards, R. Dudley. 'Venerable John Travers and the Rebellion of Silken Thomas'. *Studies: An Irish Quarterly Review* 23, no. 92 (1934): 687–99.

Edwards, R. Dudley, T. W. Moody, Jocelyn Otway-Ruthven, David B. Quinn, and H. G. Richardson. 'Parliaments and Great Councils in Ireland, 1461–1586'. *Irish Historical Studies* 3, no. 9 (1942): 60–77.

Fahy, Conor. 'The Marriage of Edward IV and Elizabeth Woodville: A New Italian Source'. *The English Historical Review* 76, no. 301 (1961): 660–72.

Findlay, Alison. 'Reproducing "Iphigenia at Aulis"'. *Early Theatre* 18, no. 2 (2015): 133–48.

Gillespie, James L. 'Ladies of the Fraternity of Saint George and of the Society of the Garter'. *Albion: A Quarterly Journal Concerned with British Studies* 17, no. 3 (1985): 259–78.

Goodman, Anthony, and Angus MacKay. 'A Castilian Report on English Affairs, 1486'. *The English Historical Review* 88, no. 346 (1973): 92–99

Graham-Matheson, Helen. 'Elisabeth Parr's Renaissance at the Mid-Tudor *Court*' *Early Modern Women* Vol. 8 Fall 2013 pp. 289–299

Green, Richard Firth. 'Historical Notes of a London Citizen, 1483–1488'. *The English Historical Review* 96, no. 380 (1981): 585–90

———. 'The Short Version of The Arrival of Edward IV'. *Speculum* 56, no. 2 (1981): 324–36

Griffiths, Ralph A. 'Local Rivalries and National Politics: The Percies, the Nevilles, and the Duke of Exeter, 1452–55'. *Speculum* 43, no. 4 (1968): 589–632

———. 'The Winchester Session of the 1449 Parliament: A Further Comment'. *Huntington Library Quarterly* 42, no. 3 (1979): 181–91

Gunn, S. J. 'The Courtiers of Henry VII'. *The English Historical Review* 108, no. 426 (1993): 23–49

———. 'The Duke of Suffolk's March on Paris in 1523'. *The English Historical Review* 101, no. 400 (1986): 596–634

Hanham, Alison. 'Richard III, Lord Hastings and the Historians'. *The English Historical Review* 87, no. 343 (1972): 233–48

———. 'Text and Subtext: Bishop John Russell's Parliamentary Sermons, 1483–1484.' *Traditio* 54 (1999): 301–22

Harris, Barbara J. 'Property, Power, and Personal Relations: Elite Mothers and Sons in Yorkist and Early Tudor England'. *Signs* 15, no. 3 (1990): 606–32.

———. 'The View from My Lady's Chamber: New Perspectives on the Early Tudor Monarchy'. *Huntington Library Quarterly* 60, no. 3 (1997): 215–47

———. 'Women and Politics in Early Tudor England'. *The Historical Journal* 33, no. 2 (1990): 259–81

Harriss, G. L. 'The Struggle for Calais: An Aspect of the Rivalry between Lancaster and York'. *The English Historical Review* 75, no. 294 (1960): 30–53

Haselden, R. B., H. C. Schulz, and The Department Of Manuscripts. 'Summary Report on the Hastings Manuscripts'. *The Huntington Library Bulletin*, no. 5 (1934): 1–67

Haugaard, William P. 'Katherine Parr: The Religious Convictions of a Renaissance Queen'. *Renaissance Quarterly* 22, no. 4 (1969): 346–59

Haward, Winifred I. 'Economic Aspects of the Wars of the Roses in East Anglia'. *The English Historical Review* 41, no. 162 (1926): 170–89

Hicks, Michael. 'Bastard Feudalism, Overmighty Subjects and Idols of the Multitude during the Wars of the Roses'. *History* 85, no. 279 (2000): 386–403

———. 'Cement or Solvent? Kinship and Politics in Late Medieval England: The Case of the Nevilles'. *History* 83, no. 269 (1998): 31–46

———. 'Crowland's World: A Westminster View of the Yorkist Age'. *History* 90, no. 2 (298) (2005): 172–90

Jones, Randolph. 'New Evidence for Edward VI's Reign in Ireland' *The Ricardian Bulletin* September 2014, pp. 43–45

———. 'Janico Markys, Dublin, and the Coronation of Edward VI' *Medieval Dublin* XIV, 2015, pp. 185–209

Jones, William R. 'Political Uses of Sorcery in Medieval Europe'. *The Historian* 34, no. 4 (1972): 670–87.

Kennedy, Edward D. 'Malory and the Marriage of Edward IV'. *Texas Studies in Literature and Language* 12, no. 2 (1970): 155–62

Kleineke, Hannes. 'The Commission De Mutuo Faciendo in the Reign of Henry VI'. *The English Historical Review* 116, no. 465 (2001): 1–30

Kujawa-Holbrook, Sheryl A., and Sheryl A. Kujawa-Holbrook. 'Katherine Parr and Reformed Religion'. *Anglican and Episcopal History* 72, no. 1 (2003): 55–78

Lander, J. R. 'Attainder and Forfeiture, 1453 to 1509'. *The Historical Journal* 4, no. 2 (1961): 119–51.

———. 'Marriage and Politics in the Fifteenth Century: The Nevilles and the Wydevilles'. *Historical Research* 36, no. 94 (1 November 1963): 119–52

Bibliography

————. 'The Crown and the Aristocracy in England, 1450–1509'. *Albion: A Quarterly Journal Concerned with British Studies* 8, no. 3 (1976): 203–18

Lester, G. A. 'Fifteenth-Century English Heraldic Narrative'. *The Yearbook of English Studies* 22 (1992): 201–12

Levine, Mortimer. 'Richard III--Usurper or Lawful King?' *Speculum* 34, no. 3 (1959): 391–401

Luckett, D. A. 'Crown Patronage and Political Morality in Early Tudor England: The Case of Giles, Lord Daubeney'. *The English Historical Review* 110, no. 437 (1995): 578–95

Manning, Roger B. 'Review Article: The Rebellions of 1549 in England'. *The Sixteenth Century Journal* 10, no. 2 (1979): 93–99

Martin, F. X. 'The Crowning of a King at Dublin, 24 May 1487'. *Hermathena*, no. 144 (1988): 7–34

McClendon, Muriel C. '"Against God's Word": Government, Religion and the Crisis of Authority in Early Reformation Norwich'. *The Sixteenth Century Journal* 25, no. 2 (1994): 353–69

Morgan, D. A. L. 'The King's Affinity in the Polity of Yorkist England'. *Transactions of the Royal Historical Society* 23 (1973): 1–25

Myers, A. R. 'The Household of Queen Elizabeth Woodville, 1466-7: I'. Bulletin of the John Rylands Library. 1967; 50(1): 207–235, 1967

Payling, S. J. 'Social Mobility, Demographic Change, and Landed Society in Late Medieval England'. *The Economic History Review* 45, no. 1 (1992): 51–73

————. 'The Ampthill Dispute: A Study in Aristocratic Lawlessness and the Breakdown of Lancastrian Government'. *The English Historical Review* 104, no. 413 (1989): 881–907

————. 'The Economics of Marriage in Late Medieval England: The Marriage of Heiresses'. *The Economic History Review* 54, no. 3 (2001): 413–29

Powell, Edward. 'Settlement of Disputes by Arbitration in Fifteenth-Century England'. *Law and History Review* 2, no. 1 (1984): 21–43

Power, Gerald, William Brabazon, Gerald Aylmer Justice, and John Alen. 'The Viceroy and his Critics. Leonard Grey's journey through the West of Ireland June-July 1538'. *Journal of the Galway Archaeological and Historical Society* 60 (2008): 78–87

Ramsay, J. H. 'The Strength of English Armies in the Middle Ages'. *The English Historical Review* 29, no. 114 (1914): 221–27

Roger, Euan. '"To Be Shut up": New Evidence for the Development of Quarantine Regulations in Tudor England'. *Social History of Medicine*, n.d.

Rosenthal, Joel T. 'Other Victims: Peeresses as War Widows, 1450–1500'. *History* 72, no. 235 (1987): 213–30

Roth, Cecil. 'Sir Edward Brampton: An Anglo-Jewish Adventurer during the Wars of the Roses'. *Transactions (Jewish Historical Society of England)* 16 (1945): 121–27

Rowney, Ian. 'Arbitration in gentry disputes of the later middle ages'. *History* 67, no. 221 (1982): 367–76

Siegel, Paul N. 'English Humanism and the New Tudor Aristocracy'. *Journal of the History of Ideas* 13, no. 4 (1952): 450–68

Sil, Narasingha Prosad. 'Sir William Herbert in Tudor Politics, 1547—53'. *Biography* 5, no. 4 (1982): 297–318

Thomson, J. A. F. '"The Arrival of Edward IV" -- The Development of the Text'. *Speculum* 46, no. 1 (1971): 84–93

————. '"Warkworth's Chronicle" Reconsidered'. *The English Historical Review* 116, no. 467 (2001): 657–64

Thorp, Malcolm R. 'Religion and the Wyatt Rebellion of 1554'. *Church History* 47, no. 4 (1978): 363–80

Wolffe, B. P. 'Hastings Reinterred'. *The English Historical Review* 91, no. 361 (1976): 813–24

Theses

Chamberlayne, Joanna L. *English Queenship 1444–1503* York, 1999

Chynoweth, John. *The Gentry of Tudor Cornwall* Exeter, n.d. BL EThOS ID 387405

Cunningham, Sean. *The establishment of the Tudor regime: Henry VII, rebellion, and the financial control of the aristocracy 1485–1509*. Lancaster 1995 BL EThOS ID 337349

Stoate, T. L. *A Survey of West Country Manors 1525*. Bristol: Stoate, 1979

Turner, G. J. 'The Justices of the Forest South of Trent'. *The English Historical Review* 18, no. 69 (1903): 112–16.

Websites

Battle of Stoke, 16 June 1487 http://www.historyofwar.org/articles/battles_stoke.html.

British History Online https://www.british-history.ac.uk/

History of the Cornish Stannaries. Cornwall For Ever! https://www.cornwallforever.co.uk/history/cornish-stannaries.

Letter to Mary | Lady Jane Grey Reference Guide. http://www.ladyjanegrey.info/

Stonor Letters and papers https://quod.lib.umich.edu/c/cme/

Tudor Chamber Books https://www.tudorchamberbooks.org/.

Vergil, Polydore. *Anglica Historica* (1555). Translated by Diana F Sutton, n.d. http://www.philological.bham.ac.uk/polverg/.

Index

Index of Places